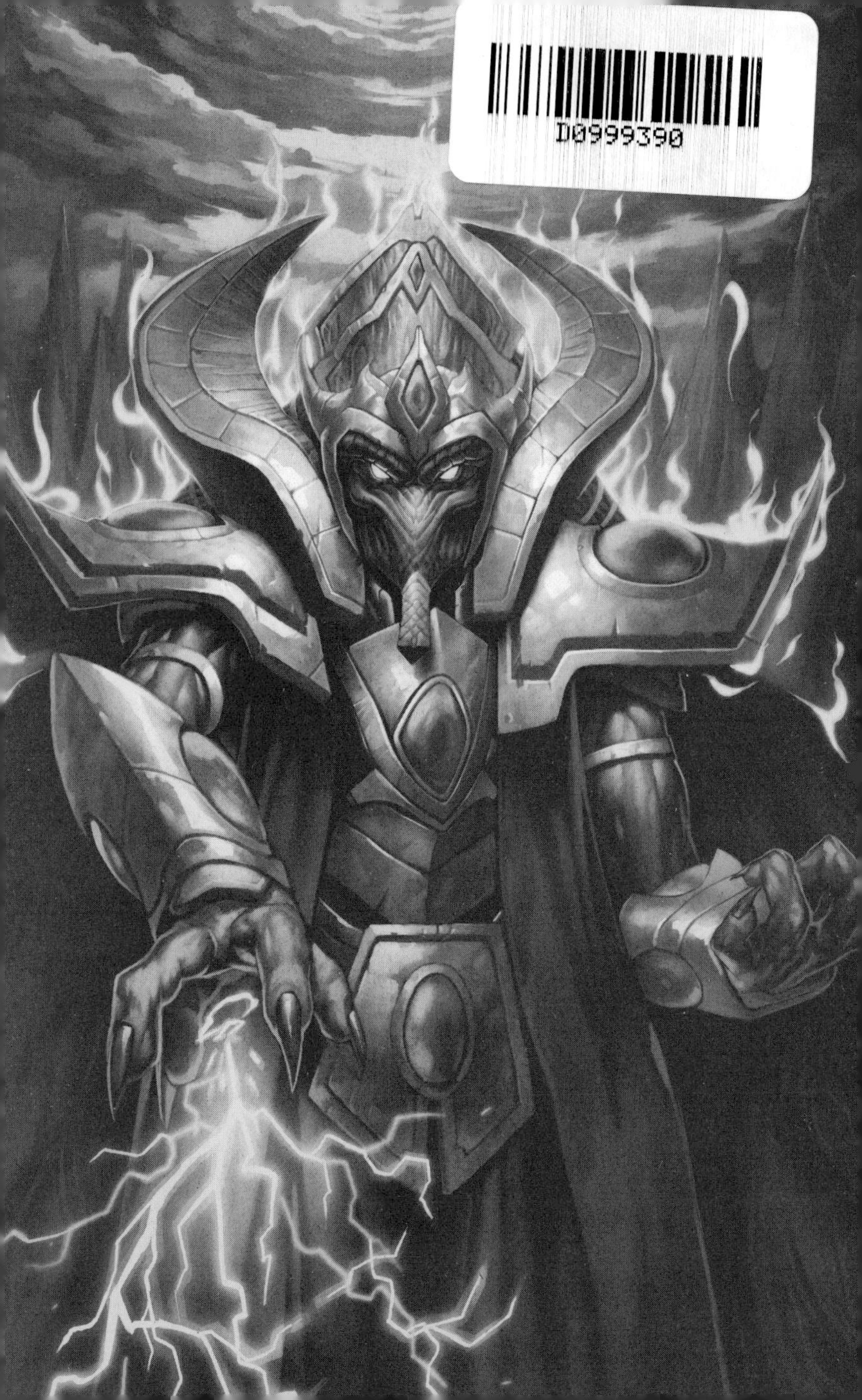

StarCraft: Frontline Vol. 3

Contributing Editor - Troy Lewter
Layout and Lettering - Michael Paolilli
Creative Consultant - Michael Paolilli
Graphic Designer - Louis Csontos
Cover Artist - UDON with Saejin Oh

Editor - Hope Donovan
Print Production Manager - Lucas Rivera
Managing Editor - Vy Nguyen
Senior Designer - Louis Csontos
Director of Sales and Manufacturing - Allyson De Simone
Associate Publisher - Marco F. Pavia
President and C.O.O. - John Parker
C.E.O. and Chief Creative Officer - Stu Levy

BLIZZARD ENTERTAINMENT

Senior Vice President, Creative Development - Chris Metzen
Director, Creative Development - Jeff Donais
Lead Developer, Licensed Products - Shawn Carnes
Publishing Lead, Creative Development - Rob Tokar
Senior Story Developer - Micky Neilson
Story Developer - James Waugh
Art Director - Glenn Rane
Director, Global Business
Development and Licensing - Cory Jones
Associate Licensing Manager - Jason Bischoff
Historian - Evelyn Fredericksen
Additional Development - Samwise Didier and Tommy Newcomer

A  Manga

TOKYOPOP and 🐢 are trademarks or registered trademarks of TOKYOPOP Inc.

TOKYOPOP Inc.
5900 Wilshire Blvd. Suite 2000
Los Angeles, CA 90036

E-mail: info@TOKYOPOP.com
Come visit us online at www.TOKYOPOP.com

ISBN: 978-1-4278-0832-5
First TOKYOPOP printing: July 2009
10 9 8 7 6 5 4 3
Printed in the USA

ЅTARCRAFT

FRONTLINE

Volume 3

HAMBURG // LONDON // LOS ANGELES // TOKYO

STARCRAFT

FRONTLINE
VOLUME 3

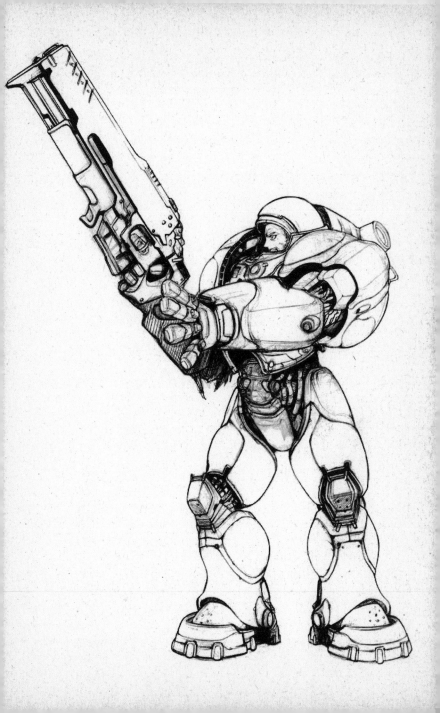

StarCraft®

Frontline™

Volume 3

War-Torn

Written by Paul Benjamin & Dave Shramek

Art by Hector Sevilla

Letterer: Michael Paolilli

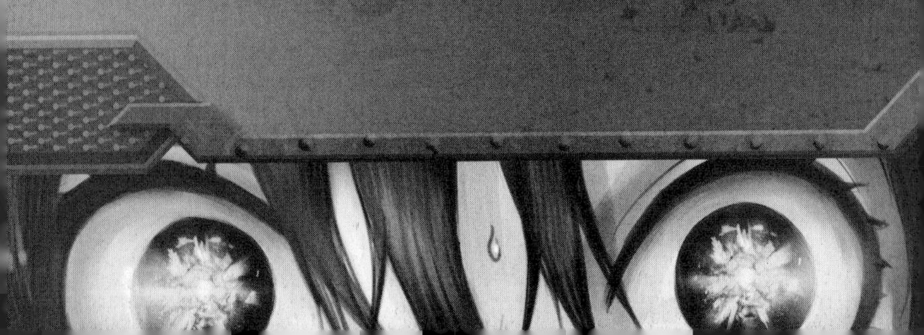

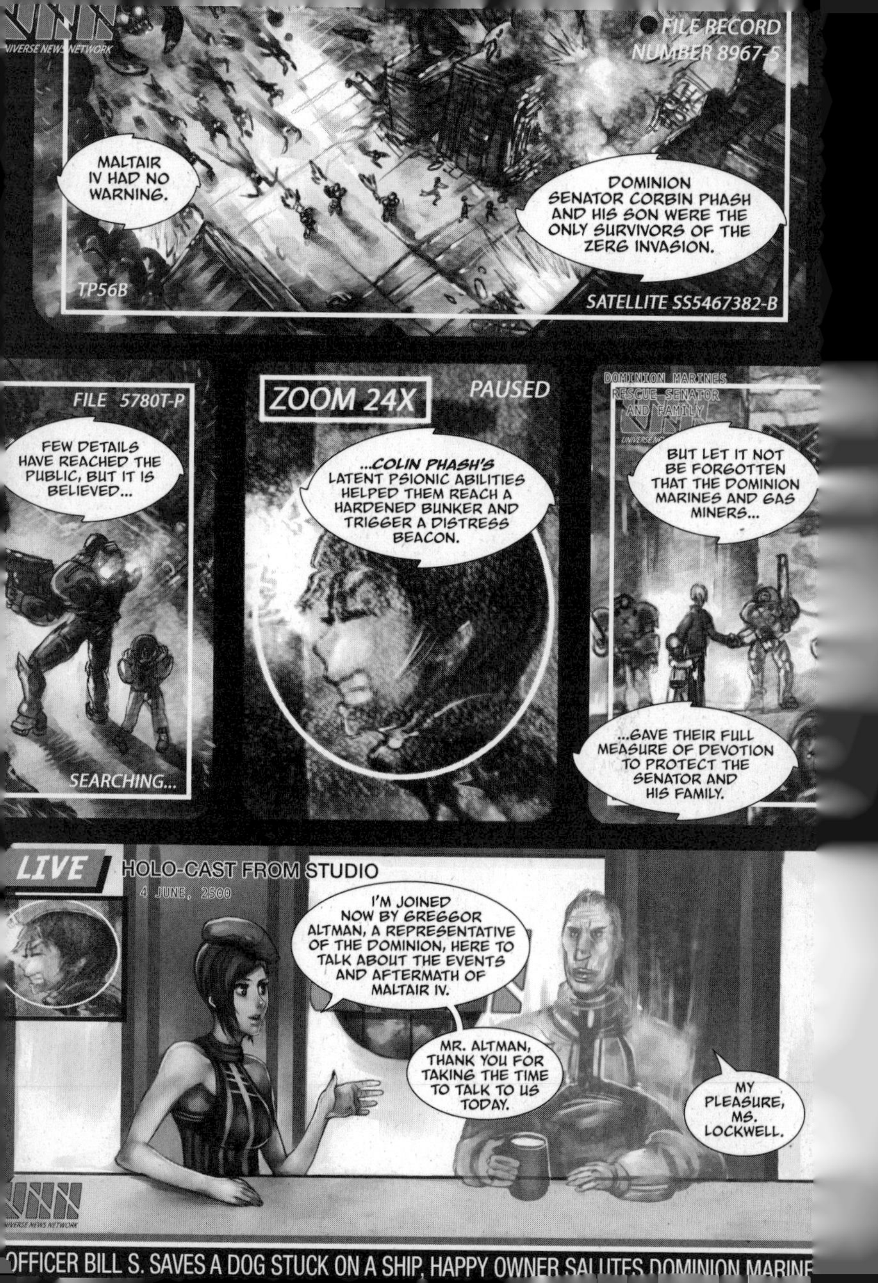
UNIVERSE NEWS NETWORK
FILE RECORD NUMBER 8967-5
MALTAIR IV HAD NO WARNING.
DOMINION SENATOR CORBIN PHASH AND HIS SON WERE THE ONLY SURVIVORS OF THE ZERG INVASION.
TP56B
SATELLITE SS5467382-B
FILE 5780T-P
FEW DETAILS HAVE REACHED THE PUBLIC, BUT IT IS BELIEVED...
SEARCHING...
ZOOM 24X
PAUSED
...COLIN PHASH'S LATENT PSIONIC ABILITIES HELPED THEM REACH A HARDENED BUNKER AND TRIGGER A DISTRESS BEACON.
DOMINION MARINES RESCUE SENATOR AND FAMILY
BUT LET IT NOT BE FORGOTTEN THAT THE DOMINION MARINES AND GAS MINERS...
...GAVE THEIR FULL MEASURE OF DEVOTION TO PROTECT THE SENATOR AND HIS FAMILY.
LIVE
HOLO-CAST FROM STUDIO
4 JUNE, 2500
I'M JOINED NOW BY GREGGOR ALTMAN, A REPRESENTATIVE OF THE DOMINION, HERE TO TALK ABOUT THE EVENTS AND AFTERMATH OF MALTAIR IV.
MR. ALTMAN, THANK YOU FOR TAKING THE TIME TO TALK TO US TODAY.
MY PLEASURE, MS. LOCKWELL.
UNIVERSE NEWS NETWORK
OFFICER BILL S. SAVES A DOG STUCK ON A SHIP, HAPPY OWNER SALUTES DOMINION MARINE

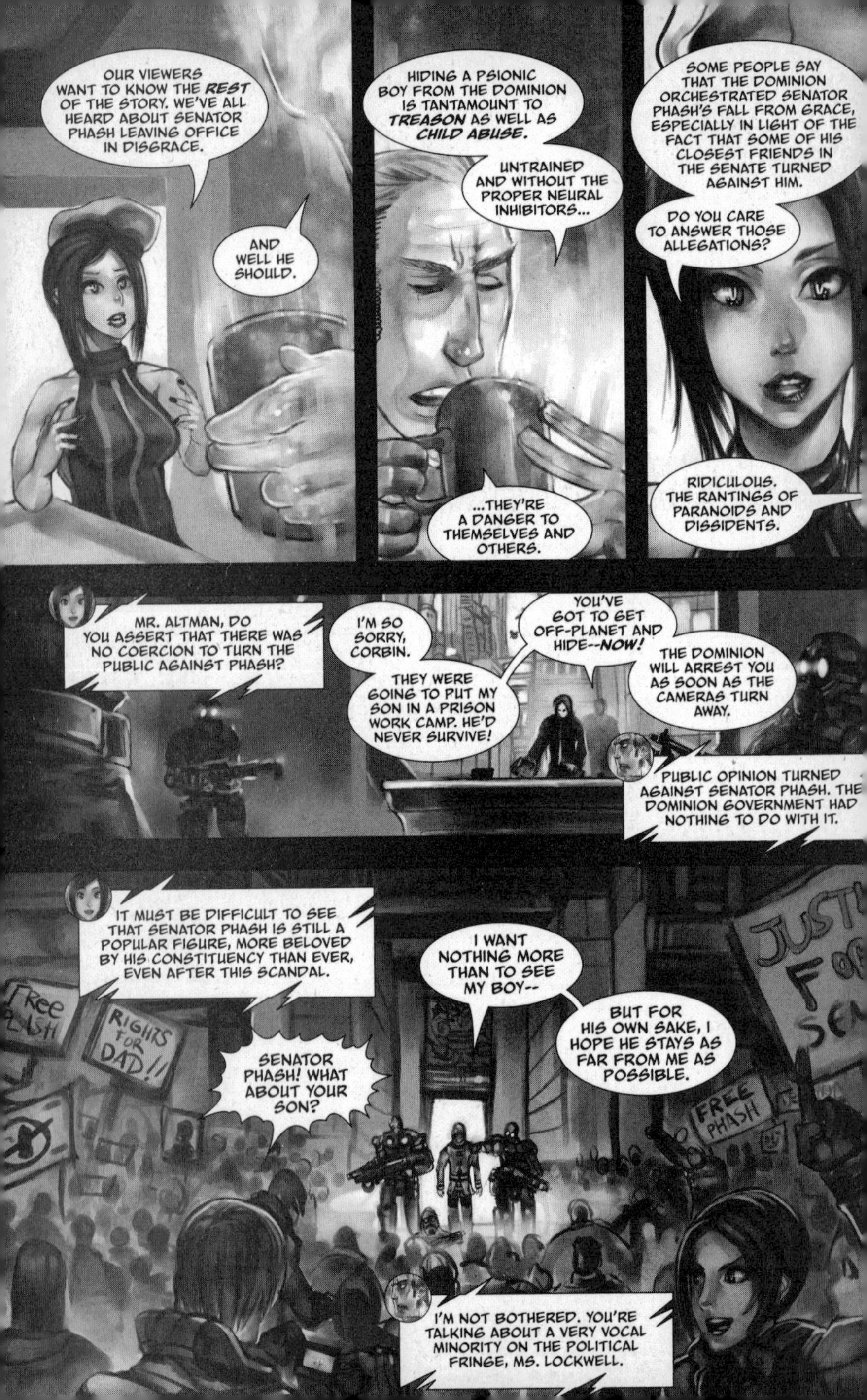
OUR VIEWERS WANT TO KNOW THE *REST* OF THE STORY. WE'VE ALL HEARD ABOUT SENATOR PHASH LEAVING OFFICE IN DISGRACE.
AND WELL HE SHOULD.
HIDING A PSIONIC BOY FROM THE DOMINION IS TANTAMOUNT TO ***TREASON*** AS WELL AS ***CHILD ABUSE.***
UNTRAINED AND WITHOUT THE PROPER NEURAL INHIBITORS...
...THEY'RE A DANGER TO THEMSELVES AND OTHERS.
SOME PEOPLE SAY THAT THE DOMINION ORCHESTRATED SENATOR PHASH'S FALL FROM GRACE, ESPECIALLY IN LIGHT OF THE FACT THAT SOME OF HIS CLOSEST FRIENDS IN THE SENATE TURNED AGAINST HIM.
DO YOU CARE TO ANSWER THOSE ALLEGATIONS?
RIDICULOUS. THE RANTINGS OF PARANOIDS AND DISSIDENTS.
MR. ALTMAN, DO YOU ASSERT THAT THERE WAS NO COERCION TO TURN THE PUBLIC AGAINST PHASH?
I'M SO SORRY, CORBIN.
THEY WERE GOING TO PUT MY SON IN A PRISON WORK CAMP. HE'D NEVER SURVIVE!
YOU'VE GOT TO GET OFF-PLANET AND HIDE--***NOW!***
THE DOMINION WILL ARREST YOU AS SOON AS THE CAMERAS TURN AWAY.
PUBLIC OPINION TURNED AGAINST SENATOR PHASH. THE DOMINION GOVERNMENT HAD NOTHING TO DO WITH IT.
IT MUST BE DIFFICULT TO SEE THAT SENATOR PHASH IS STILL A POPULAR FIGURE, MORE BELOVED BY HIS CONSTITUENCY THAN EVER, EVEN AFTER THIS SCANDAL.
FREE PHASH
RIGHTS FOR DAD!!
SENATOR PHASH! WHAT ABOUT YOUR SON?
I WANT NOTHING MORE THAN TO SEE MY BOY--
BUT FOR HIS OWN SAKE, I HOPE HE STAYS AS FAR FROM ME AS POSSIBLE.
FREE PHASH
I'M NOT BOTHERED. YOU'RE TALKING ABOUT A VERY VOCAL MINORITY ON THE POLITICAL FRINGE, MS. LOCKWELL.

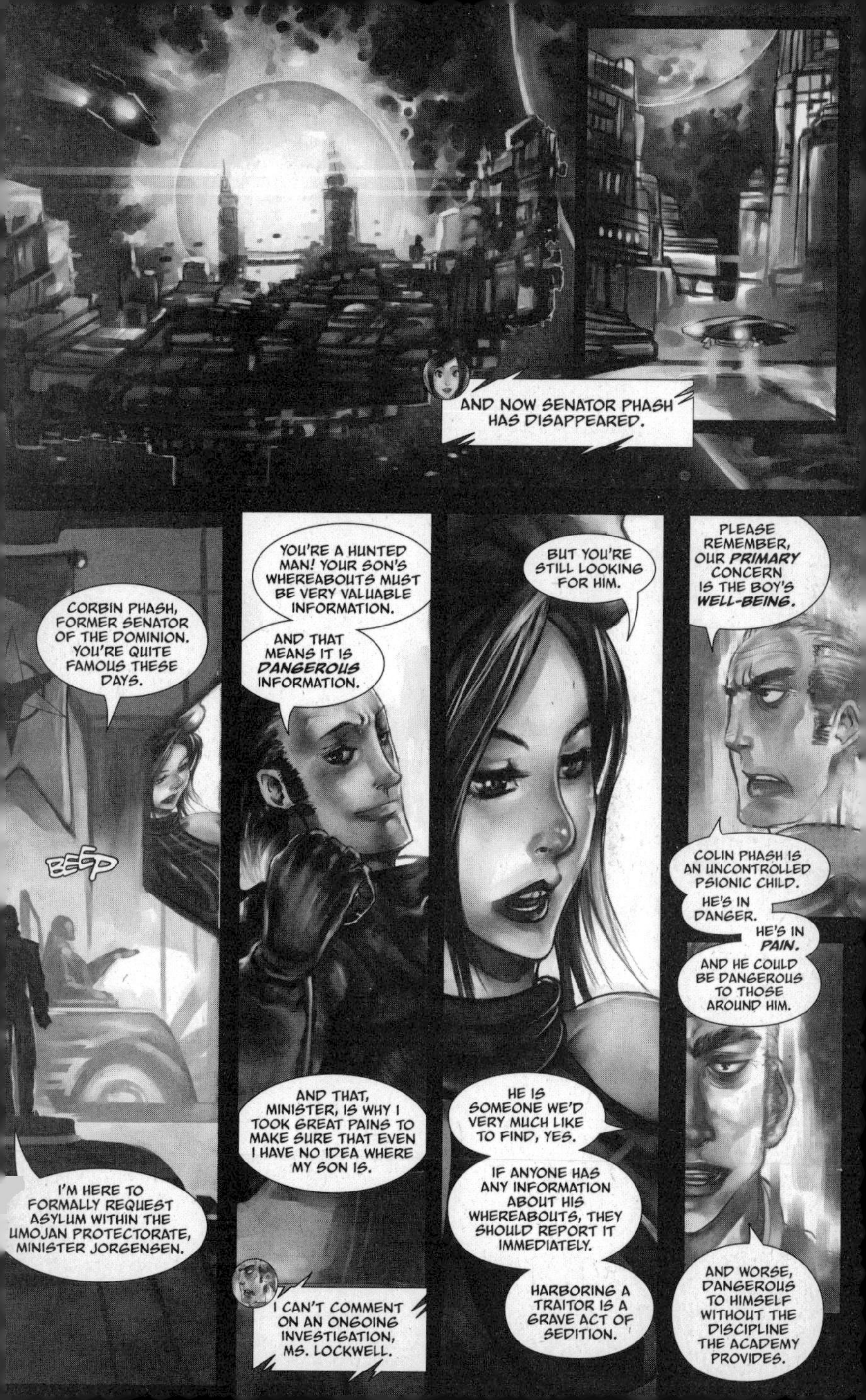
AND NOW SENATOR PHASH HAS DISAPPEARED.
CORBIN PHASH, FORMER SENATOR OF THE DOMINION. YOU'RE QUITE FAMOUS THESE DAYS.
BEEP
I'M HERE TO FORMALLY REQUEST ASYLUM WITHIN THE UMOJAN PROTECTORATE, MINISTER JORGENSEN.
YOU'RE A HUNTED MAN! YOUR SON'S WHEREABOUTS MUST BE VERY VALUABLE INFORMATION.
AND THAT MEANS IT IS *DANGEROUS* INFORMATION.
AND THAT, MINISTER, IS WHY I TOOK GREAT PAINS TO MAKE SURE THAT EVEN I HAVE NO IDEA WHERE MY SON IS.
I CAN'T COMMENT ON AN ONGOING INVESTIGATION, MS. LOCKWELL.
BUT YOU'RE STILL LOOKING FOR HIM.
HE IS SOMEONE WE'D VERY MUCH LIKE TO FIND, YES.
IF ANYONE HAS ANY INFORMATION ABOUT HIS WHEREABOUTS, THEY SHOULD REPORT IT IMMEDIATELY.
HARBORING A TRAITOR IS A GRAVE ACT OF SEDITION.
PLEASE REMEMBER, OUR *PRIMARY* CONCERN IS THE BOY'S *WELL-BEING.*
COLIN PHASH IS AN UNCONTROLLED PSIONIC CHILD.
HE'S IN DANGER.
HE'S IN *PAIN.*
AND HE COULD BE DANGEROUS TO THOSE AROUND HIM.
AND WORSE, DANGEROUS TO HIMSELF WITHOUT THE DISCIPLINE THE ACADEMY PROVIDES.

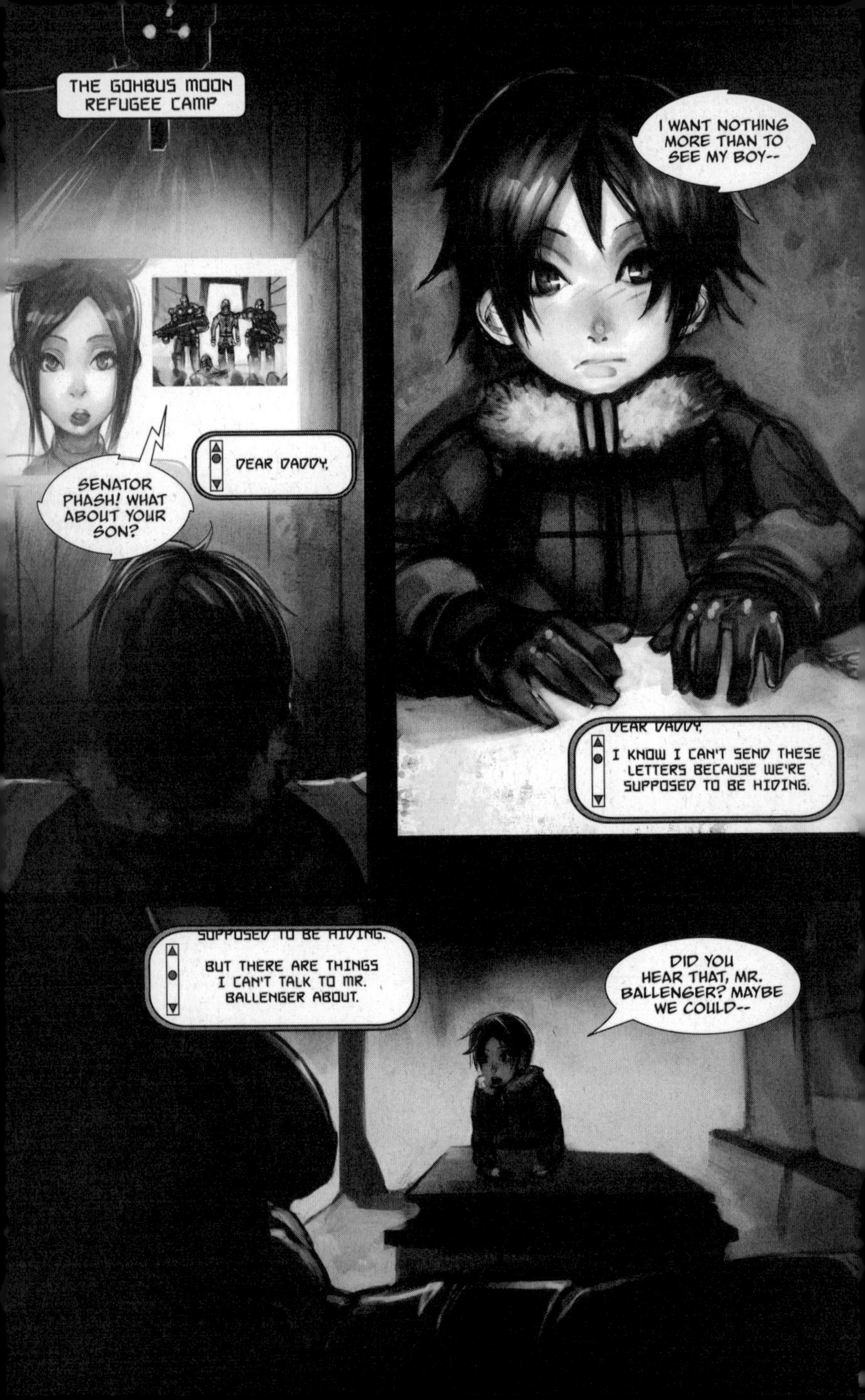
THE GOHBUS MOON REFUGEE CAMP
SENATOR PHASH! WHAT ABOUT YOUR SON?
DEAR DADDY,
I WANT NOTHING MORE THAN TO SEE MY BOY--
DEAR DADDY,
I KNOW I CAN'T SEND THESE LETTERS BECAUSE WE'RE SUPPOSED TO BE HIDING.
SUPPOSED TO BE HIDING.
BUT THERE ARE THINGS I CAN'T TALK TO MR. BALLENGER ABOUT.
DID YOU HEAR THAT, MR. BALLENGER? MAYBE WE COULD--

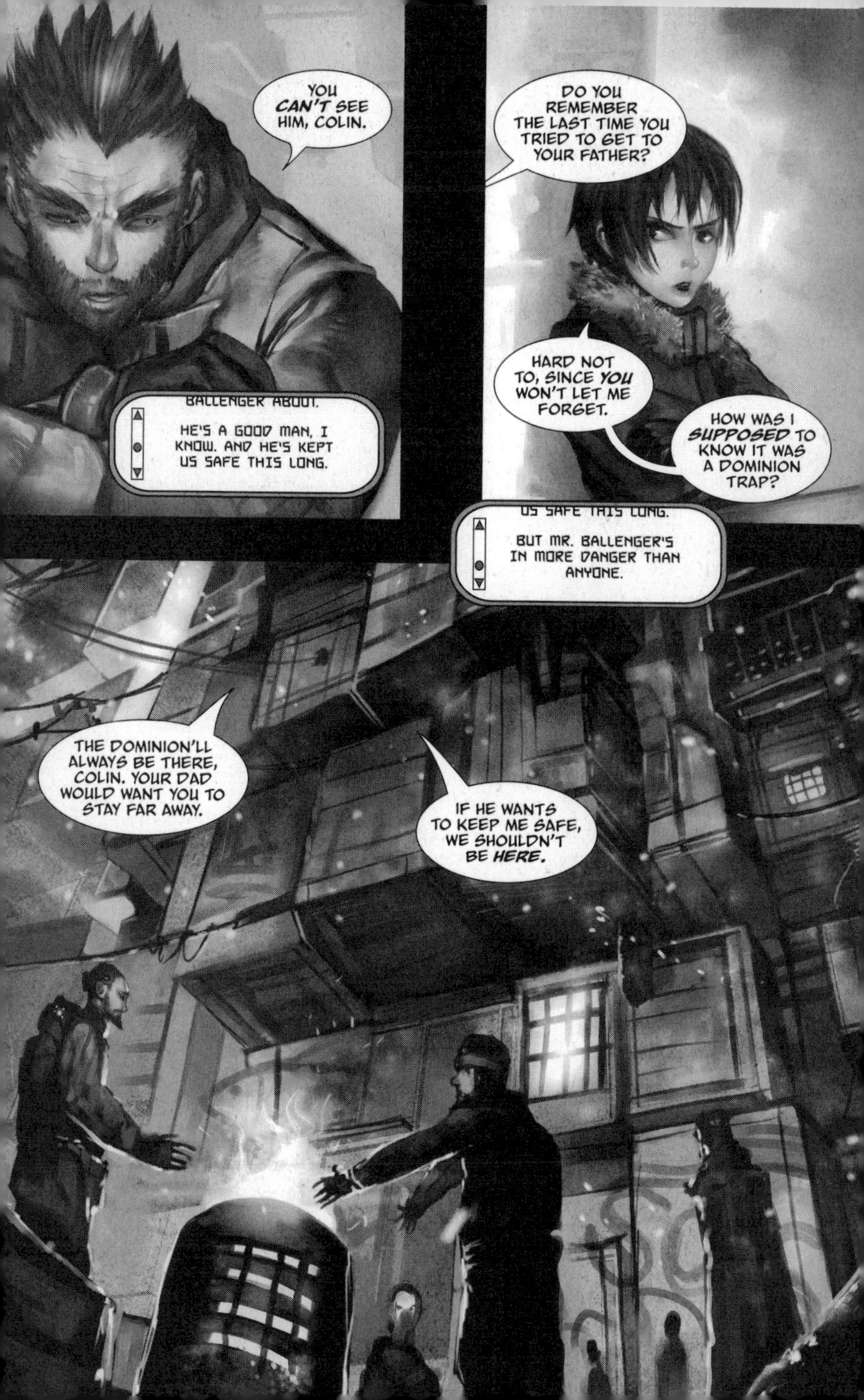

YOU *CAN'T* SEE HIM, COLIN.
BALLENGER ABOUT.
HE'S A GOOD MAN, I KNOW. AND HE'S KEPT US SAFE THIS LONG.
DO YOU REMEMBER THE LAST TIME YOU TRIED TO GET TO YOUR FATHER?
HARD NOT TO, SINCE *YOU* WON'T LET ME FORGET.
HOW WAS I *SUPPOSED* TO KNOW IT WAS A DOMINION TRAP?
US SAFE THIS LONG.
BUT MR. BALLENGER'S IN MORE DANGER THAN ANYONE.
THE DOMINION'LL ALWAYS BE THERE, COLIN. YOUR DAD WOULD WANT YOU TO STAY FAR AWAY.
IF HE WANTS TO KEEP ME SAFE, WE SHOULDN'T BE *HERE*.

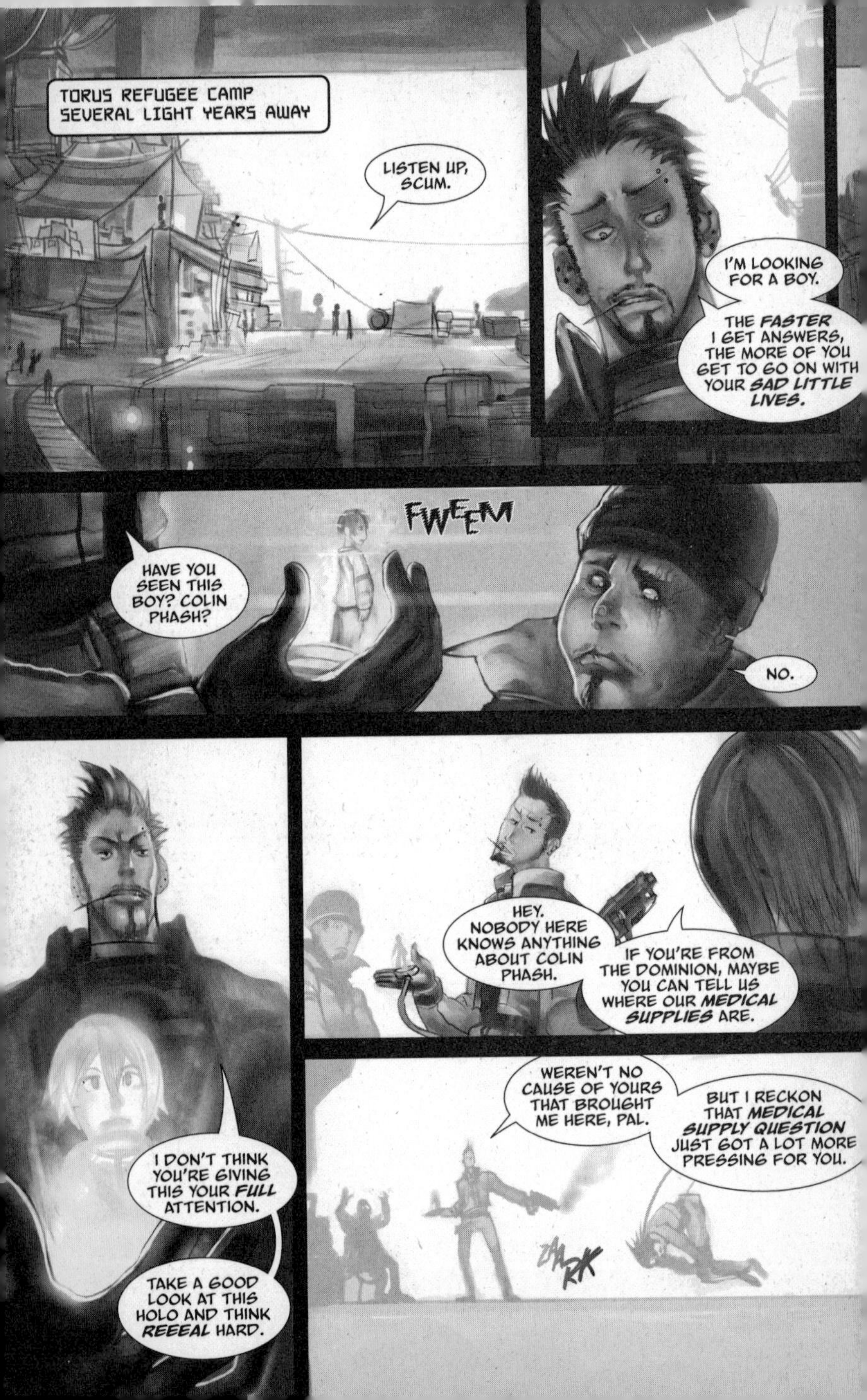
TORUS REFUGEE CAMP
SEVERAL LIGHT YEARS AWAY
LISTEN UP, SCUM.
I'M LOOKING FOR A BOY.
THE *FASTER* I GET ANSWERS, THE MORE OF YOU GET TO GO ON WITH YOUR ***SAD LITTLE LIVES.***
FWEEM
HAVE YOU SEEN THIS BOY? COLIN PHASH?
NO.
I DON'T THINK YOU'RE GIVING THIS YOUR *FULL* ATTENTION.
TAKE A GOOD LOOK AT THIS HOLO AND THINK *REEEAL* HARD.
HEY. NOBODY HERE KNOWS ANYTHING ABOUT COLIN PHASH.
IF YOU'RE FROM THE DOMINION, MAYBE YOU CAN TELL US WHERE OUR *MEDICAL SUPPLIES* ARE.
WEREN'T NO CAUSE OF YOURS THAT BROUGHT ME HERE, PAL.
BUT I RECKON THAT *MEDICAL SUPPLY QUESTION* JUST GOT A LOT MORE PRESSING FOR YOU.

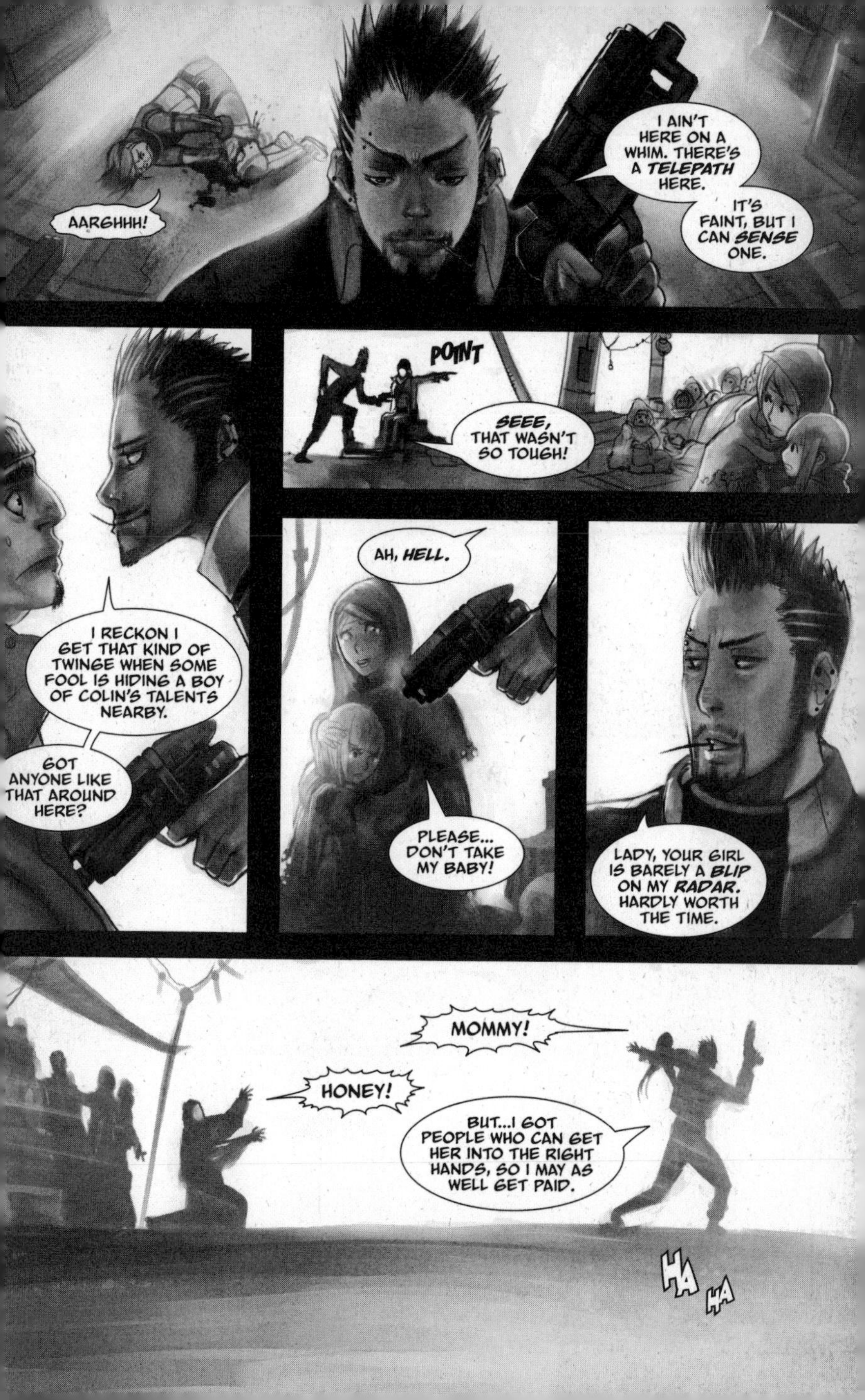
AARGHHH!
I AIN'T HERE ON A WHIM. THERE'S A *TELEPATH* HERE.
IT'S FAINT, BUT I CAN *SENSE* ONE.
I RECKON I GET THAT KIND OF TWINGE WHEN SOME FOOL IS HIDING A BOY OF COLIN'S TALENTS NEARBY.
GOT ANYONE LIKE THAT AROUND HERE?
POINT
SEEE, THAT WASN'T SO TOUGH!
AH, *HELL.*
PLEASE... DON'T TAKE MY BABY!
LADY, YOUR GIRL IS BARELY A *BLIP* ON MY *RADAR.* HARDLY WORTH THE TIME.
MOMMY!
HONEY!
BUT...I GOT PEOPLE WHO CAN GET HER INTO THE RIGHT HANDS, SO I MAY AS WELL GET PAID.
HA HA

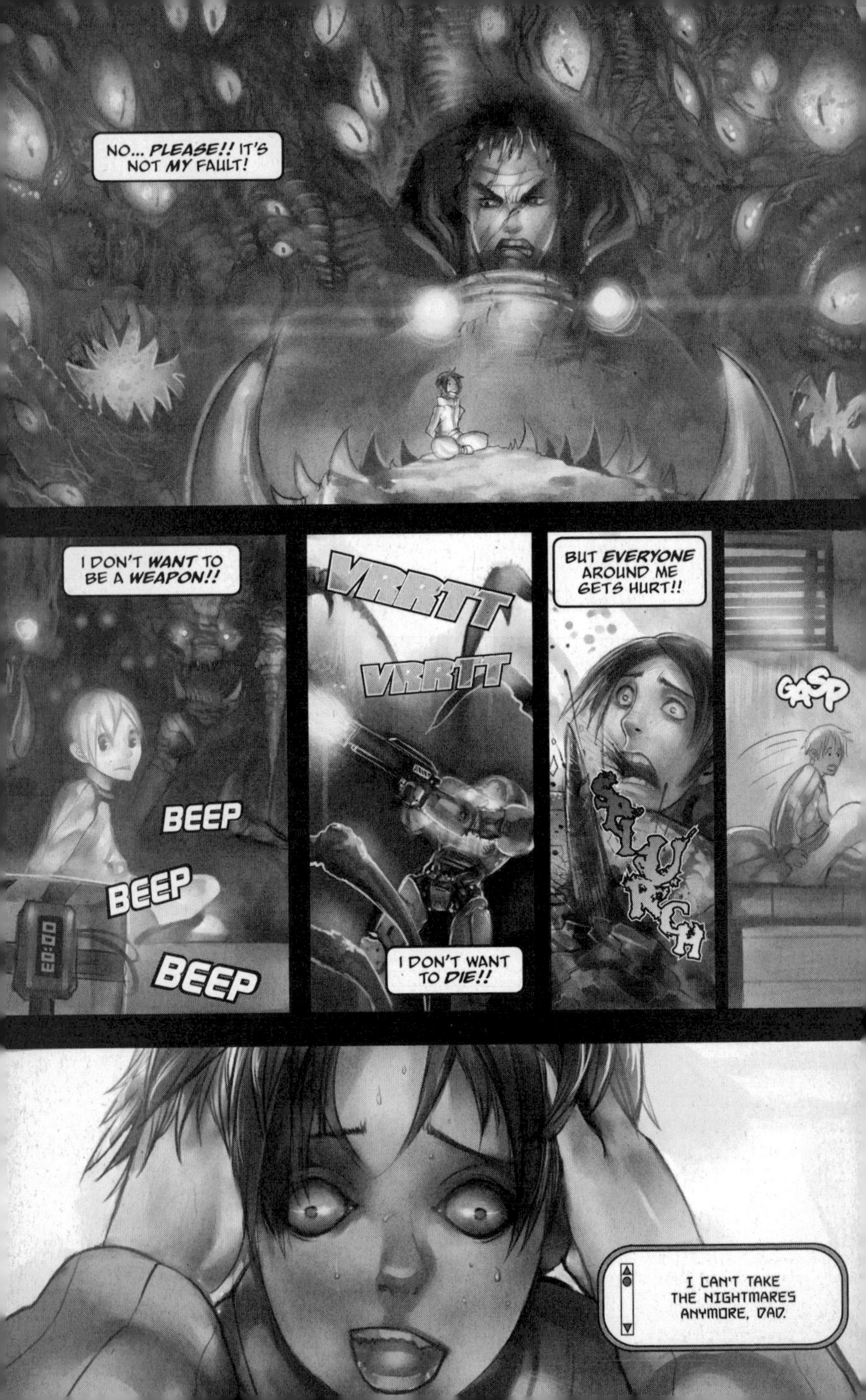
NO... PLEASE!! IT'S NOT MY FAULT!
I DON'T WANT TO BE A WEAPON!!
BEEP
BEEP
BEEP
VRRTT
VRRTT
I DON'T WANT TO DIE!!
BUT EVERYONE AROUND ME GETS HURT!!
GASP
I CAN'T TAKE THE NIGHTMARES ANYMORE, DAD.

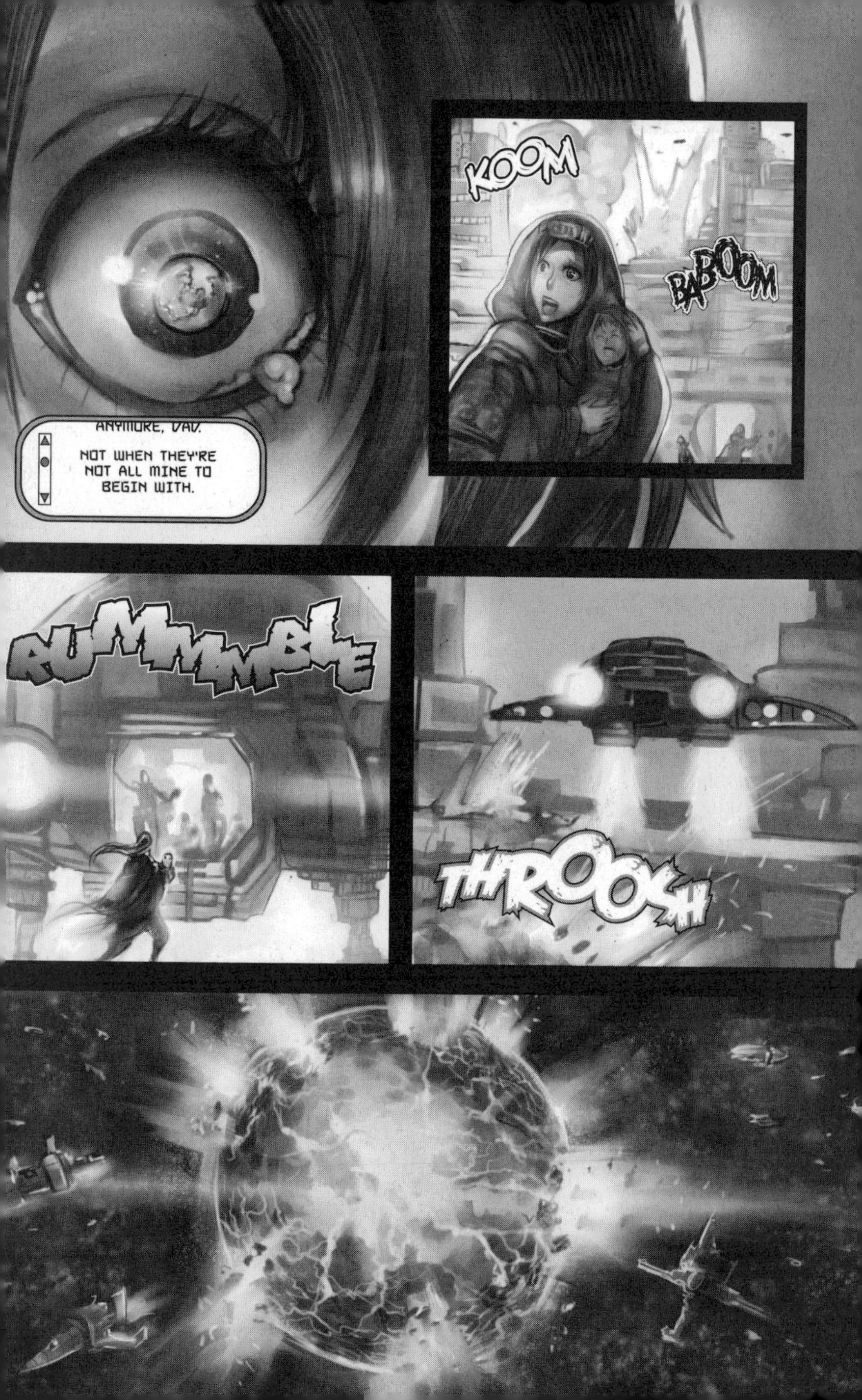
ANYMORE, DAD.
NOT WHEN THEY'RE NOT ALL MINE TO BEGIN WITH.
KOOM
BABOOM
RUMMMMBLE
THROOSH

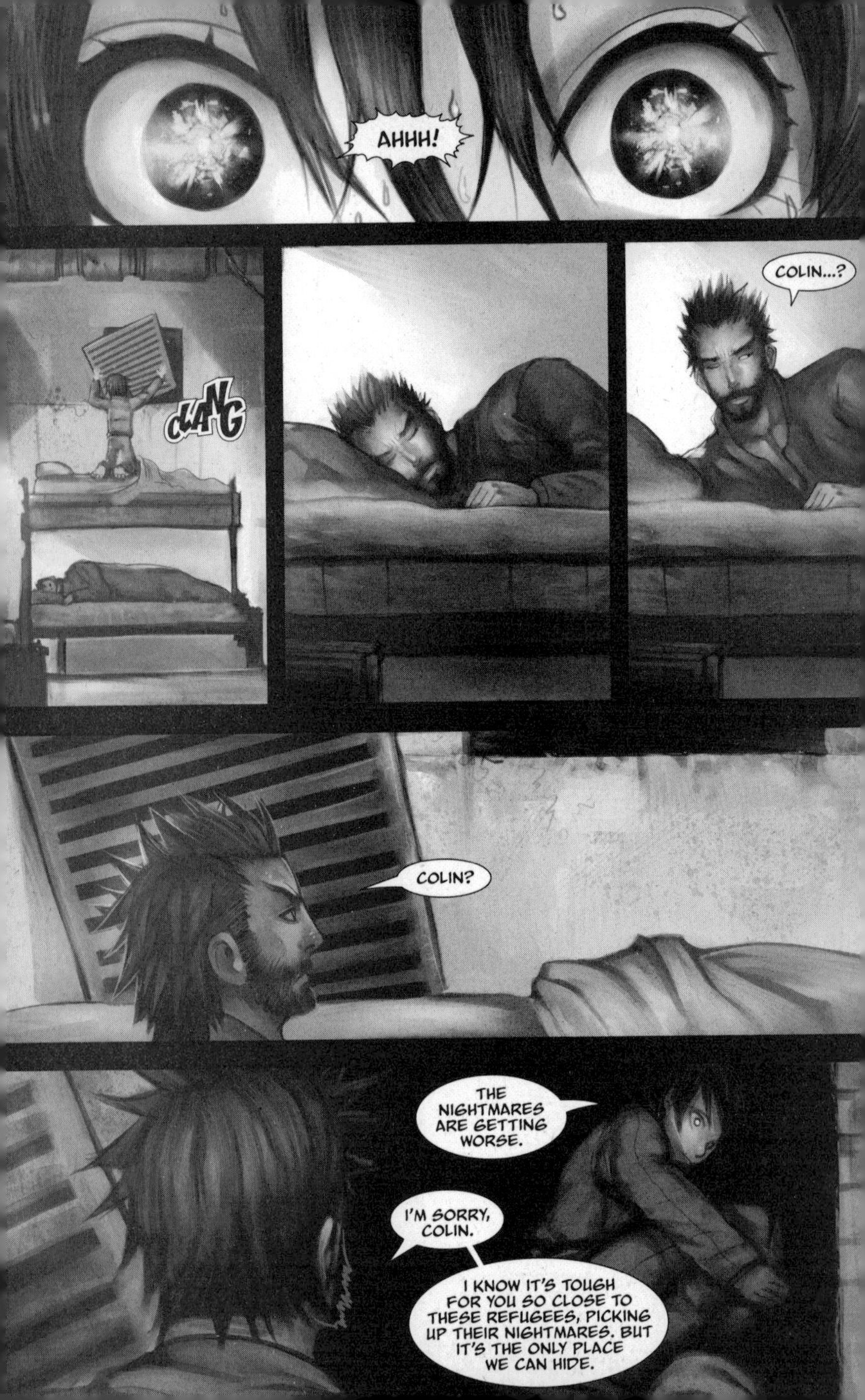
AHHH!
CLANG
COLIN...?
COLIN?
THE NIGHTMARES ARE GETTING WORSE.
I'M SORRY, COLIN.
I KNOW IT'S TOUGH FOR YOU SO CLOSE TO THESE REFUGEES, PICKING UP THEIR NIGHTMARES. BUT IT'S THE ONLY PLACE WE CAN HIDE.

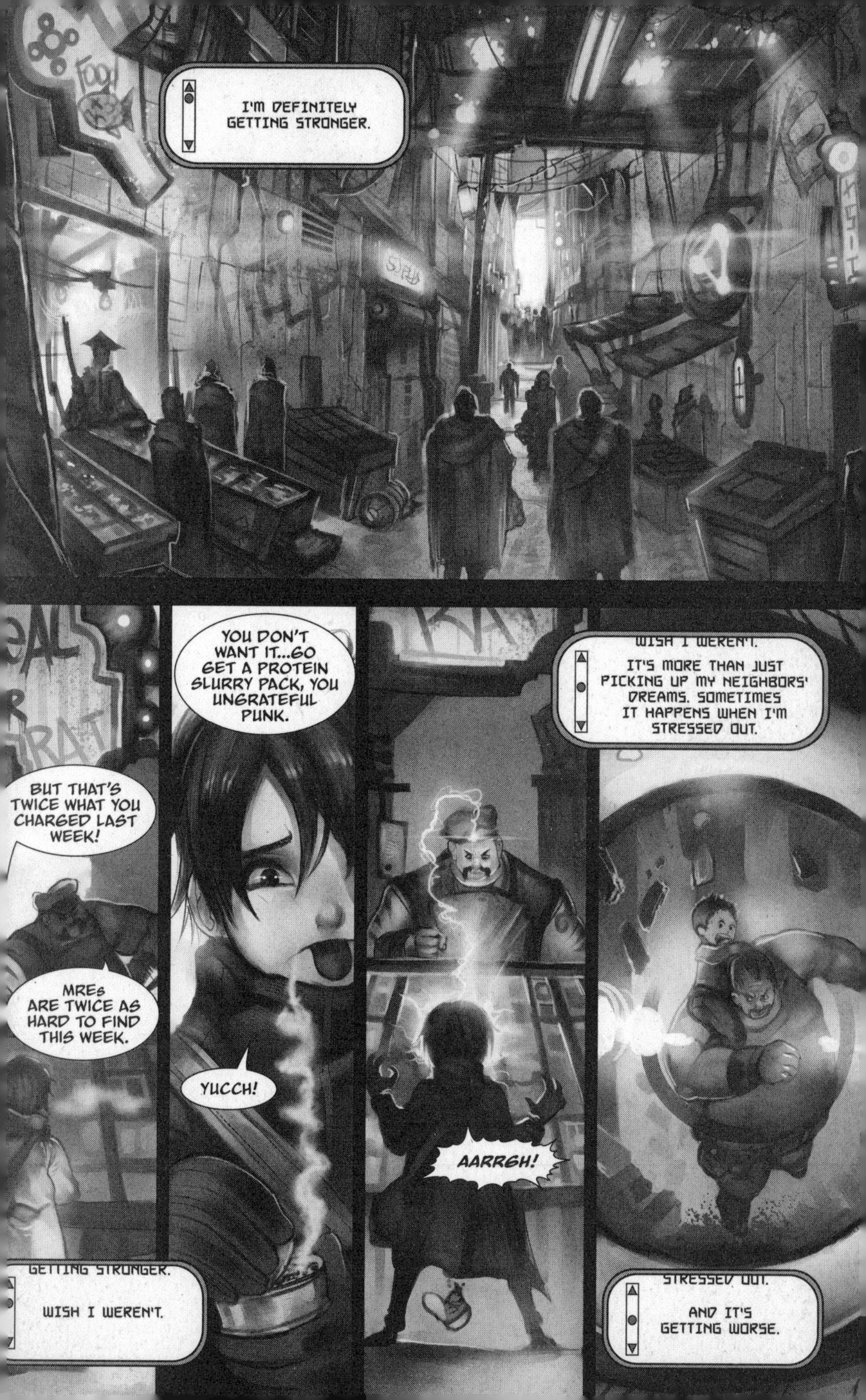
I'M DEFINITELY GETTING STRONGER.
BUT THAT'S TWICE WHAT YOU CHARGED LAST WEEK!
MREs ARE TWICE AS HARD TO FIND THIS WEEK.
GETTING STRONGER.
WISH I WEREN'T.
YOU DON'T WANT IT...GO GET A PROTEIN SLURRY PACK, YOU UNGRATEFUL PUNK.
YUCCH!
AARRGH!
WISH I WEREN'T.
IT'S MORE THAN JUST PICKING UP MY NEIGHBORS' DREAMS. SOMETIMES IT HAPPENS WHEN I'M STRESSED OUT.
STRESSED OUT.
AND IT'S GETTING WORSE.

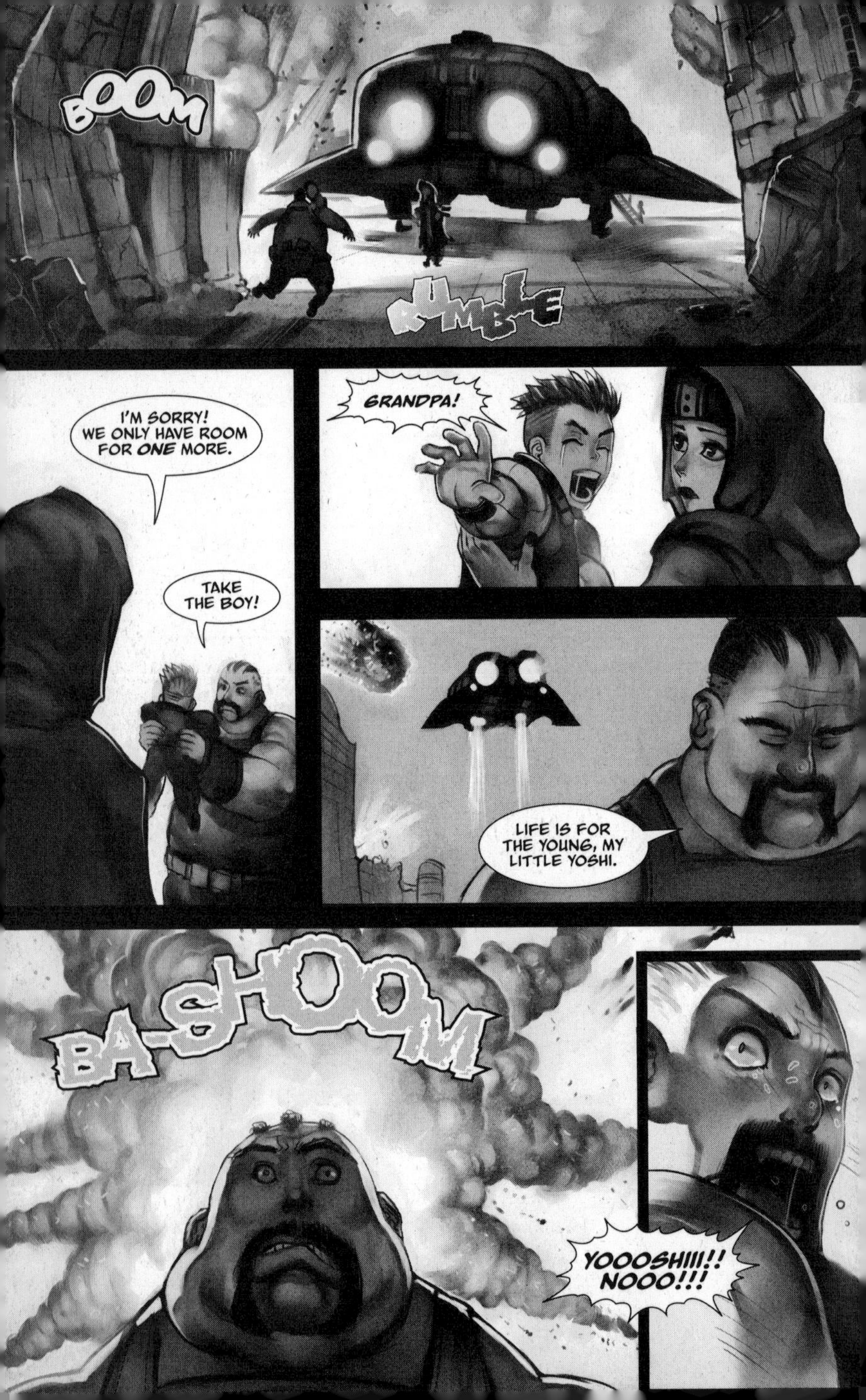
BOOM
RUMBLE
I'M SORRY! WE ONLY HAVE ROOM FOR *ONE* MORE.
TAKE THE BOY!
GRANDPA!
LIFE IS FOR THE YOUNG, MY LITTLE YOSHI.
BA-SHOOM
YOOOSHI!!!! NOOO!!!

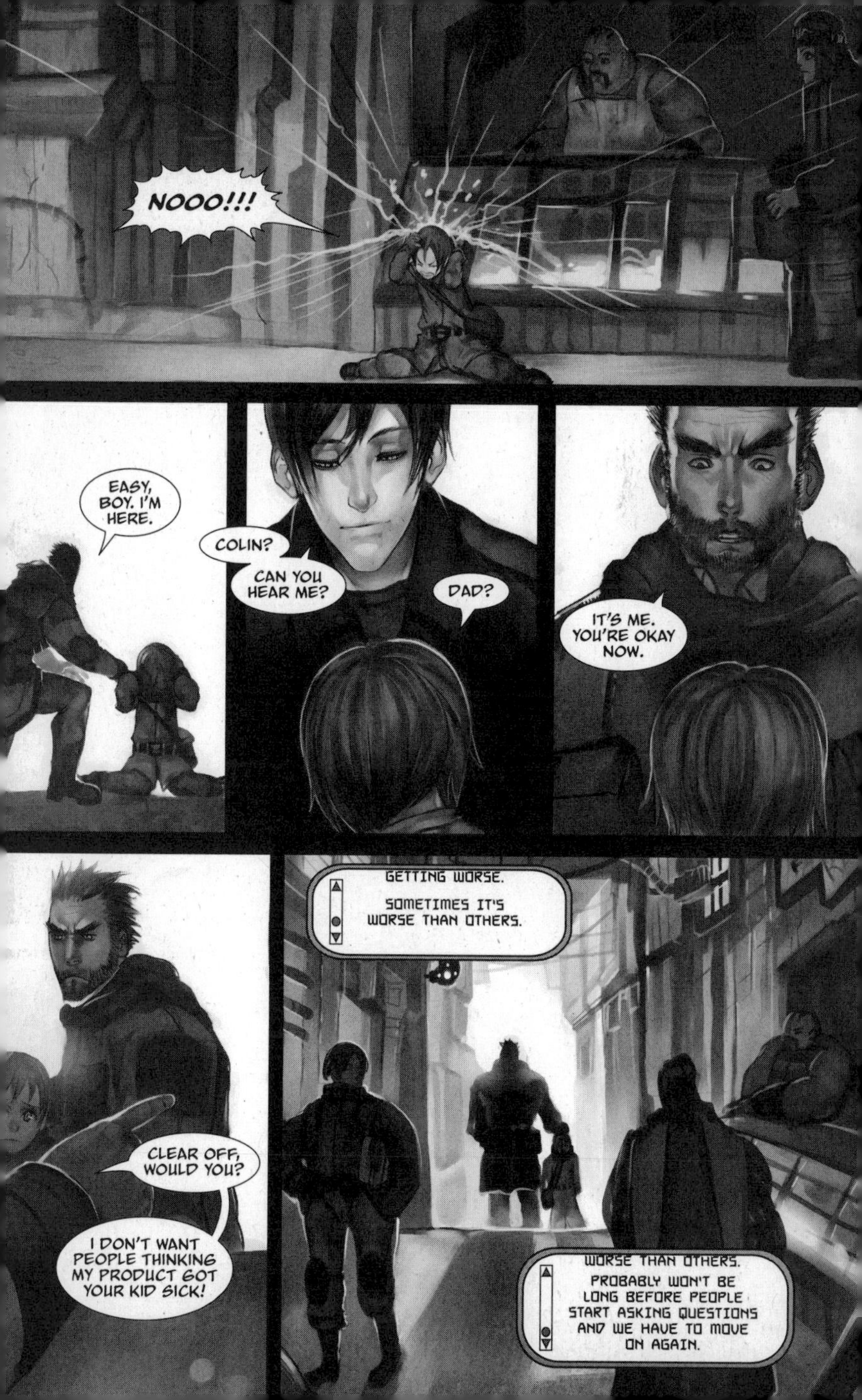
NOOO!!!
EASY, BOY. I'M HERE.
COLIN?
CAN YOU HEAR ME?
DAD?
IT'S ME. YOU'RE OKAY NOW.
CLEAR OFF, WOULD YOU?
I DON'T WANT PEOPLE THINKING MY PRODUCT GOT YOUR KID SICK!
GETTING WORSE.
SOMETIMES IT'S WORSE THAN OTHERS.
WORSE THAN OTHERS.
PROBABLY WON'T BE LONG BEFORE PEOPLE START ASKING QUESTIONS AND WE HAVE TO MOVE ON AGAIN.

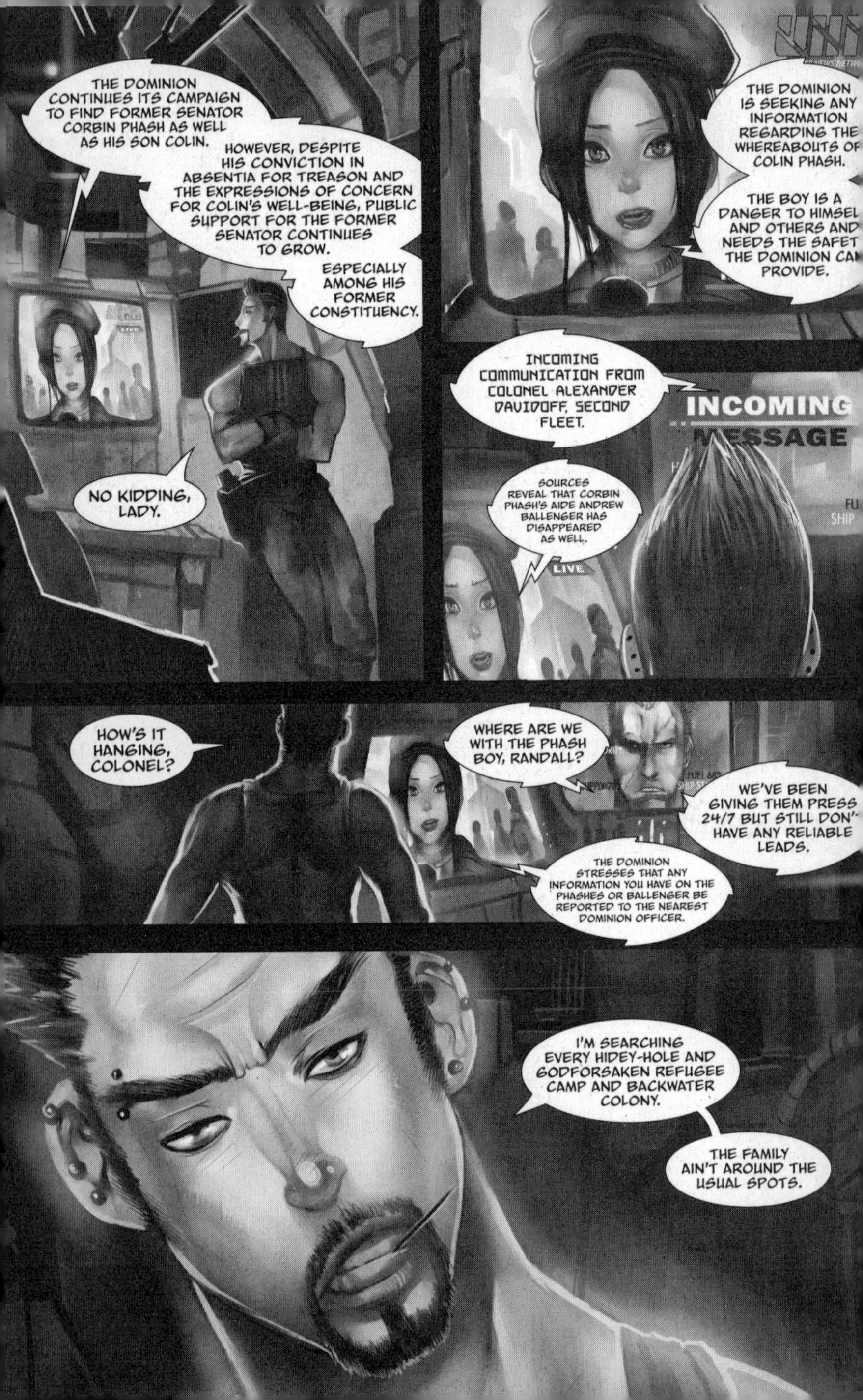
THE DOMINION CONTINUES ITS CAMPAIGN TO FIND FORMER SENATOR CORBIN PHASH AS WELL AS HIS SON COLIN.
HOWEVER, DESPITE HIS CONVICTION IN ABSENTIA FOR TREASON AND THE EXPRESSIONS OF CONCERN FOR COLIN'S WELL-BEING, PUBLIC SUPPORT FOR THE FORMER SENATOR CONTINUES TO GROW.
ESPECIALLY AMONG HIS FORMER CONSTITUENCY.
NO KIDDING, LADY.
THE DOMINION IS SEEKING ANY INFORMATION REGARDING THE WHEREABOUTS OF COLIN PHASH.
THE BOY IS A DANGER TO HIMSEL AND OTHERS AND NEEDS THE SAFET THE DOMINION CA PROVIDE.
INCOMING COMMUNICATION FROM COLONEL ALEXANDER DAVIDOFF, SECOND FLEET.
INCOMING MESSAGE
SOURCES REVEAL THAT CORBIN PHASH'S AIDE ANDREW BALLENGER HAS DISAPPEARED AS WELL.
LIVE
HOW'S IT HANGING, COLONEL?
WHERE ARE WE WITH THE PHASH BOY, RANDALL?
WE'VE BEEN GIVING THEM PRESS 24/7 BUT STILL DON' HAVE ANY RELIABLE LEADS.
THE DOMINION STRESSES THAT ANY INFORMATION YOU HAVE ON THE PHASHES OR BALLENGER BE REPORTED TO THE NEAREST DOMINION OFFICER.
I'M SEARCHING EVERY HIDEY-HOLE AND GODFORSAKEN REFUGEE CAMP AND BACKWATER COLONY.
THE FAMILY AIN'T AROUND THE USUAL SPOTS.

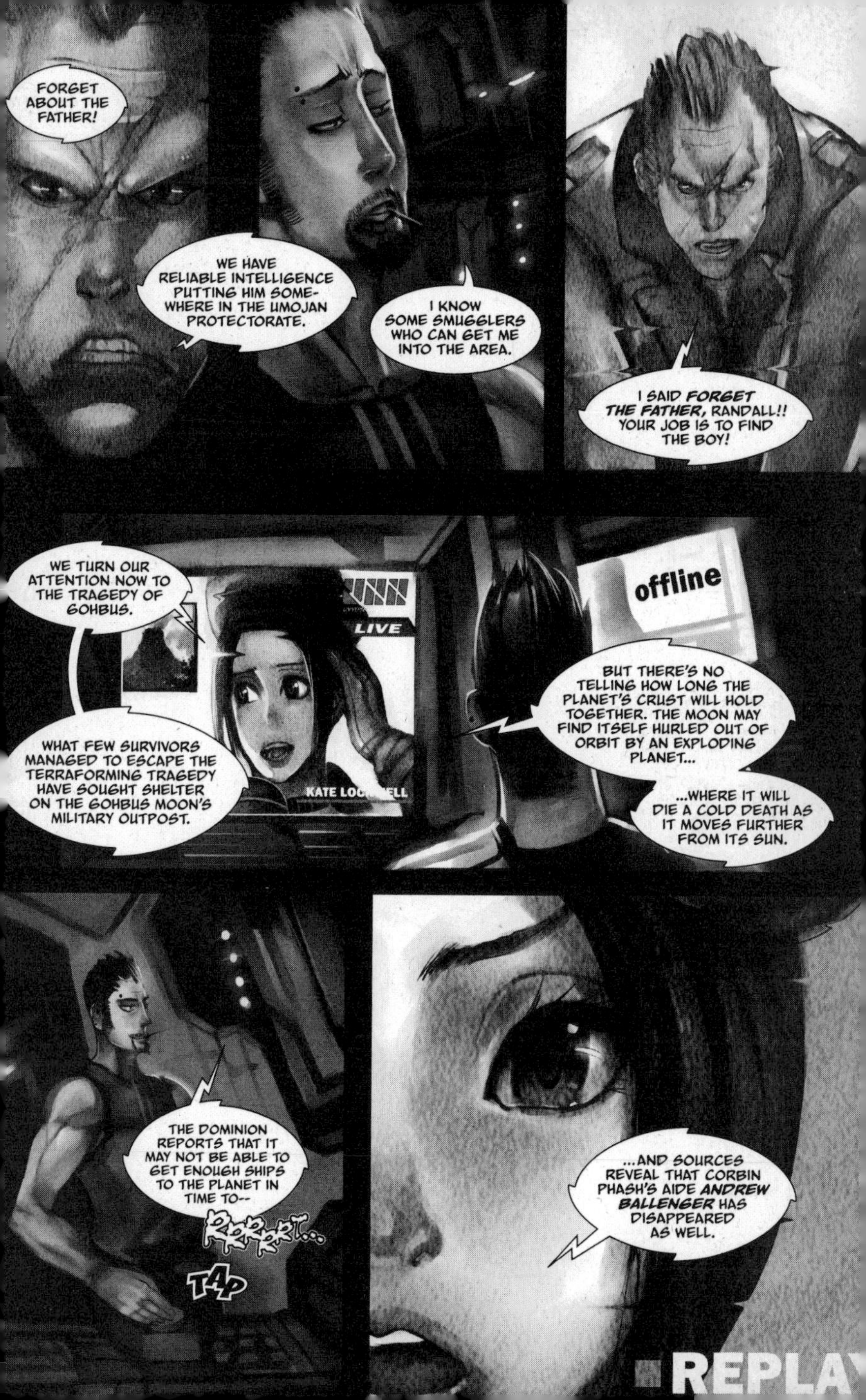
FORGET ABOUT THE FATHER!
WE HAVE RELIABLE INTELLIGENCE PUTTING HIM SOME-WHERE IN THE UMOJAN PROTECTORATE.
I KNOW SOME SMUGGLERS WHO CAN GET ME INTO THE AREA.
I SAID *FORGET THE FATHER,* RANDALL!! YOUR JOB IS TO FIND THE BOY!
WE TURN OUR ATTENTION NOW TO THE TRAGEDY OF GOHBUS.
LIVE
WHAT FEW SURVIVORS MANAGED TO ESCAPE THE TERRAFORMING TRAGEDY HAVE SOUGHT SHELTER ON THE GOHBUS MOON'S MILITARY OUTPOST.
offline
BUT THERE'S NO TELLING HOW LONG THE PLANET'S CRUST WILL HOLD TOGETHER. THE MOON MAY FIND ITSELF HURLED OUT OF ORBIT BY AN EXPLODING PLANET...
...WHERE IT WILL DIE A COLD DEATH AS IT MOVES FURTHER FROM ITS SUN.
THE DOMINION REPORTS THAT IT MAY NOT BE ABLE TO GET ENOUGH SHIPS TO THE PLANET IN TIME TO--
TAP
...AND SOURCES REVEAL THAT CORBIN PHASH'S AIDE *ANDREW BALLENGER* HAS DISAPPEARED AS WELL.
REPLAY

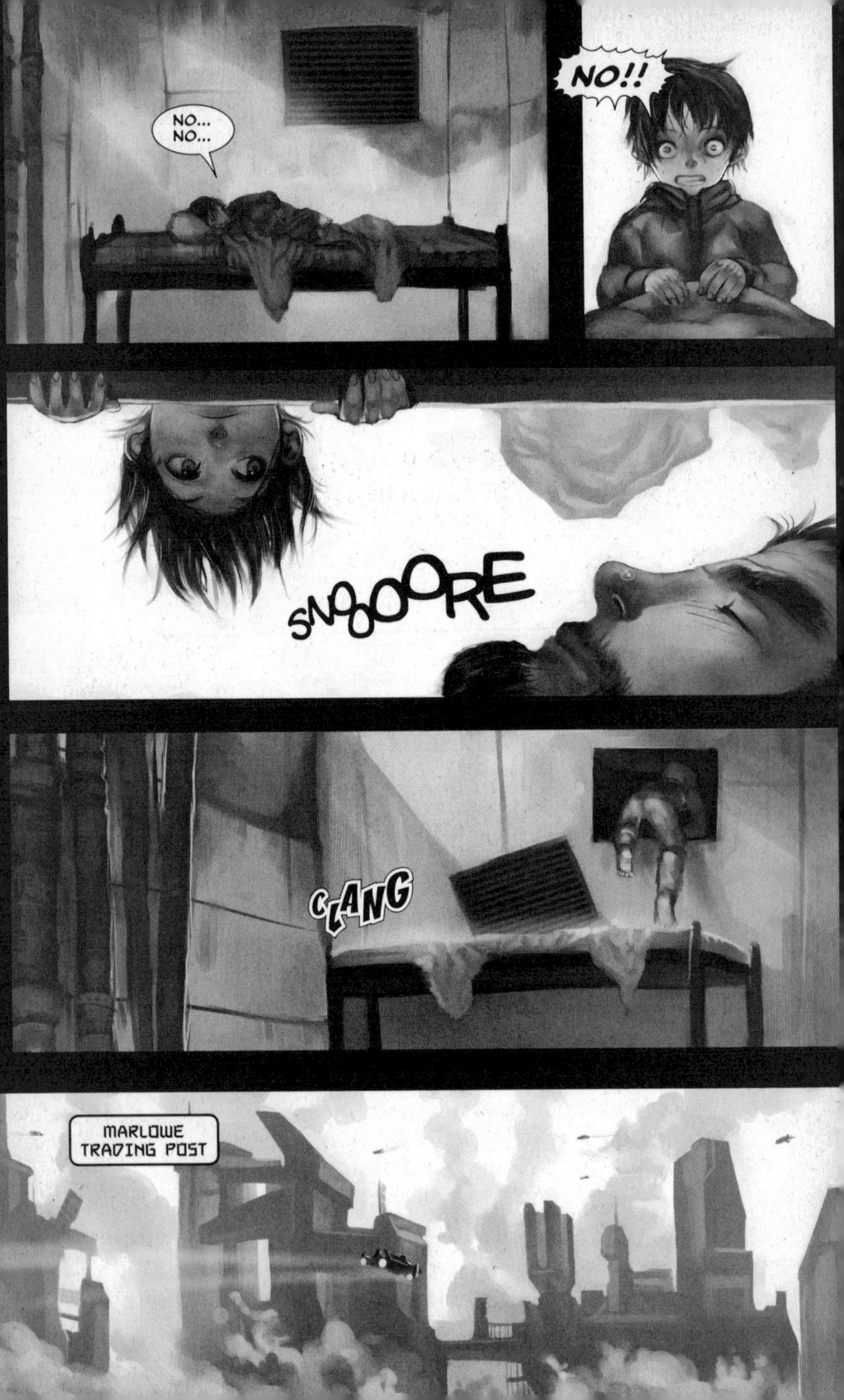
NO...
NO...
NO!!
SNOOOORE
CLANG
MARLOWE
TRADING POST

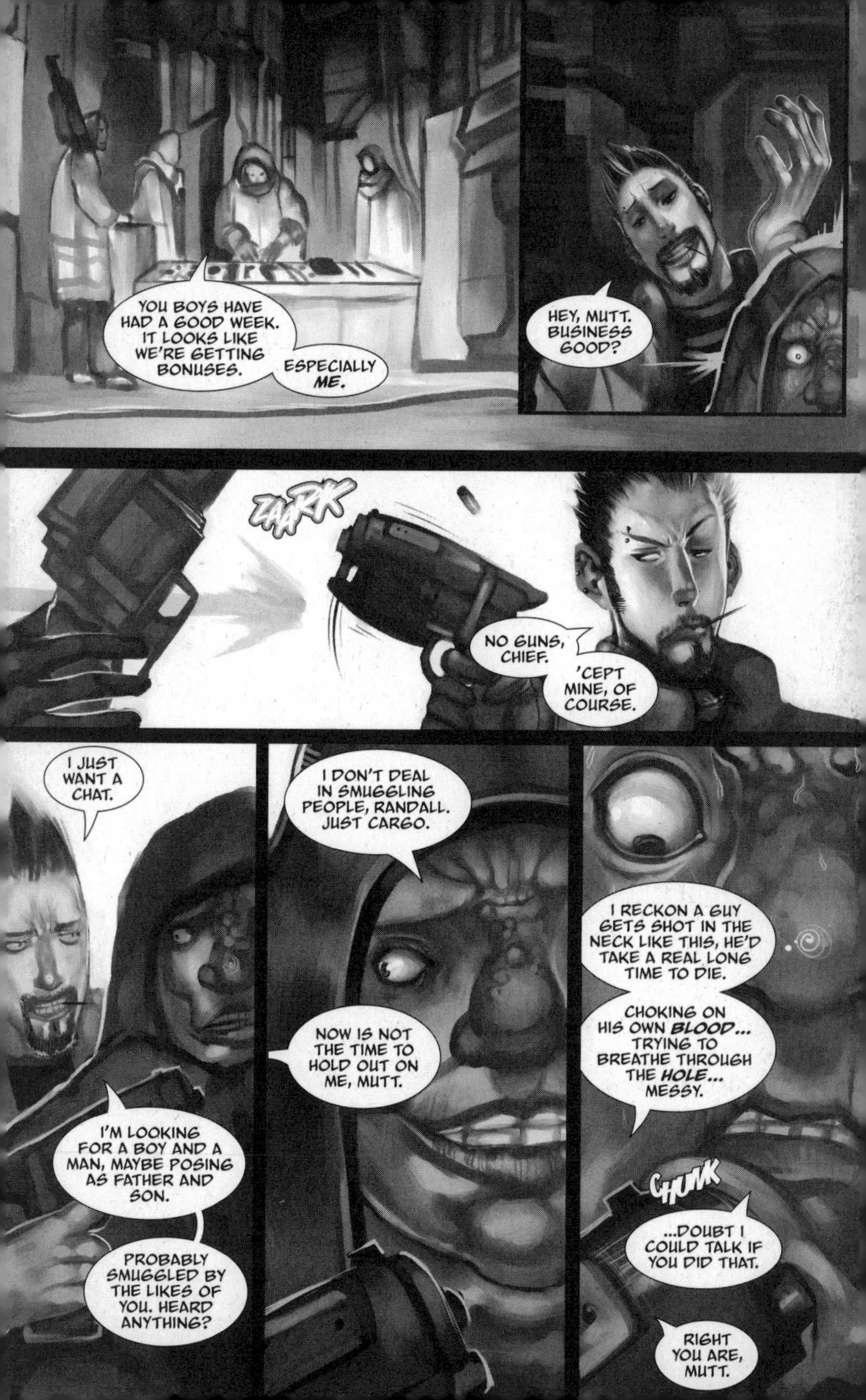
YOU BOYS HAVE HAD A GOOD WEEK. IT LOOKS LIKE WE'RE GETTING BONUSES.
ESPECIALLY *ME.*
HEY, MUTT. BUSINESS GOOD?
ZAARK
NO GUNS, CHIEF.
'CEPT MINE, OF COURSE.
I JUST WANT A CHAT.
I'M LOOKING FOR A BOY AND A MAN, MAYBE POSING AS FATHER AND SON.
PROBABLY SMUGGLED BY THE LIKES OF YOU. HEARD ANYTHING?
I DON'T DEAL IN SMUGGLING PEOPLE, RANDALL. JUST CARGO.
NOW IS NOT THE TIME TO HOLD OUT ON ME, MUTT.
I RECKON A GUY GETS SHOT IN THE NECK LIKE THIS, HE'D TAKE A REAL LONG TIME TO DIE.
CHOKING ON HIS OWN *BLOOD*... TRYING TO BREATHE THROUGH THE *HOLE*... MESSY.
CHUNK
...DOUBT I COULD TALK IF YOU DID THAT.
RIGHT YOU ARE, MUTT.

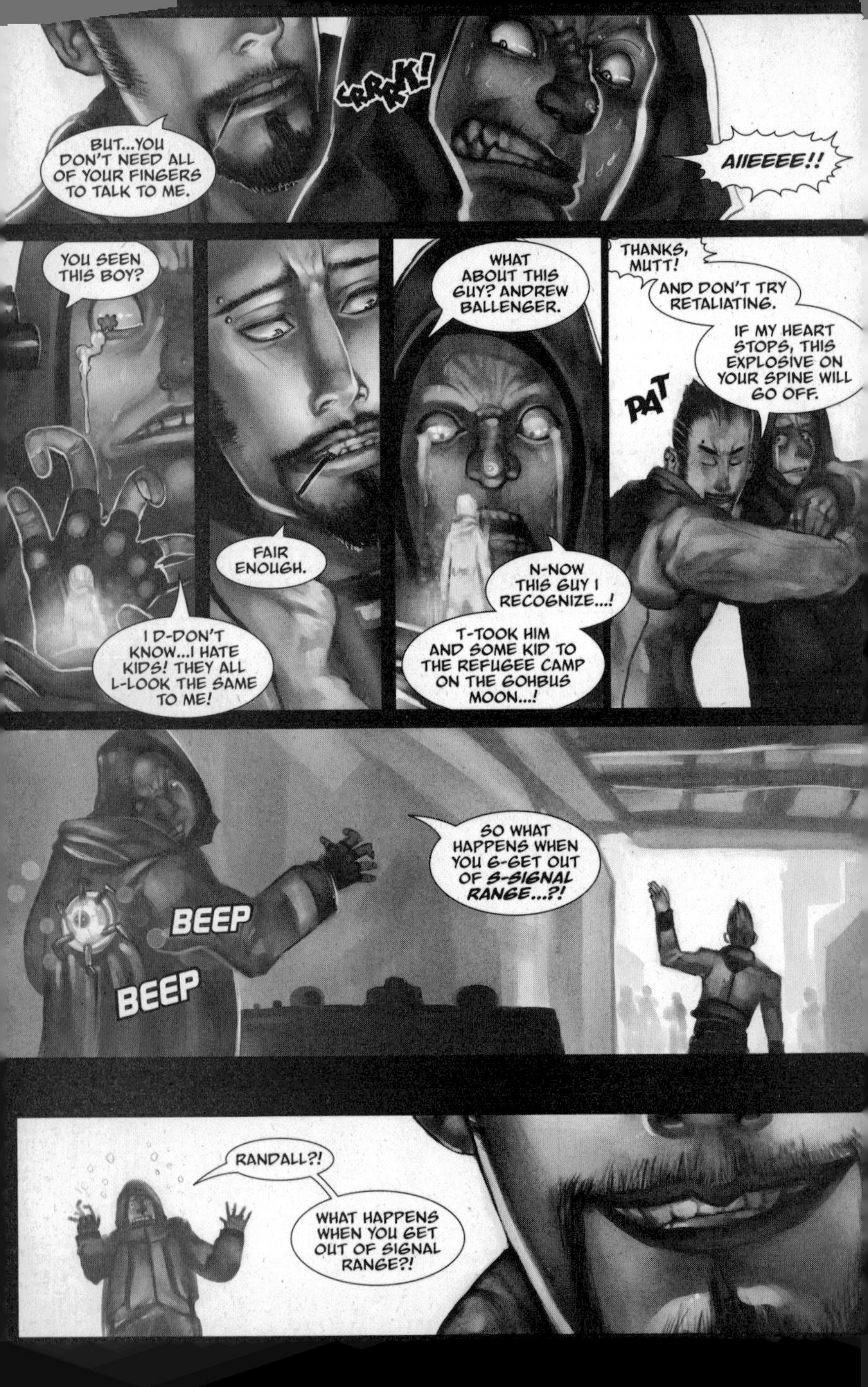
BUT...YOU DON'T NEED ALL OF YOUR FINGERS TO TALK TO ME.
CRRAK!
AIIEEEE!!
YOU SEEN THIS BOY?
I D-DON'T KNOW...I HATE KIDS! THEY ALL L-LOOK THE SAME TO ME!
FAIR ENOUGH.
WHAT ABOUT THIS GUY? ANDREW BALLENGER.
N-NOW THIS GUY I RECOGNIZE...!
T-TOOK HIM AND SOME KID TO THE REFUGEE CAMP ON THE GOHBUS MOON...!
THANKS, MUTT!
AND DON'T TRY RETALIATING.
IF MY HEART STOPS, THIS EXPLOSIVE ON YOUR SPINE WILL GO OFF.
PAT
BEEP
BEEP
SO WHAT HAPPENS WHEN YOU G-GET OUT OF S-SIGNAL RANGE...?!
RANDALL?!
WHAT HAPPENS WHEN YOU GET OUT OF SIGNAL RANGE?!

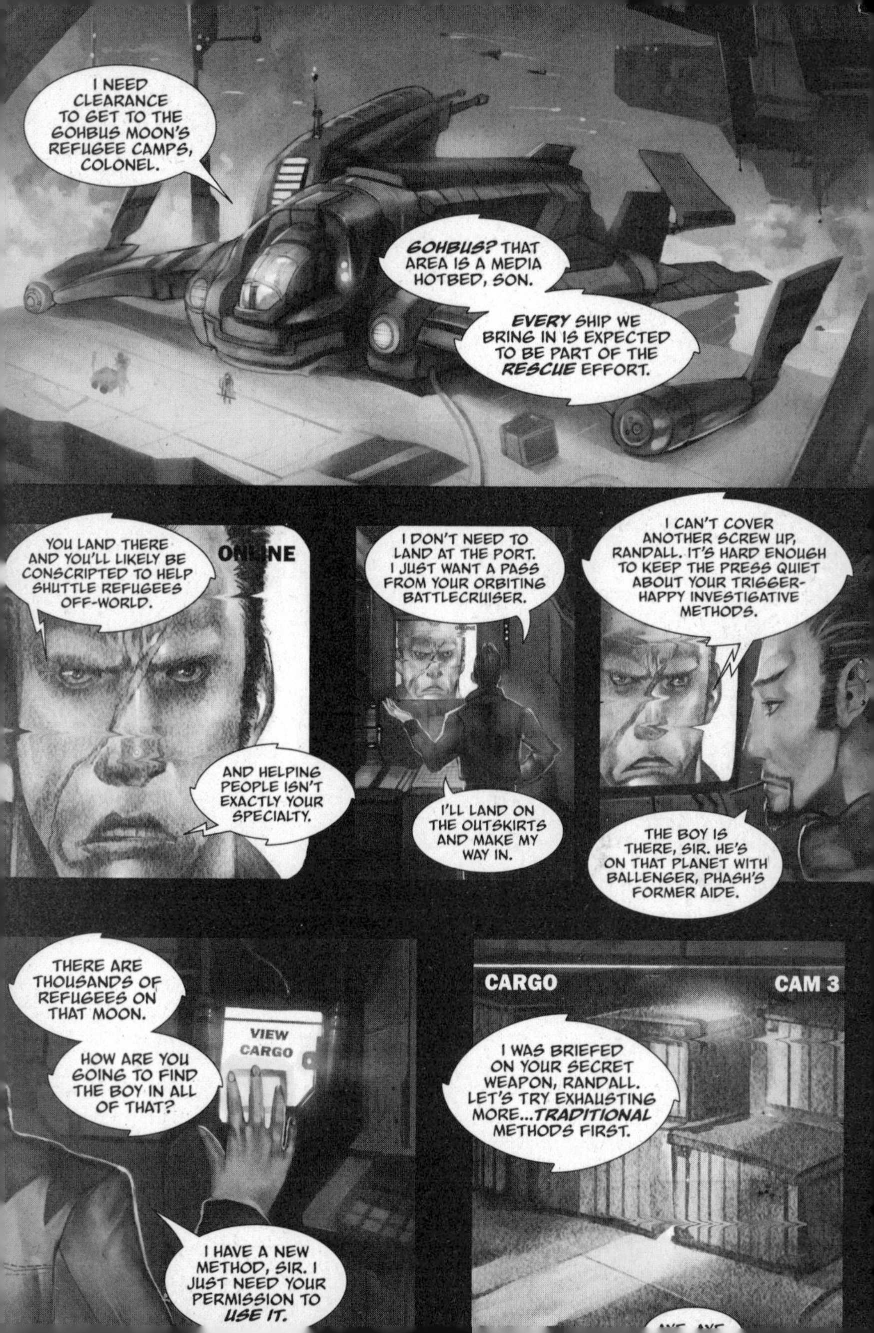

I NEED CLEARANCE TO GET TO THE GOHBUS MOON'S REFUGEE CAMPS, COLONEL.
GOHBUS? THAT AREA IS A MEDIA HOTBED, SON.
EVERY SHIP WE BRING IN IS EXPECTED TO BE PART OF THE RESCUE EFFORT.
YOU LAND THERE AND YOU'LL LIKELY BE CONSCRIPTED TO HELP SHUTTLE REFUGEES OFF-WORLD.
ONLINE
AND HELPING PEOPLE ISN'T EXACTLY YOUR SPECIALTY.
I DON'T NEED TO LAND AT THE PORT. I JUST WANT A PASS FROM YOUR ORBITING BATTLECRUISER.
I'LL LAND ON THE OUTSKIRTS AND MAKE MY WAY IN.
I CAN'T COVER ANOTHER SCREW UP, RANDALL. IT'S HARD ENOUGH TO KEEP THE PRESS QUIET ABOUT YOUR TRIGGER-HAPPY INVESTIGATIVE METHODS.
THE BOY IS THERE, SIR. HE'S ON THAT PLANET WITH BALLENGER, PHASH'S FORMER AIDE.
THERE ARE THOUSANDS OF REFUGEES ON THAT MOON.
HOW ARE YOU GOING TO FIND THE BOY IN ALL OF THAT?
VIEW CARGO
I HAVE A NEW METHOD, SIR. I JUST NEED YOUR PERMISSION TO USE IT.
CARGO
CAM 3
I WAS BRIEFED ON YOUR SECRET WEAPON, RANDALL. LET'S TRY EXHAUSTING MORE...TRADITIONAL METHODS FIRST.

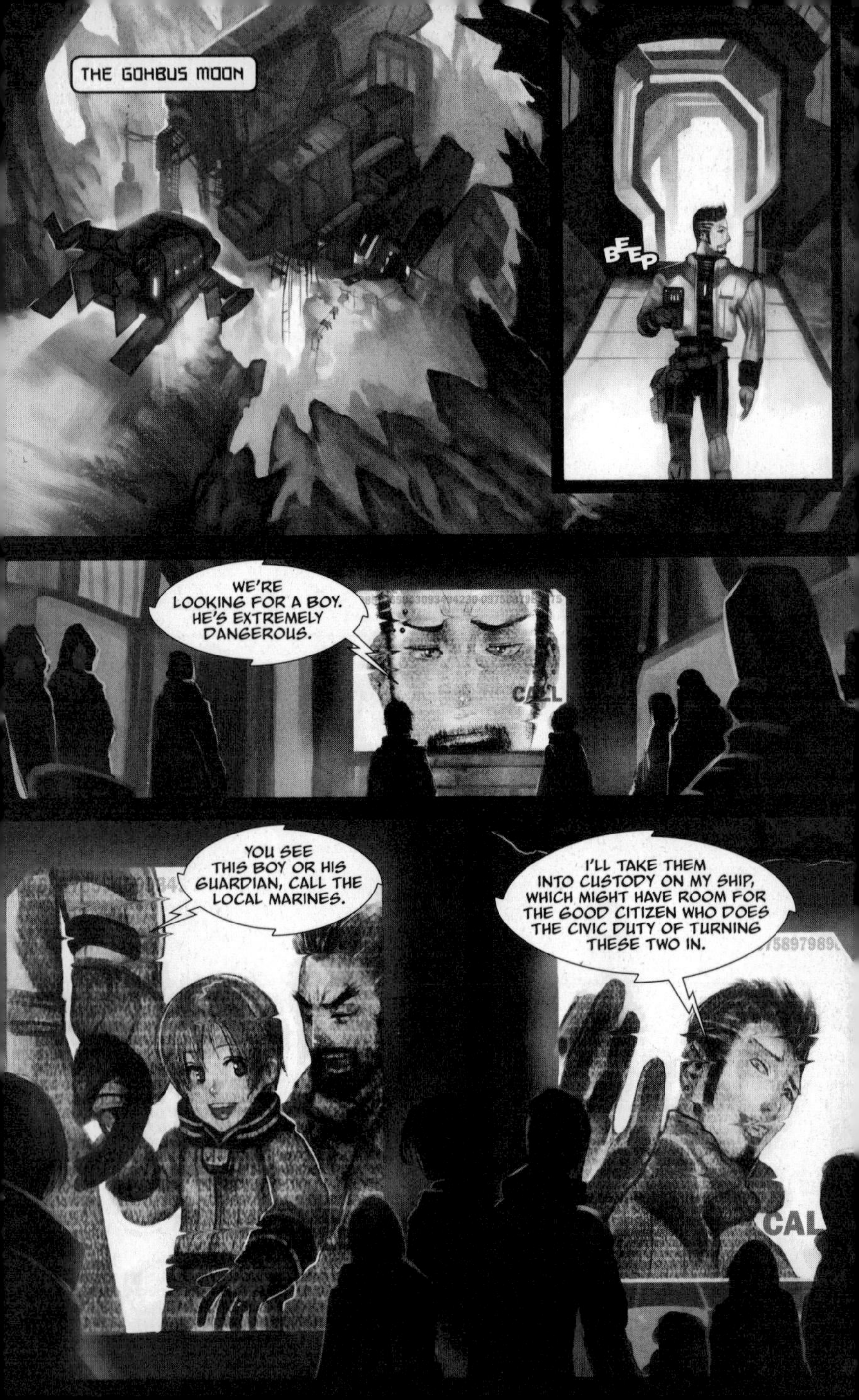
THE GOHBUS MOON
BEEP
WE'RE LOOKING FOR A BOY. HE'S EXTREMELY DANGEROUS.
CALL
YOU SEE THIS BOY OR HIS GUARDIAN, CALL THE LOCAL MARINES.
I'LL TAKE THEM INTO CUSTODY ON MY SHIP, WHICH MIGHT HAVE ROOM FOR THE GOOD CITIZEN WHO DOES THE CIVIC DUTY OF TURNING THESE TWO IN.
CAL

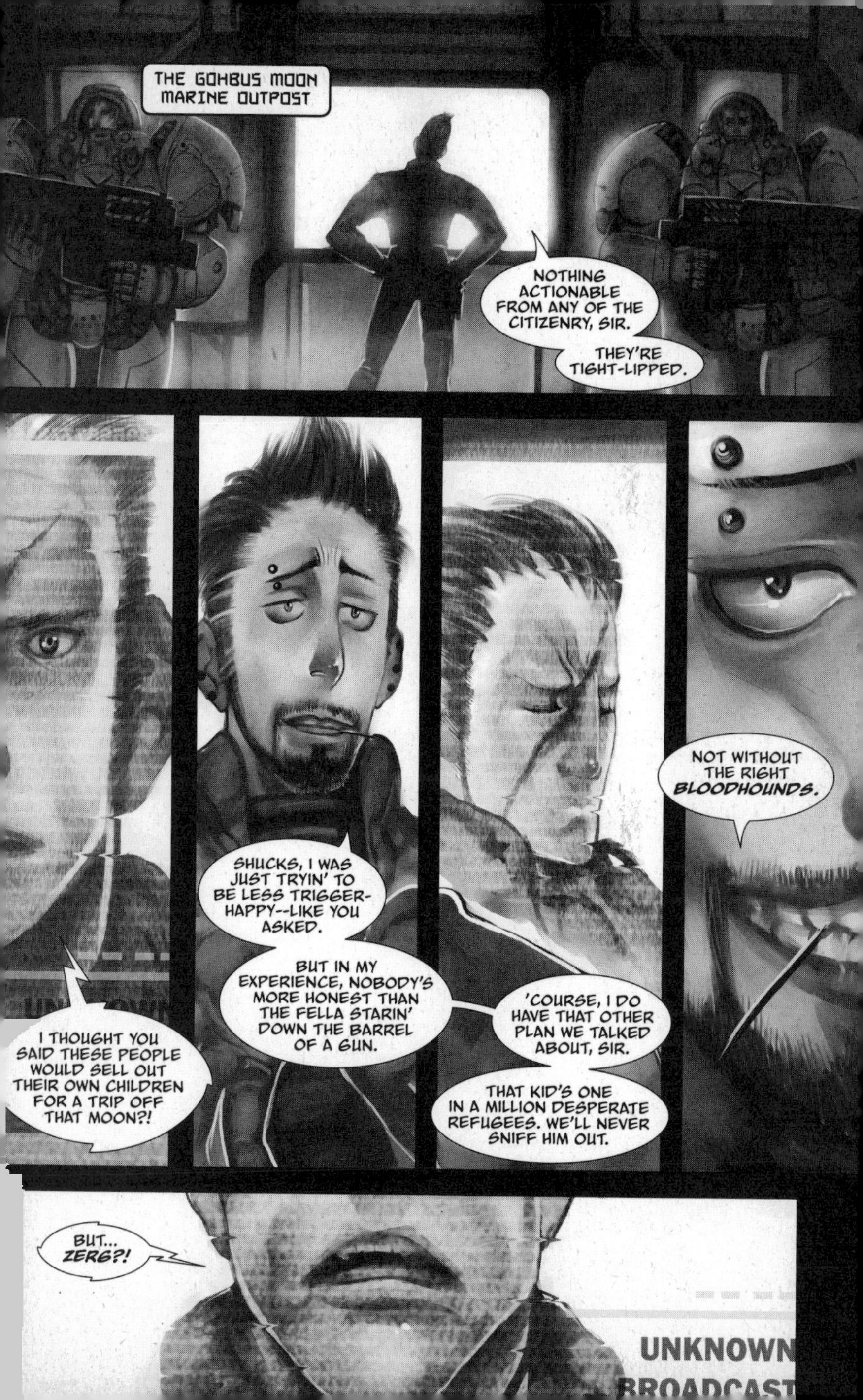
THE GOHBUS MOON MARINE OUTPOST
NOTHING ACTIONABLE FROM ANY OF THE CITIZENRY, SIR.
THEY'RE TIGHT-LIPPED.
I THOUGHT YOU SAID THESE PEOPLE WOULD SELL OUT THEIR OWN CHILDREN FOR A TRIP OFF THAT MOON?!
SHUCKS, I WAS JUST TRYIN' TO BE LESS TRIGGER-HAPPY--LIKE YOU ASKED.
BUT IN MY EXPERIENCE, NOBODY'S MORE HONEST THAN THE FELLA STARIN' DOWN THE BARREL OF A GUN.
'COURSE, I DO HAVE THAT OTHER PLAN WE TALKED ABOUT, SIR.
THAT KID'S ONE IN A MILLION DESPERATE REFUGEES. WE'LL NEVER SNIFF HIM OUT.
NOT WITHOUT THE RIGHT *BLOODHOUNDS*.
BUT... *ZERG?!*
UNKNOWN
BROADCAST

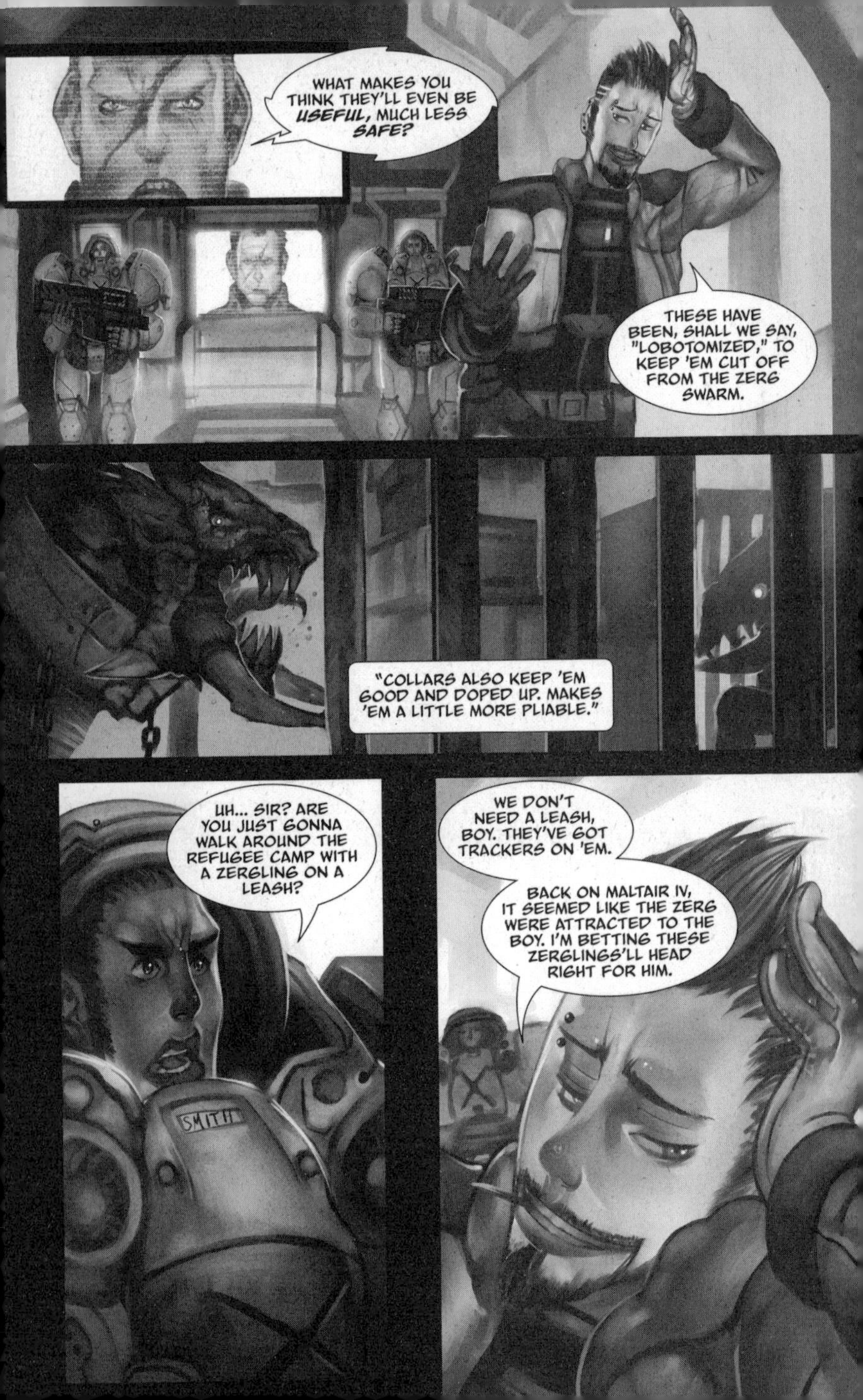
WHAT MAKES YOU THINK THEY'LL EVEN BE USEFUL, MUCH LESS SAFE?
THESE HAVE BEEN, SHALL WE SAY, "LOBOTOMIZED," TO KEEP 'EM CUT OFF FROM THE ZERG SWARM.
"COLLARS ALSO KEEP 'EM GOOD AND DOPED UP. MAKES 'EM A LITTLE MORE PLIABLE."
UH... SIR? ARE YOU JUST GONNA WALK AROUND THE REFUGEE CAMP WITH A ZERGLING ON A LEASH?
SMITH
WE DON'T NEED A LEASH, BOY. THEY'VE GOT TRACKERS ON 'EM.
BACK ON MALTAIR IV, IT SEEMED LIKE THE ZERG WERE ATTRACTED TO THE BOY. I'M BETTING THESE ZERGLINGS'LL HEAD RIGHT FOR HIM.

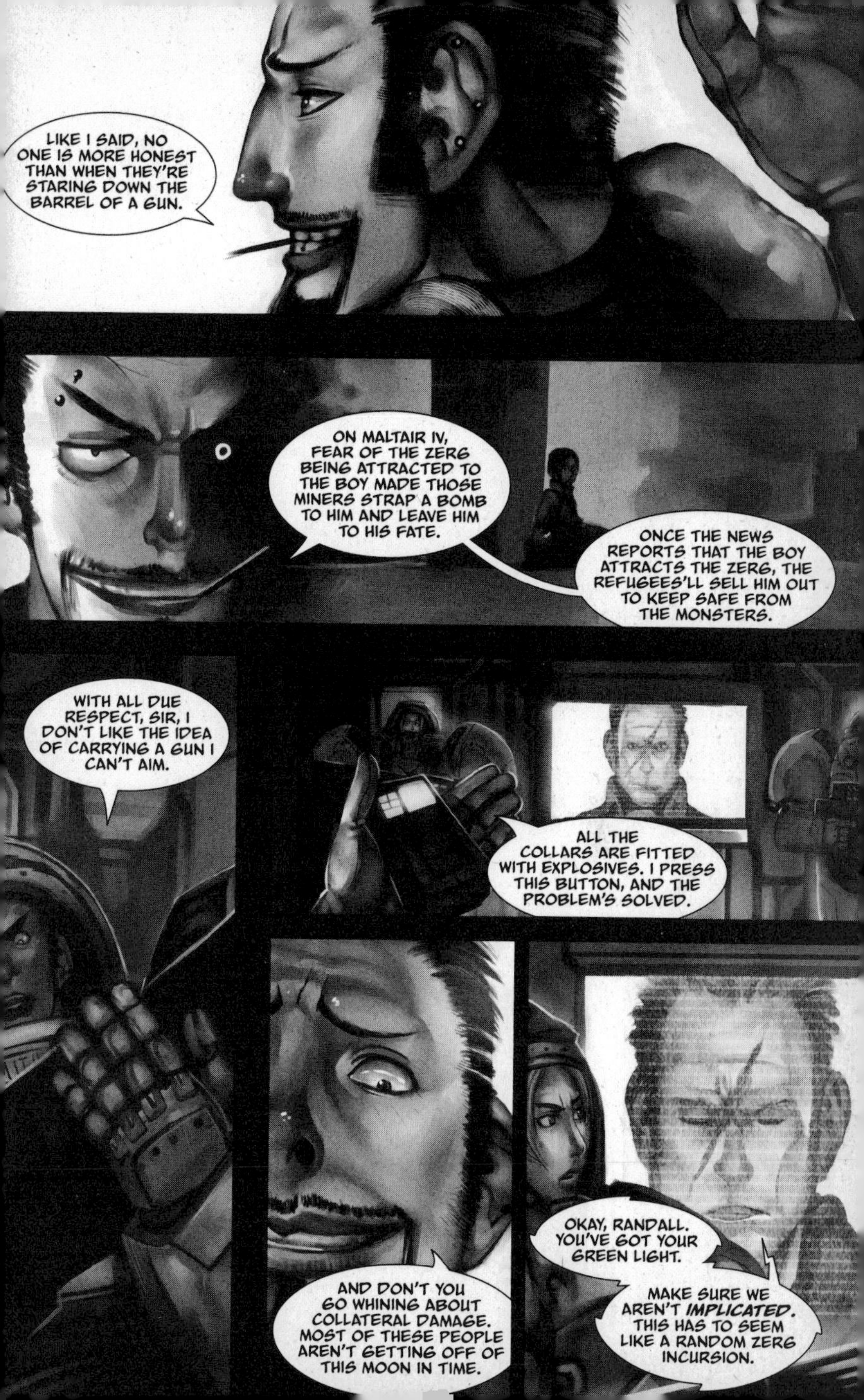
LIKE I SAID, NO ONE IS MORE HONEST THAN WHEN THEY'RE STARING DOWN THE BARREL OF A GUN.
ON MALTAIR IV, FEAR OF THE ZERG BEING ATTRACTED TO THE BOY MADE THOSE MINERS STRAP A BOMB TO HIM AND LEAVE HIM TO HIS FATE.
ONCE THE NEWS REPORTS THAT THE BOY ATTRACTS THE ZERG, THE REFUGEES'LL SELL HIM OUT TO KEEP SAFE FROM THE MONSTERS.
WITH ALL DUE RESPECT, SIR, I DON'T LIKE THE IDEA OF CARRYING A GUN I CAN'T AIM.
ALL THE COLLARS ARE FITTED WITH EXPLOSIVES. I PRESS THIS BUTTON, AND THE PROBLEM'S SOLVED.
AND DON'T YOU GO WHINING ABOUT COLLATERAL DAMAGE. MOST OF THESE PEOPLE AREN'T GETTING OFF OF THIS MOON IN TIME.
OKAY, RANDALL. YOU'VE GOT YOUR GREEN LIGHT.
MAKE SURE WE AREN'T *IMPLICATED*. THIS HAS TO SEEM LIKE A RANDOM ZERG INCURSION.

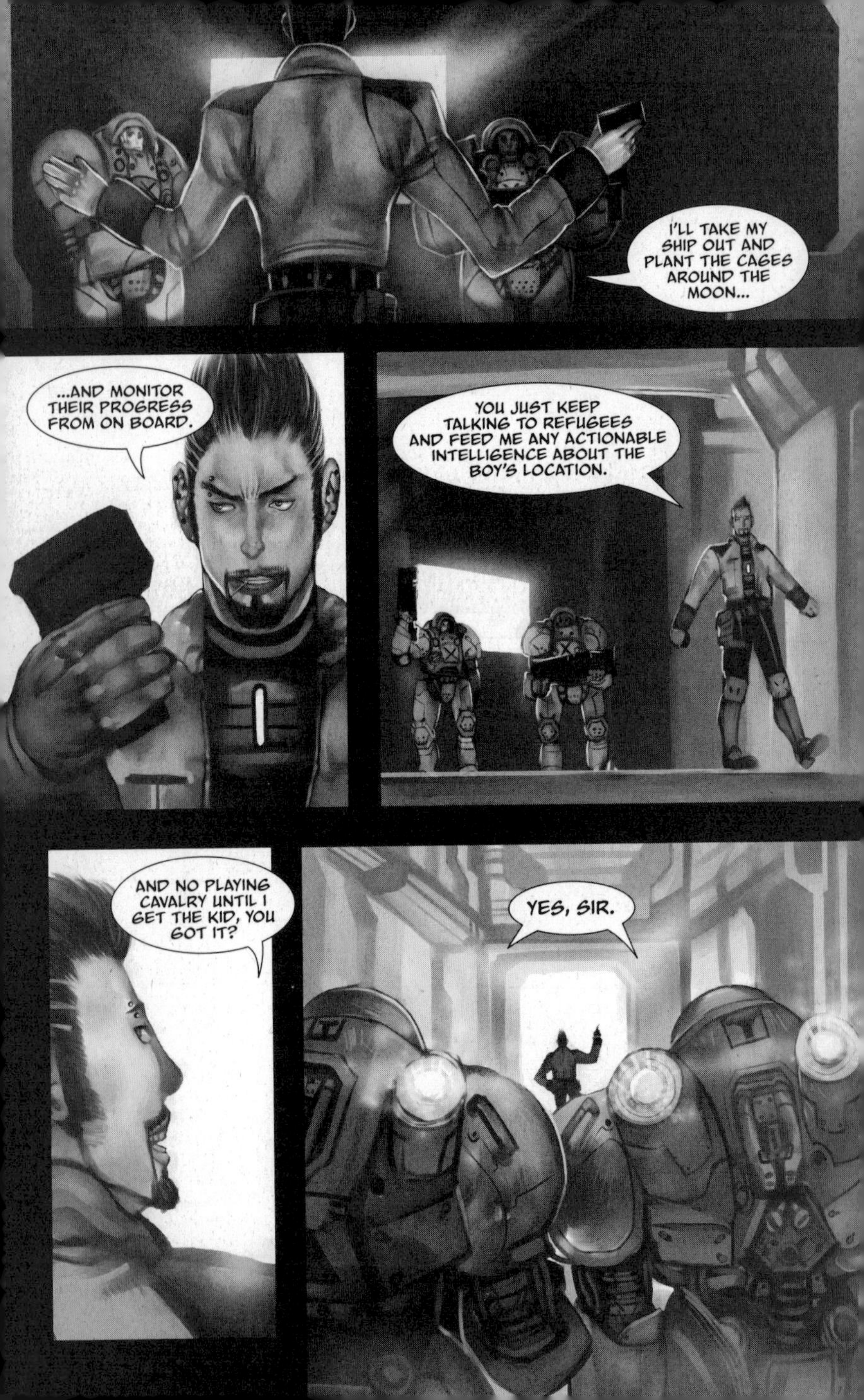
I'LL TAKE MY SHIP OUT AND PLANT THE CAGES AROUND THE MOON...
...AND MONITOR THEIR PROGRESS FROM ON BOARD.
YOU JUST KEEP TALKING TO REFUGEES AND FEED ME ANY ACTIONABLE INTELLIGENCE ABOUT THE BOY'S LOCATION.
AND NO PLAYING CAVALRY UNTIL I GET THE KID, YOU GOT IT?
YES, SIR.

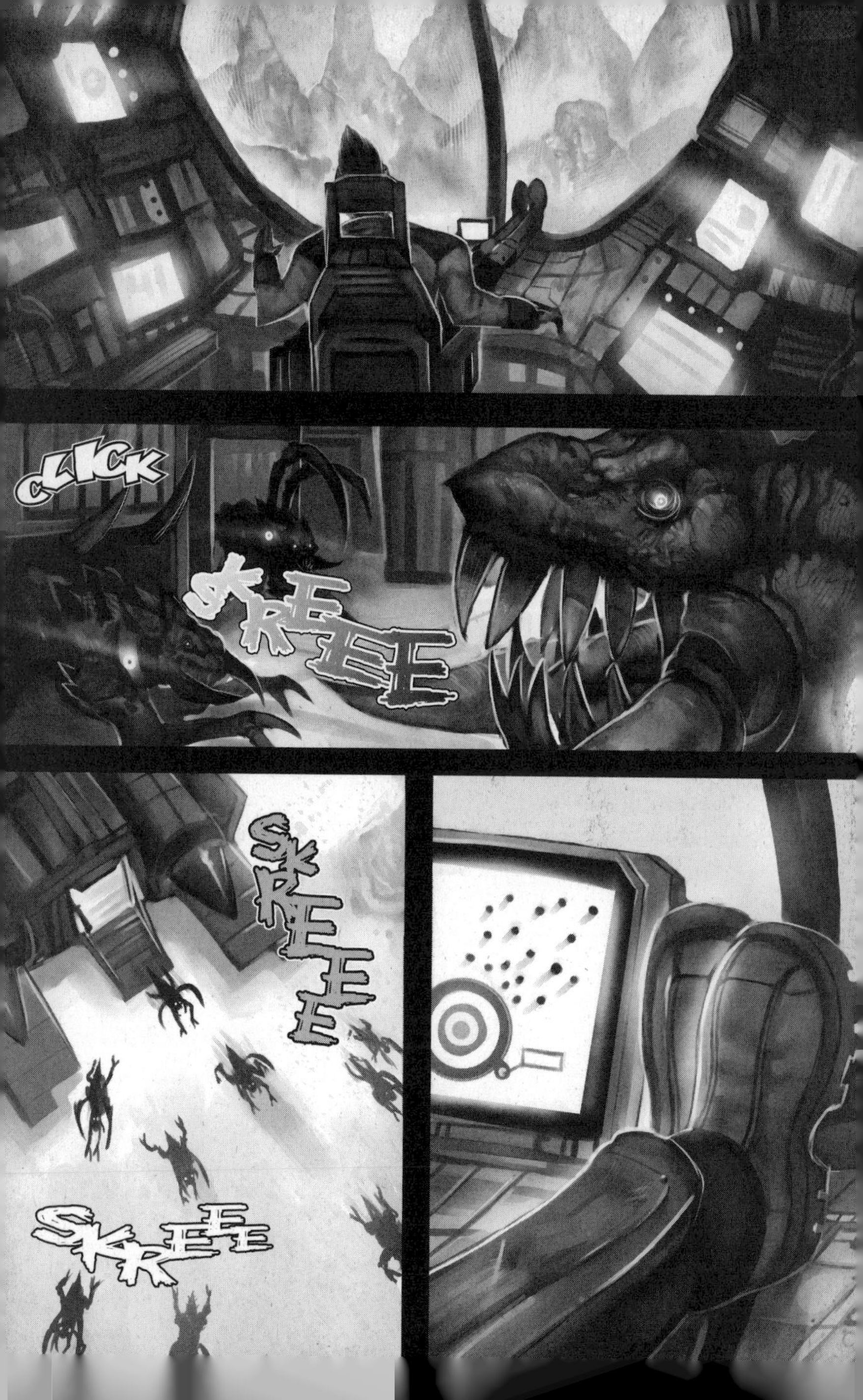
CLICK
SKREEE
SKREEE
SKREEE

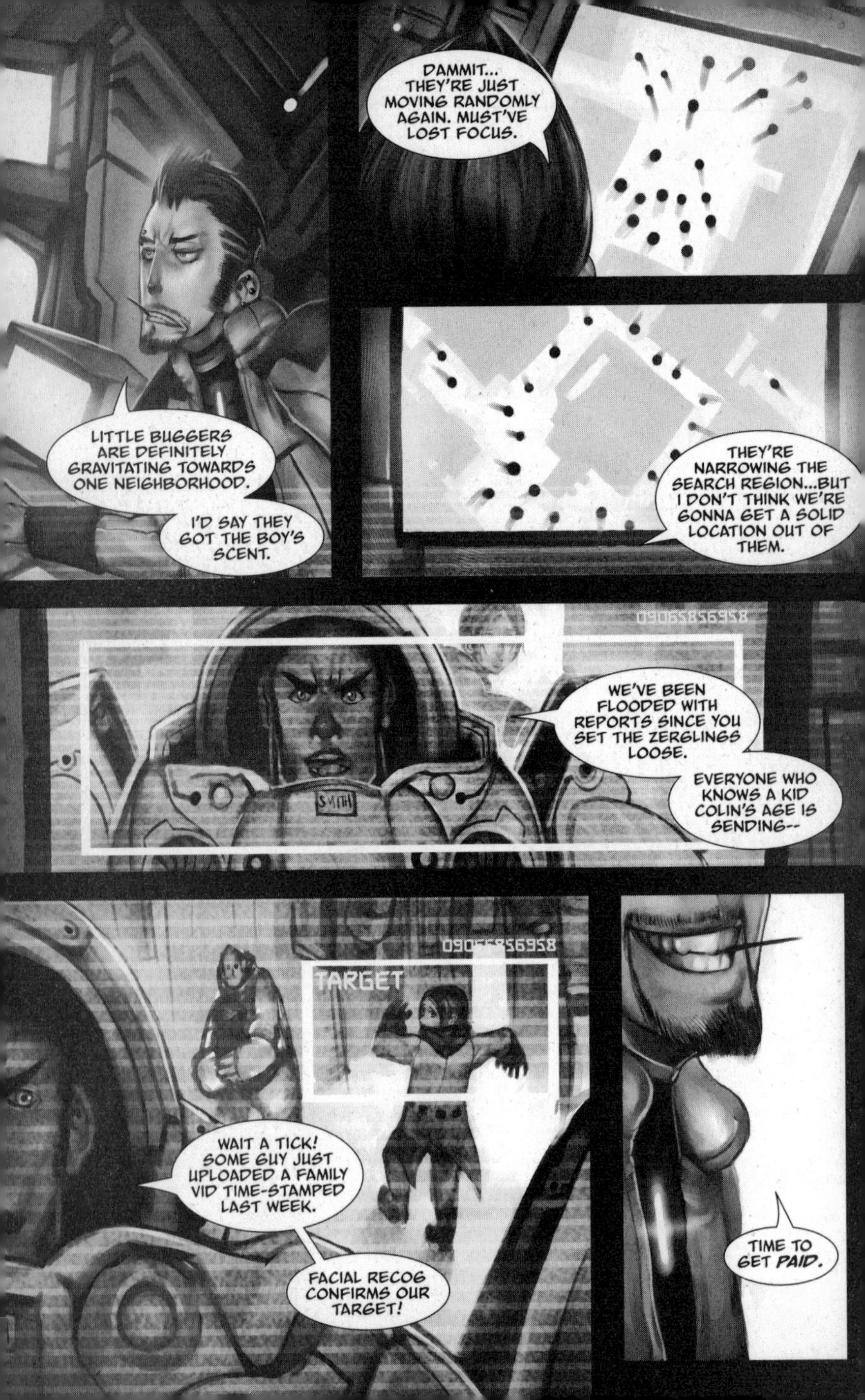
DAMMIT... THEY'RE JUST MOVING RANDOMLY AGAIN. MUST'VE LOST FOCUS.
LITTLE BUGGERS ARE DEFINITELY GRAVITATING TOWARDS ONE NEIGHBORHOOD.
I'D SAY THEY GOT THE BOY'S SCENT.
THEY'RE NARROWING THE SEARCH REGION...BUT I DON'T THINK WE'RE GONNA GET A SOLID LOCATION OUT OF THEM.
09065856958
SMITH
WE'VE BEEN FLOODED WITH REPORTS SINCE YOU SET THE ZERGLINGS LOOSE.
EVERYONE WHO KNOWS A KID COLIN'S AGE IS SENDING--
TARGET
WAIT A TICK! SOME GUY JUST UPLOADED A FAMILY VID TIME-STAMPED LAST WEEK.
FACIAL RECOG CONFIRMS OUR TARGET!
TIME TO GET *PAID*.

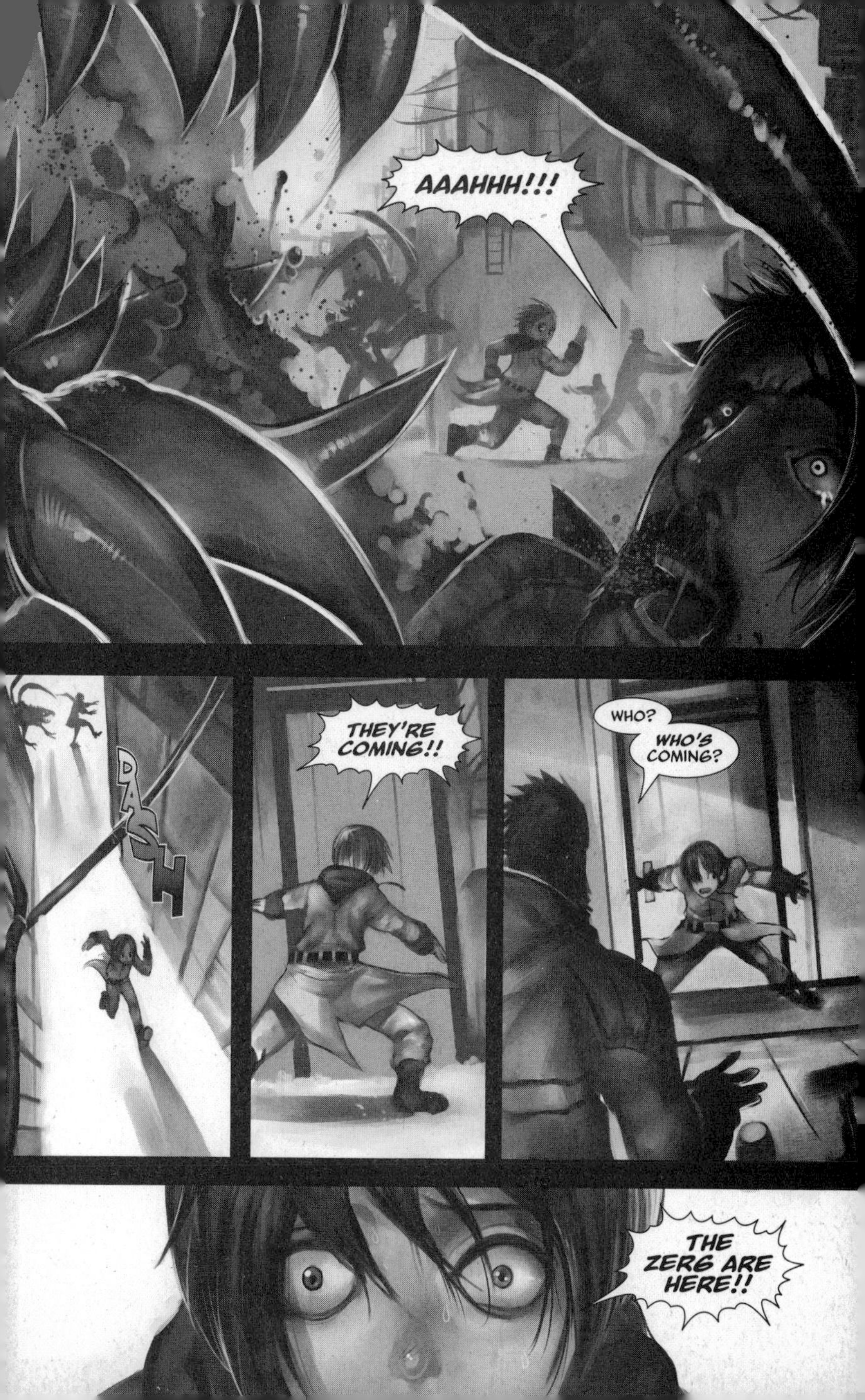
AAAHHH!!!
DASH
THEY'RE COMING!!
WHO?
WHO'S COMING?
THE ZERG ARE HERE!!

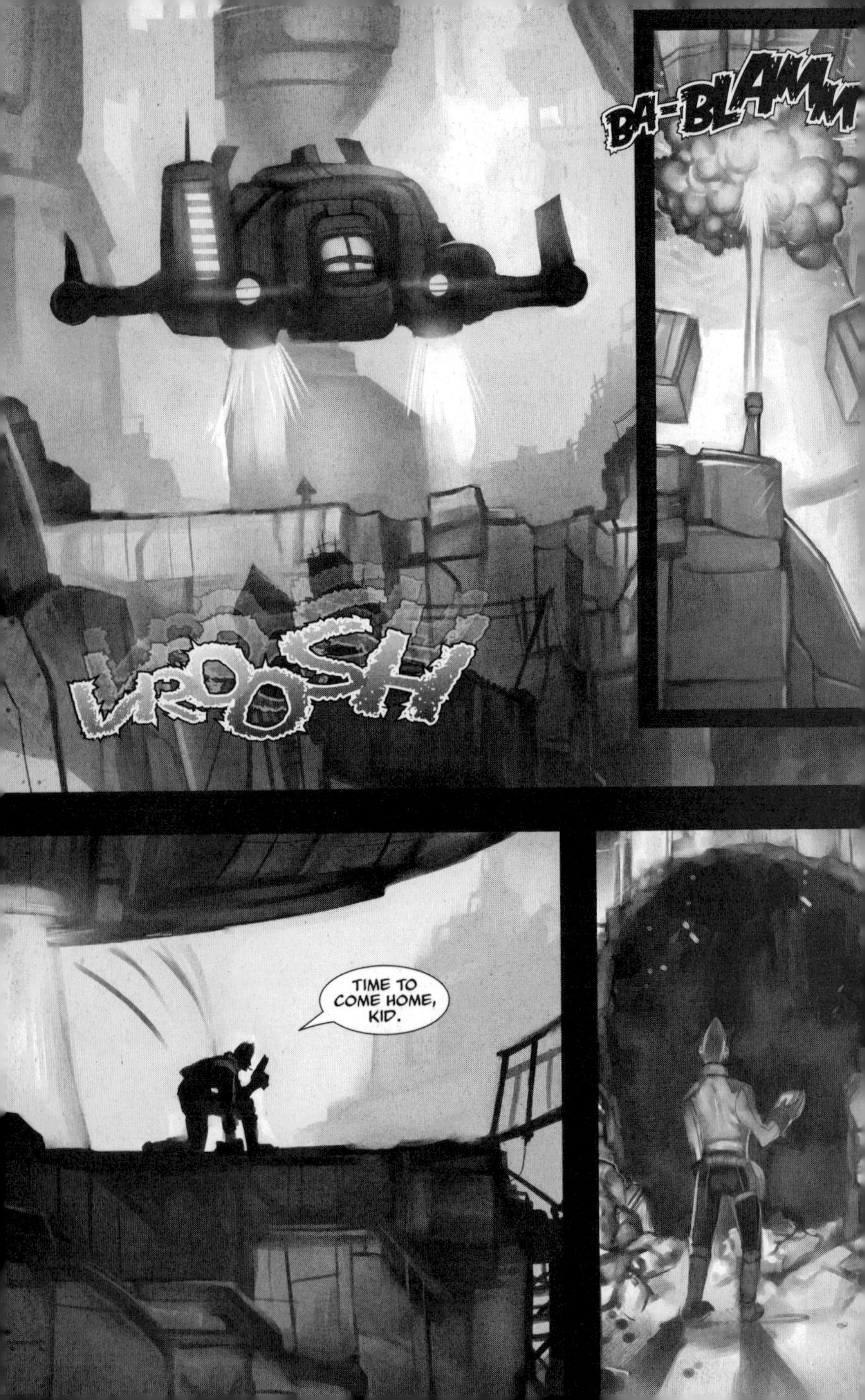
VROOSH
BA-BLAMM
TIME TO COME HOME, KID.

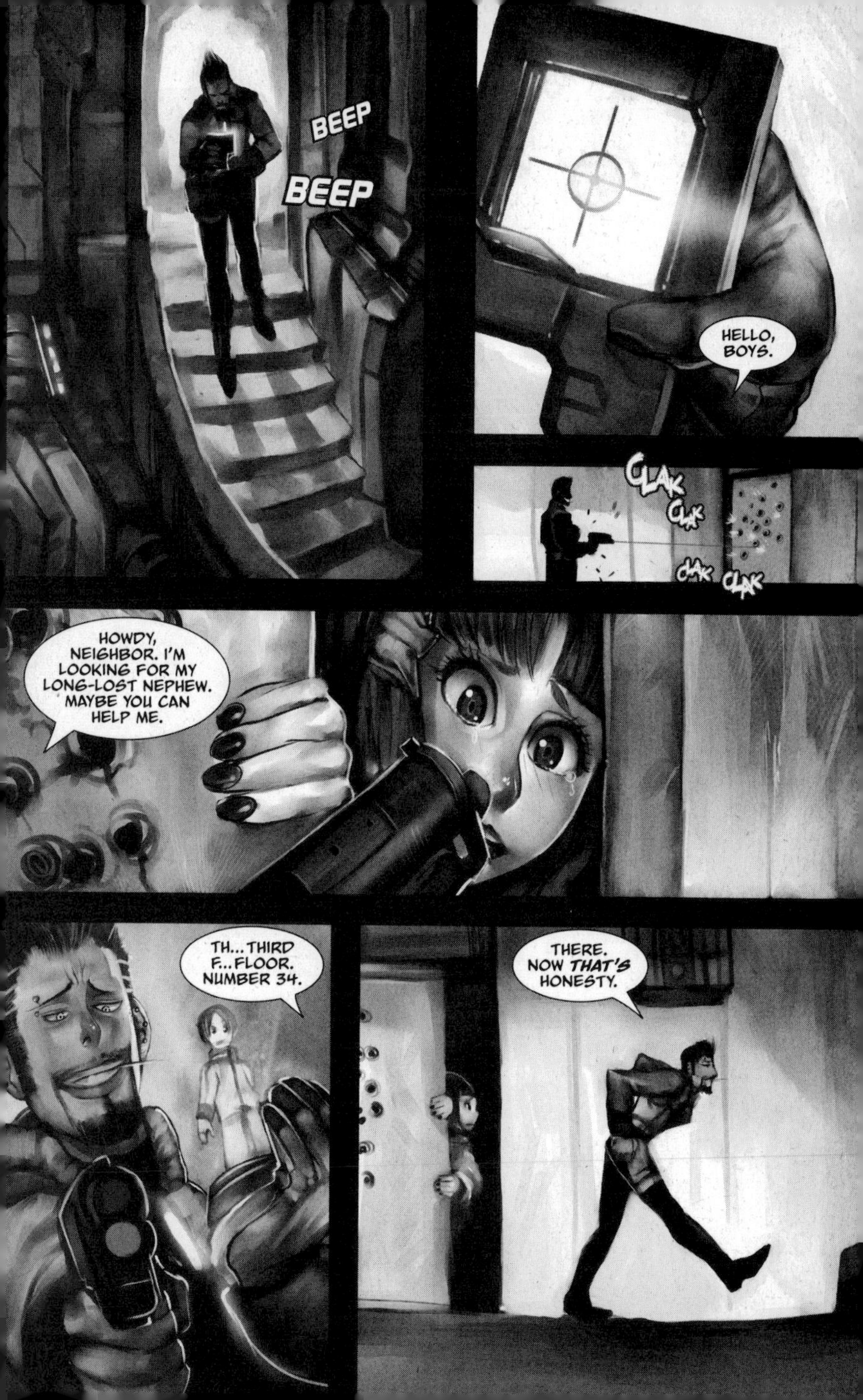
BEEP
BEEP
HELLO, BOYS.
CLAK
CLAK
CLAK
CLAK
HOWDY, NEIGHBOR. I'M LOOKING FOR MY LONG-LOST NEPHEW. MAYBE YOU CAN HELP ME.
TH...THIRD F...FLOOR. NUMBER 34.
THERE. NOW *THAT'S* HONESTY.

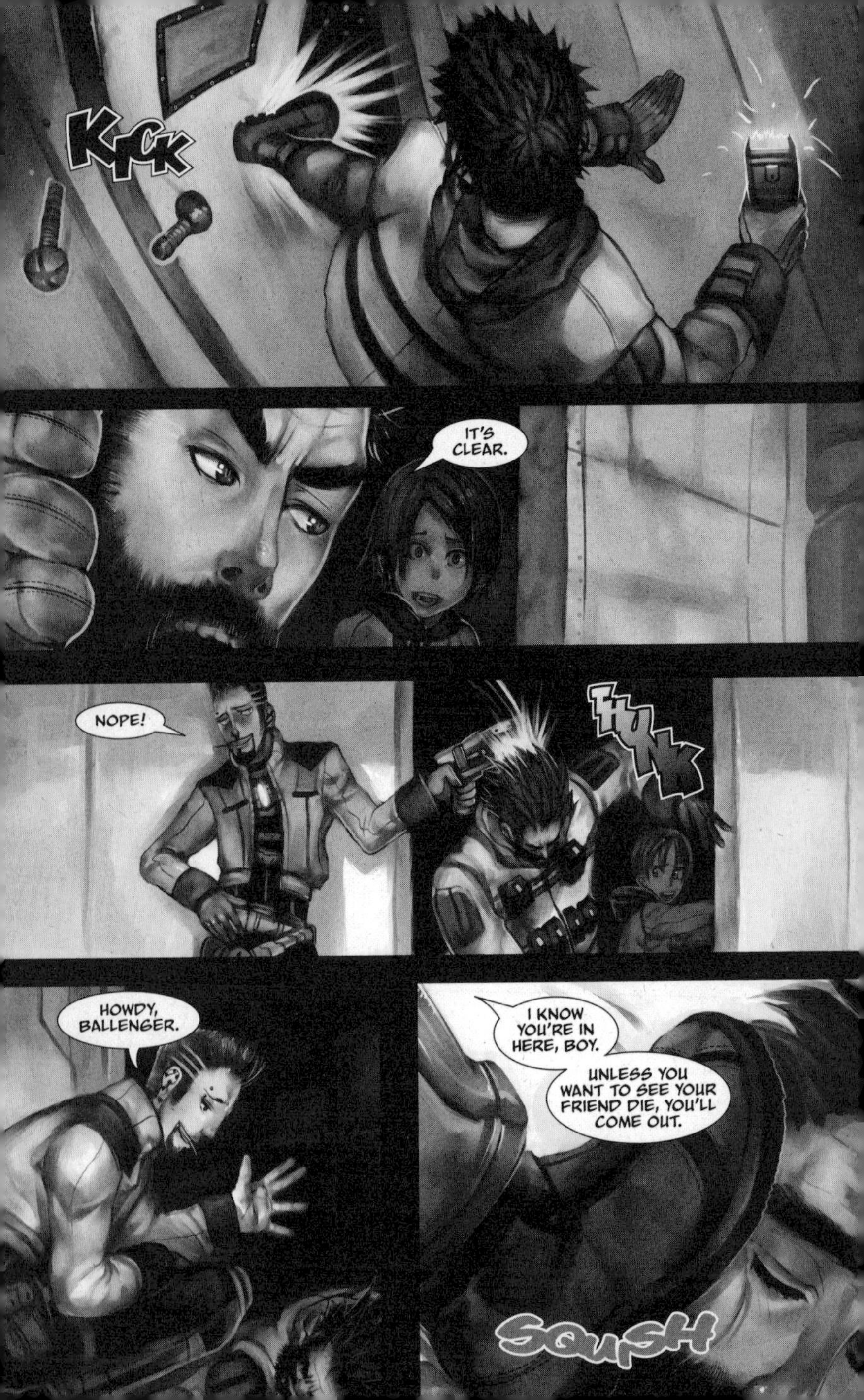
KYCK
IT'S CLEAR.
NOPE!
THUNK
HOWDY, BALLENGER.
I KNOW YOU'RE IN HERE, BOY.
UNLESS YOU WANT TO SEE YOUR FRIEND DIE, YOU'LL COME OUT.
SQUISH

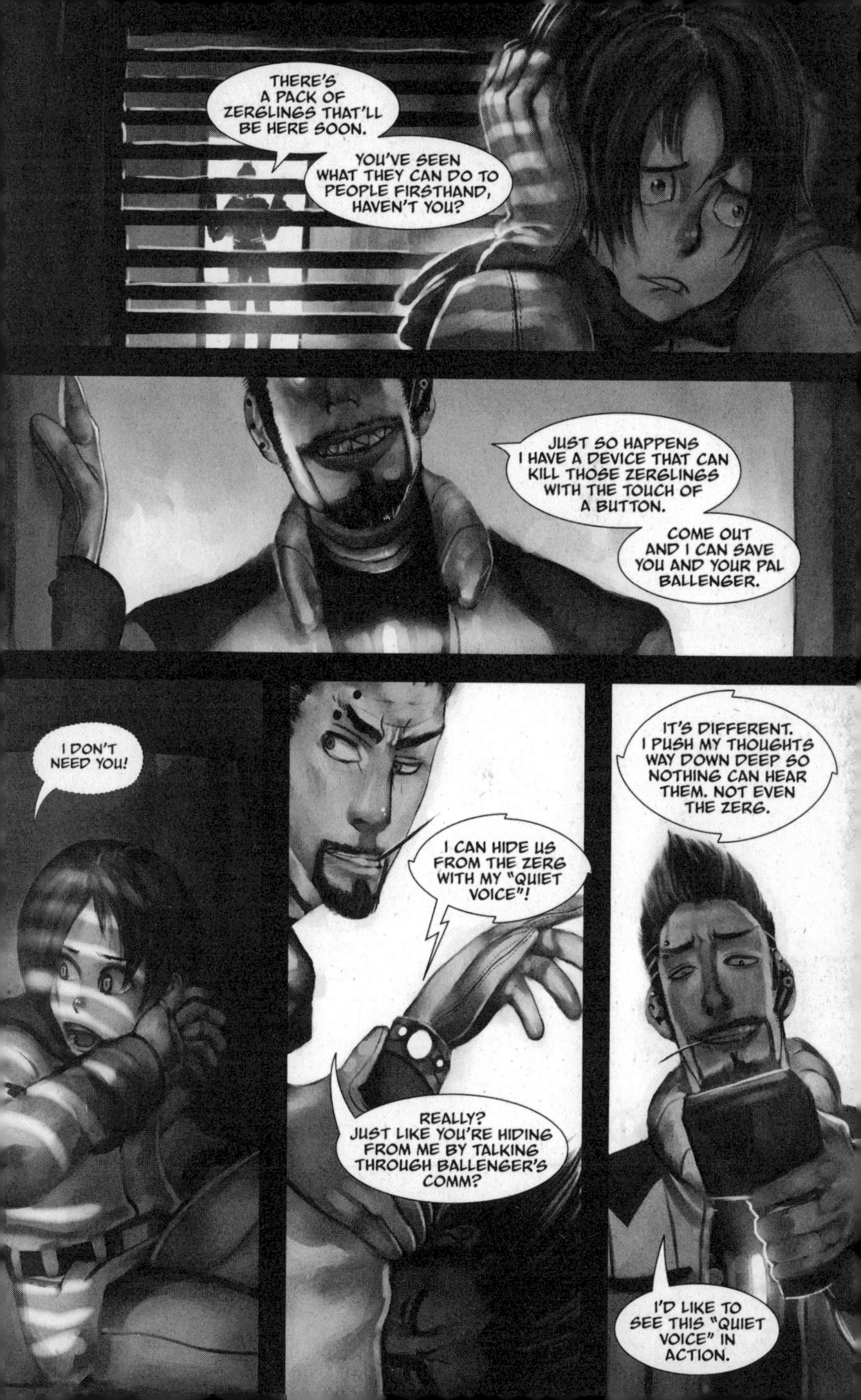
THERE'S A PACK OF ZERGLINGS THAT'LL BE HERE SOON.
YOU'VE SEEN WHAT THEY CAN DO TO PEOPLE FIRSTHAND, HAVEN'T YOU?
JUST SO HAPPENS I HAVE A DEVICE THAT CAN KILL THOSE ZERGLINGS WITH THE TOUCH OF A BUTTON.
COME OUT AND I CAN SAVE YOU AND YOUR PAL BALLENGER.
I DON'T NEED YOU!
I CAN HIDE US FROM THE ZERG WITH MY "QUIET VOICE"!
REALLY? JUST LIKE YOU'RE HIDING FROM ME BY TALKING THROUGH BALLENGER'S COMM?
IT'S DIFFERENT. I PUSH MY THOUGHTS WAY DOWN DEEP SO NOTHING CAN HEAR THEM. NOT EVEN THE ZERG.
I'D LIKE TO SEE THIS "QUIET VOICE" IN ACTION.

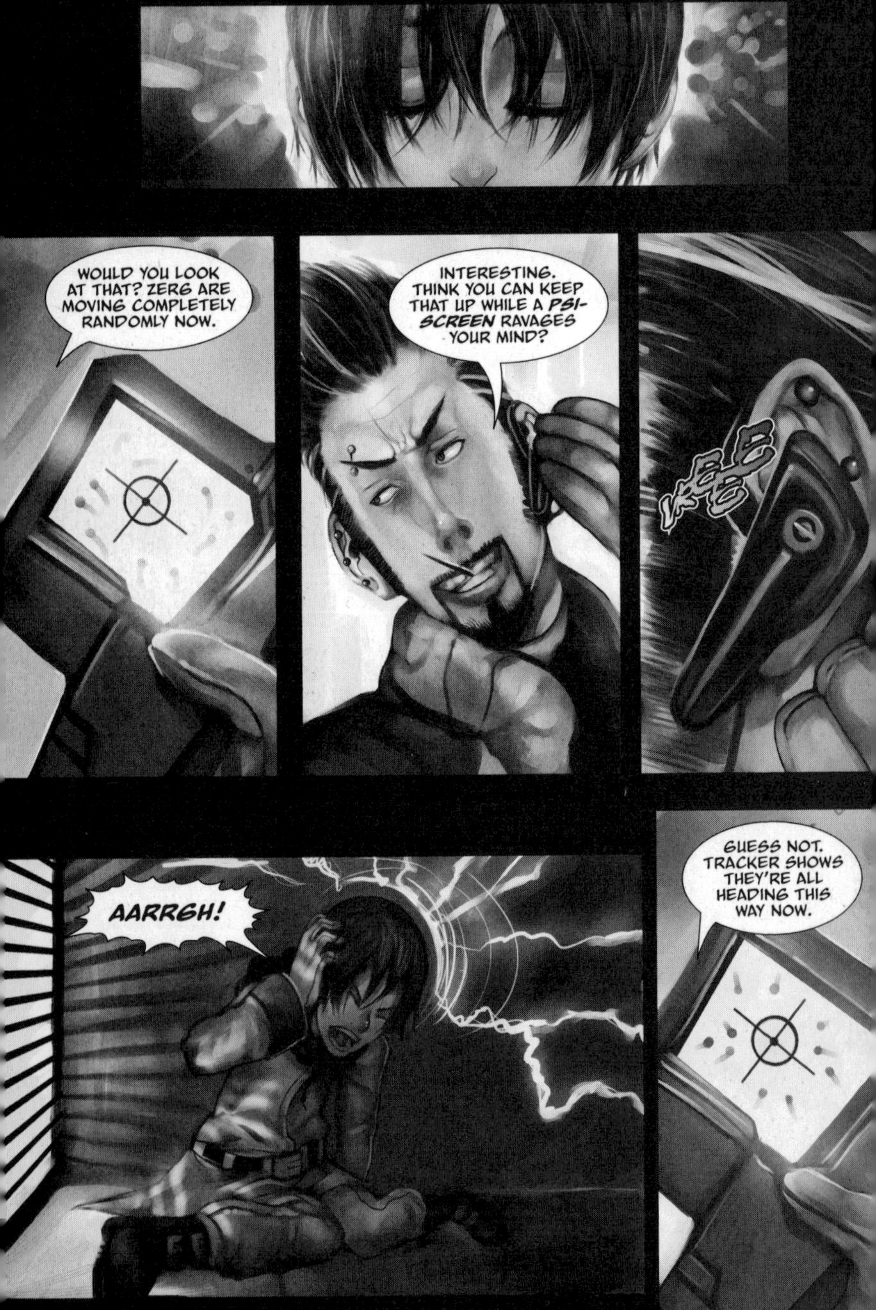
WOULD YOU LOOK AT THAT? ZERG ARE MOVING COMPLETELY RANDOMLY NOW.
INTERESTING. THINK YOU CAN KEEP THAT UP WHILE A *PSI-SCREEN* RAVAGES YOUR MIND?
AARRGH!
GUESS NOT. TRACKER SHOWS THEY'RE ALL HEADING THIS WAY NOW.

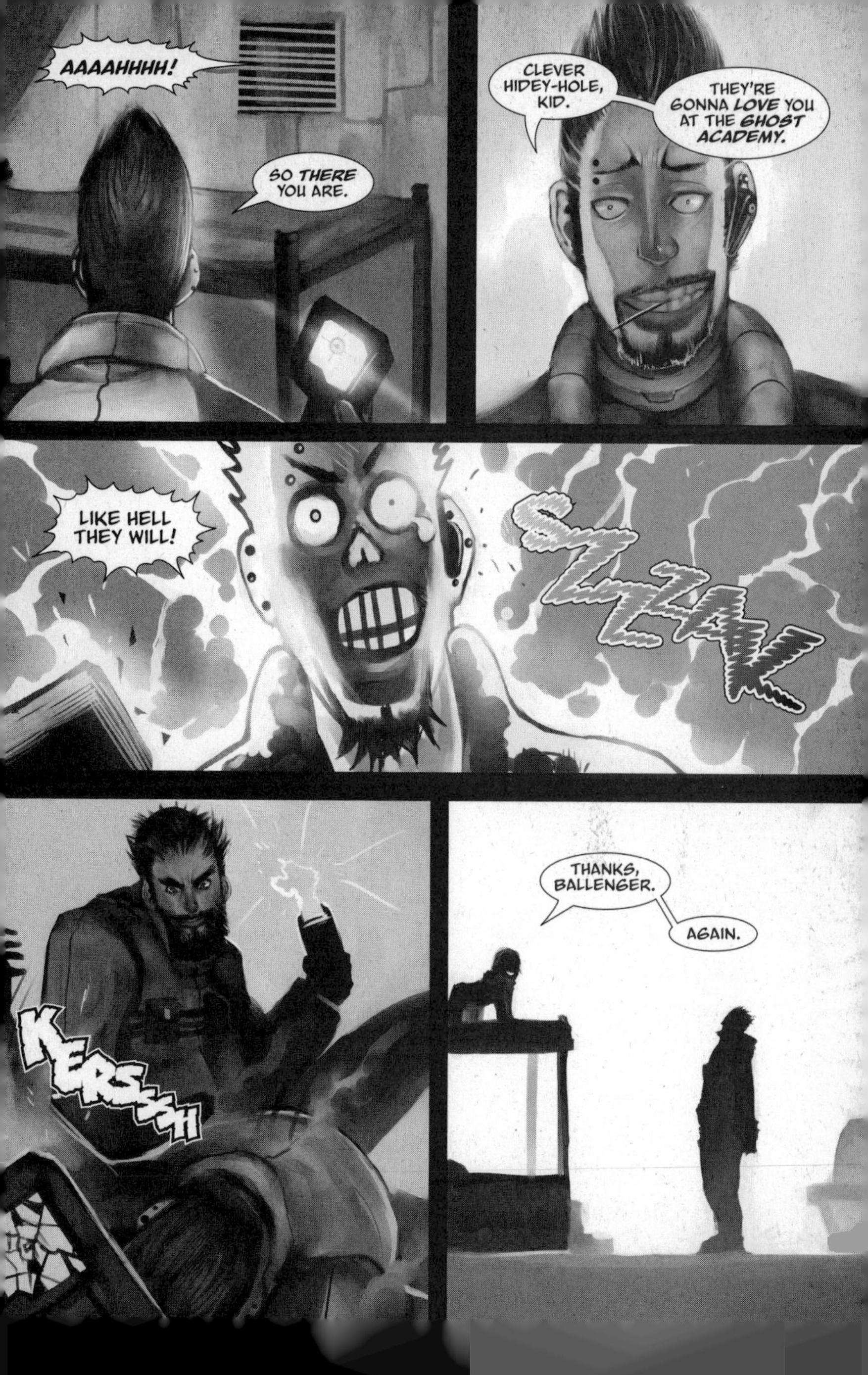

AAAAHHHH!
SO THERE YOU ARE.
CLEVER HIDEY-HOLE, KID.
THEY'RE GONNA LOVE YOU AT THE GHOST ACADEMY.
LIKE HELL THEY WILL!
SZZZAK
KERSSSH
THANKS, BALLENGER.
AGAIN.

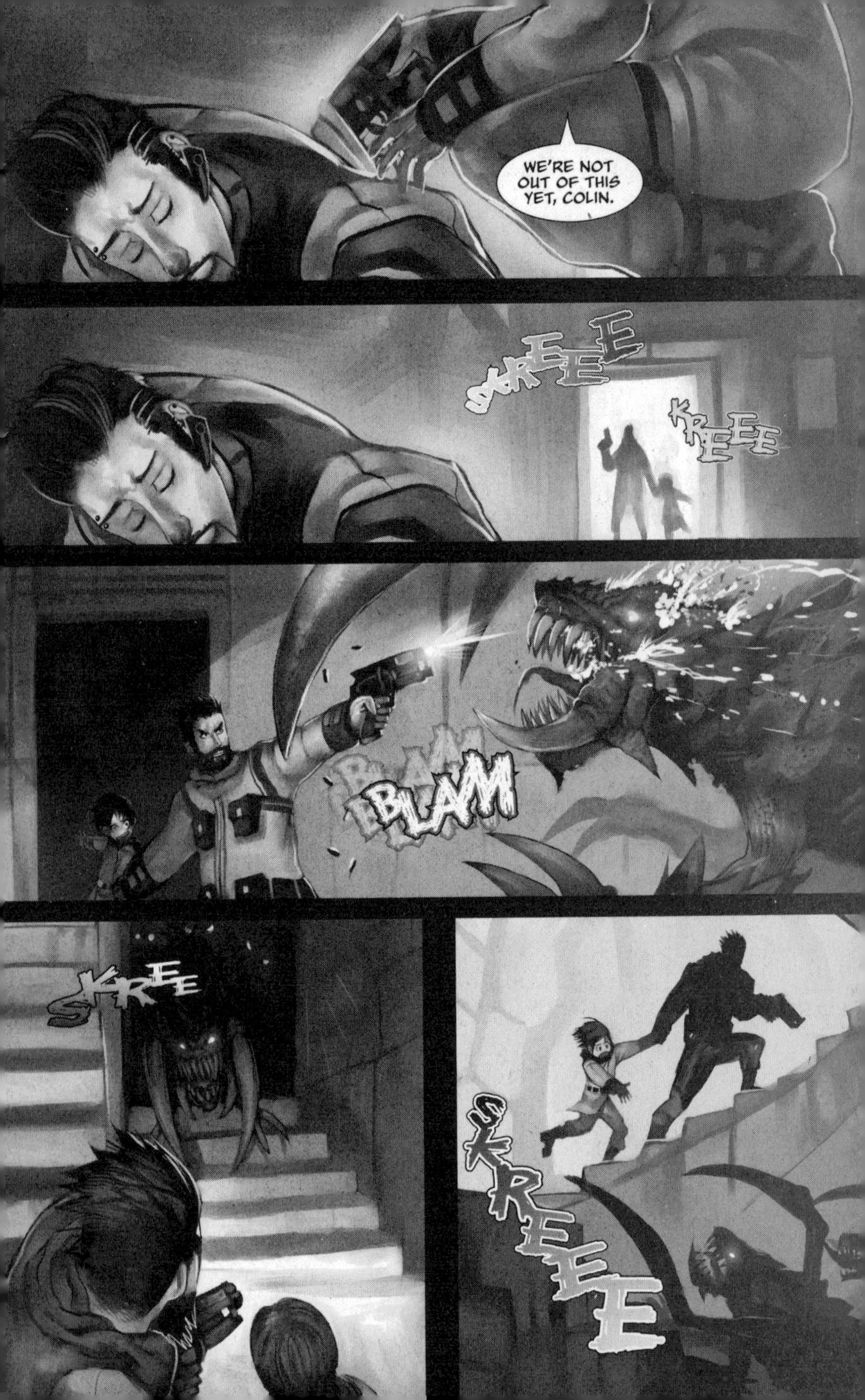
WE'RE NOT OUT OF THIS YET, COLIN.
SKREEE
KREEE
BLAM
SKREE
SKREEEE

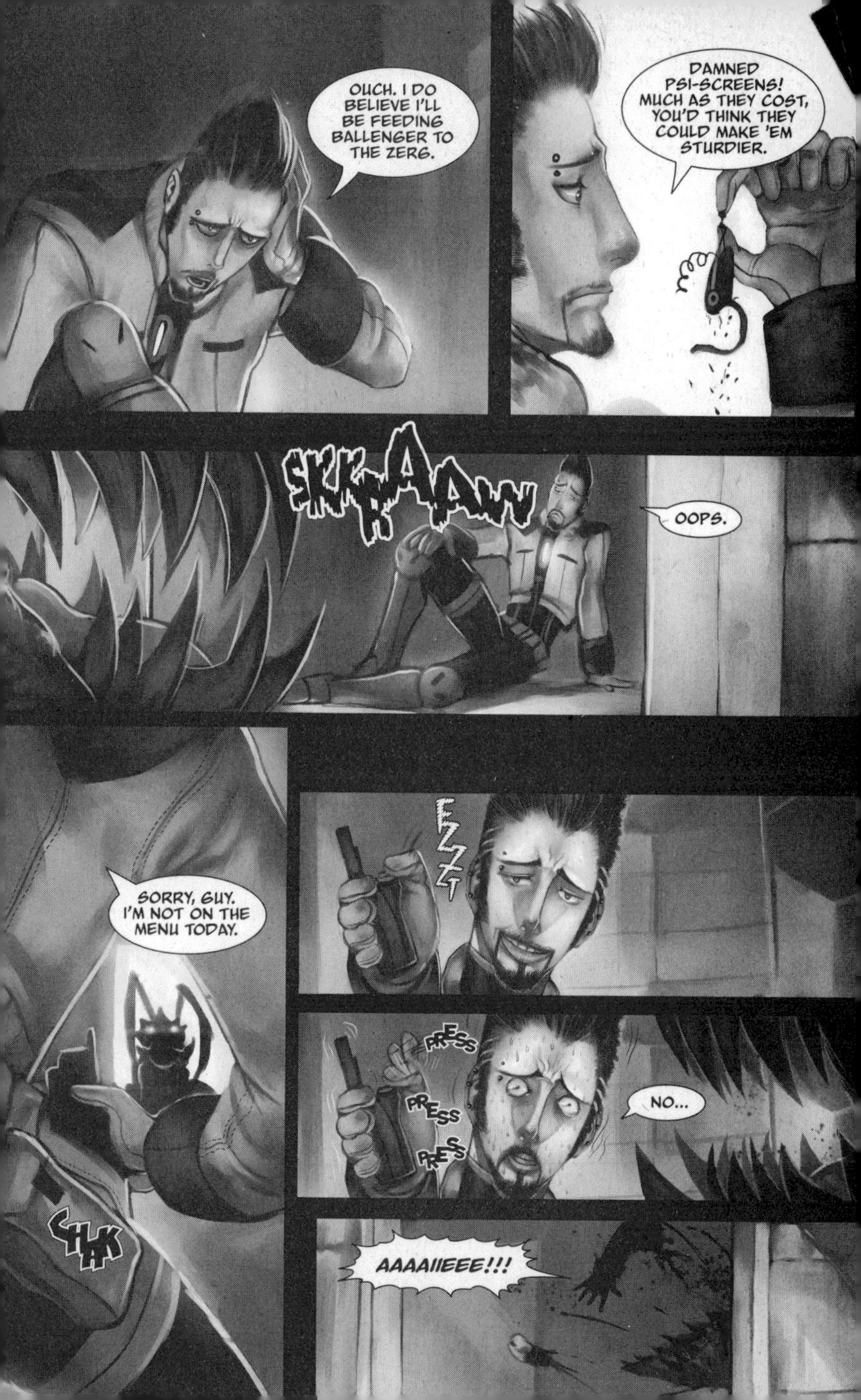
OUCH. I DO BELIEVE I'LL BE FEEDING BALLENGER TO THE ZERG.
DAMNED PSI-SCREENS! MUCH AS THEY COST, YOU'D THINK THEY COULD MAKE 'EM STURDIER.
SKKRAAAWW
OOPS.
SORRY, GUY. I'M NOT ON THE MENU TODAY.
CHAK
FZZZT
PRESS
PRESS
PRESS
NO...
AAAAIIEEE!!!

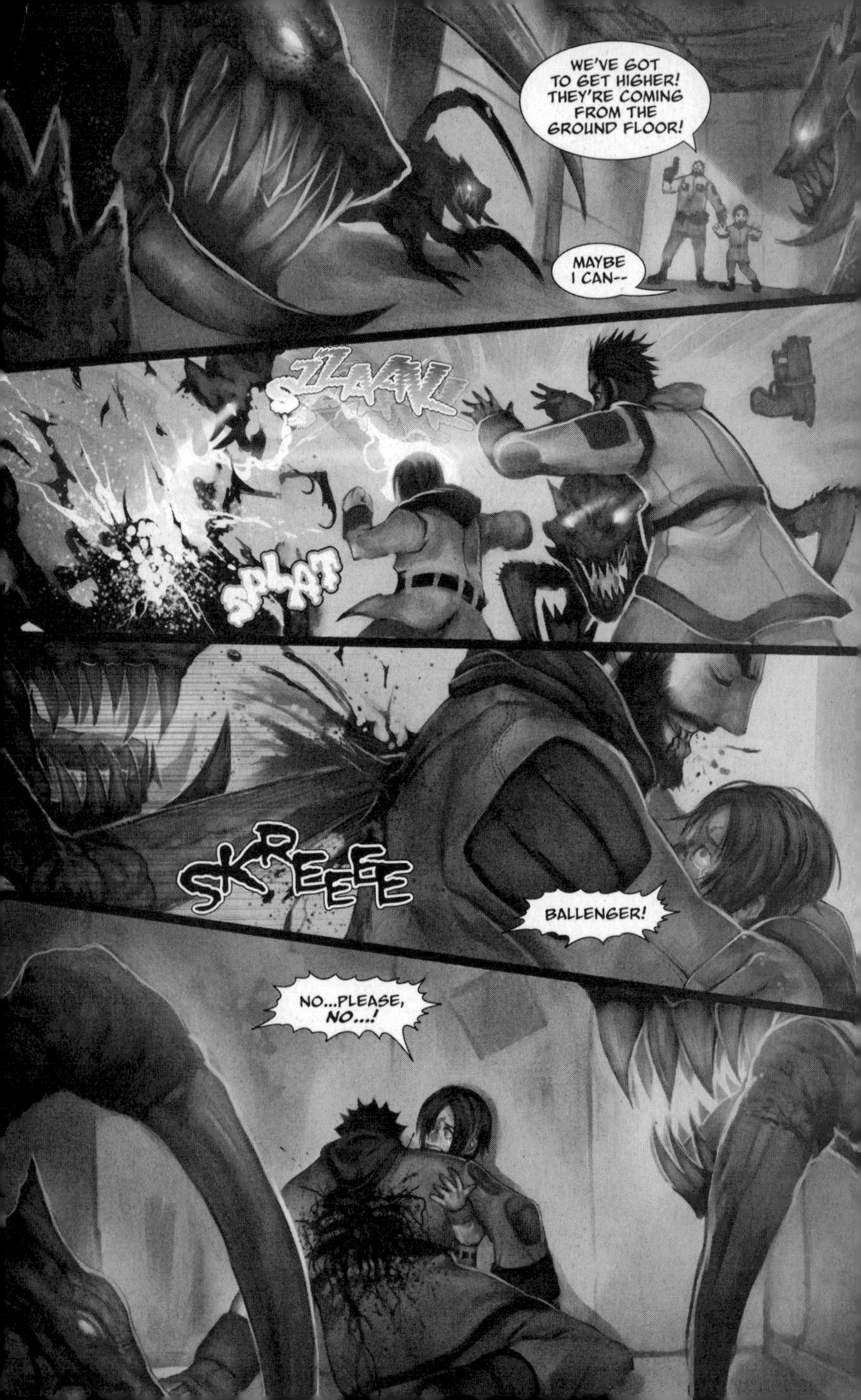
WE'VE GOT TO GET HIGHER! THEY'RE COMING FROM THE GROUND FLOOR!
MAYBE I CAN--
SZZAAK!
SPLAT
SKREEEE
BALLENGER!
NO...PLEASE, NO...!

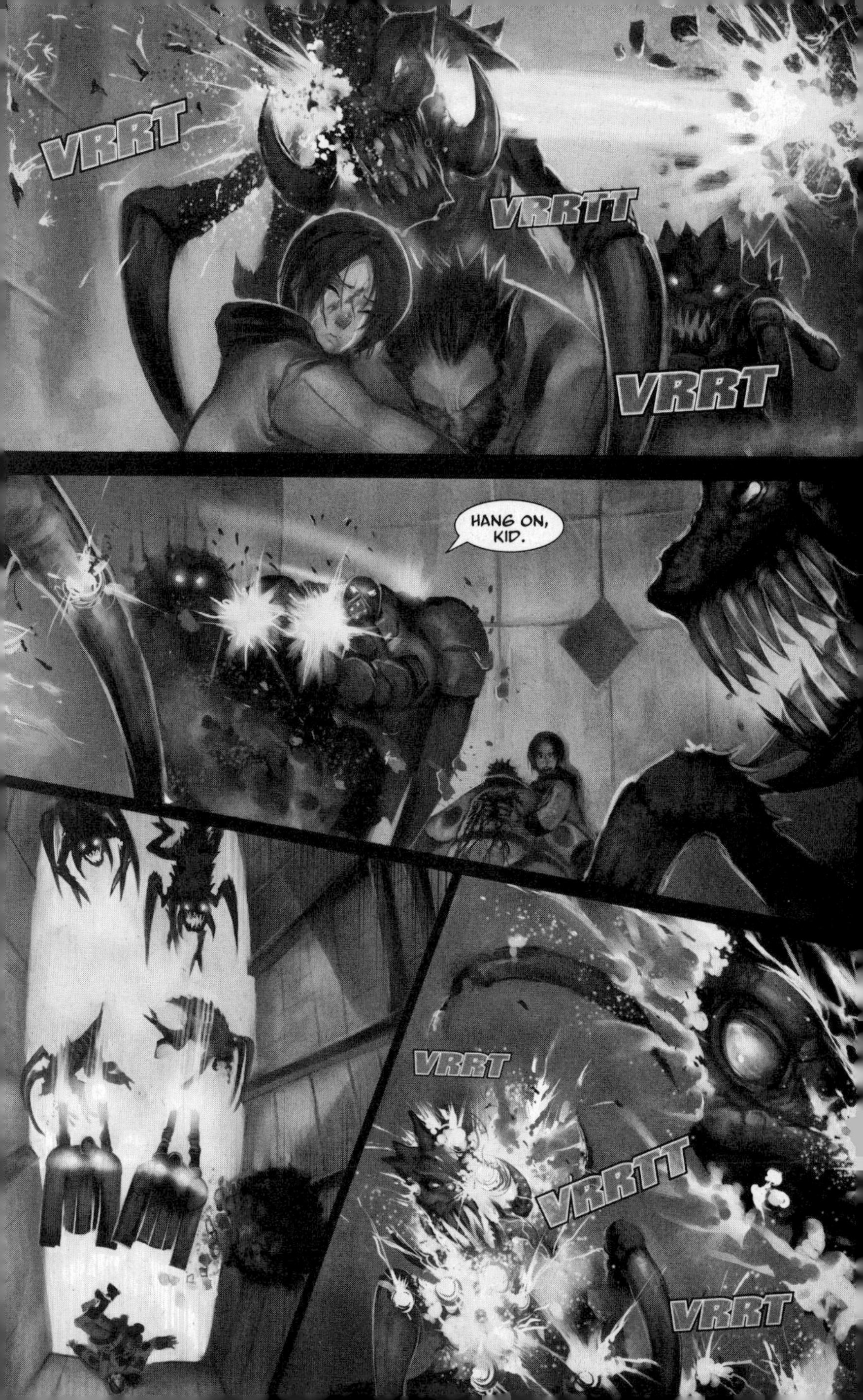
VRRT
VRRTT
VRRT
HANG ON, KID.
VRRT
VRRTT
VRRT

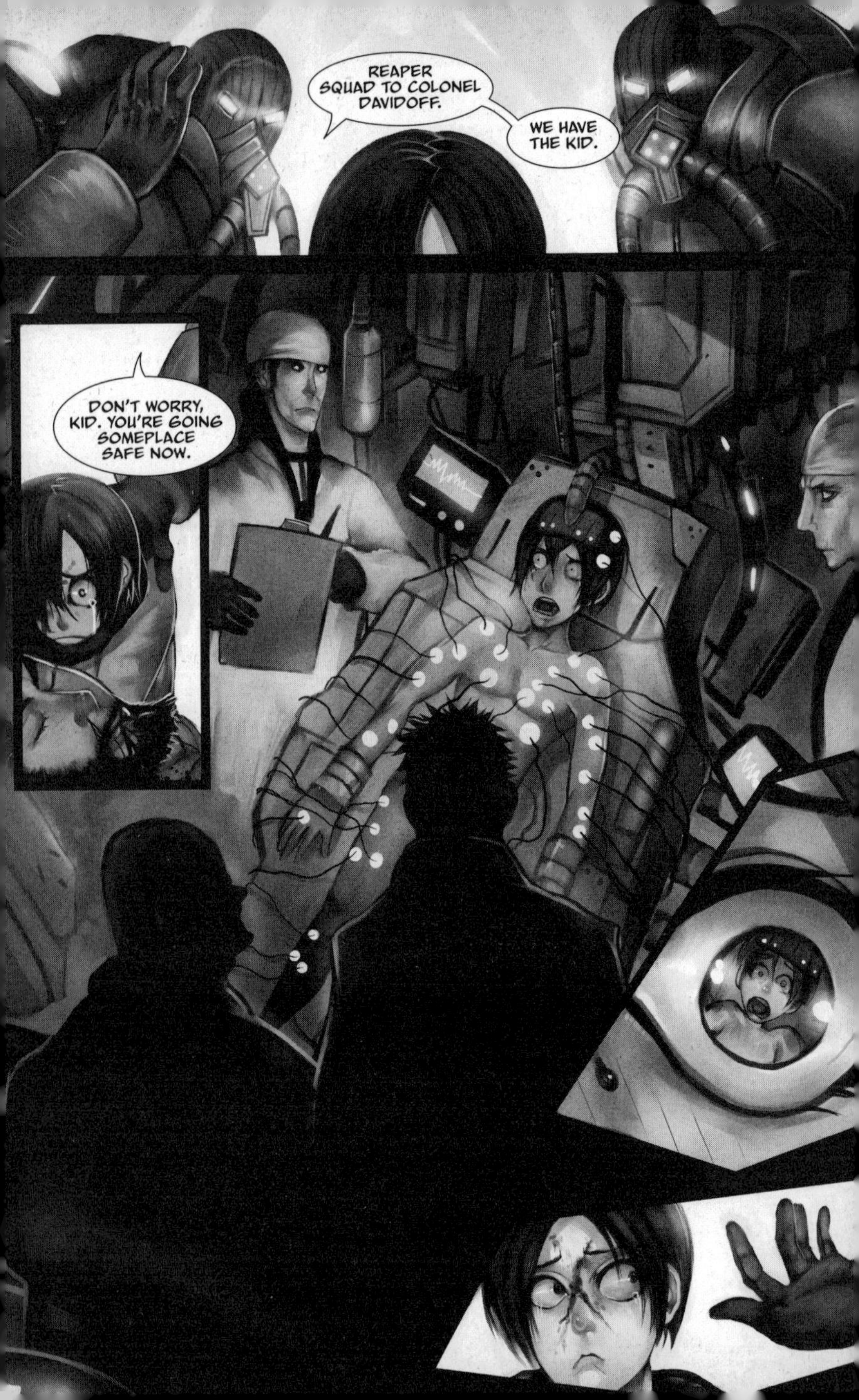
REAPER SQUAD TO COLONEL DAVIDOFF.
WE HAVE THE KID.
DON'T WORRY, KID. YOU'RE GOING SOMEPLACE SAFE NOW.

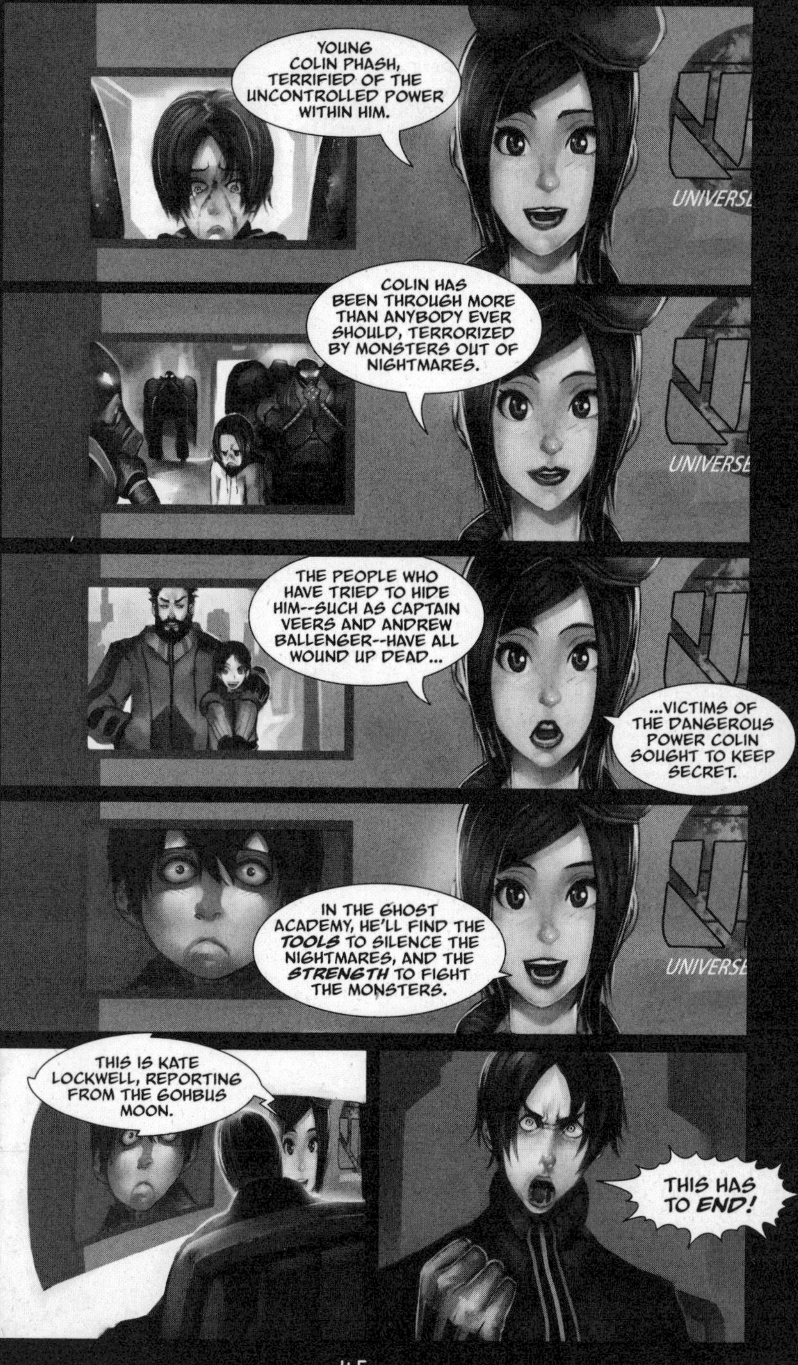
YOUNG COLIN PHASH, TERRIFIED OF THE UNCONTROLLED POWER WITHIN HIM.
COLIN HAS BEEN THROUGH MORE THAN ANYBODY EVER SHOULD, TERRORIZED BY MONSTERS OUT OF NIGHTMARES.
THE PEOPLE WHO HAVE TRIED TO HIDE HIM--SUCH AS CAPTAIN VEERS AND ANDREW BALLENGER--HAVE ALL WOUND UP DEAD...
...VICTIMS OF THE DANGEROUS POWER COLIN SOUGHT TO KEEP SECRET.
IN THE GHOST ACADEMY, HE'LL FIND THE ***TOOLS*** TO SILENCE THE NIGHTMARES, AND THE ***STRENGTH*** TO FIGHT THE MONSTERS.
THIS IS KATE LOCKWELL, REPORTING FROM THE GOHBUS MOON.
THIS HAS TO ***END!***

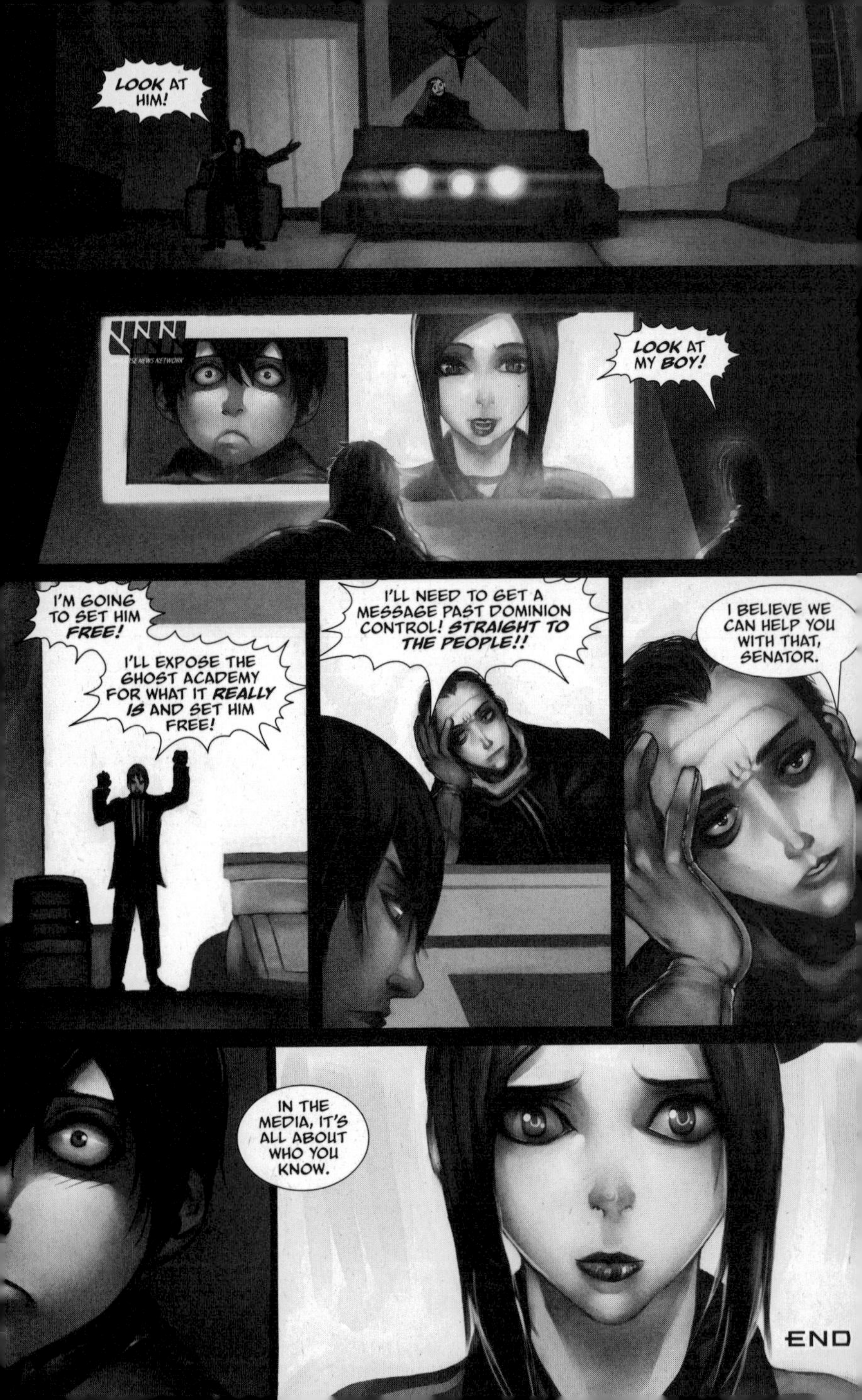
LOOK AT HIM!
LOOK AT MY BOY!
I'M GOING TO SET HIM FREE!
I'LL EXPOSE THE GHOST ACADEMY FOR WHAT IT REALLY IS AND SET HIM FREE!
I'LL NEED TO GET A MESSAGE PAST DOMINION CONTROL! STRAIGHT TO THE PEOPLE!!
I BELIEVE WE CAN HELP YOU WITH THAT, SENATOR.
IN THE MEDIA, IT'S ALL ABOUT WHO YOU KNOW.
END

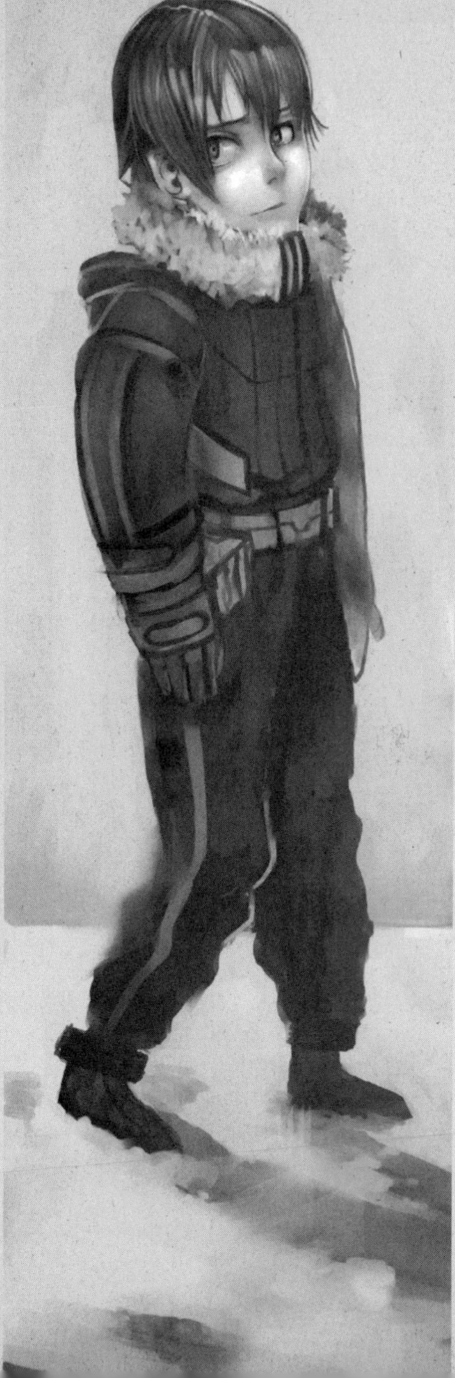

STARCRAFT

FRONTLINE
VOLUME 3

DO NO HARM

Written by Josh Elder

Pencils by Ramanda Kamarga
Inks by Angie Nathalia and Junaidi of Caravan Studio
Tones by Erfian Asafat of Caravan Studio and Beatusvir

Letterer: Michael Paolilli

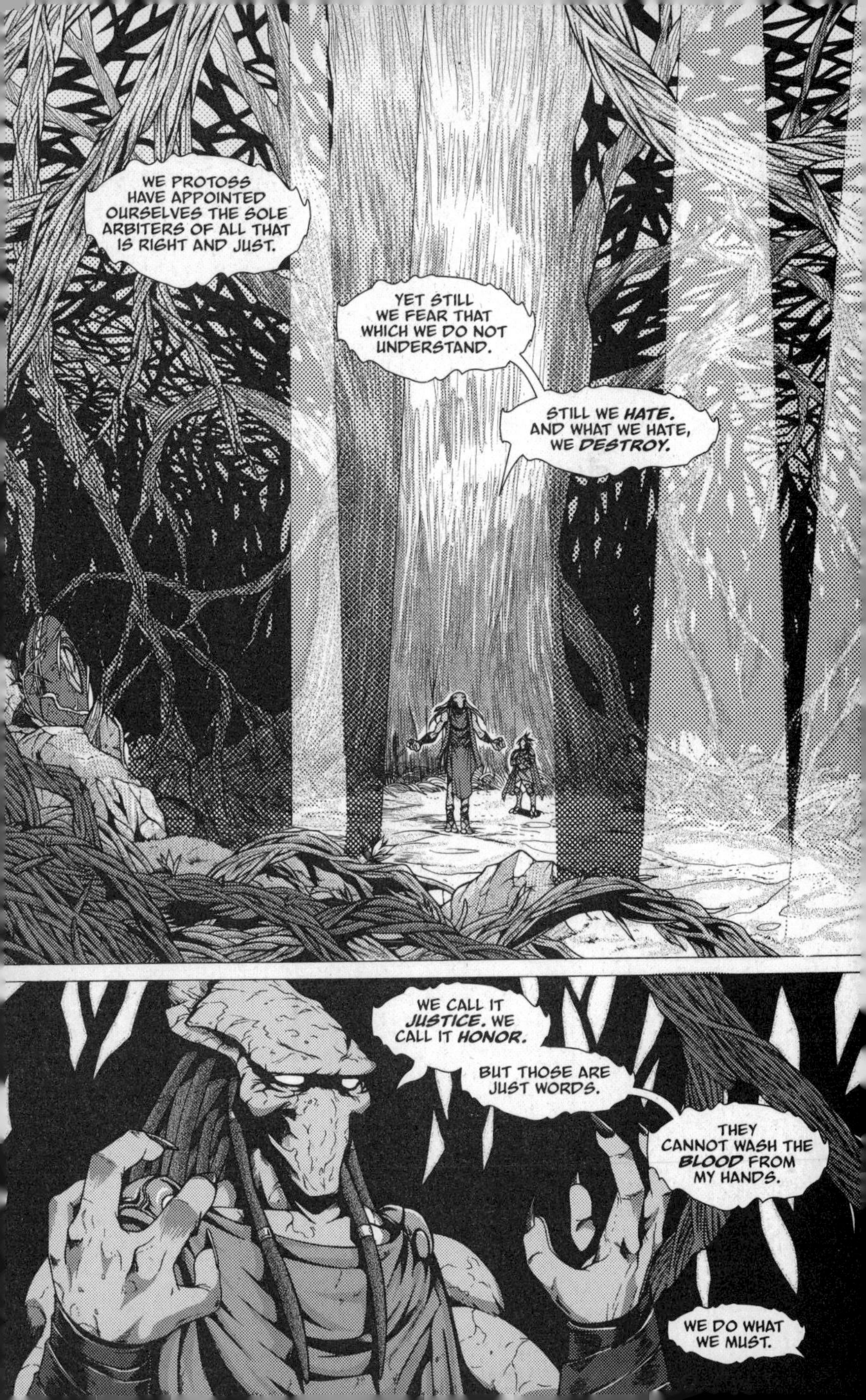

WE PROTOSS HAVE APPOINTED OURSELVES THE SOLE ARBITERS OF ALL THAT IS RIGHT AND JUST.
YET STILL WE FEAR THAT WHICH WE DO NOT UNDERSTAND.
STILL WE HATE. AND WHAT WE HATE, WE DESTROY.
WE CALL IT JUSTICE. WE CALL IT HONOR.
BUT THOSE ARE JUST WORDS.
THEY CANNOT WASH THE BLOOD FROM MY HANDS.
WE DO WHAT WE MUST.

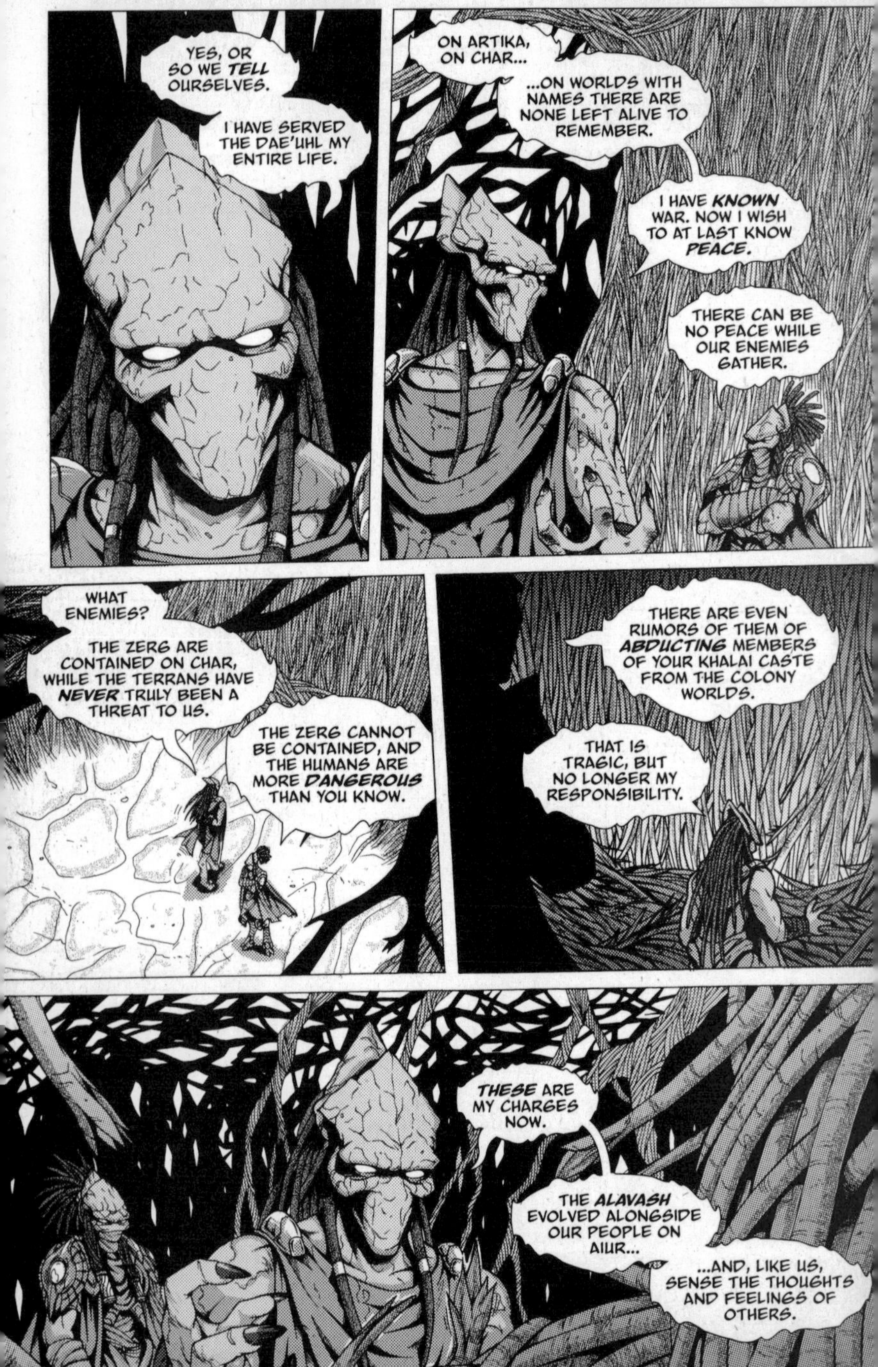
YES, OR SO WE TELL OURSELVES.
I HAVE SERVED THE DAE'UHL MY ENTIRE LIFE.
ON ARTIKA, ON CHAR...
...ON WORLDS WITH NAMES THERE ARE NONE LEFT ALIVE TO REMEMBER.
I HAVE KNOWN WAR. NOW I WISH TO AT LAST KNOW PEACE.
THERE CAN BE NO PEACE WHILE OUR ENEMIES GATHER.
WHAT ENEMIES?
THE ZERG ARE CONTAINED ON CHAR, WHILE THE TERRANS HAVE NEVER TRULY BEEN A THREAT TO US.
THE ZERG CANNOT BE CONTAINED, AND THE HUMANS ARE MORE DANGEROUS THAN YOU KNOW.
THERE ARE EVEN RUMORS OF THEM OF ABDUCTING MEMBERS OF YOUR KHALAI CASTE FROM THE COLONY WORLDS.
THAT IS TRAGIC, BUT NO LONGER MY RESPONSIBILITY.
THESE ARE MY CHARGES NOW.
THE ALAVASH EVOLVED ALONGSIDE OUR PEOPLE ON AIUR...
...AND, LIKE US, SENSE THE THOUGHTS AND FEELINGS OF OTHERS.

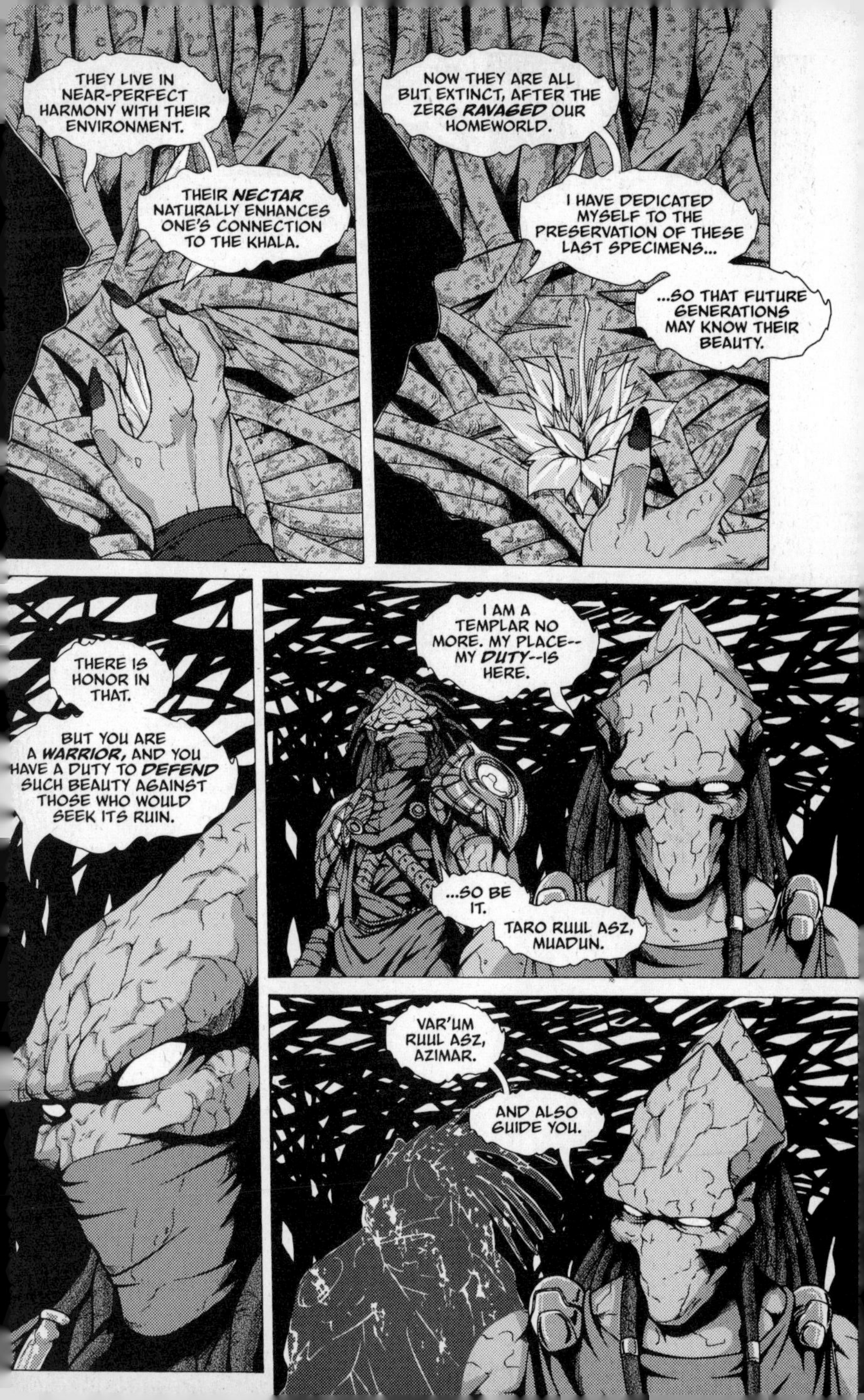
THEY LIVE IN NEAR-PERFECT HARMONY WITH THEIR ENVIRONMENT.
THEIR NECTAR NATURALLY ENHANCES ONE'S CONNECTION TO THE KHALA.
NOW THEY ARE ALL BUT EXTINCT, AFTER THE ZERG RAVAGED OUR HOMEWORLD.
I HAVE DEDICATED MYSELF TO THE PRESERVATION OF THESE LAST SPECIMENS...
...SO THAT FUTURE GENERATIONS MAY KNOW THEIR BEAUTY.
THERE IS HONOR IN THAT.
BUT YOU ARE A WARRIOR, AND YOU HAVE A DUTY TO DEFEND SUCH BEAUTY AGAINST THOSE WHO WOULD SEEK ITS RUIN.
I AM A TEMPLAR NO MORE. MY PLACE--MY DUTY--IS HERE.
...SO BE IT.
TARO RUUL ASZ, MUADUN.
VAR'UM RUUL ASZ, AZIMAR.
AND ALSO GUIDE YOU.

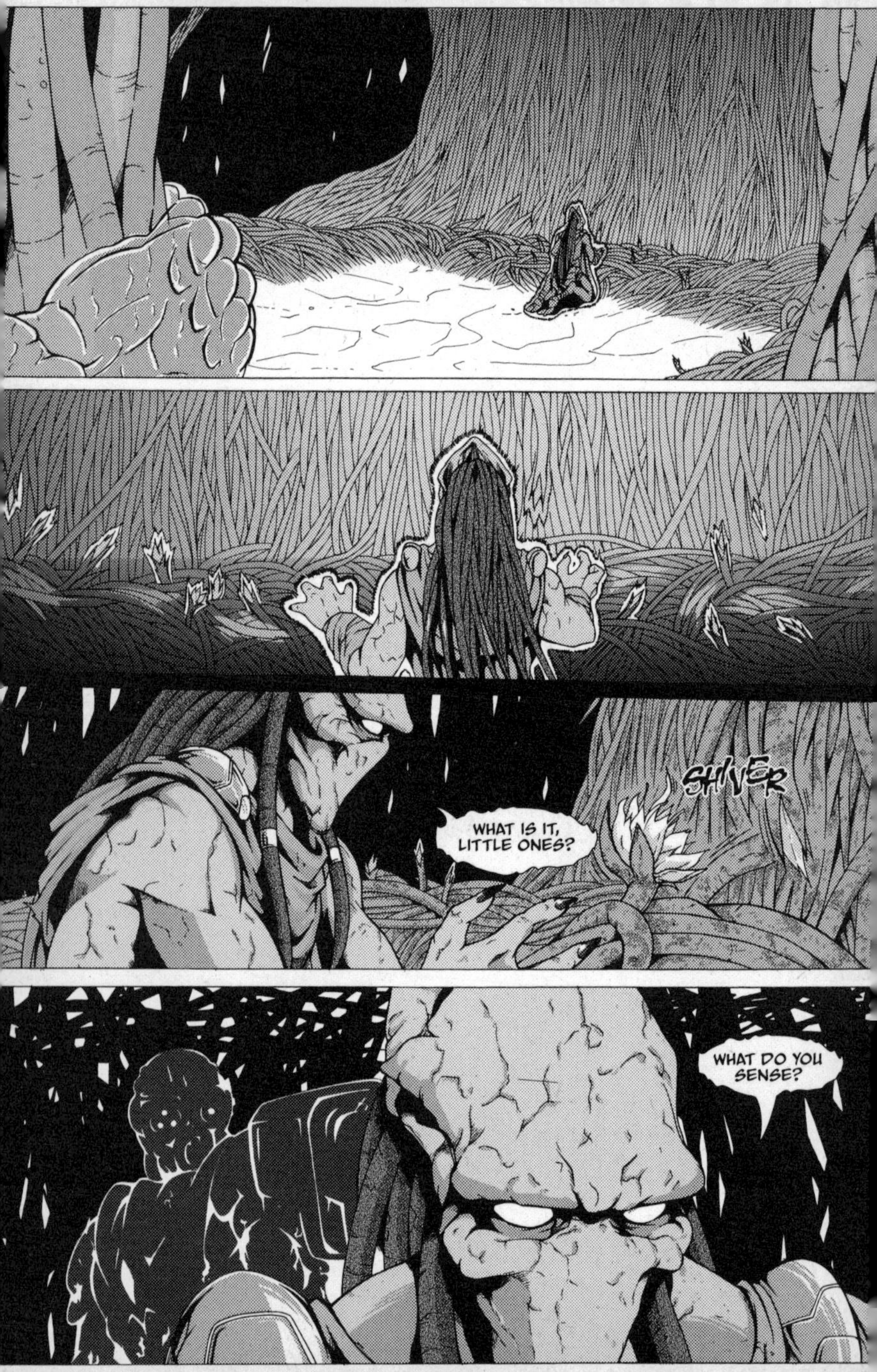
SHIVER
WHAT IS IT, LITTLE ONES?
WHAT DO YOU SENSE?

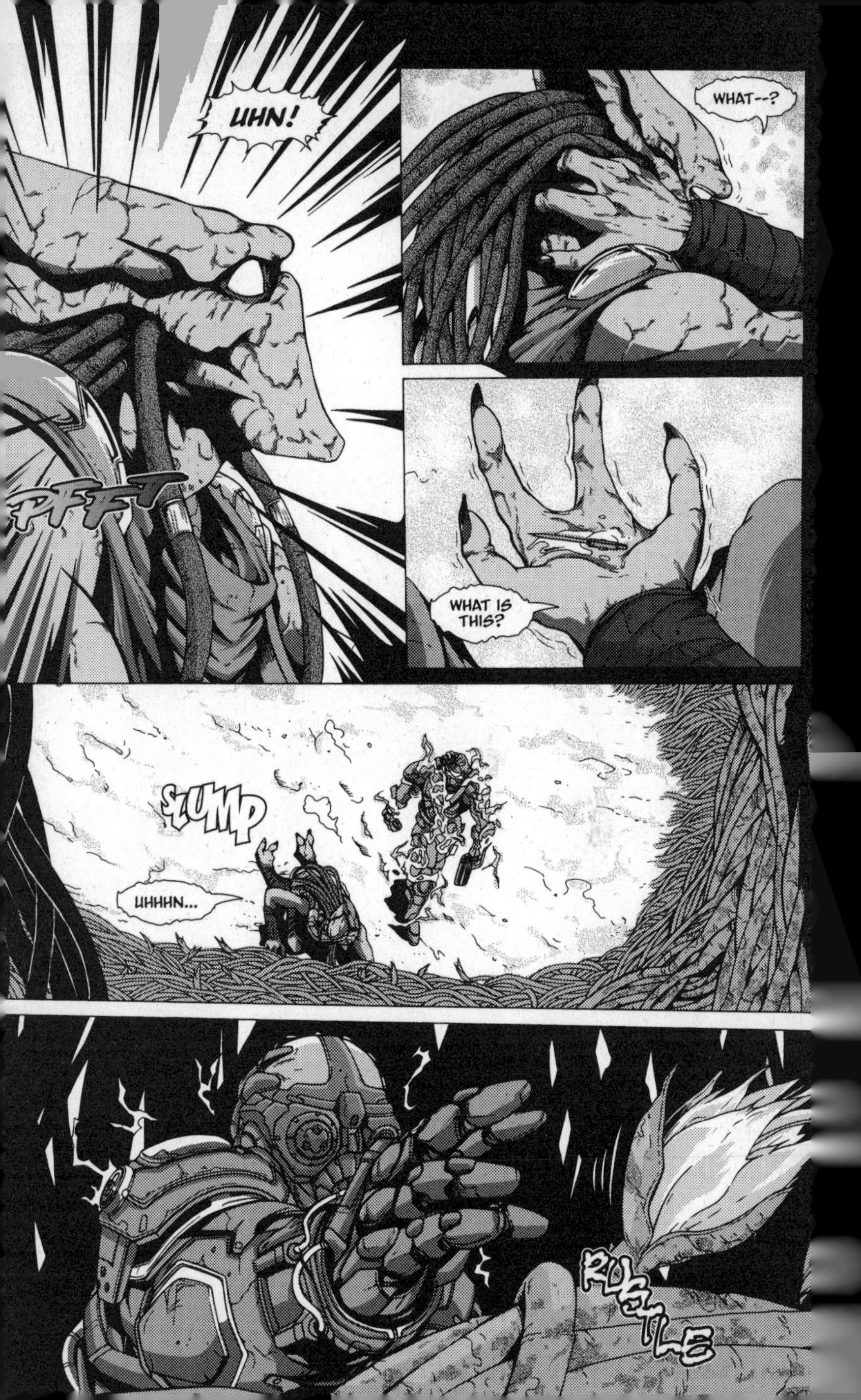
UHN!
PFFT
WHAT--?
WHAT IS THIS?
SLUMP
UHHHN...
RUSTLE

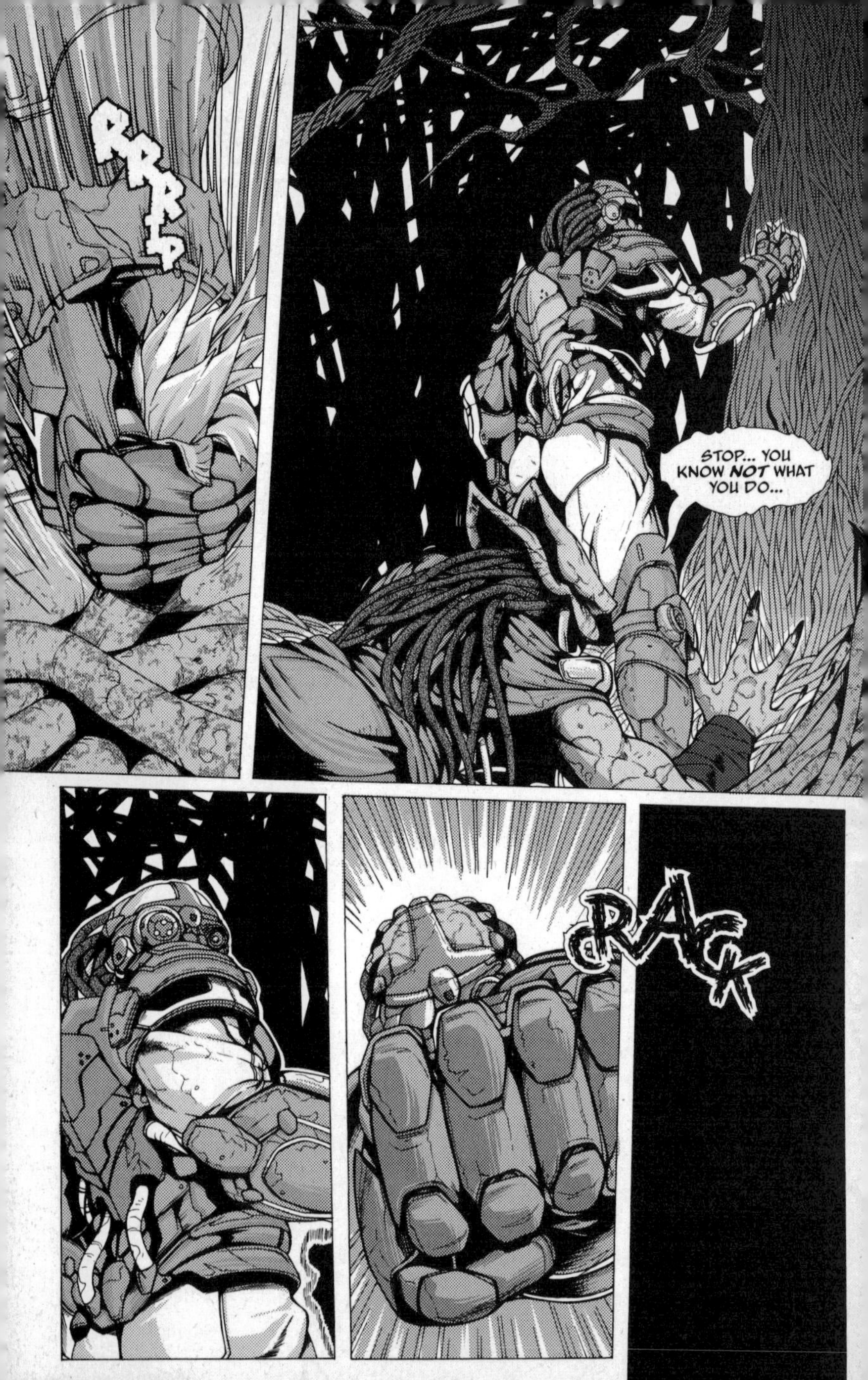
RRRIP
STOP... YOU KNOW NOT WHAT YOU DO...
CRACK

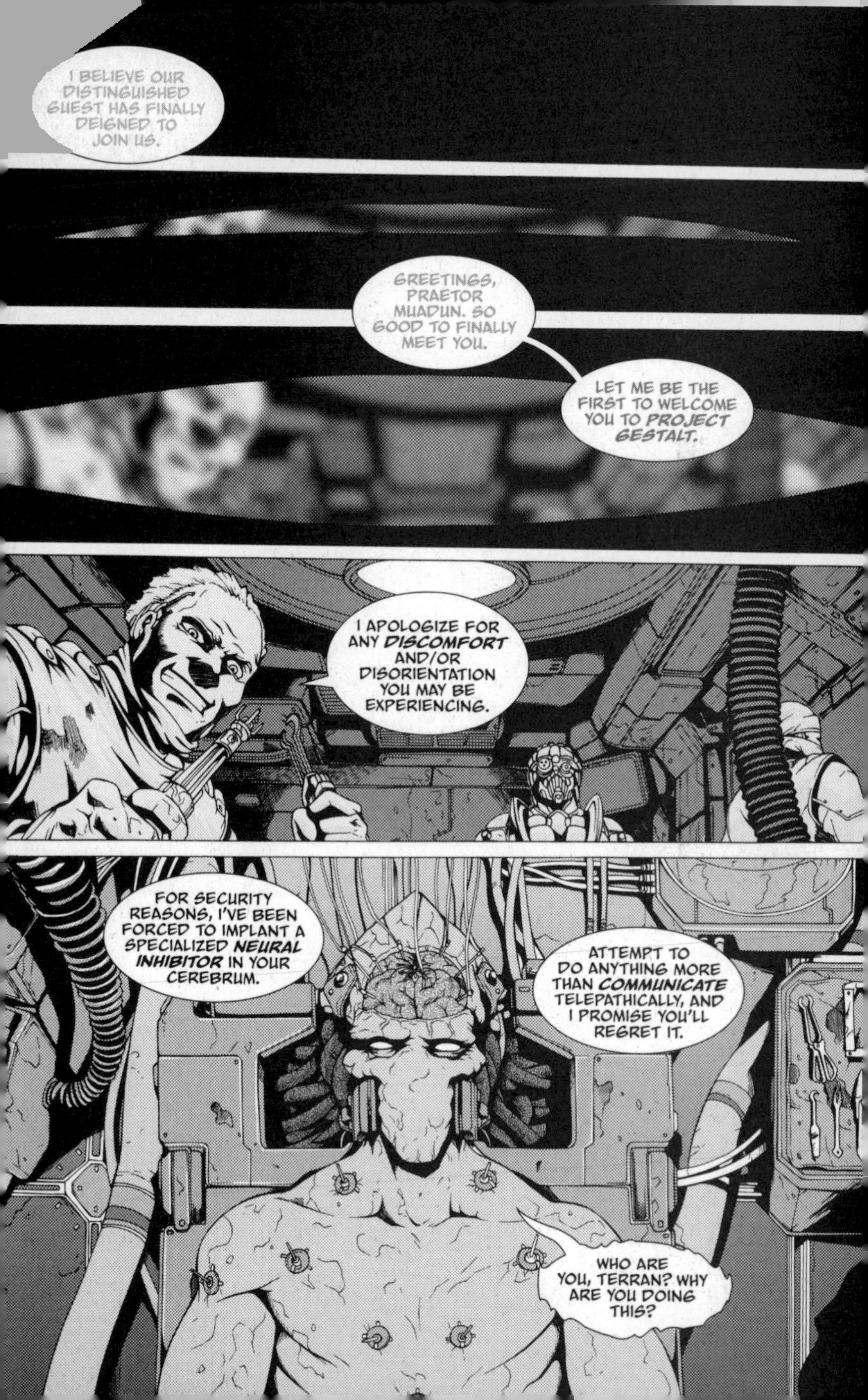
I BELIEVE OUR DISTINGUISHED GUEST HAS FINALLY DEIGNED TO JOIN US.
GREETINGS, PRAETOR MUADUN. SO GOOD TO FINALLY MEET YOU.
LET ME BE THE FIRST TO WELCOME YOU TO PROJECT GESTALT.
I APOLOGIZE FOR ANY DISCOMFORT AND/OR DISORIENTATION YOU MAY BE EXPERIENCING.
FOR SECURITY REASONS, I'VE BEEN FORCED TO IMPLANT A SPECIALIZED NEURAL INHIBITOR IN YOUR CEREBRUM.
ATTEMPT TO DO ANYTHING MORE THAN COMMUNICATE TELEPATHICALLY, AND I PROMISE YOU'LL REGRET IT.
WHO ARE YOU, TERRAN? WHY ARE YOU DOING THIS?

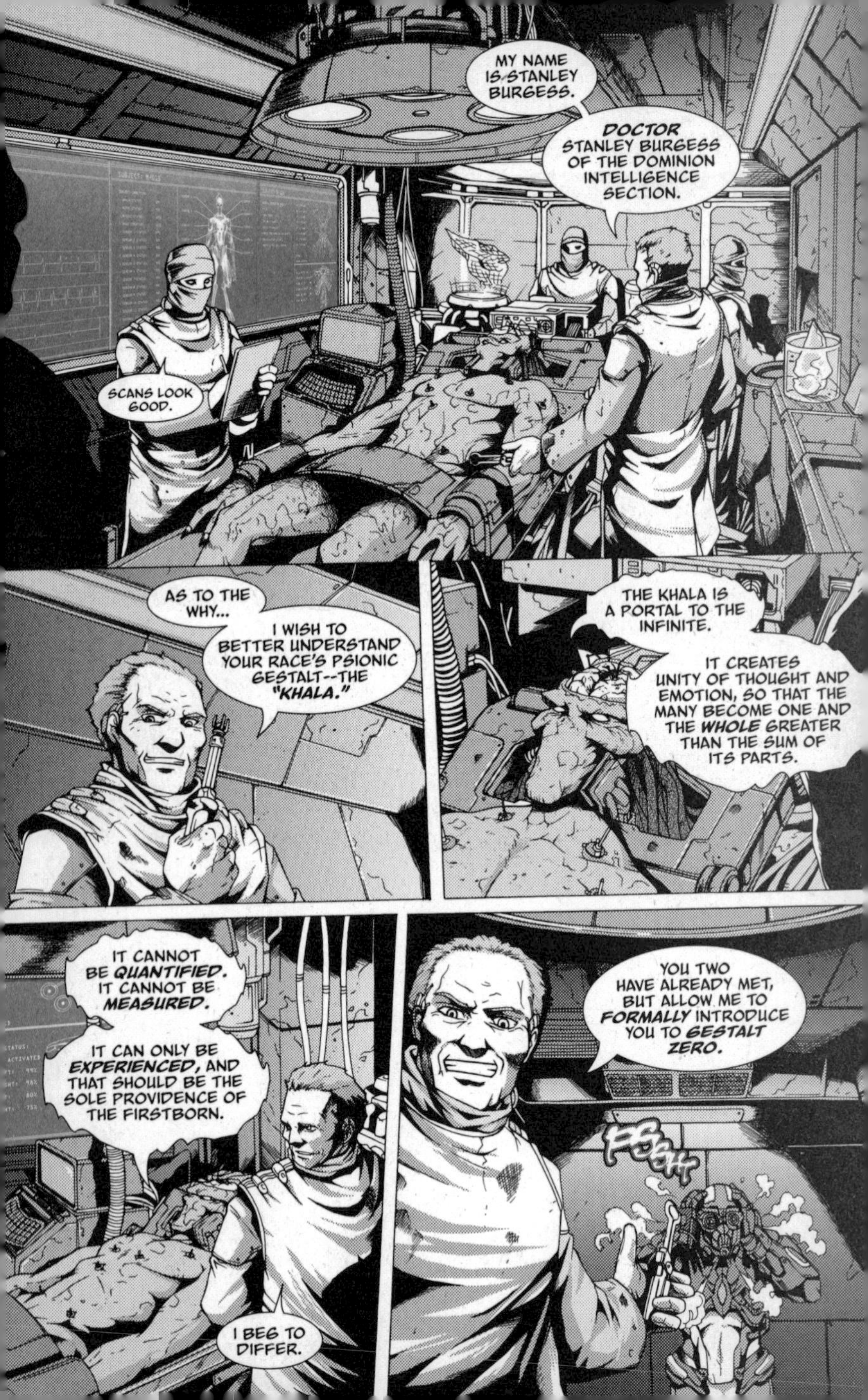
MY NAME IS STANLEY BURGESS.
DOCTOR STANLEY BURGESS OF THE DOMINION INTELLIGENCE SECTION.
SCANS LOOK GOOD.
AS TO THE WHY...
I WISH TO BETTER UNDERSTAND YOUR RACE'S PSIONIC GESTALT--THE "KHALA."
THE KHALA IS A PORTAL TO THE INFINITE.
IT CREATES UNITY OF THOUGHT AND EMOTION, SO THAT THE MANY BECOME ONE AND THE WHOLE GREATER THAN THE SUM OF ITS PARTS.
IT CANNOT BE QUANTIFIED. IT CANNOT BE MEASURED.
IT CAN ONLY BE EXPERIENCED, AND THAT SHOULD BE THE SOLE PROVIDENCE OF THE FIRSTBORN.
I BEG TO DIFFER.
YOU TWO HAVE ALREADY MET, BUT ALLOW ME TO FORMALLY INTRODUCE YOU TO GESTALT ZERO.
PSSH

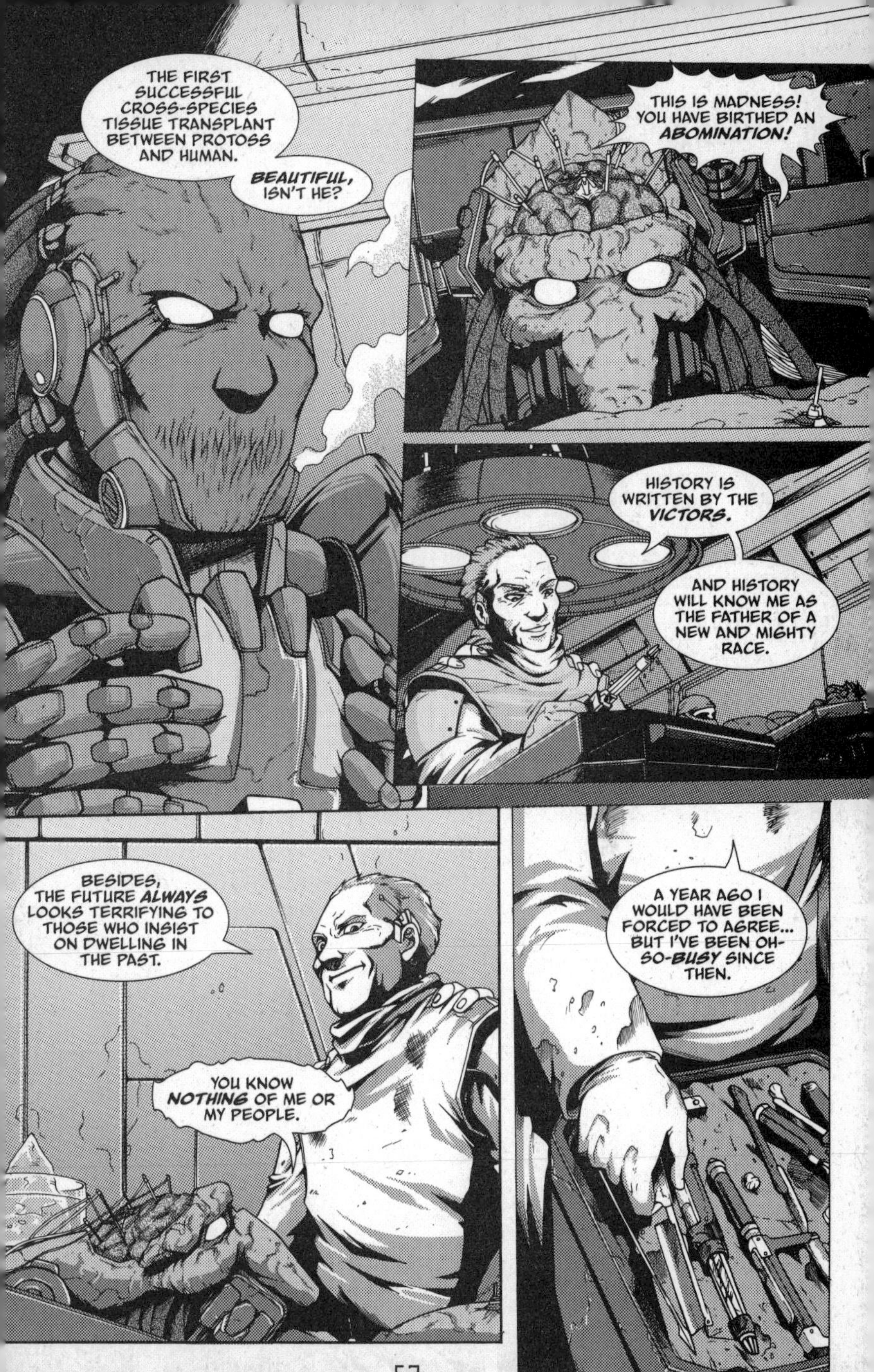
THE FIRST SUCCESSFUL CROSS-SPECIES TISSUE TRANSPLANT BETWEEN PROTOSS AND HUMAN.
BEAUTIFUL, ISN'T HE?
THIS IS MADNESS! YOU HAVE BIRTHED AN ABOMINATION!
HISTORY IS WRITTEN BY THE VICTORS.
AND HISTORY WILL KNOW ME AS THE FATHER OF A NEW AND MIGHTY RACE.
BESIDES, THE FUTURE ALWAYS LOOKS TERRIFYING TO THOSE WHO INSIST ON DWELLING IN THE PAST.
YOU KNOW NOTHING OF ME OR MY PEOPLE.
A YEAR AGO I WOULD HAVE BEEN FORCED TO AGREE... BUT I'VE BEEN OH-SO-BUSY SINCE THEN.

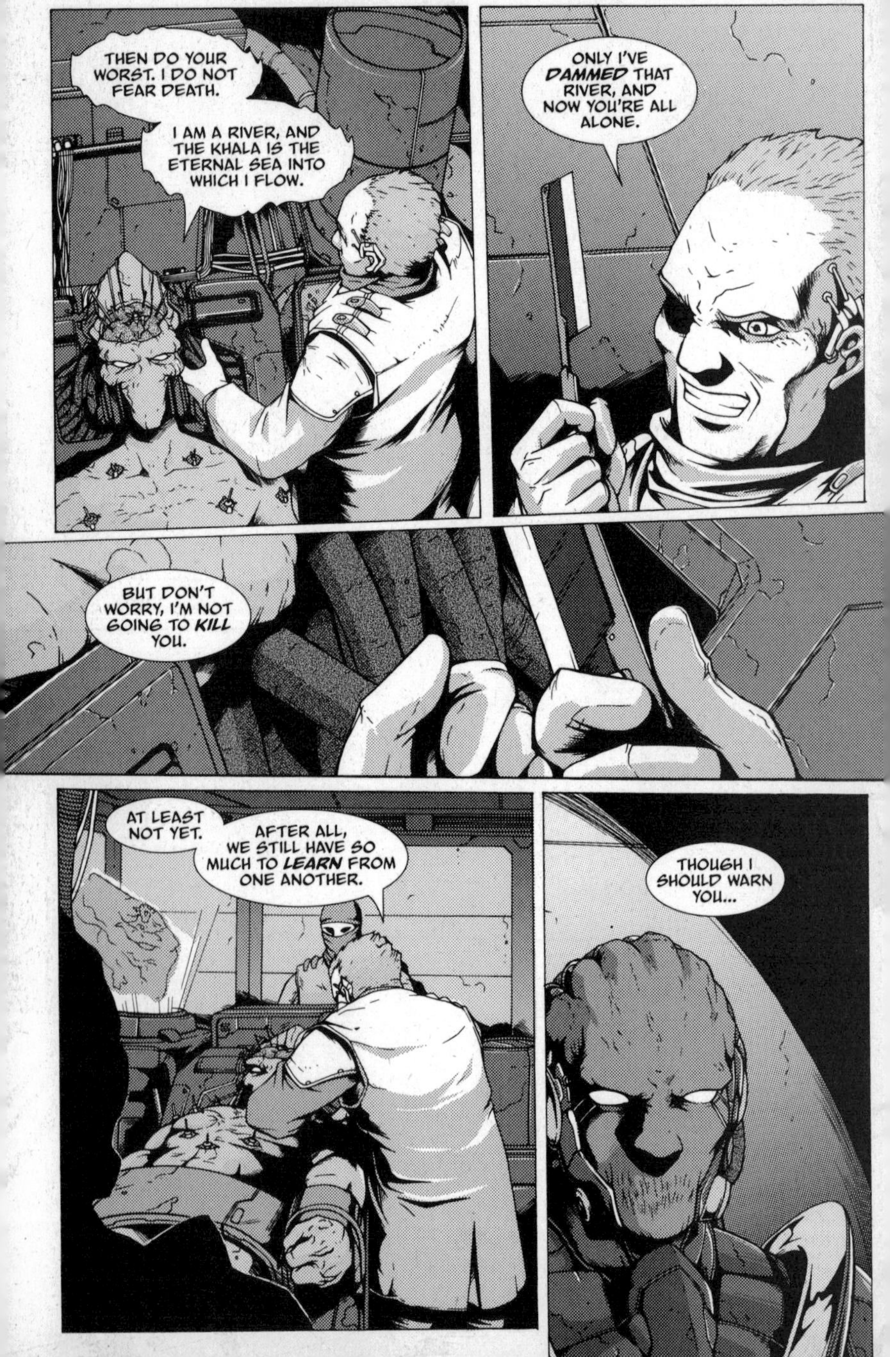
THEN DO YOUR WORST. I DO NOT FEAR DEATH.
I AM A RIVER, AND THE KHALA IS THE ETERNAL SEA INTO WHICH I FLOW.
ONLY I'VE *DAMMED* THAT RIVER, AND NOW YOU'RE ALL ALONE.
BUT DON'T WORRY, I'M NOT GOING TO *KILL* YOU.
AT LEAST NOT YET.
AFTER ALL, WE STILL HAVE SO MUCH TO *LEARN* FROM ONE ANOTHER.
THOUGH I SHOULD WARN YOU...

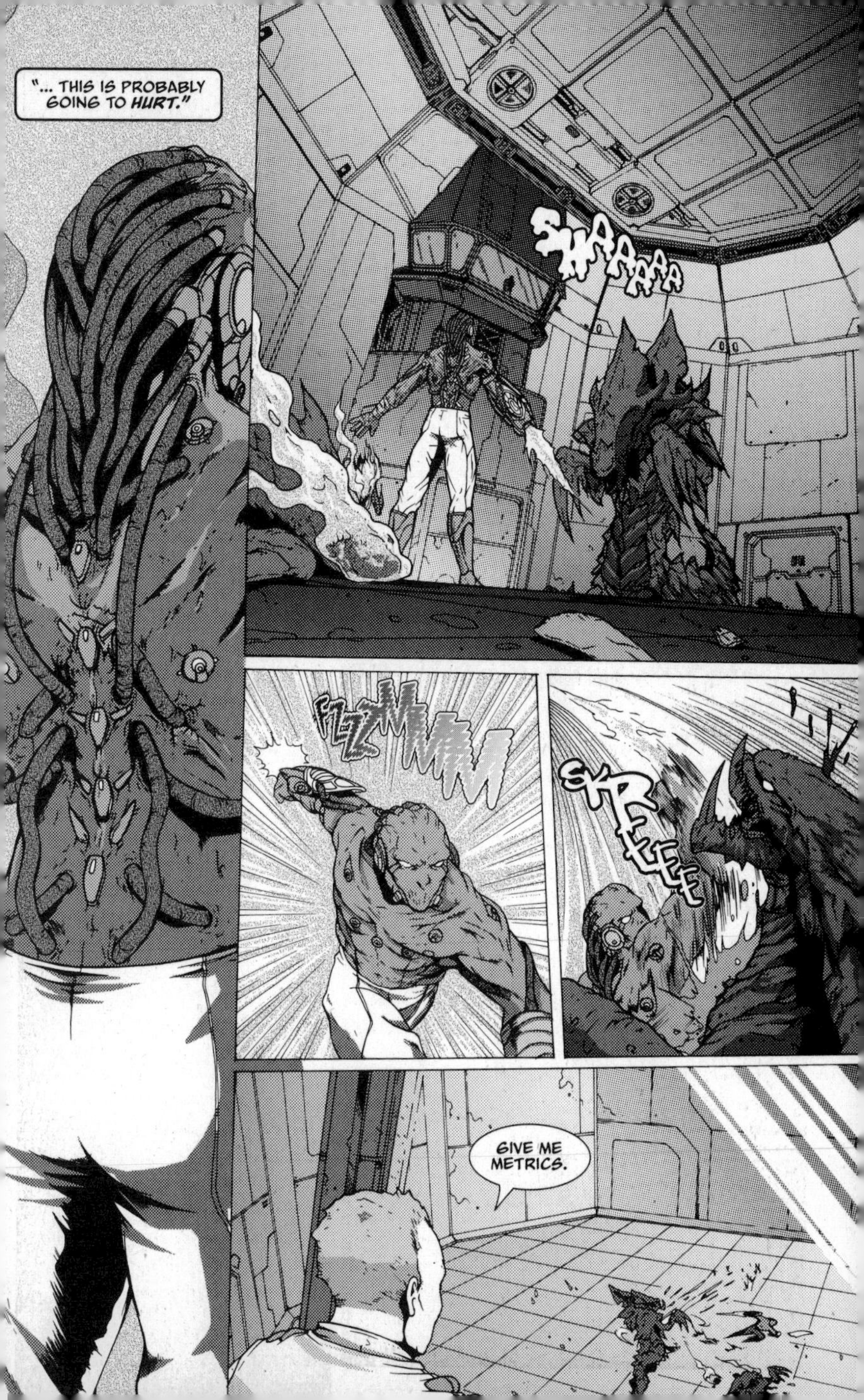
"... THIS IS PROBABLY GOING TO HURT."
SHAAAAA
FZZMMMM
SKREEEE
GIVE ME METRICS.

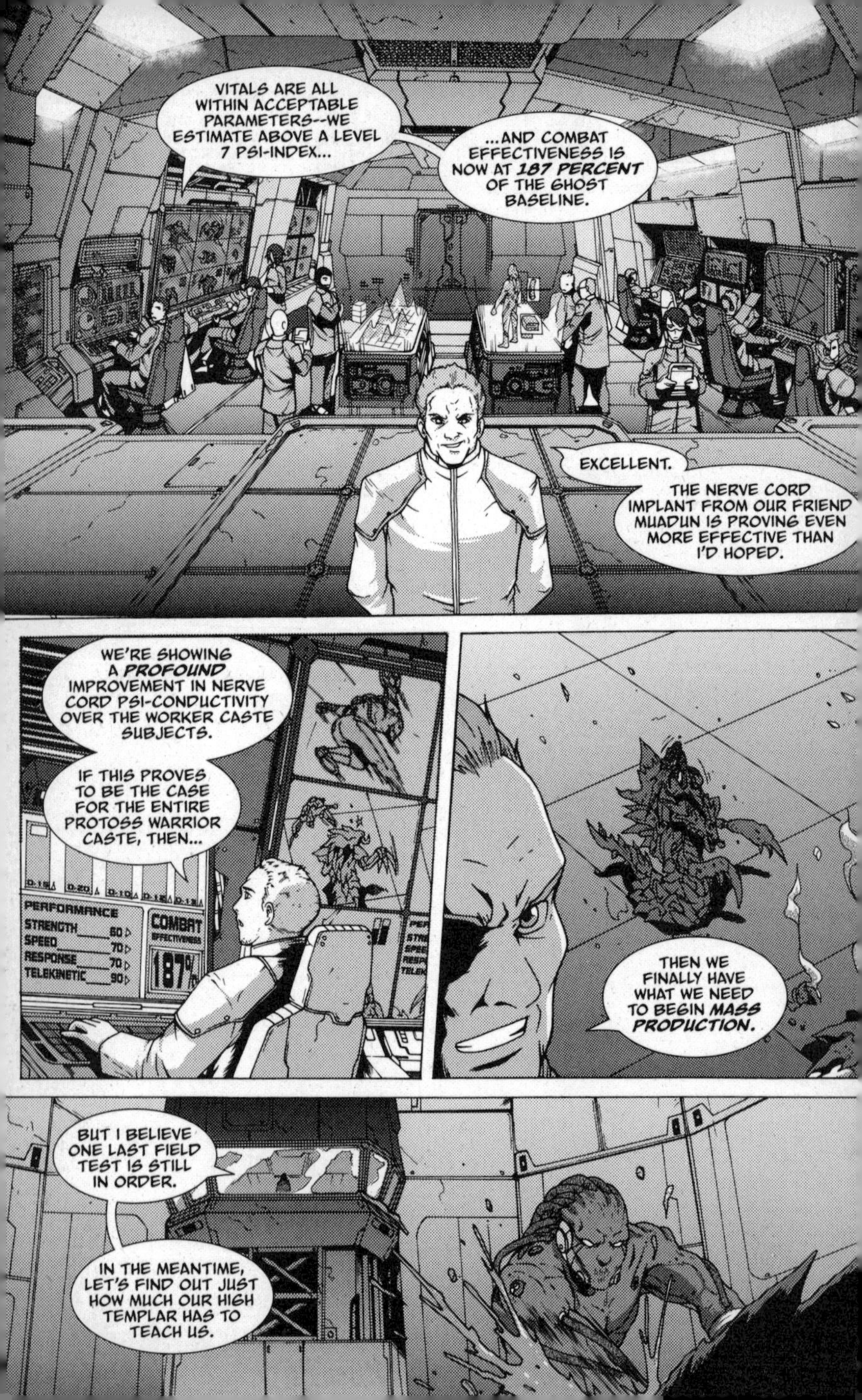
VITALS ARE ALL WITHIN ACCEPTABLE PARAMETERS--WE ESTIMATE ABOVE A LEVEL 7 PSI-INDEX...
...AND COMBAT EFFECTIVENESS IS NOW AT *187 PERCENT* OF THE GHOST BASELINE.
EXCELLENT.
THE NERVE CORD IMPLANT FROM OUR FRIEND MUADUN IS PROVING EVEN MORE EFFECTIVE THAN I'D HOPED.
WE'RE SHOWING A *PROFOUND* IMPROVEMENT IN NERVE CORD PSI-CONDUCTIVITY OVER THE WORKER CASTE SUBJECTS.
IF THIS PROVES TO BE THE CASE FOR THE ENTIRE PROTOSS WARRIOR CASTE, THEN...
PERFORMANCE
STRENGTH 60
SPEED 70
RESPONSE 70
TELEKINETIC 90
COMBAT EFFECTIVENESS
187%
THEN WE FINALLY HAVE WHAT WE NEED TO BEGIN *MASS PRODUCTION.*
BUT I BELIEVE ONE LAST FIELD TEST IS STILL IN ORDER.
IN THE MEANTIME, LET'S FIND OUT JUST HOW MUCH OUR HIGH TEMPLAR HAS TO TEACH US.

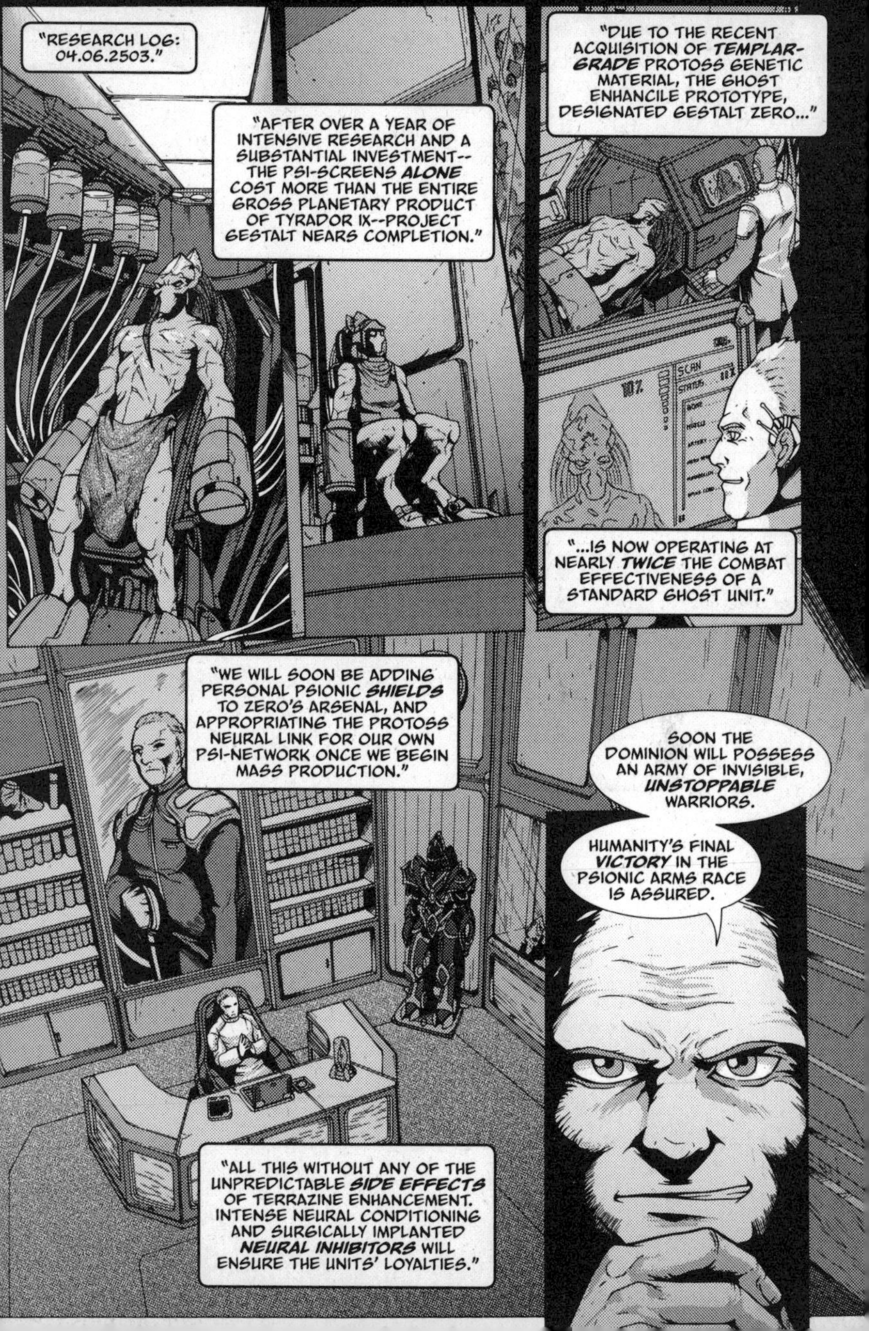
"RESEARCH LOG: 04.06.2503."
"AFTER OVER A YEAR OF INTENSIVE RESEARCH AND A SUBSTANTIAL INVESTMENT-- THE PSI-SCREENS ALONE COST MORE THAN THE ENTIRE GROSS PLANETARY PRODUCT OF TYRADOR IX--PROJECT GESTALT NEARS COMPLETION."
"DUE TO THE RECENT ACQUISITION OF TEMPLAR-GRADE PROTOSS GENETIC MATERIAL, THE GHOST ENHANCILE PROTOTYPE, DESIGNATED GESTALT ZERO..."
SCAN
STATUS
"...IS NOW OPERATING AT NEARLY TWICE THE COMBAT EFFECTIVENESS OF A STANDARD GHOST UNIT."
"WE WILL SOON BE ADDING PERSONAL PSIONIC SHIELDS TO ZERO'S ARSENAL, AND APPROPRIATING THE PROTOSS NEURAL LINK FOR OUR OWN PSI-NETWORK ONCE WE BEGIN MASS PRODUCTION."
"ALL THIS WITHOUT ANY OF THE UNPREDICTABLE SIDE EFFECTS OF TERRAZINE ENHANCEMENT. INTENSE NEURAL CONDITIONING AND SURGICALLY IMPLANTED NEURAL INHIBITORS WILL ENSURE THE UNITS' LOYALTIES."
SOON THE DOMINION WILL POSSESS AN ARMY OF INVISIBLE, UNSTOPPABLE WARRIORS.
HUMANITY'S FINAL VICTORY IN THE PSIONIC ARMS RACE IS ASSURED.

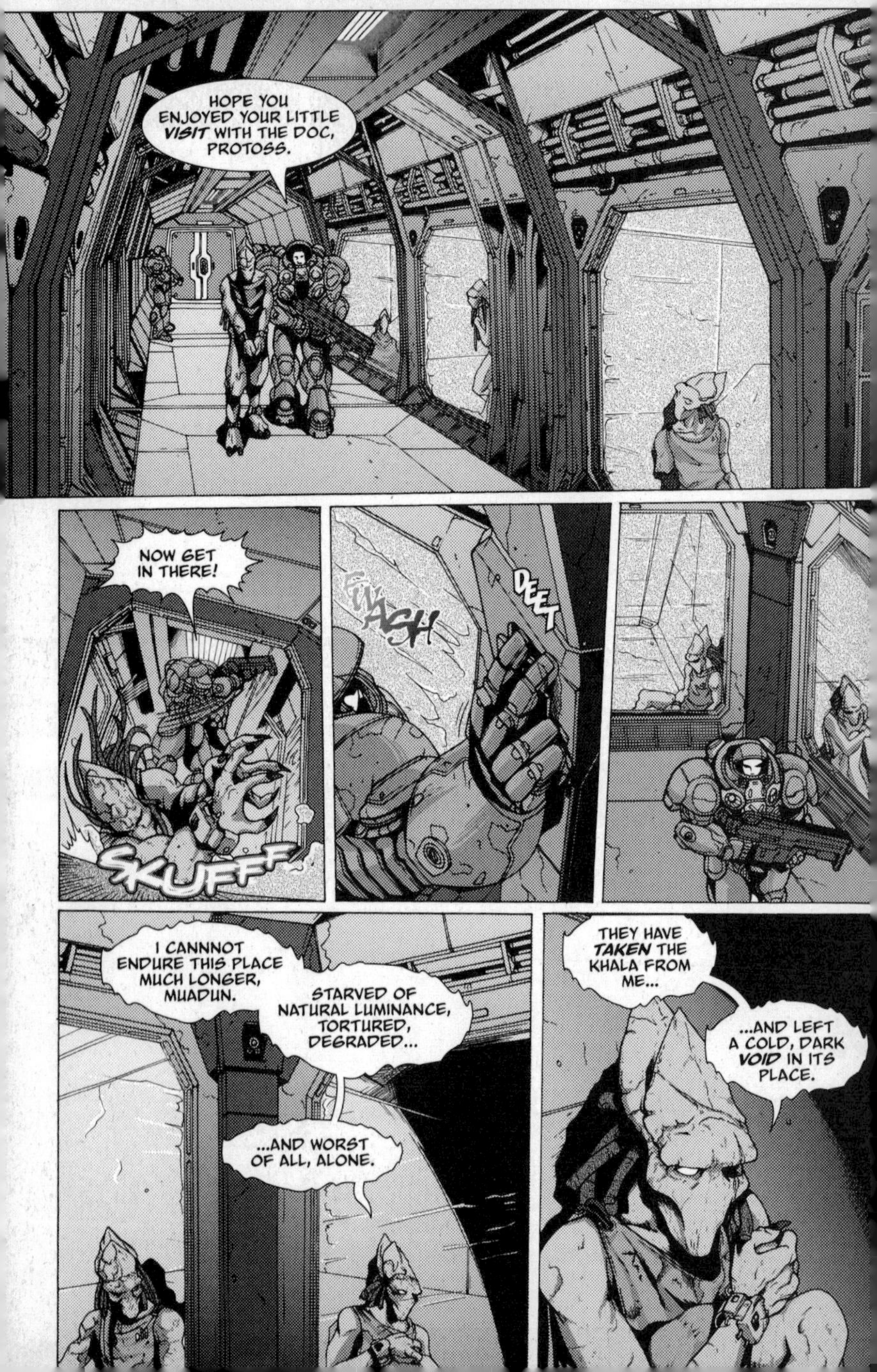
HOPE YOU ENJOYED YOUR LITTLE VISIT WITH THE DOC, PROTOSS.
NOW GET IN THERE!
SKUFFF
FWASH!
DEET
I CANNNOT ENDURE THIS PLACE MUCH LONGER, MUADUN.
STARVED OF NATURAL LUMINANCE, TORTURED, DEGRADED...
...AND WORST OF ALL, ALONE.
THEY HAVE TAKEN THE KHALA FROM ME...
...AND LEFT A COLD, DARK VOID IN ITS PLACE.

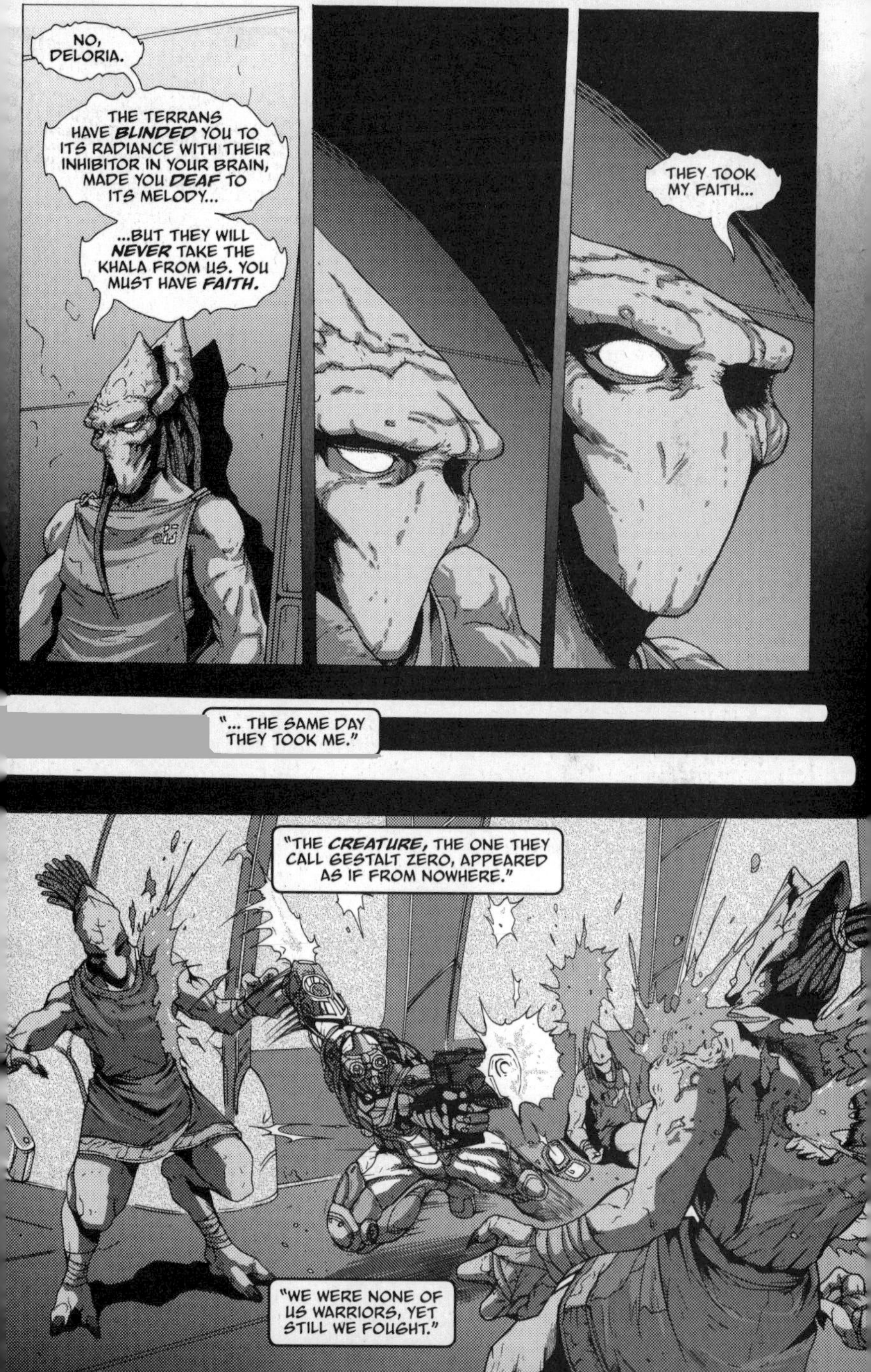
NO, DELORIA.
THE TERRANS HAVE BLINDED YOU TO ITS RADIANCE WITH THEIR INHIBITOR IN YOUR BRAIN, MADE YOU DEAF TO ITS MELODY...
...BUT THEY WILL NEVER TAKE THE KHALA FROM US. YOU MUST HAVE FAITH.
THEY TOOK MY FAITH...
"... THE SAME DAY THEY TOOK ME."
"THE CREATURE, THE ONE THEY CALL GESTALT ZERO, APPEARED AS IF FROM NOWHERE."
"WE WERE NONE OF US WARRIORS, YET STILL WE FOUGHT."

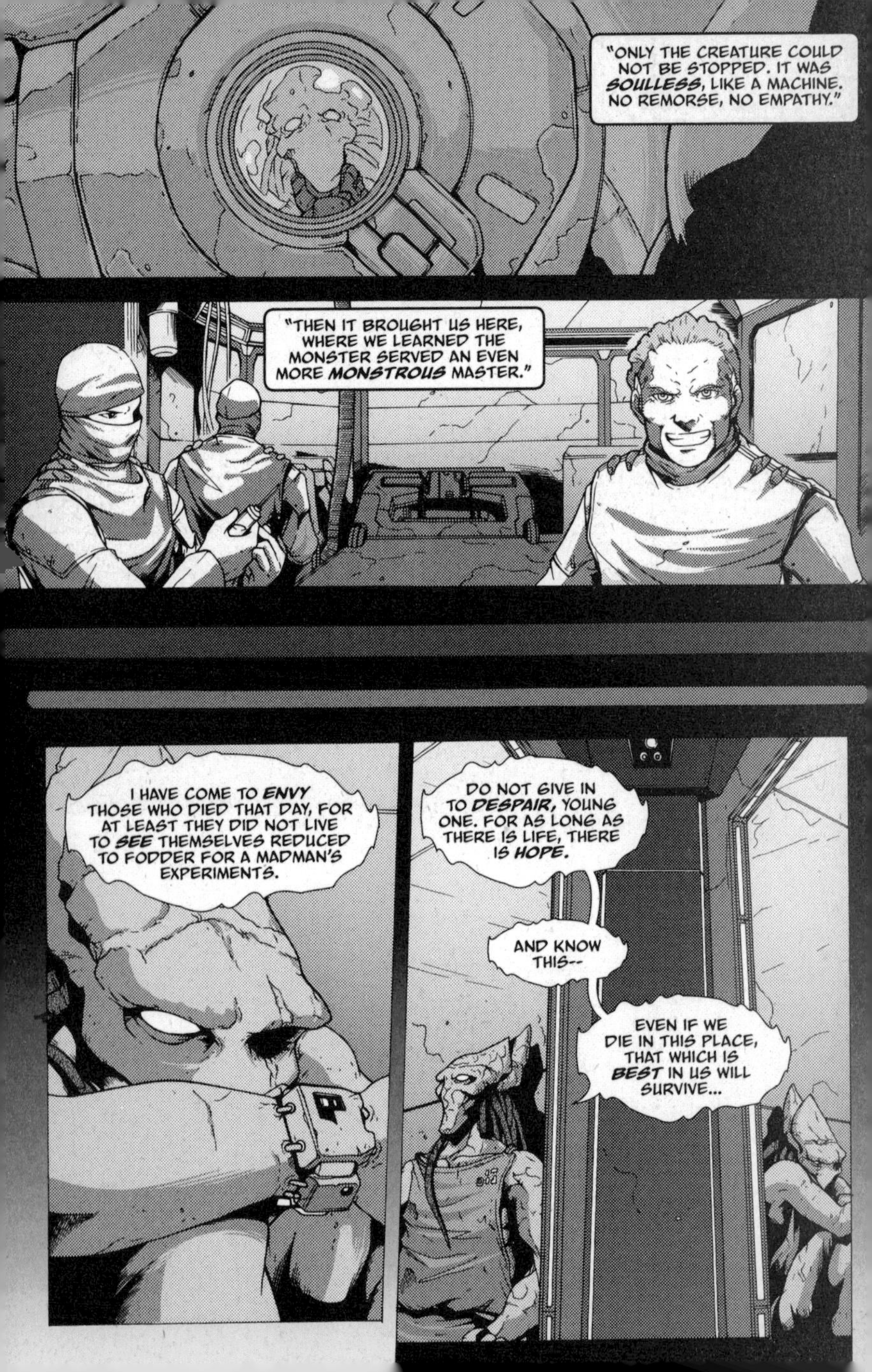
"ONLY THE CREATURE COULD NOT BE STOPPED. IT WAS SOULLESS, LIKE A MACHINE. NO REMORSE, NO EMPATHY."
"THEN IT BROUGHT US HERE, WHERE WE LEARNED THE MONSTER SERVED AN EVEN MORE MONSTROUS MASTER."
I HAVE COME TO ENVY THOSE WHO DIED THAT DAY, FOR AT LEAST THEY DID NOT LIVE TO SEE THEMSELVES REDUCED TO FODDER FOR A MADMAN'S EXPERIMENTS.
DO NOT GIVE IN TO DESPAIR, YOUNG ONE. FOR AS LONG AS THERE IS LIFE, THERE IS HOPE.
AND KNOW THIS--
EVEN IF WE DIE IN THIS PLACE, THAT WHICH IS BEST IN US WILL SURVIVE...

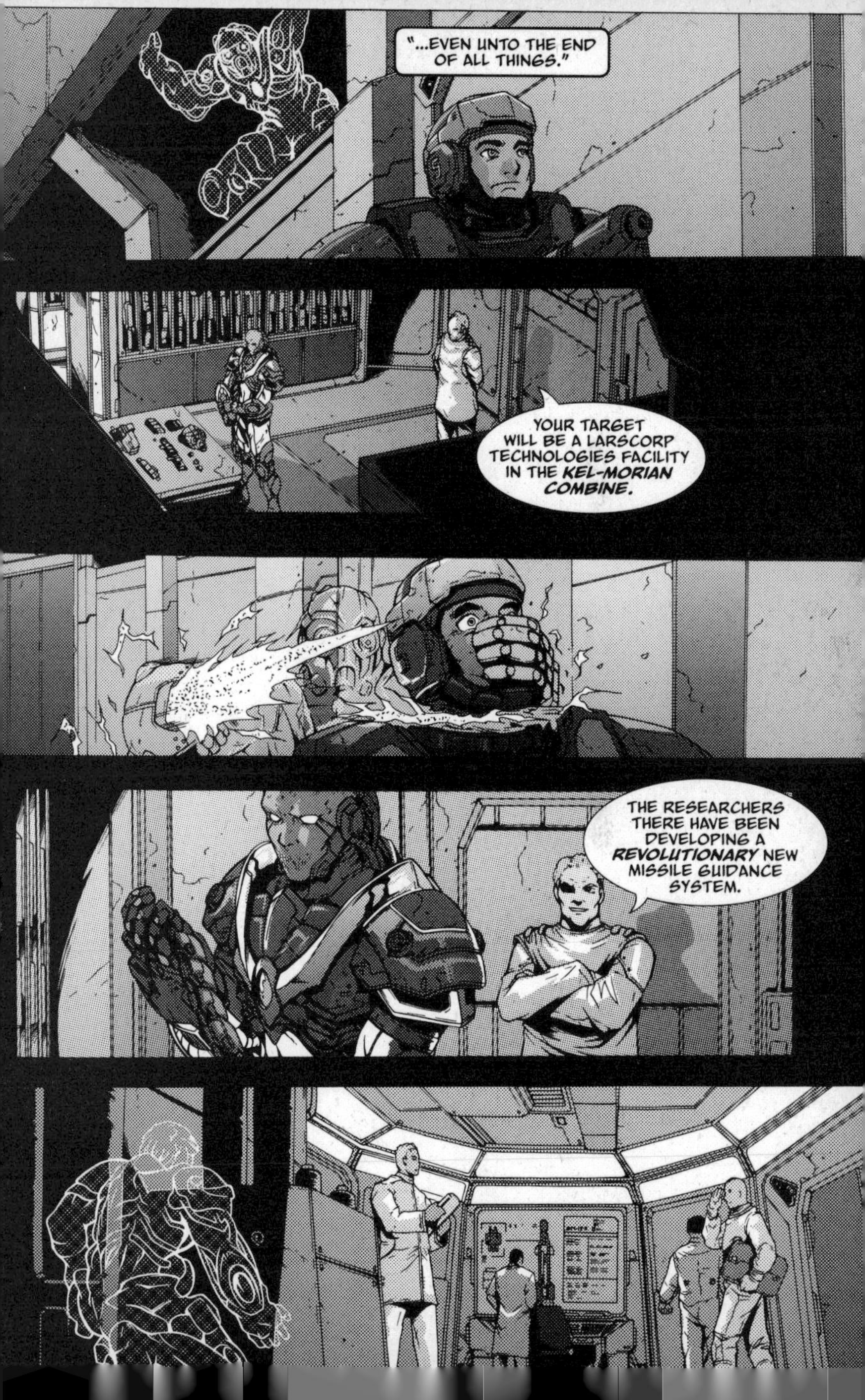
"...EVEN UNTO THE END OF ALL THINGS."
YOUR TARGET WILL BE A LARSCORP TECHNOLOGIES FACILITY IN THE KEL-MORIAN COMBINE.
THE RESEARCHERS THERE HAVE BEEN DEVELOPING A REVOLUTIONARY NEW MISSILE GUIDANCE SYSTEM.

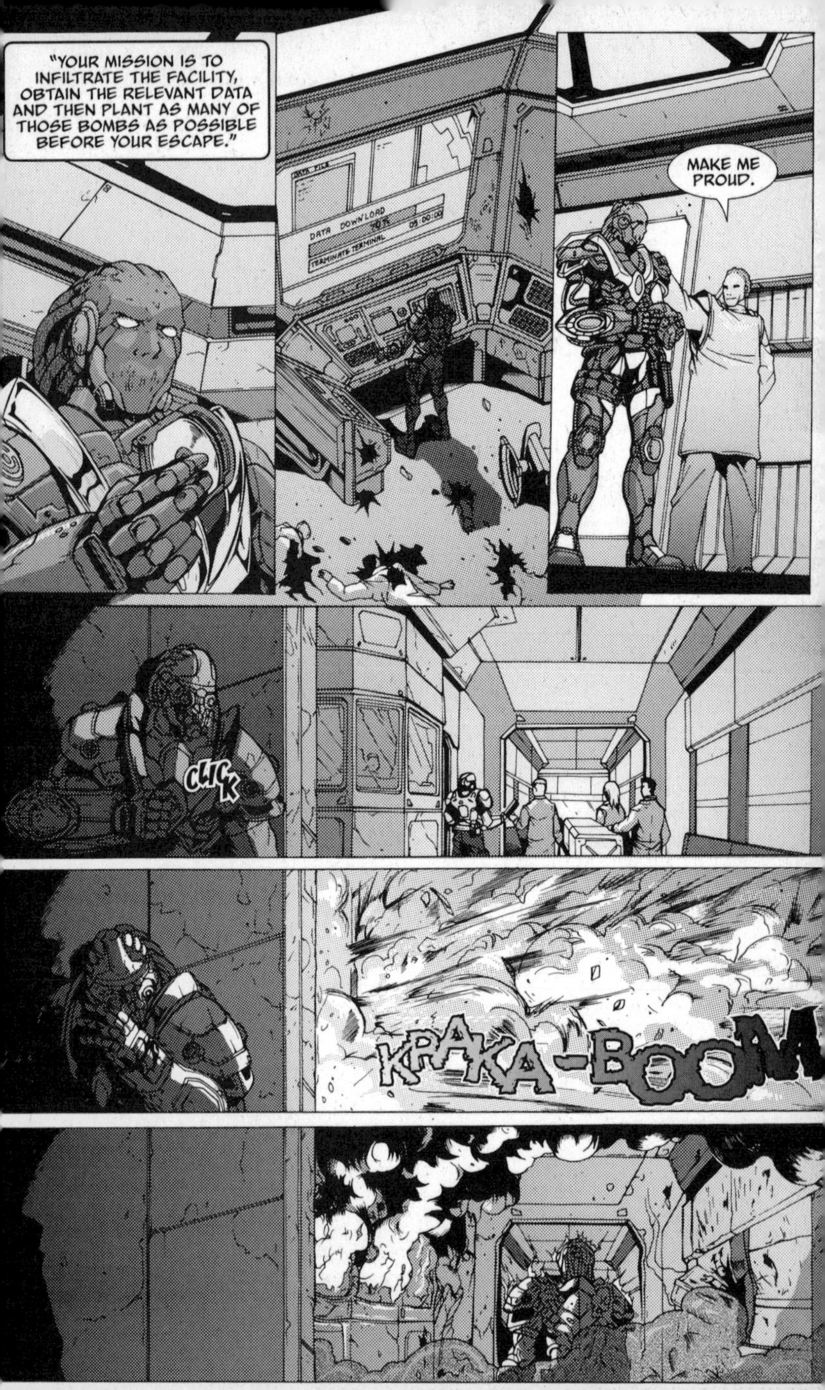
"YOUR MISSION IS TO INFILTRATE THE FACILITY, OBTAIN THE RELEVANT DATA AND THEN PLANT AS MANY OF THOSE BOMBS AS POSSIBLE BEFORE YOUR ESCAPE."
DATA FILE
DATA DOWNLOAD
TERMINATE TERMINAL
MAKE ME PROUD.
CLICK
KRAKA-BOOM

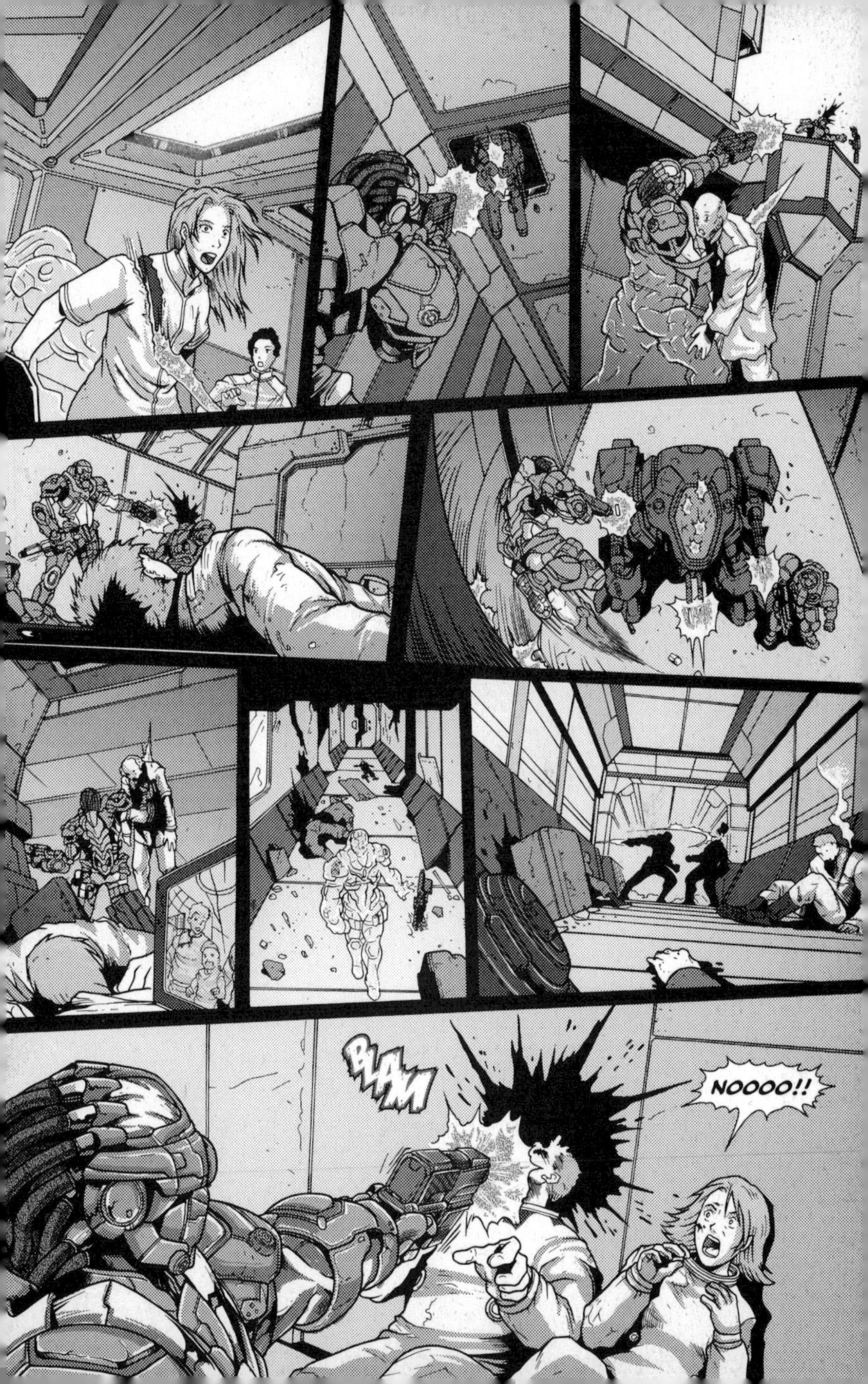
BLAM
NOOOO!!

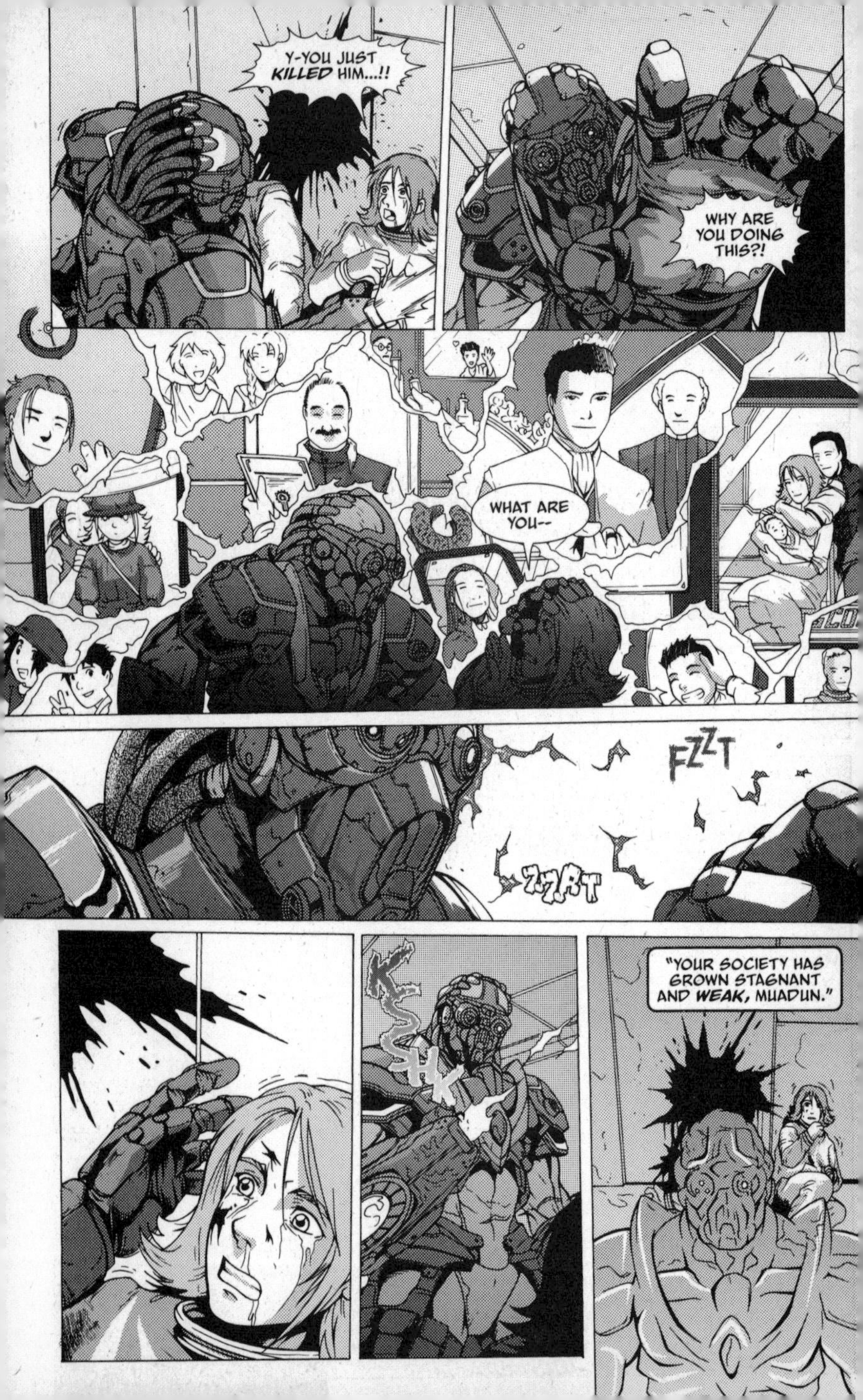
Y-YOU JUST *KILLED* HIM...!!
WHY ARE YOU DOING THIS?!
WHAT ARE YOU--
FZZT
ZZZRT
KSHK
"YOUR SOCIETY HAS GROWN STAGNANT AND *WEAK*, MUADUN."

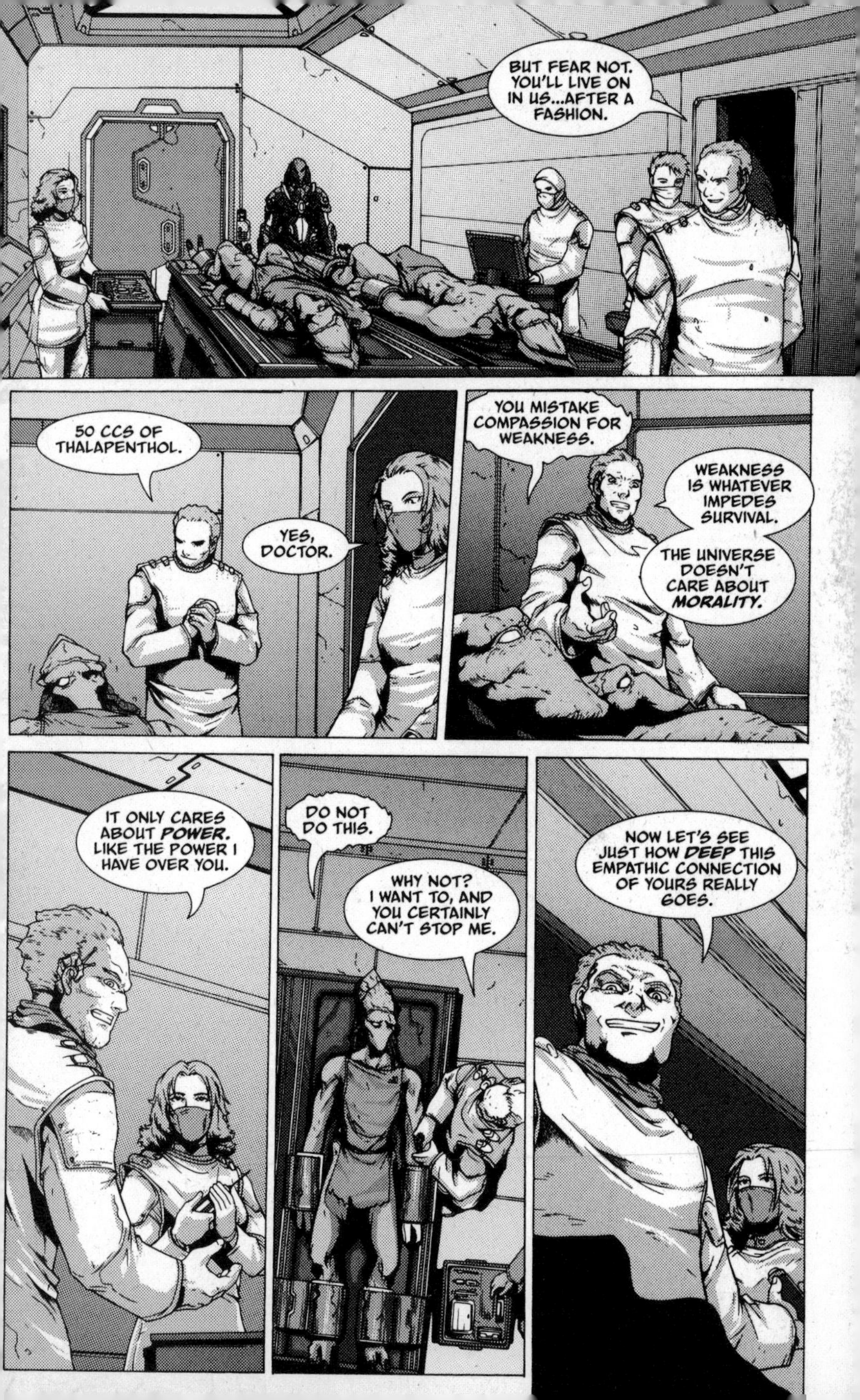
BUT FEAR NOT. YOU'LL LIVE ON IN US...AFTER A FASHION.
50 CCS OF THALAPENTHOL.
YES, DOCTOR.
YOU MISTAKE COMPASSION FOR WEAKNESS.
WEAKNESS IS WHATEVER IMPEDES SURVIVAL.
THE UNIVERSE DOESN'T CARE ABOUT *MORALITY.*
IT ONLY CARES ABOUT *POWER.* LIKE THE POWER I HAVE OVER YOU.
DO NOT DO THIS.
WHY NOT? I WANT TO, AND YOU CERTAINLY CAN'T STOP ME.
NOW LET'S SEE JUST HOW *DEEP* THIS EMPATHIC CONNECTION OF YOURS REALLY GOES.

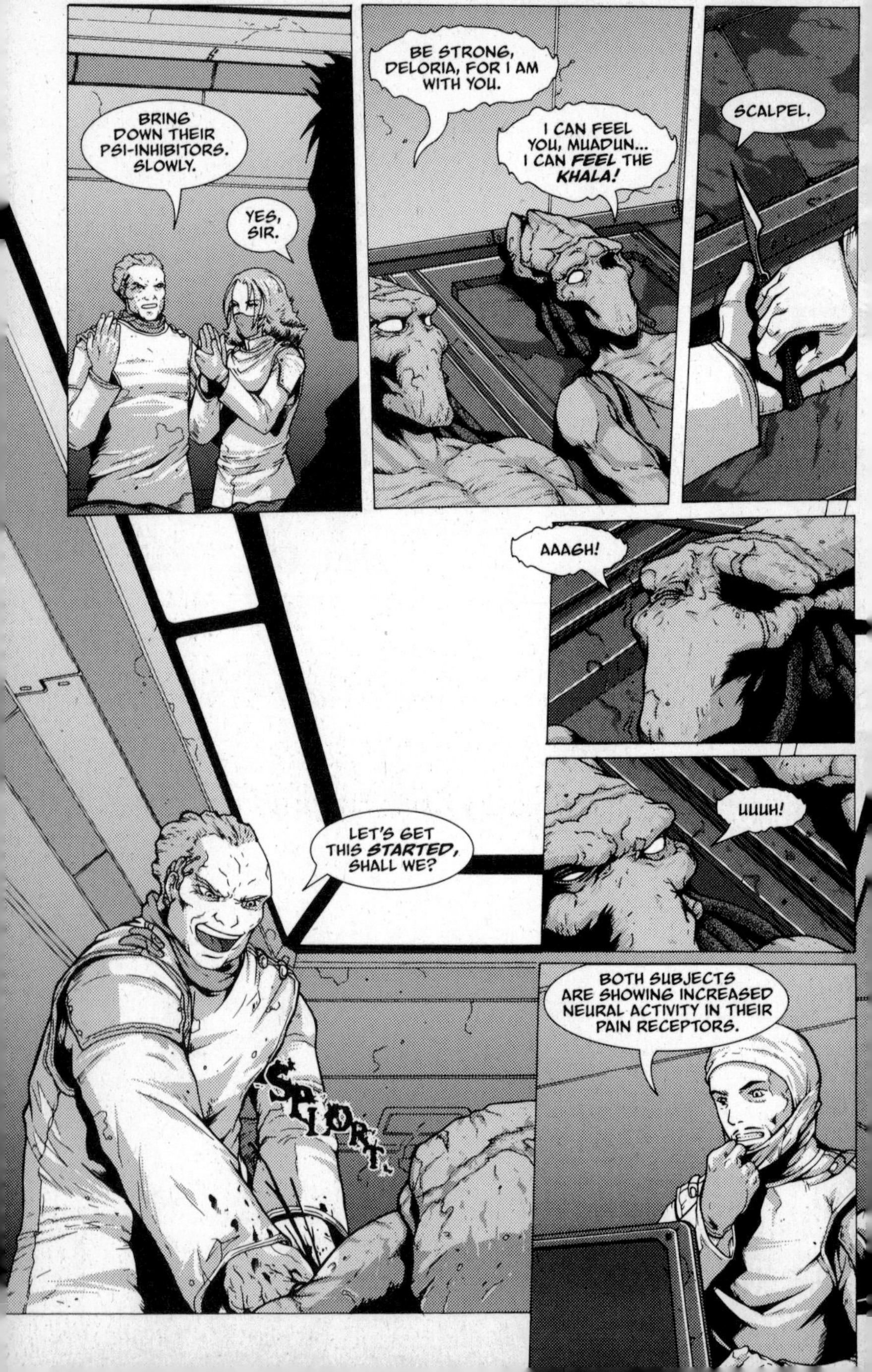

BRING DOWN THEIR PSI-INHIBITORS. SLOWLY.
YES, SIR.
BE STRONG, DELORIA, FOR I AM WITH YOU.
I CAN FEEL YOU, MUADUN... I CAN *FEEL* THE *KHALA!*
SCALPEL.
AAAGH!
LET'S GET THIS *STARTED*, SHALL WE?
SPLORT.
UUUH!
BOTH SUBJECTS ARE SHOWING INCREASED NEURAL ACTIVITY IN THEIR PAIN RECEPTORS.

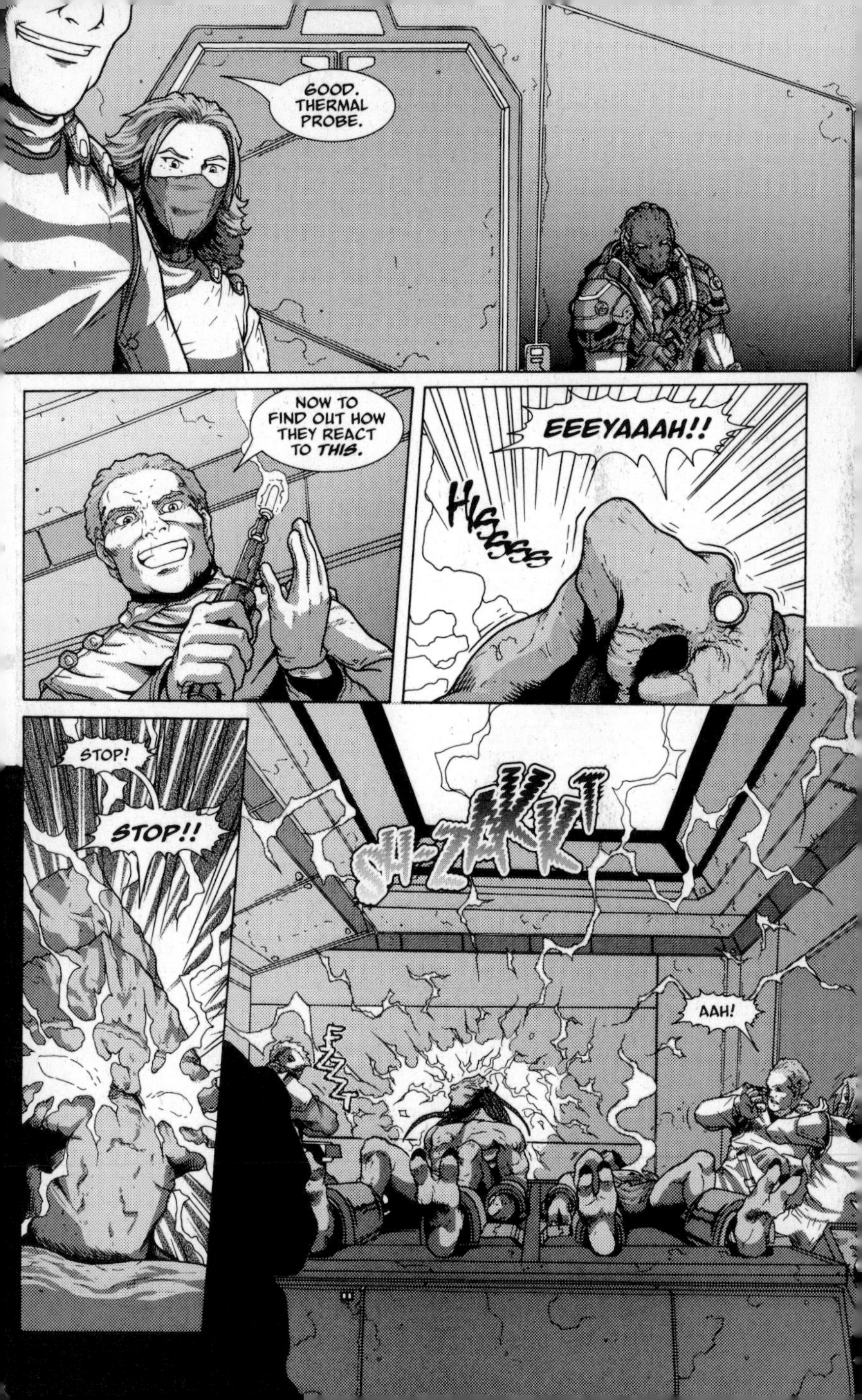
GOOD. THERMAL PROBE.
NOW TO FIND OUT HOW THEY REACT TO *THIS*.
EEEYAAAH!!
HISSSSS
STOP!
STOP!!
SH-ZAKK!
AAH!
FZZZT

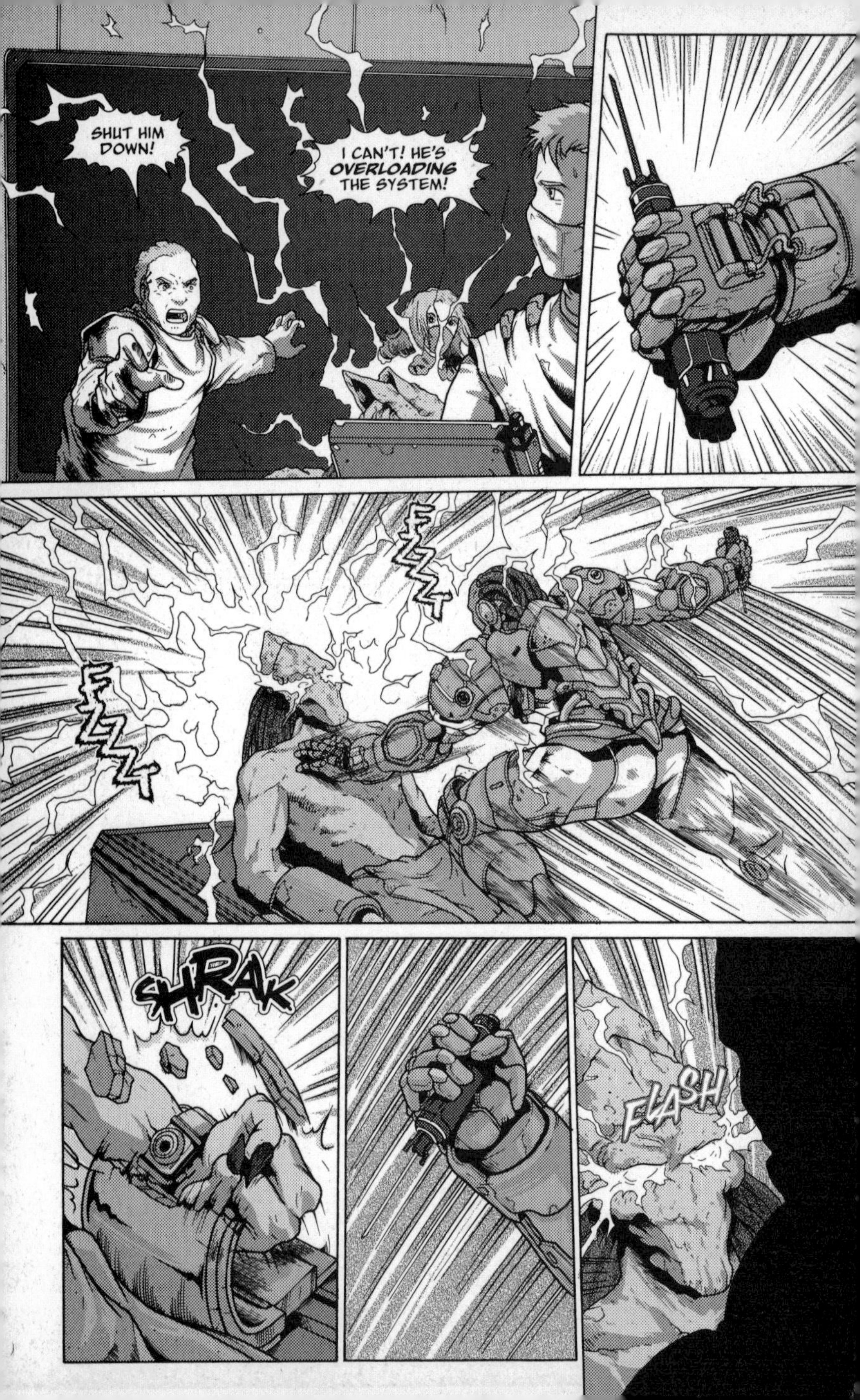
SHUT HIM DOWN!
I CAN'T! HE'S *OVERLOADING* THE SYSTEM!
FZZZT
FZZZT
SHRAK
FLASH

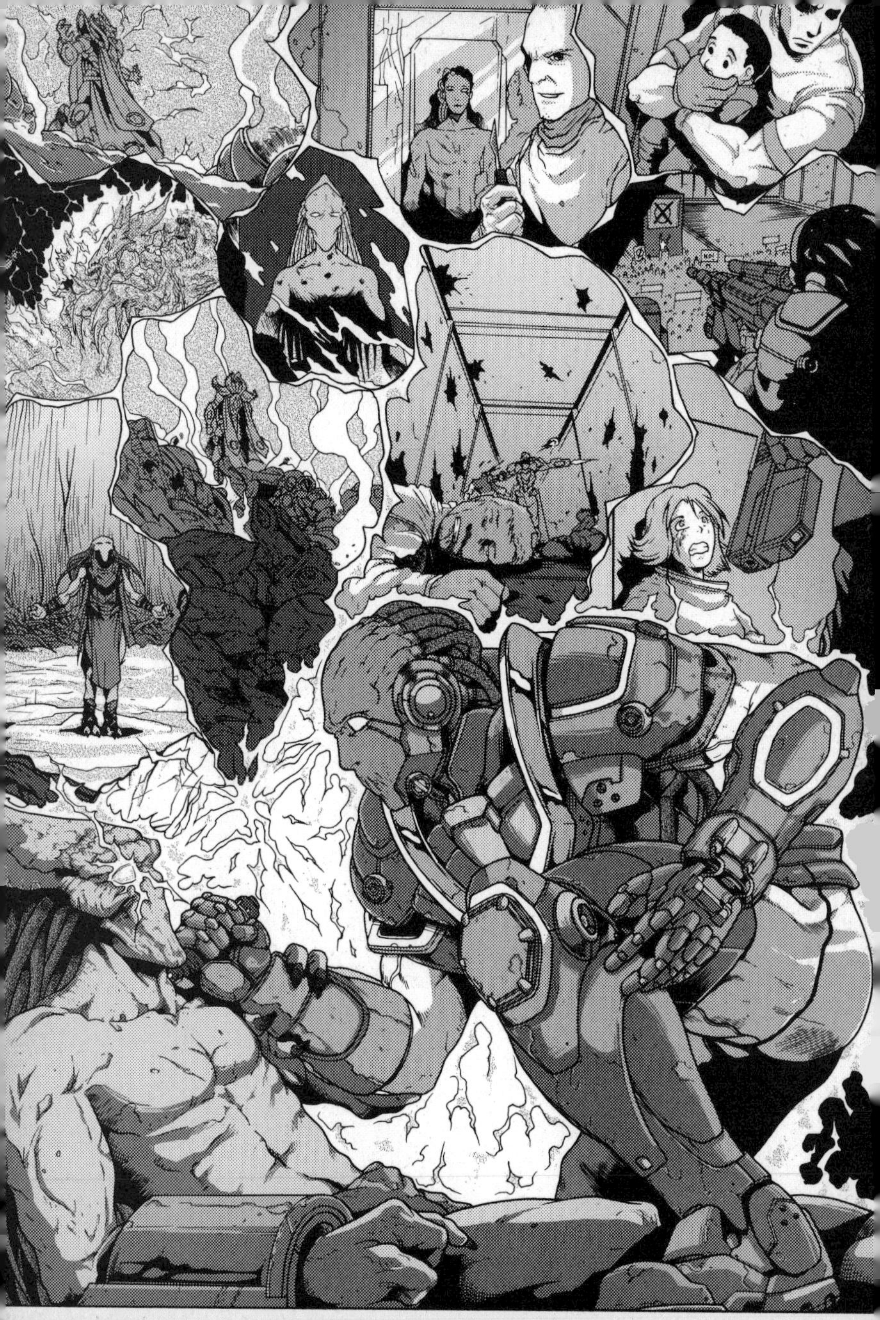

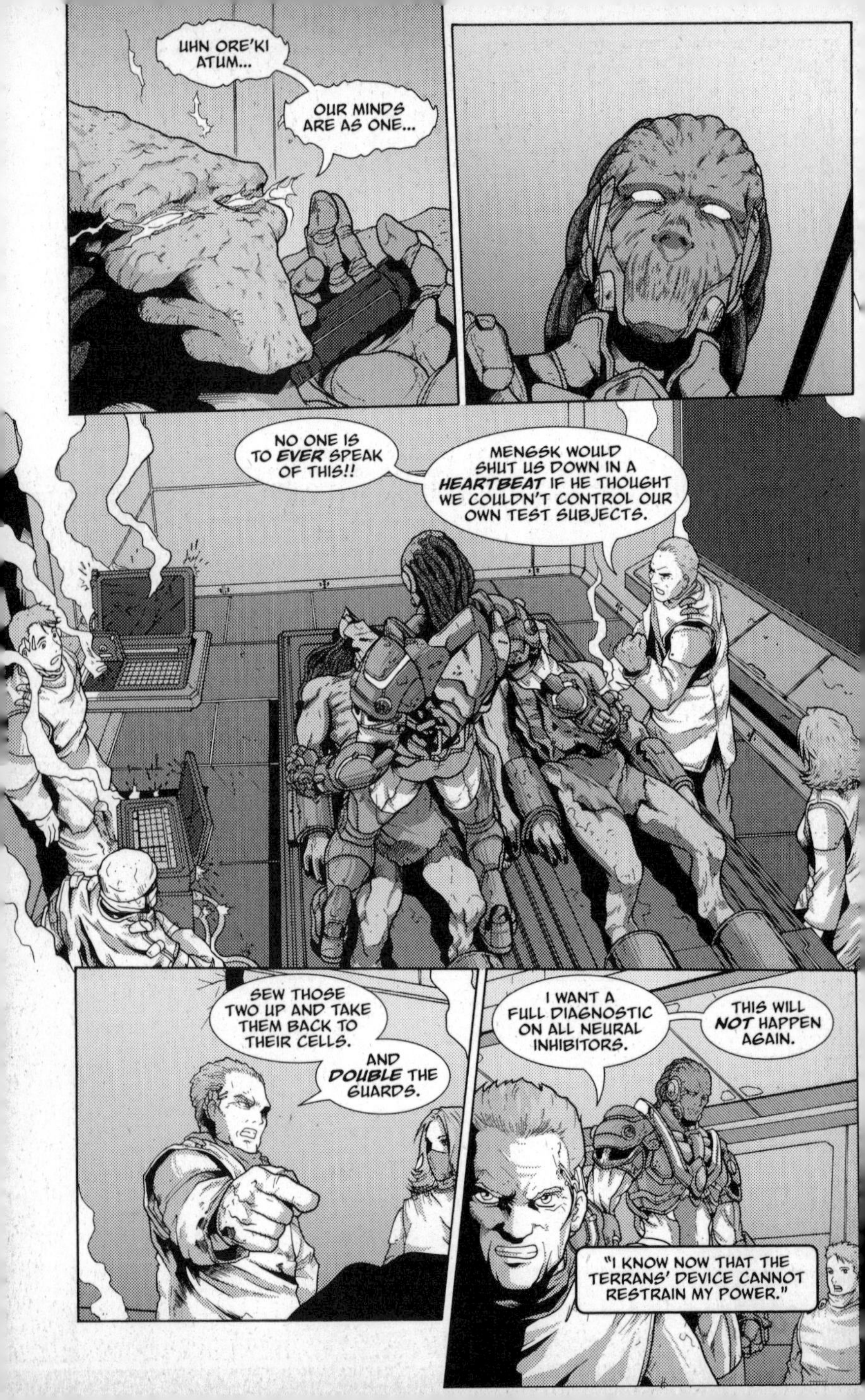
UHN ORE'KI ATUM...
OUR MINDS ARE AS ONE...
NO ONE IS TO ***EVER*** SPEAK OF THIS!!
MENGSK WOULD SHUT US DOWN IN A ***HEARTBEAT*** IF HE THOUGHT WE COULDN'T CONTROL OUR OWN TEST SUBJECTS.
SEW THOSE TWO UP AND TAKE THEM BACK TO THEIR CELLS.
AND ***DOUBLE*** THE GUARDS.
I WANT A FULL DIAGNOSTIC ON ALL NEURAL INHIBITORS.
THIS WILL ***NOT*** HAPPEN AGAIN.
"I KNOW NOW THAT THE TERRANS' DEVICE CANNOT RESTRAIN MY POWER."

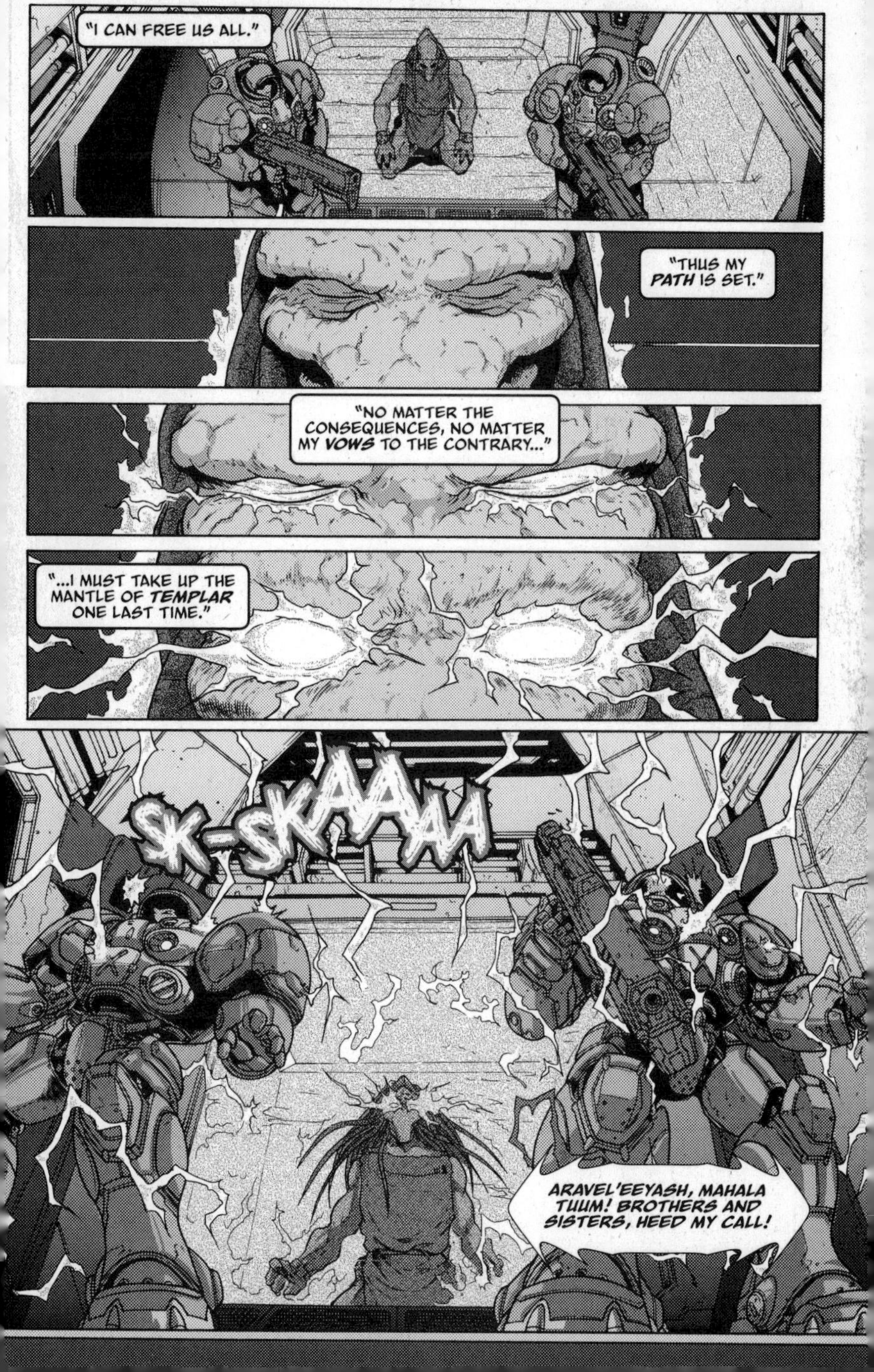
"I CAN FREE US ALL."
"THUS MY PATH IS SET."
"NO MATTER THE CONSEQUENCES, NO MATTER MY VOWS TO THE CONTRARY..."
"...I MUST TAKE UP THE MANTLE OF TEMPLAR ONE LAST TIME."
SK-SKAAAAA
ARAVEL'EEYASH, MAHALA TUUM! BROTHERS AND SISTERS, HEED MY CALL!

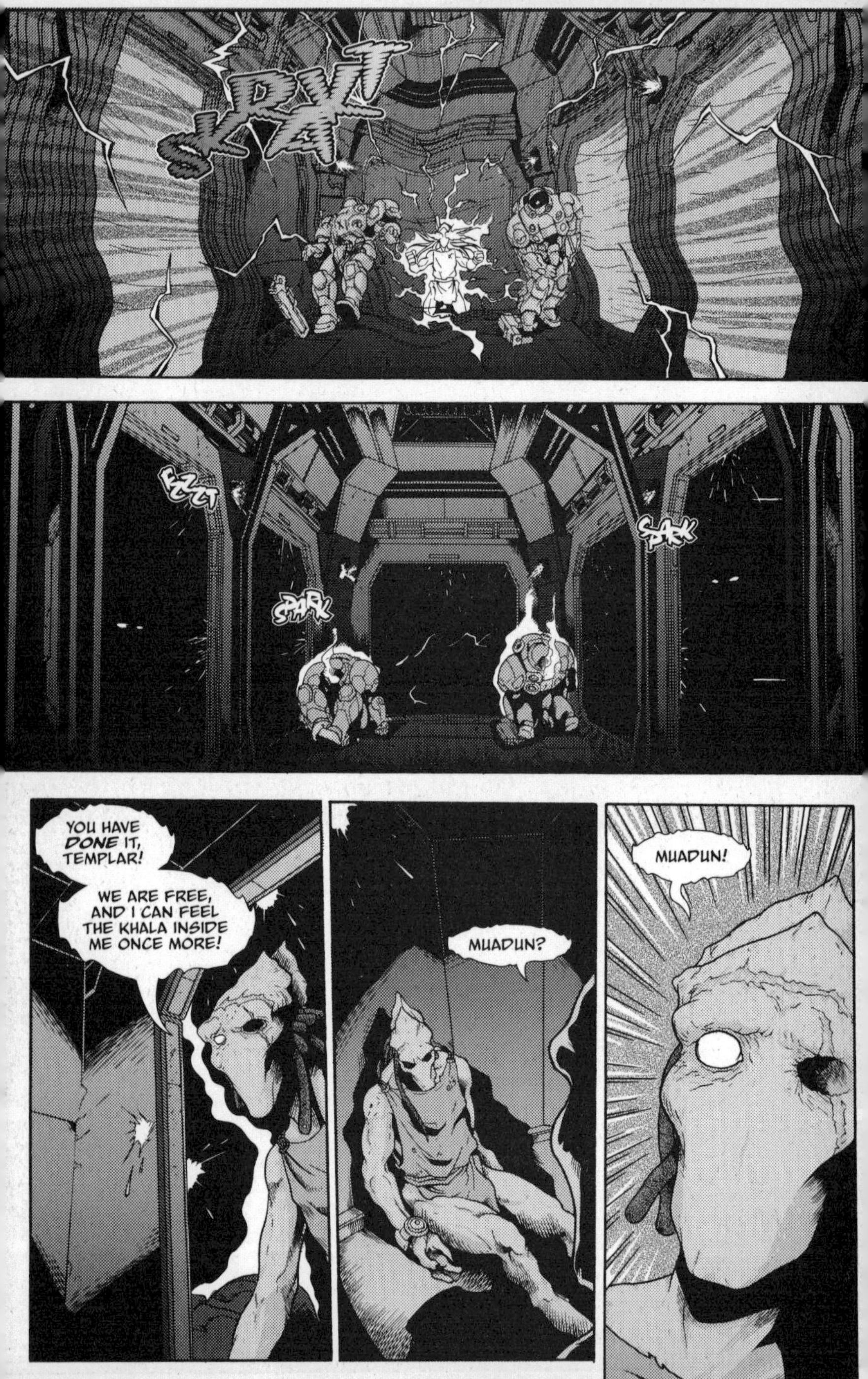
SKPXT
EZZZT
SPARK
SPARK
YOU HAVE DONE IT, TEMPLAR!
WE ARE FREE, AND I CAN FEEL THE KHALA INSIDE ME ONCE MORE!
MUADUN?
MUADUN!

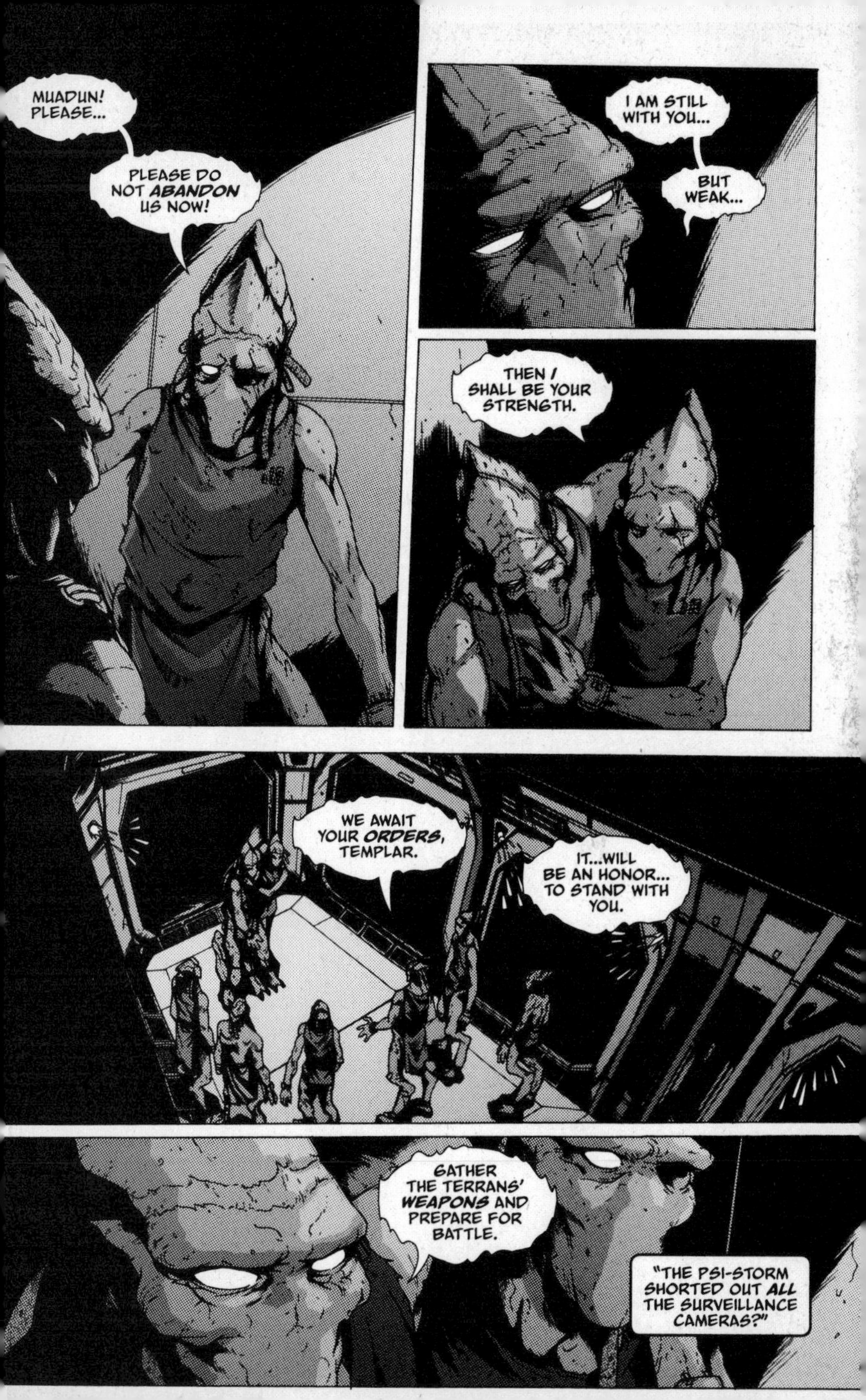
MUADUN! PLEASE...
PLEASE DO NOT *ABANDON* US NOW!
I AM STILL WITH YOU...
BUT WEAK...
THEN *I* SHALL BE YOUR STRENGTH.
WE AWAIT YOUR ***ORDERS***, TEMPLAR.
IT...WILL BE AN HONOR... TO STAND WITH YOU.
GATHER THE TERRANS' ***WEAPONS*** AND PREPARE FOR BATTLE.
"THE PSI-STORM SHORTED OUT *ALL* THE SURVEILLANCE CAMERAS?"

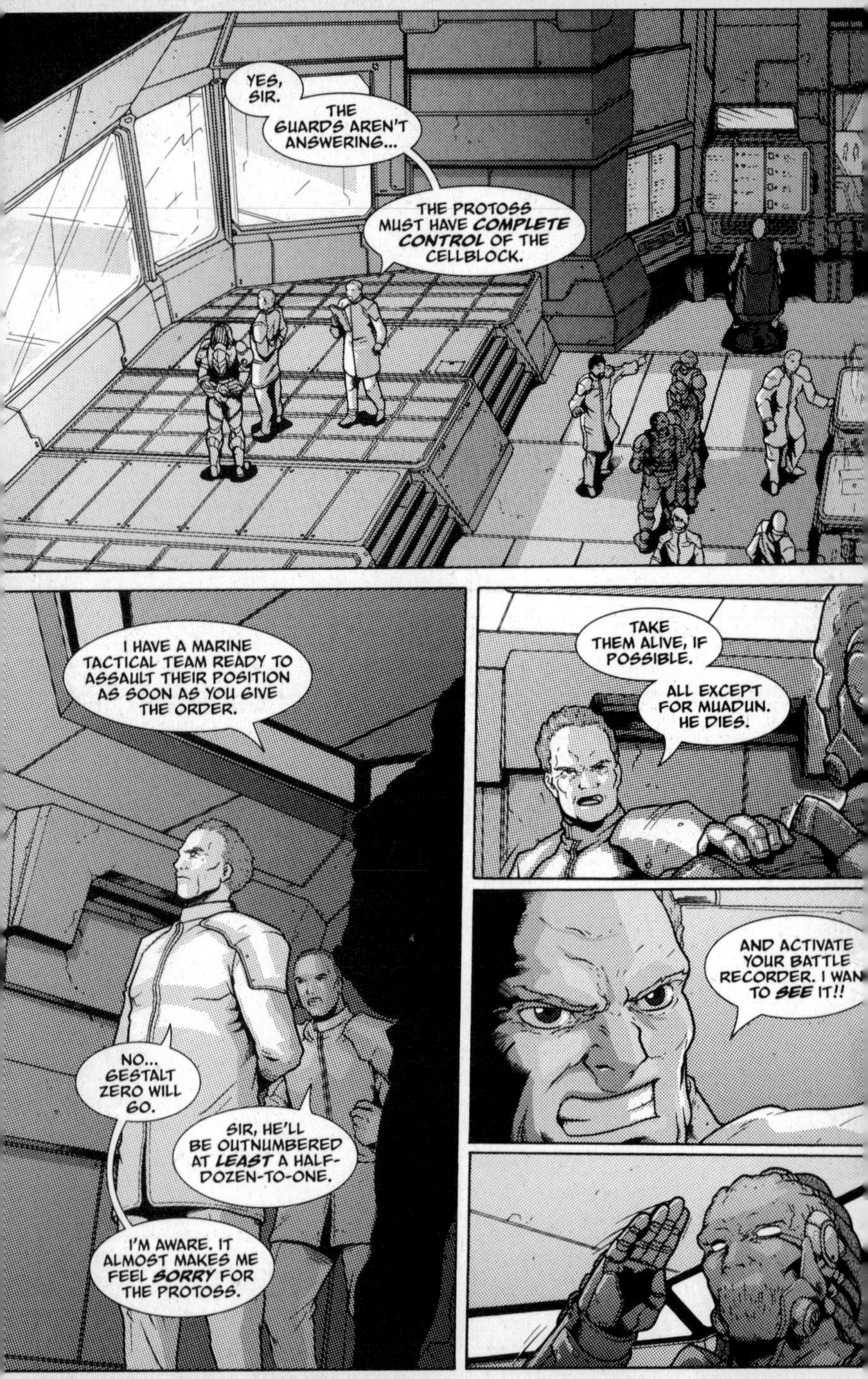
YES, SIR.
THE GUARDS AREN'T ANSWERING...
THE PROTOSS MUST HAVE COMPLETE CONTROL OF THE CELLBLOCK.
I HAVE A MARINE TACTICAL TEAM READY TO ASSAULT THEIR POSITION AS SOON AS YOU GIVE THE ORDER.
NO... GESTALT ZERO WILL GO.
SIR, HE'LL BE OUTNUMBERED AT LEAST A HALF-DOZEN-TO-ONE.
I'M AWARE. IT ALMOST MAKES ME FEEL SORRY FOR THE PROTOSS.
TAKE THEM ALIVE, IF POSSIBLE.
ALL EXCEPT FOR MUADUN. HE DIES.
AND ACTIVATE YOUR BATTLE RECORDER. I WAN TO SEE IT!!

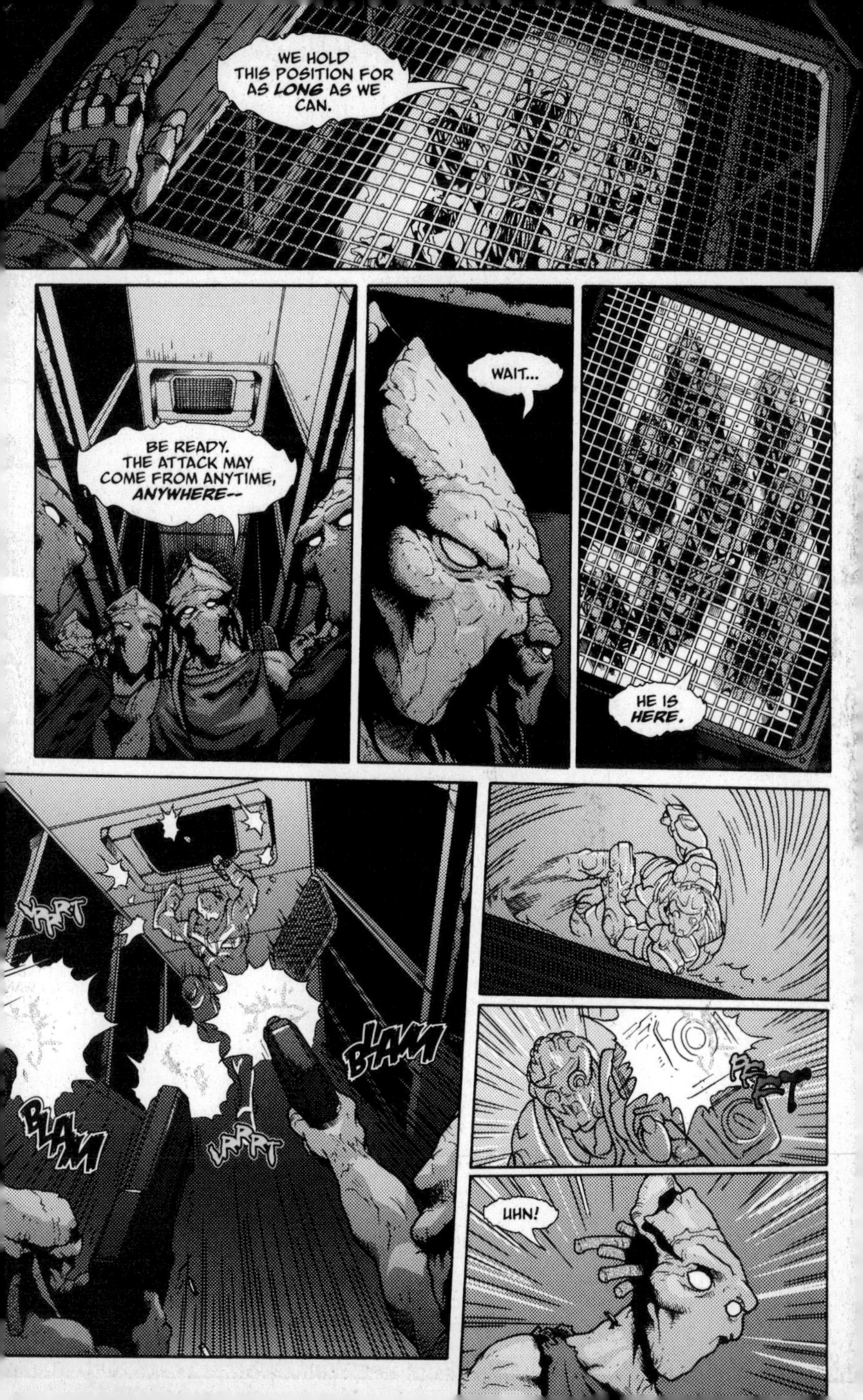
WE HOLD THIS POSITION FOR AS LONG AS WE CAN.
BE READY. THE ATTACK MAY COME FROM ANYTIME, ANYWHERE--
WAIT...
HE IS HERE.
VRRRT
BLAM
BLAM
VRRRT
UHN!

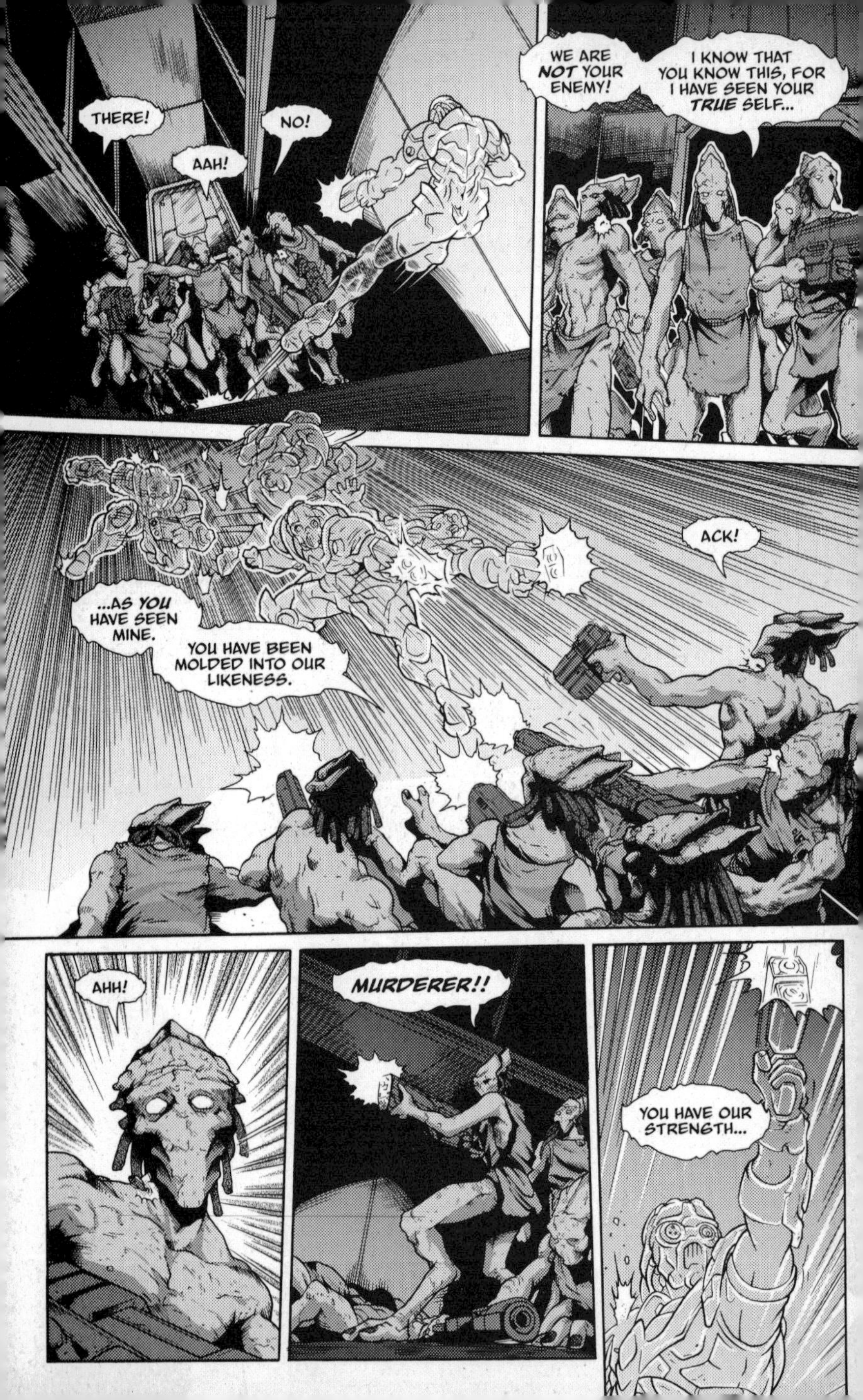
THERE!
AAH!
NO!
WE ARE *NOT* YOUR ENEMY!
I KNOW THAT YOU KNOW THIS, FOR I HAVE SEEN YOUR *TRUE* SELF...
ACK!
...AS *YOU* HAVE SEEN MINE.
YOU HAVE BEEN MOLDED INTO OUR LIKENESS.
AHH!
MURDERER!!
YOU HAVE OUR STRENGTH...

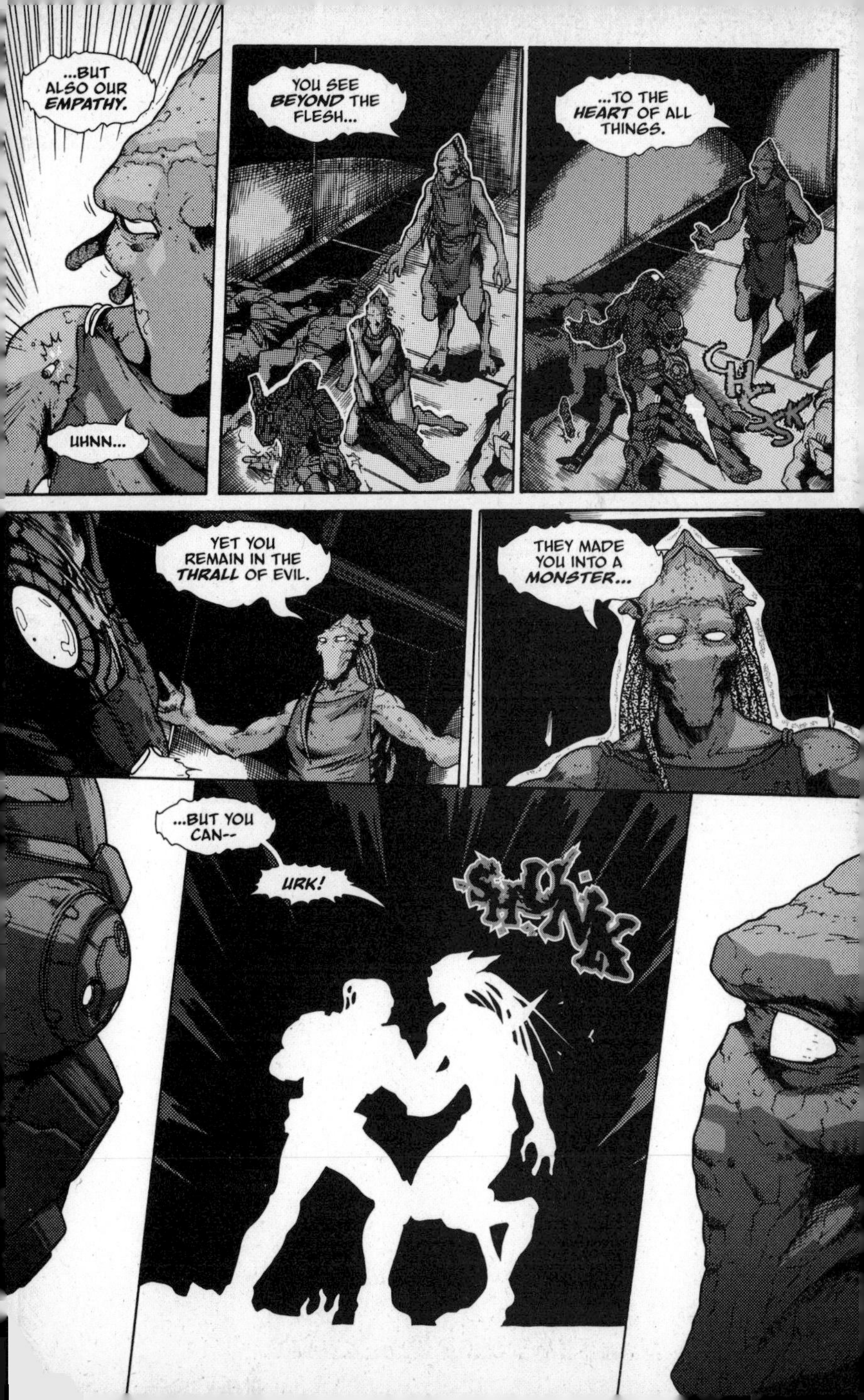
...BUT ALSO OUR *EMPATHY.*
UHNN...
YOU SEE *BEYOND* THE FLESH...
...TO THE *HEART* OF ALL THINGS.
CHSK
YET YOU REMAIN IN THE *THRALL* OF EVIL.
THEY MADE YOU INTO A *MONSTER...*
...BUT YOU CAN--
URK!

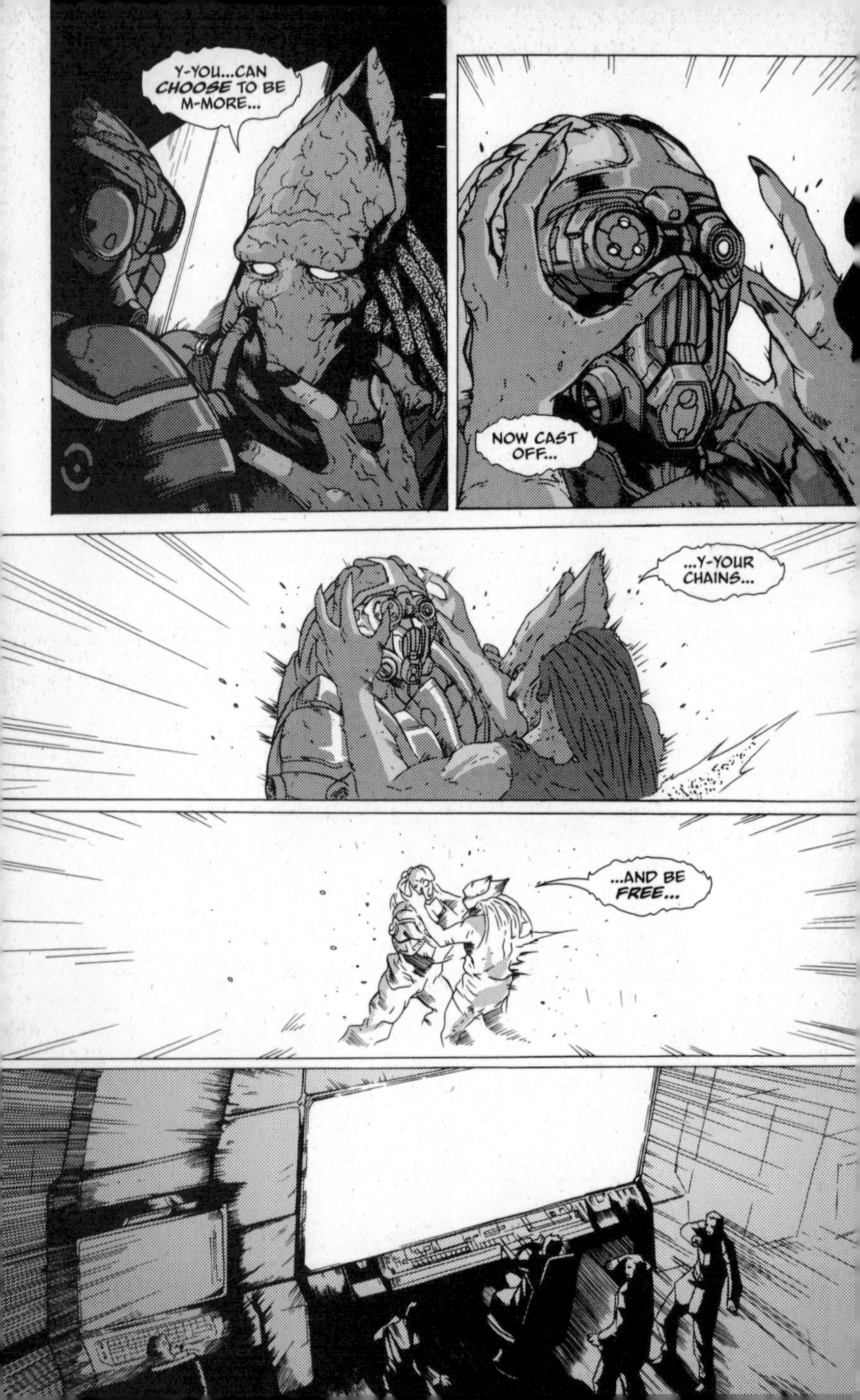
Y-YOU...CAN CHOOSE TO BE M-MORE...
NOW CAST OFF...
...Y-YOUR CHAINS...
...AND BE FREE...

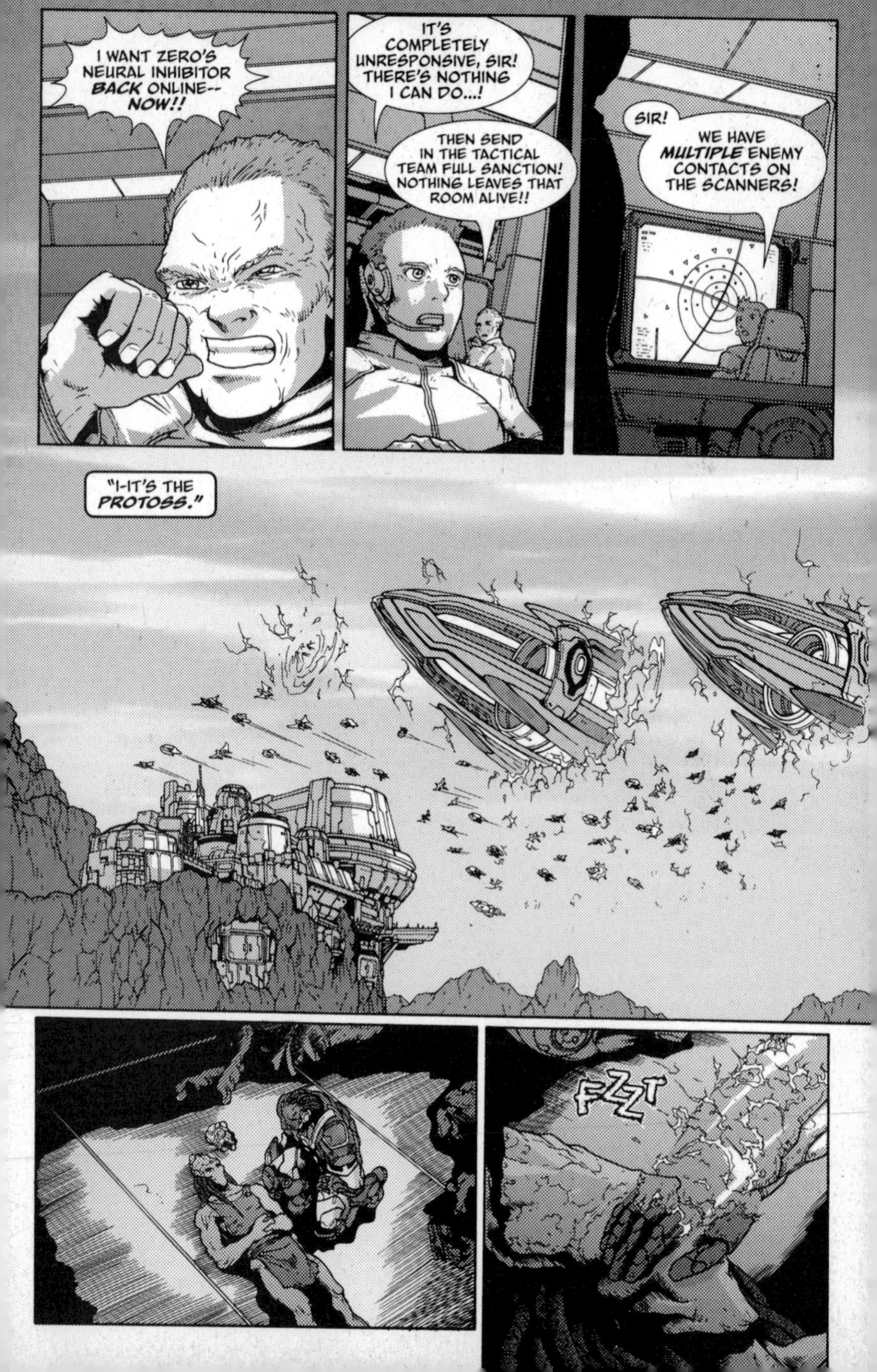

I WANT ZERO'S NEURAL INHIBITOR *BACK* ONLINE-- *NOW!!*
IT'S COMPLETELY UNRESPONSIVE, SIR! THERE'S NOTHING I CAN DO...!
THEN SEND IN THE TACTICAL TEAM FULL SANCTION! NOTHING LEAVES THAT ROOM ALIVE!!
SIR!
WE HAVE *MULTIPLE* ENEMY CONTACTS ON THE SCANNERS!
"I-IT'S THE *PROTOSS.*"
FZZT

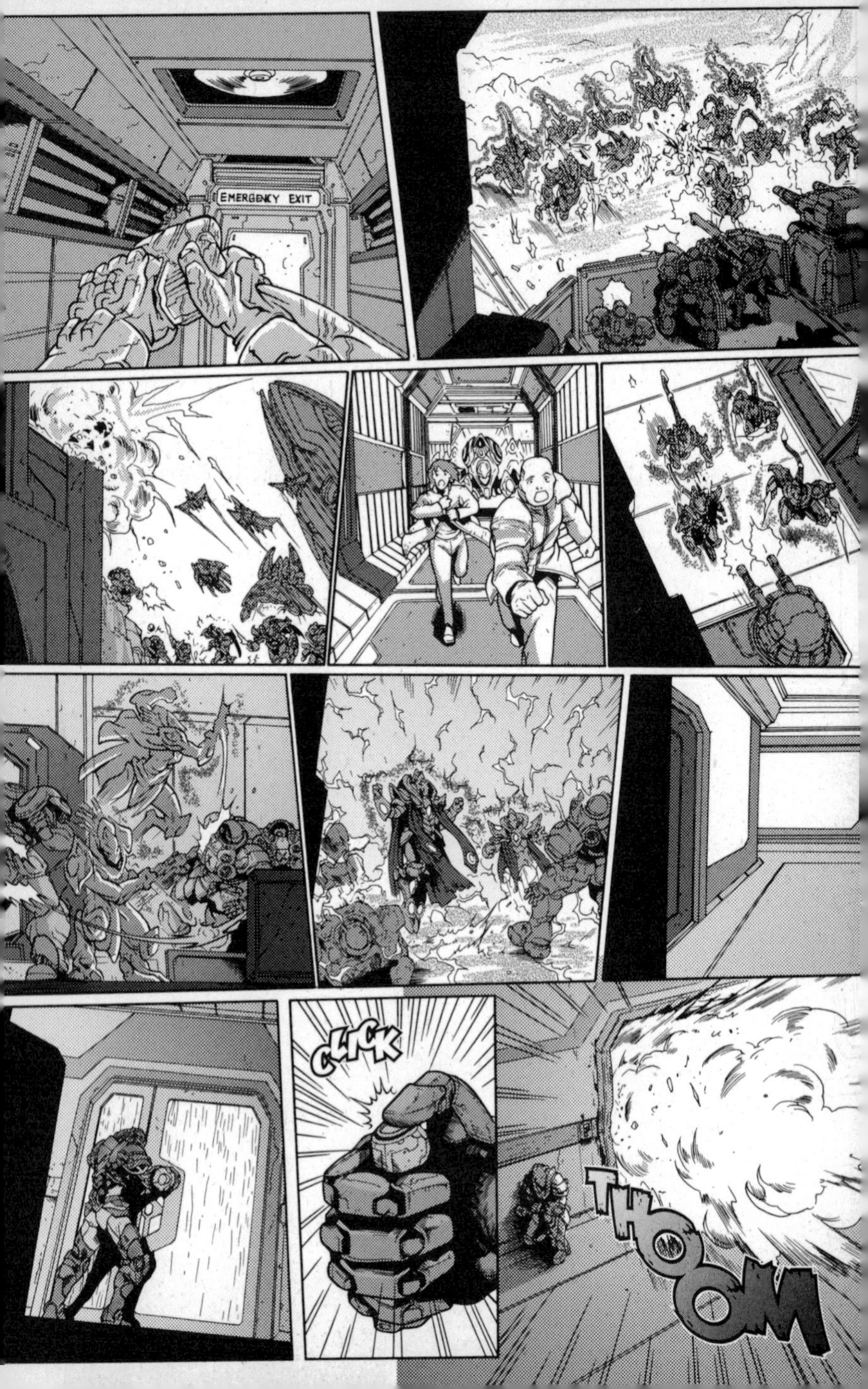
EMERGENCY EXIT
CLICK
THOOM

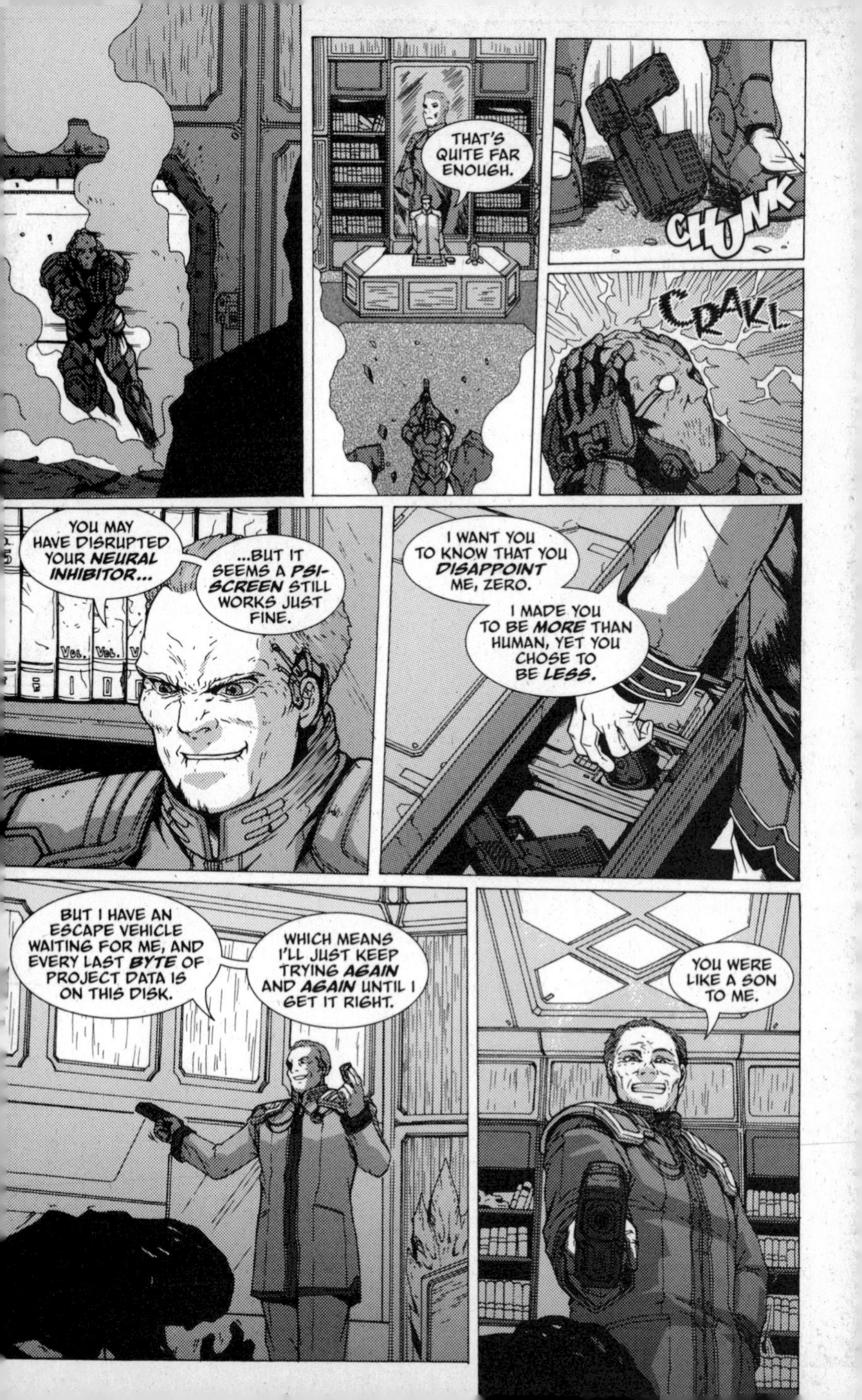
THAT'S QUITE FAR ENOUGH.
CHUNK
CRAKL
YOU MAY HAVE DISRUPTED YOUR NEURAL INHIBITOR...
...BUT IT SEEMS A PSI-SCREEN STILL WORKS JUST FINE.
I WANT YOU TO KNOW THAT YOU DISAPPOINT ME, ZERO.
I MADE YOU TO BE MORE THAN HUMAN, YET YOU CHOSE TO BE LESS.
BUT I HAVE AN ESCAPE VEHICLE WAITING FOR ME, AND EVERY LAST BYTE OF PROJECT DATA IS ON THIS DISK.
WHICH MEANS I'LL JUST KEEP TRYING AGAIN AND AGAIN UNTIL I GET IT RIGHT.
YOU WERE LIKE A SON TO ME.

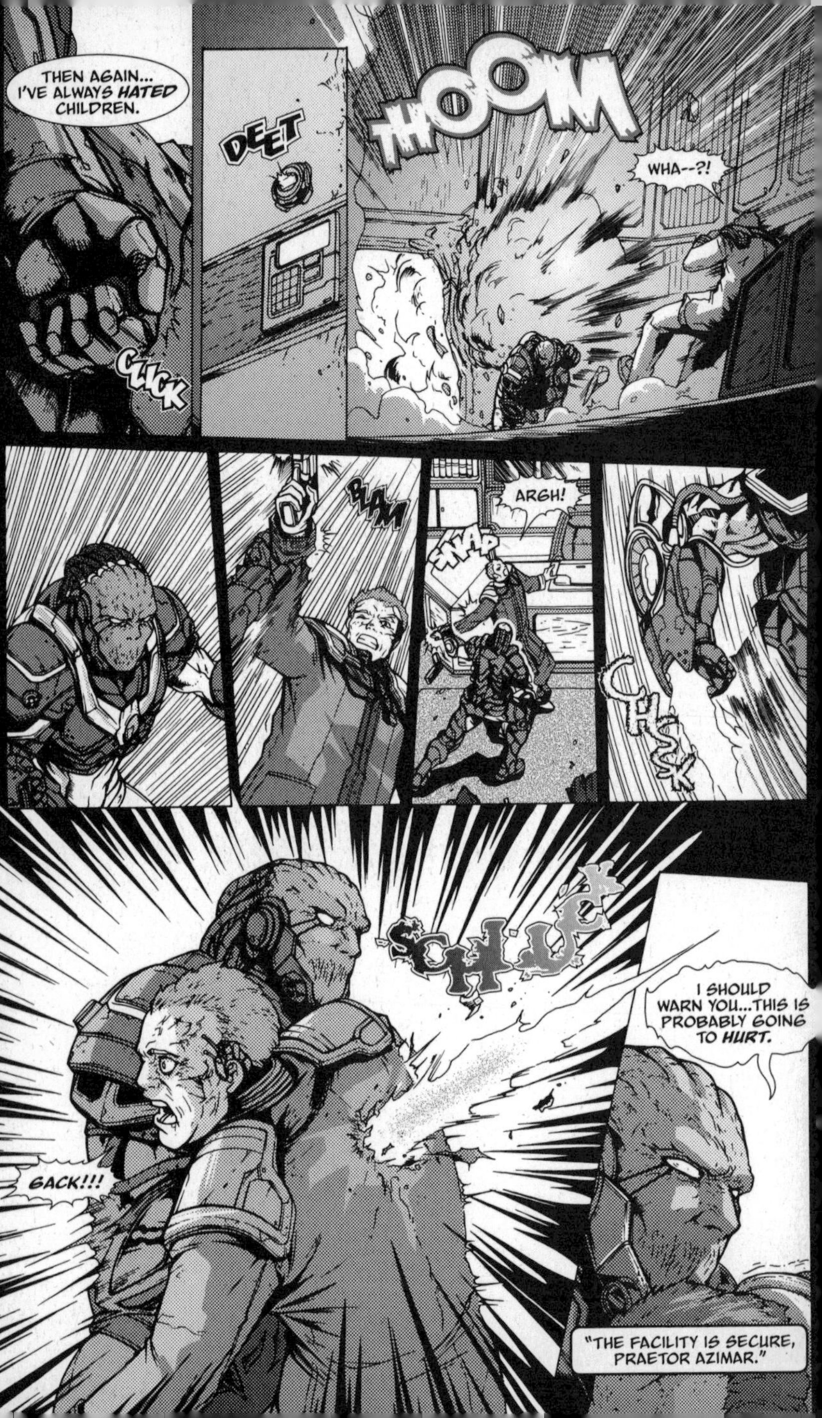
THEN AGAIN... I'VE ALWAYS HATED CHILDREN.
CLICK
DEET
THOOM
WHA--?!
BLAM
ARGH!
SNAP
CHSK
SCHLUCK
GACK!!!
I SHOULD WARN YOU...THIS IS PROBABLY GOING TO HURT.
"THE FACILITY IS SECURE, PRAETOR AZIMAR."

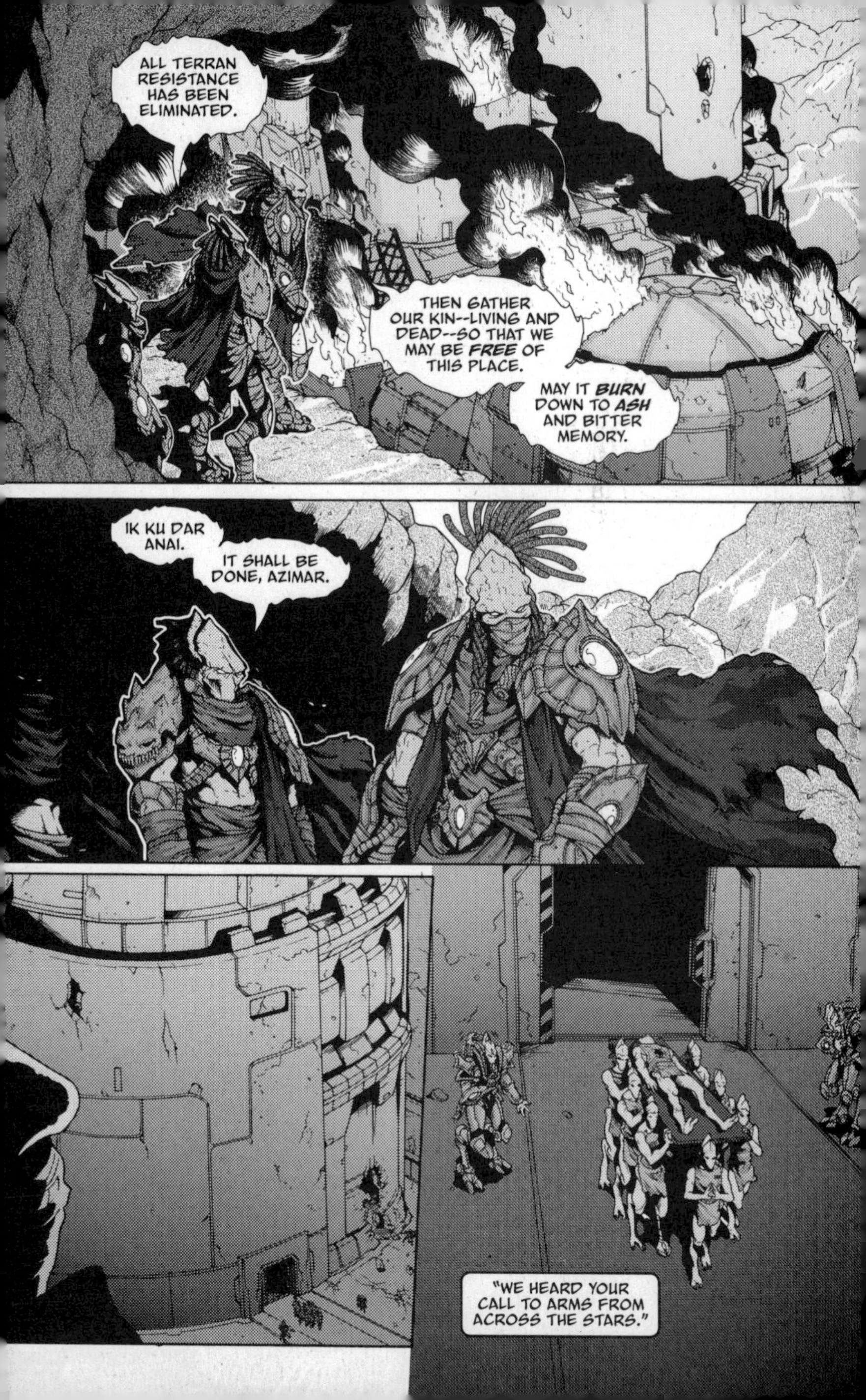
ALL TERRAN RESISTANCE HAS BEEN ELIMINATED.
THEN GATHER OUR KIN--LIVING AND DEAD--SO THAT WE MAY BE *FREE* OF THIS PLACE.
MAY IT *BURN* DOWN TO *ASH* AND BITTER MEMORY.
IK KU DAR ANAI.
IT SHALL BE DONE, AZIMAR.
"WE HEARD YOUR CALL TO ARMS FROM ACROSS THE STARS."

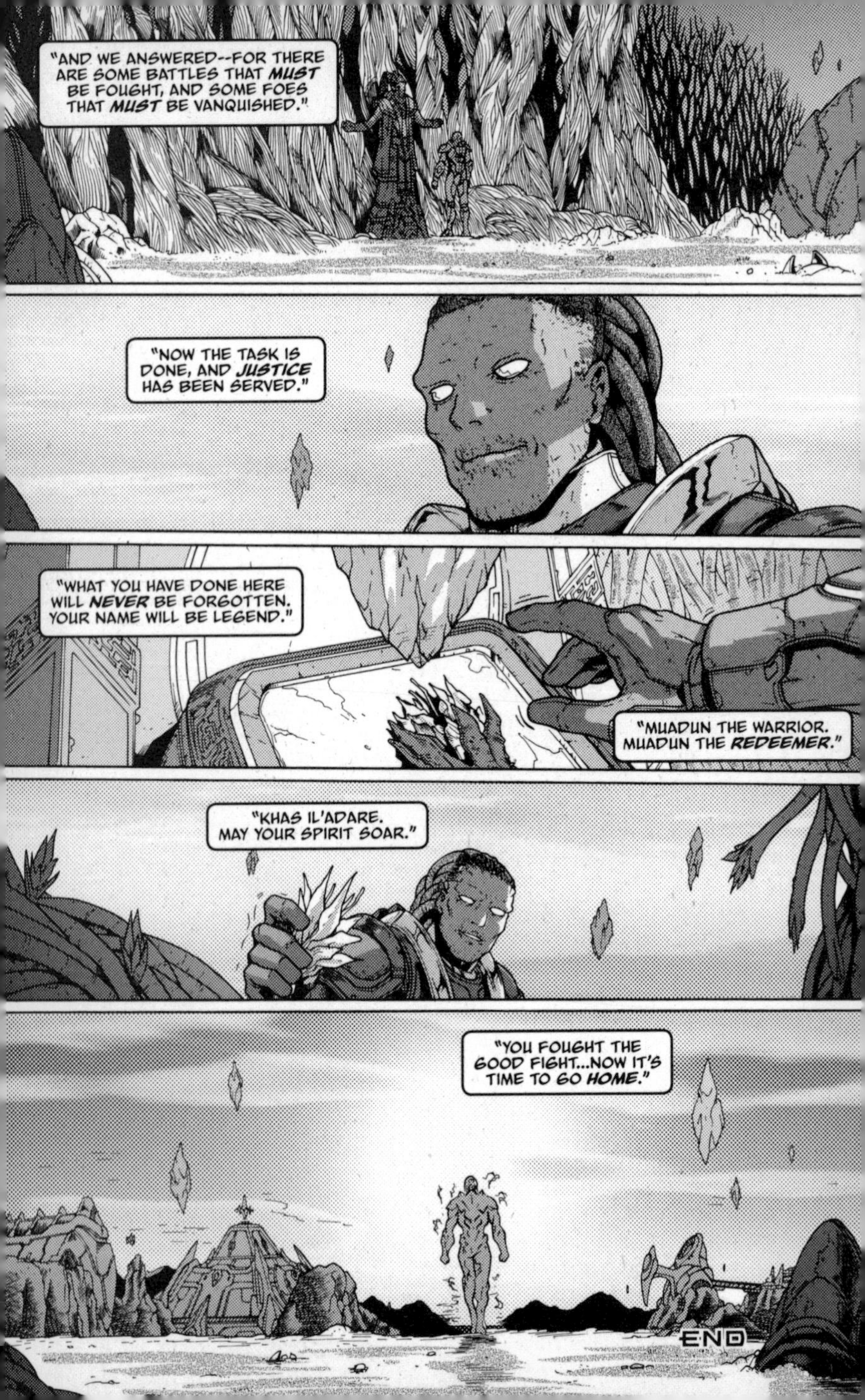
"AND WE ANSWERED--FOR THERE ARE SOME BATTLES THAT MUST BE FOUGHT, AND SOME FOES THAT MUST BE VANQUISHED."
"NOW THE TASK IS DONE, AND JUSTICE HAS BEEN SERVED."
"WHAT YOU HAVE DONE HERE WILL NEVER BE FORGOTTEN. YOUR NAME WILL BE LEGEND."
"MUADUN THE WARRIOR. MUADUN THE REDEEMER."
"KHAS IL'ADARE. MAY YOUR SPIRIT SOAR."
"YOU FOUGHT THE GOOD FIGHT...NOW IT'S TIME TO GO HOME."
END

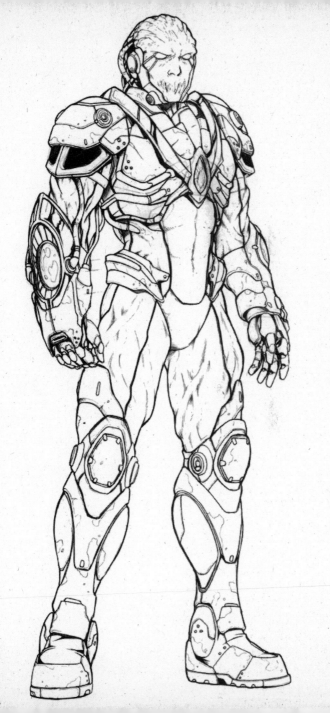

StarCraft

Frontline™

Volume 3

Last Call

Written by Grace Randolph

Art by Seung-hui Kye

Letterer: Michael Paolilli

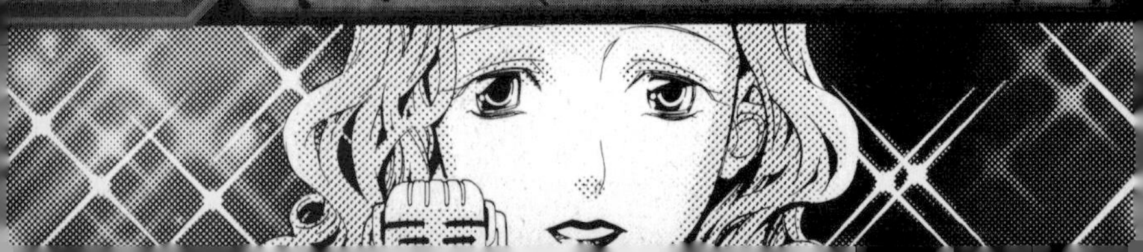

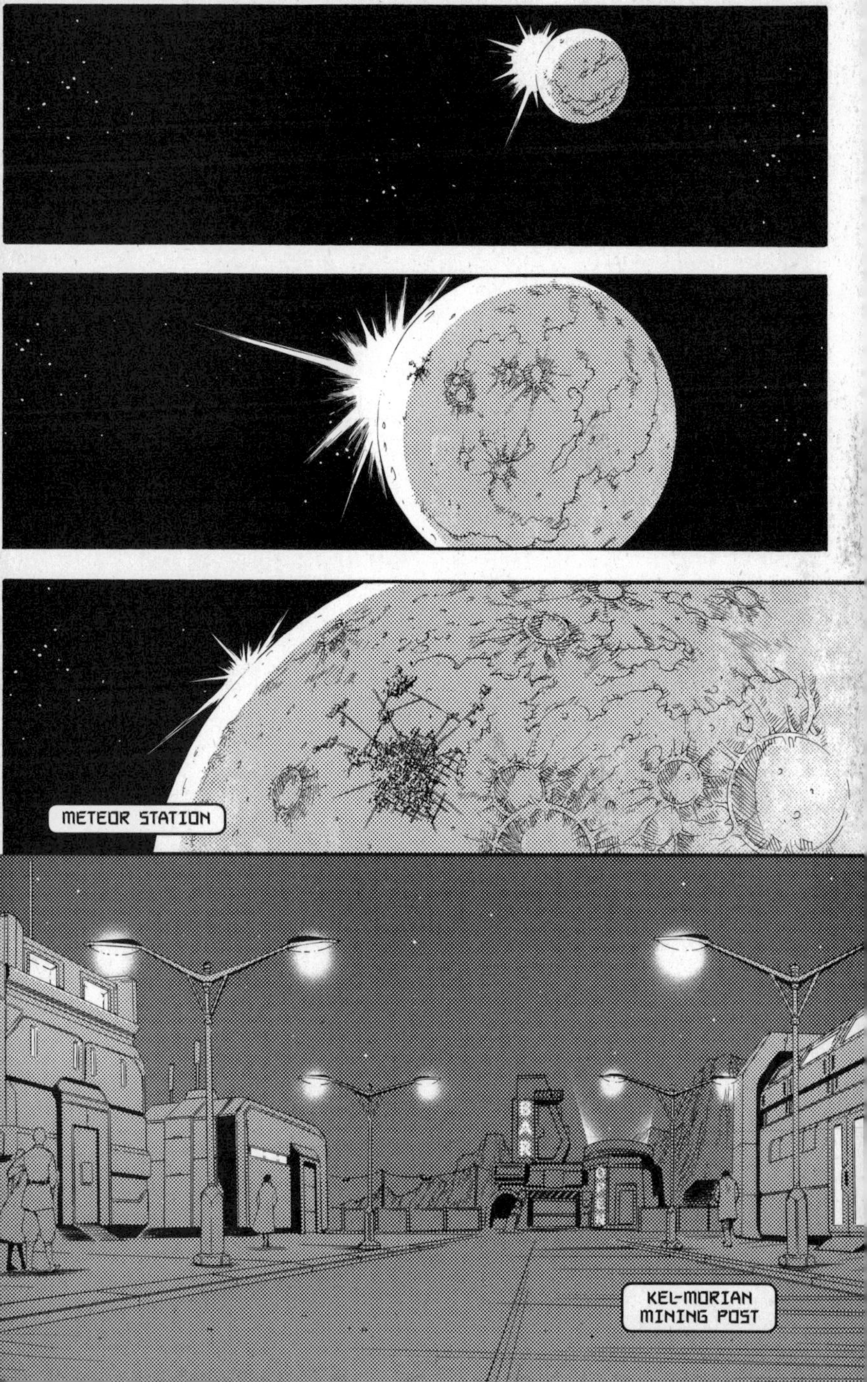
METEOR STATION
BAR
KEL-MORIAN
MINING POST

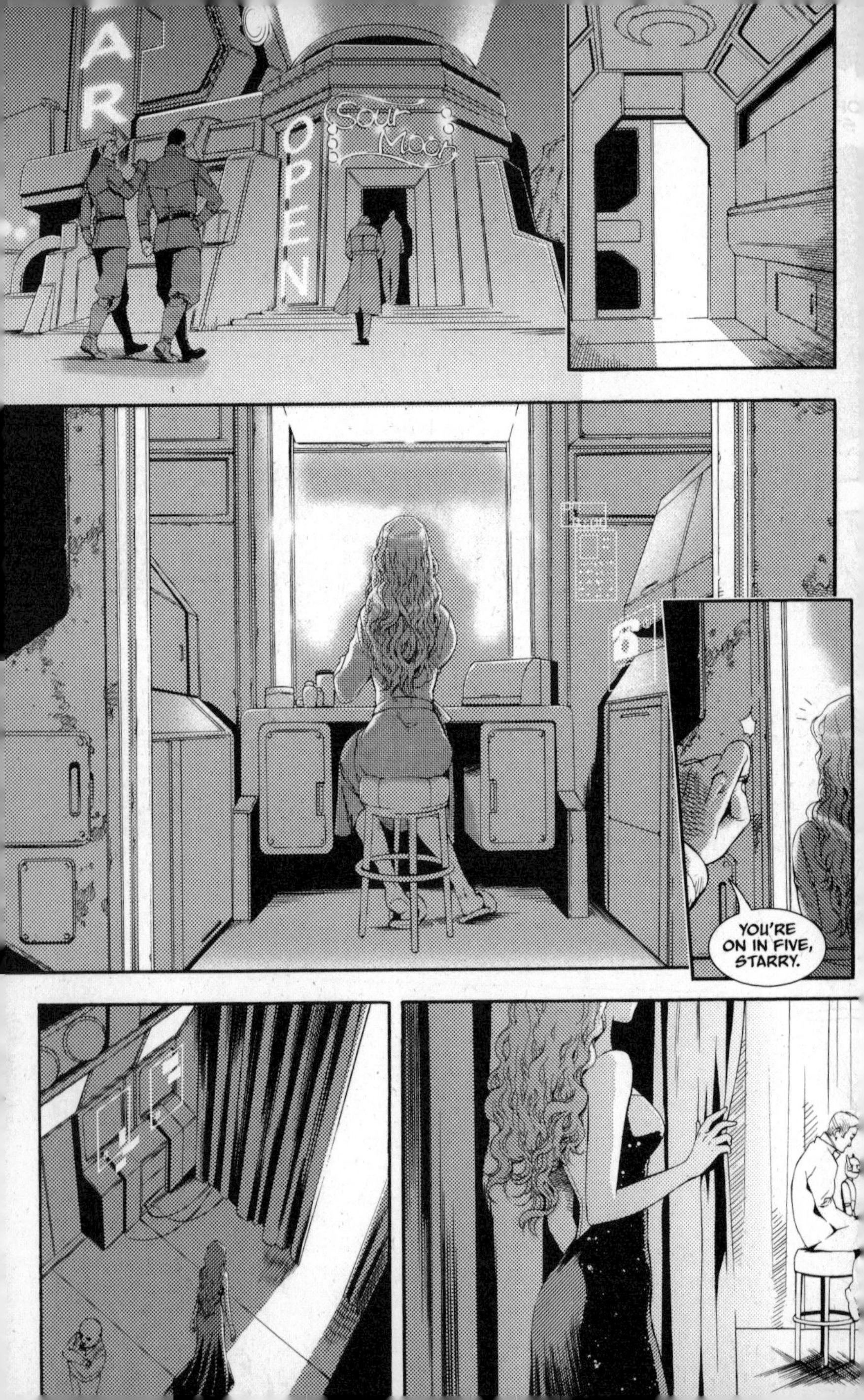
BAR
Sour Moon
OPEN
YOU'RE ON IN FIVE, STARRY.

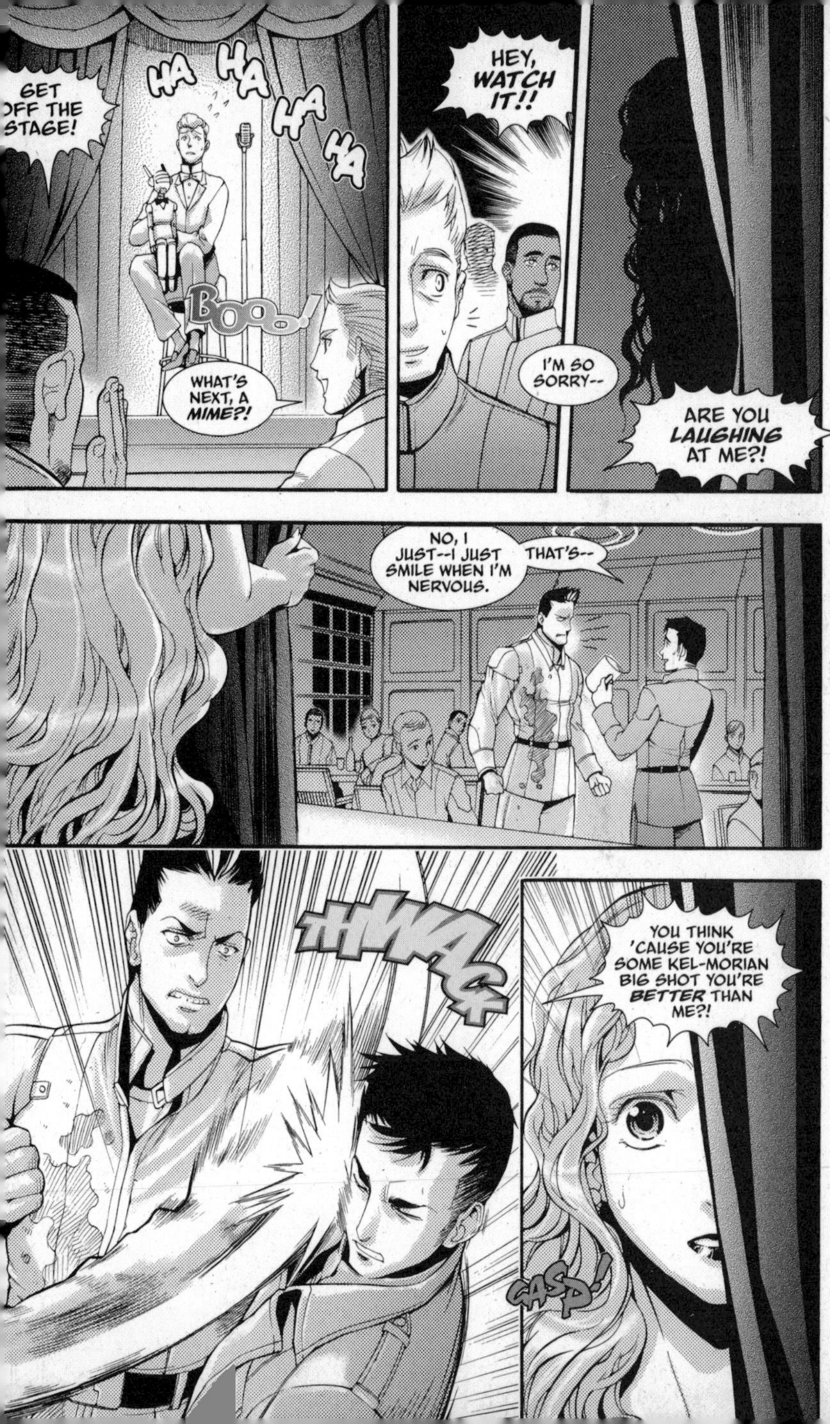
GET OFF THE STAGE!
HA HA HA HA
BOOO!
WHAT'S NEXT, A *MIME?!*
HEY, *WATCH IT!!*
I'M SO SORRY--
ARE YOU *LAUGHING* AT ME?!
NO, I JUST--I JUST SMILE WHEN I'M NERVOUS.
THAT'S--
THWACK
YOU THINK 'CAUSE YOU'RE SOME KEL-MORIAN BIG SHOT YOU'RE *BETTER* THAN ME?!
GASP!

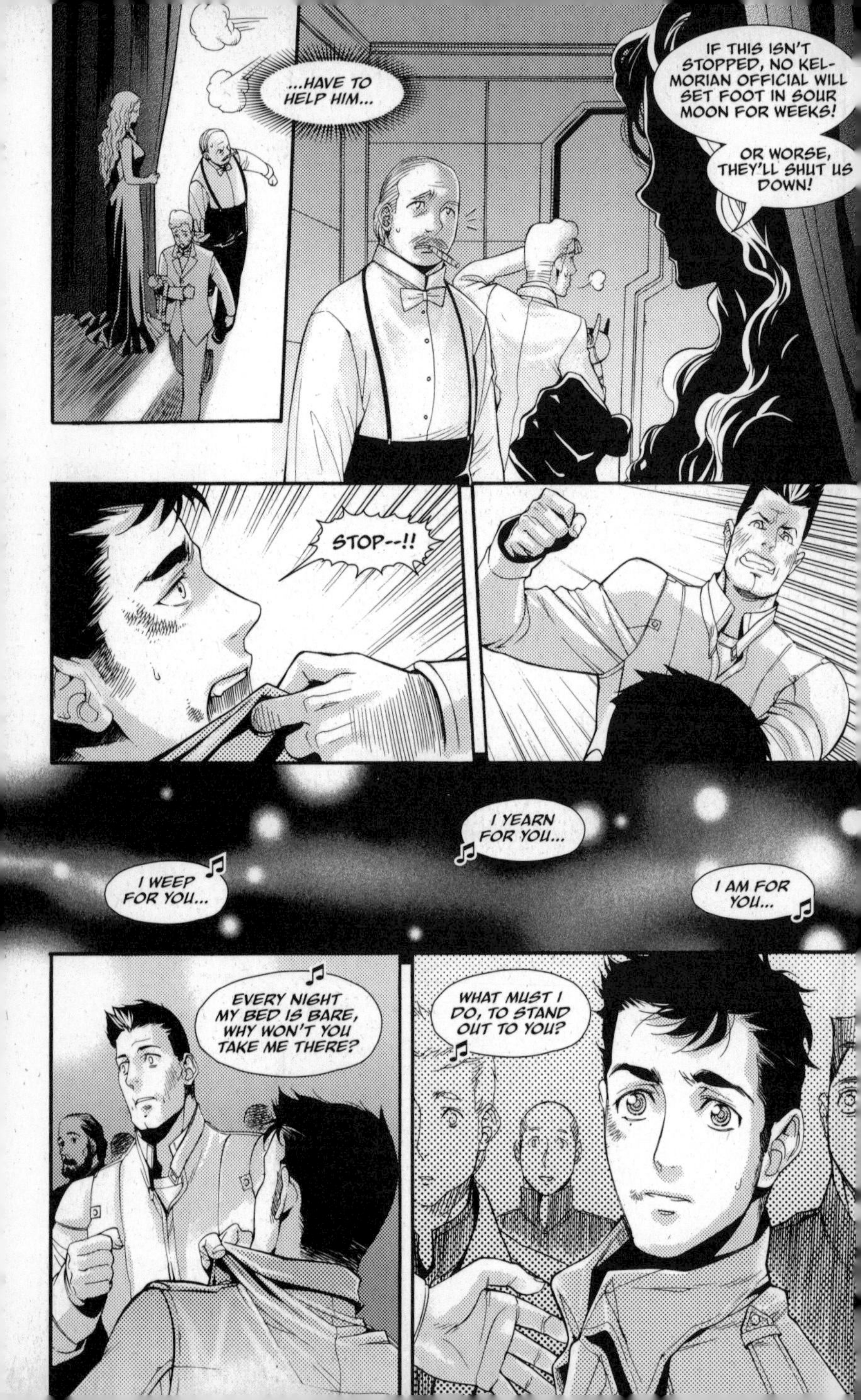
...HAVE TO HELP HIM...
IF THIS ISN'T STOPPED, NO KEL-MORIAN OFFICIAL WILL SET FOOT IN SOUR MOON FOR WEEKS!
OR WORSE, THEY'LL SHUT US DOWN!
STOP--!!
I WEEP FOR YOU...
I YEARN FOR YOU...
I AM FOR YOU...
EVERY NIGHT MY BED IS BARE, WHY WON'T YOU TAKE ME THERE?
WHAT MUST I DO, TO STAND OUT TO YOU?

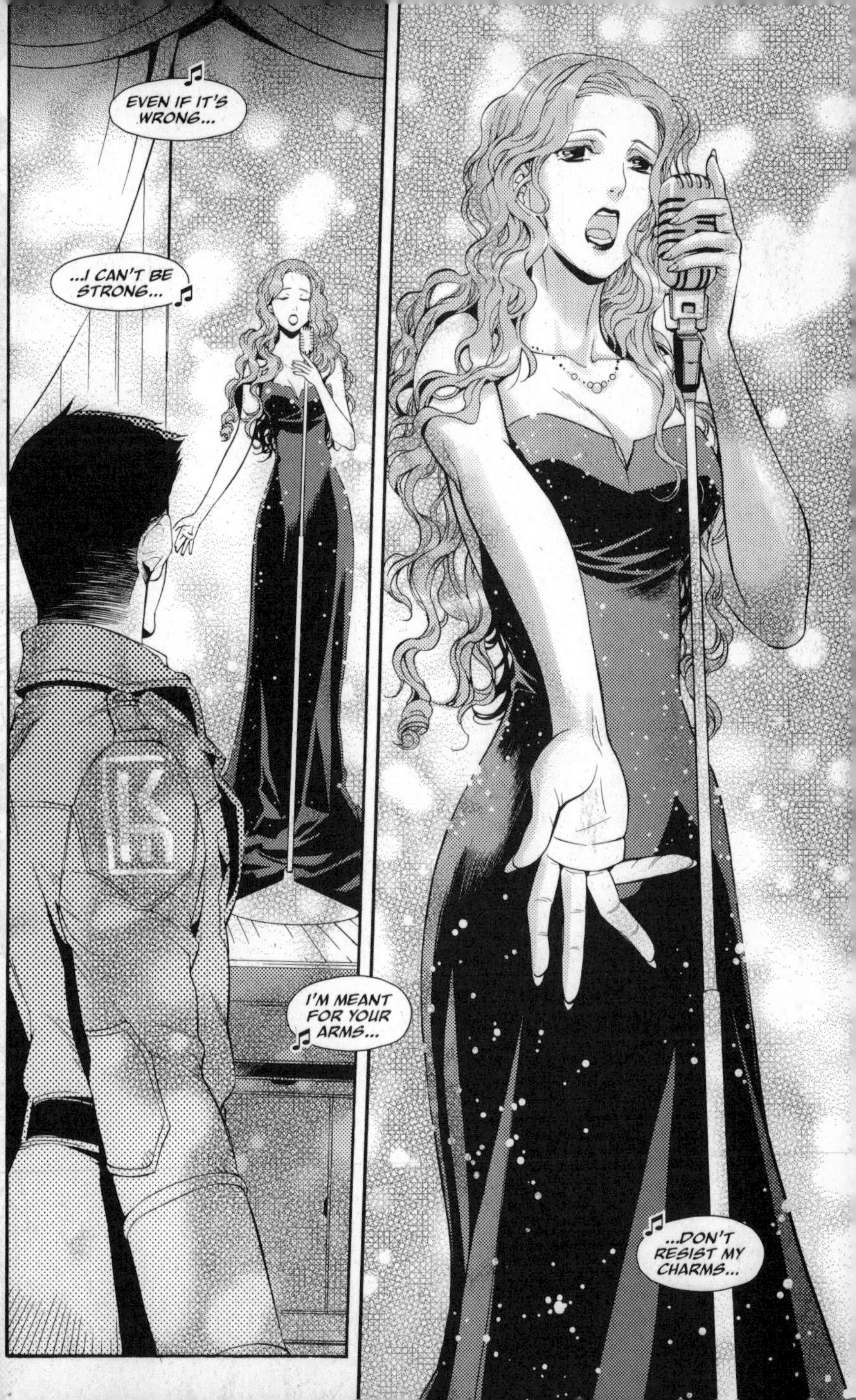
EVEN IF IT'S WRONG...
...I CAN'T BE STRONG...
I'M MEANT FOR YOUR ARMS...
...DON'T RESIST MY CHARMS...

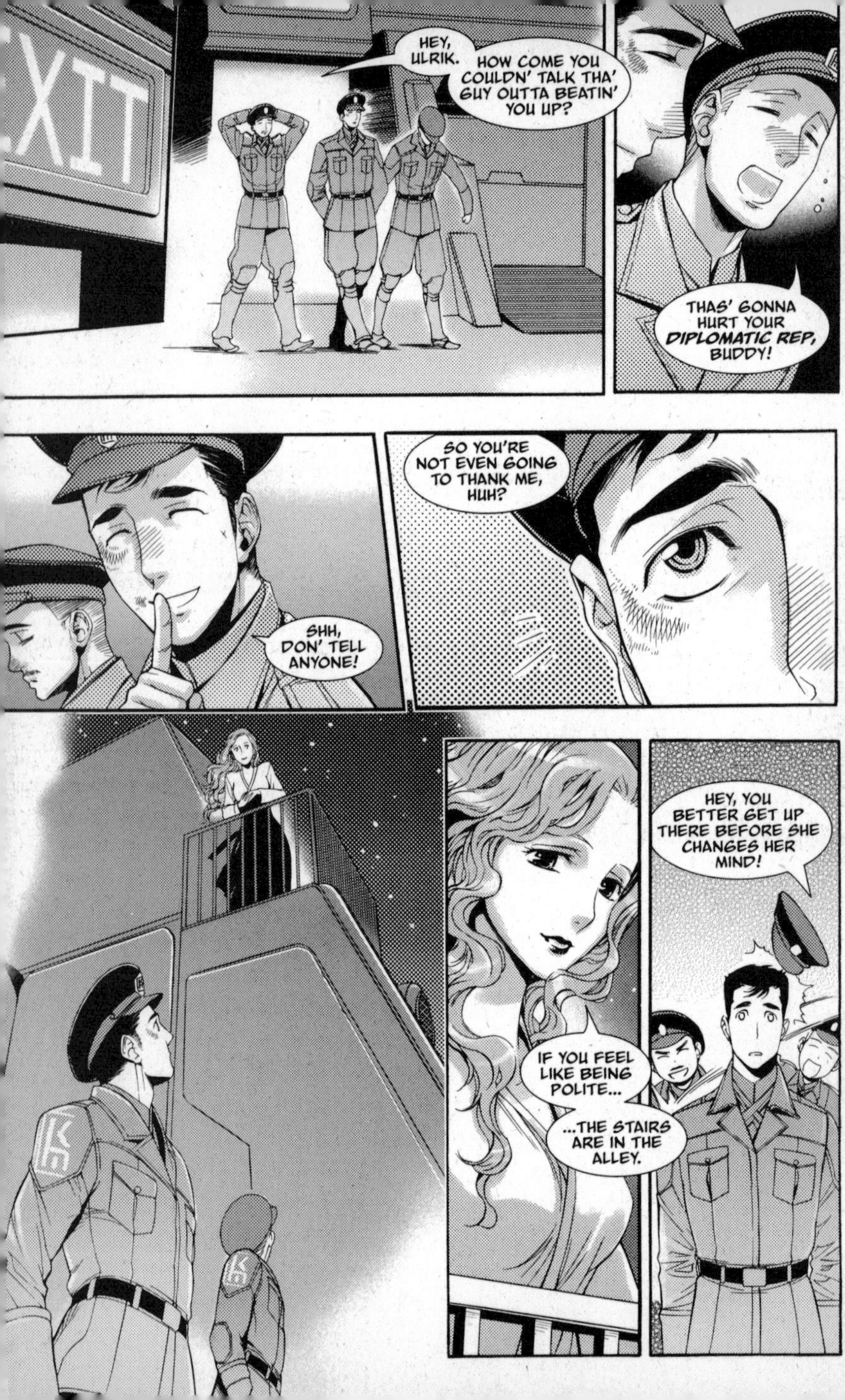
HEY, ULRIK.
HOW COME YOU COULDN' TALK THA' GUY OUTTA BEATIN' YOU UP?
THAS' GONNA HURT YOUR DIPLOMATIC REP, BUDDY!
SHH, DON' TELL ANYONE!
SO YOU'RE NOT EVEN GOING TO THANK ME, HUH?
IF YOU FEEL LIKE BEING POLITE...
...THE STAIRS ARE IN THE ALLEY.
HEY, YOU BETTER GET UP THERE BEFORE SHE CHANGES HER MIND!

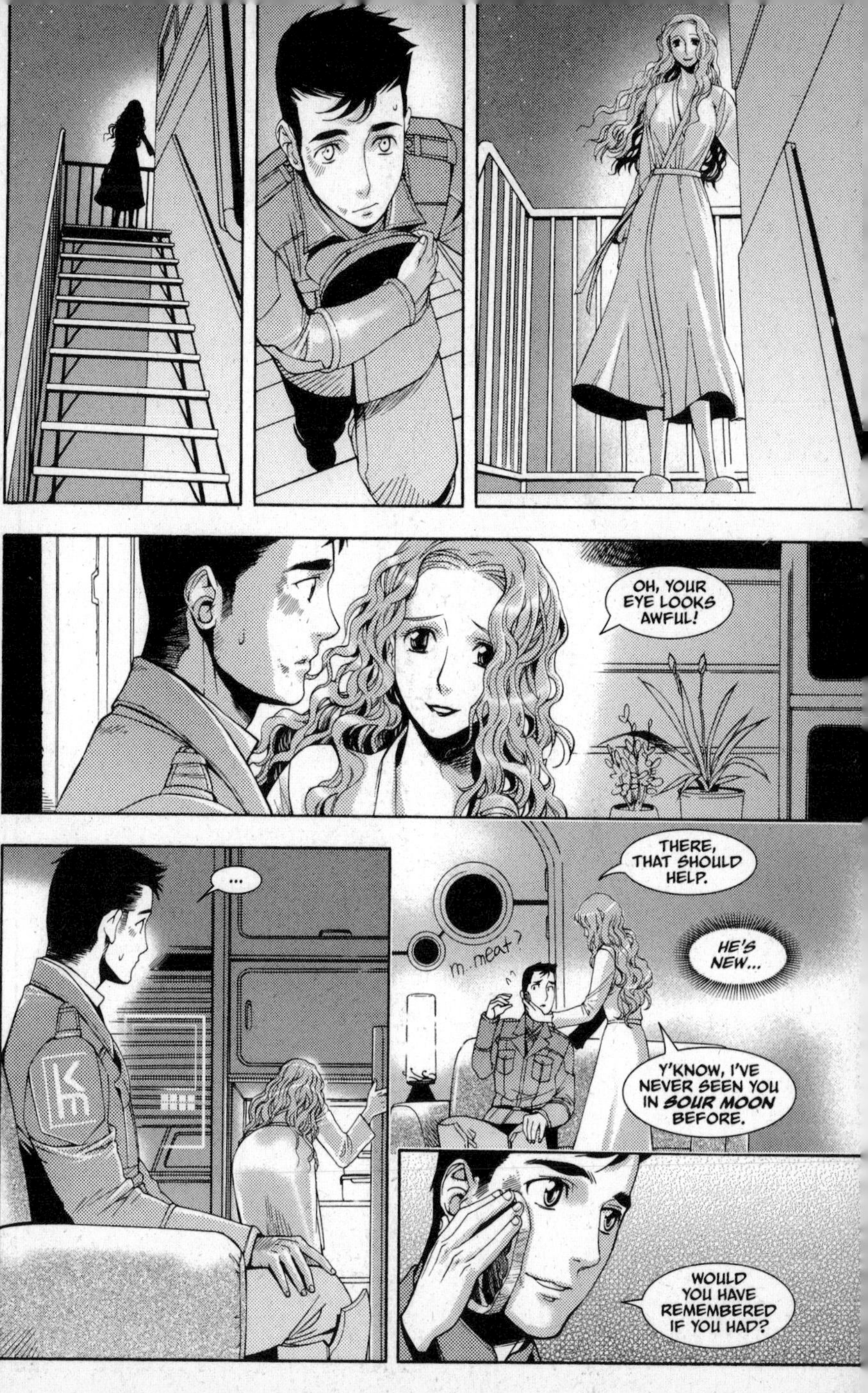
OH, YOUR EYE LOOKS AWFUL!
...
THERE, THAT SHOULD HELP.
HE'S NEW...
Y'KNOW, I'VE NEVER SEEN YOU IN SOUR MOON BEFORE.
WOULD YOU HAVE REMEMBERED IF YOU HAD?

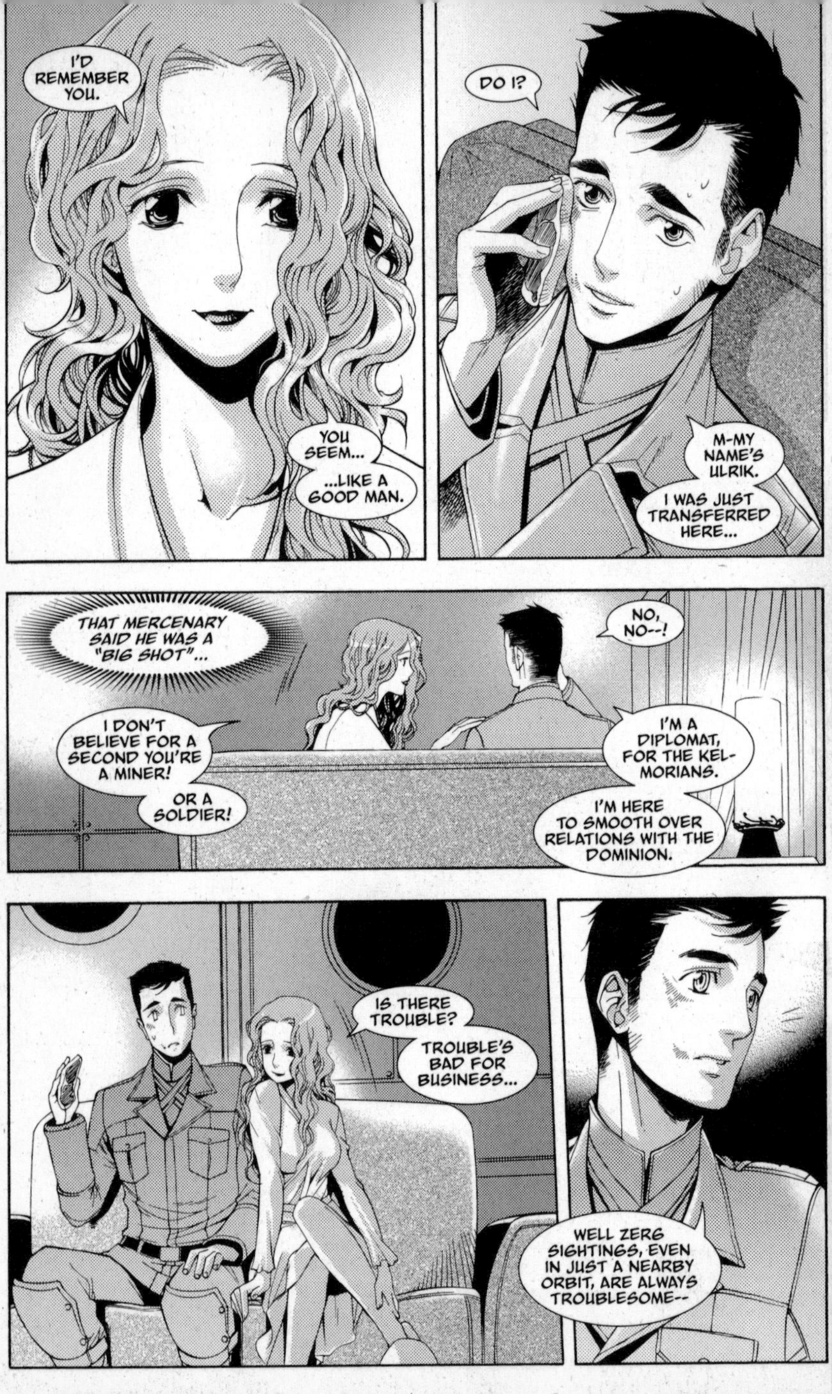

I'D REMEMBER YOU.
YOU SEEM... ...LIKE A GOOD MAN.
DO I?
M-MY NAME'S ULRIK.
I WAS JUST TRANSFERRED HERE...
THAT MERCENARY SAID HE WAS A "BIG SHOT"...
I DON'T BELIEVE FOR A SECOND YOU'RE A MINER!
OR A SOLDIER!
NO, NO--!
I'M A DIPLOMAT, FOR THE KEL-MORIANS.
I'M HERE TO SMOOTH OVER RELATIONS WITH THE DOMINION.
IS THERE TROUBLE?
TROUBLE'S BAD FOR BUSINESS...
WELL ZERG SIGHTINGS, EVEN IN JUST A NEARBY ORBIT, ARE ALWAYS TROUBLESOME--

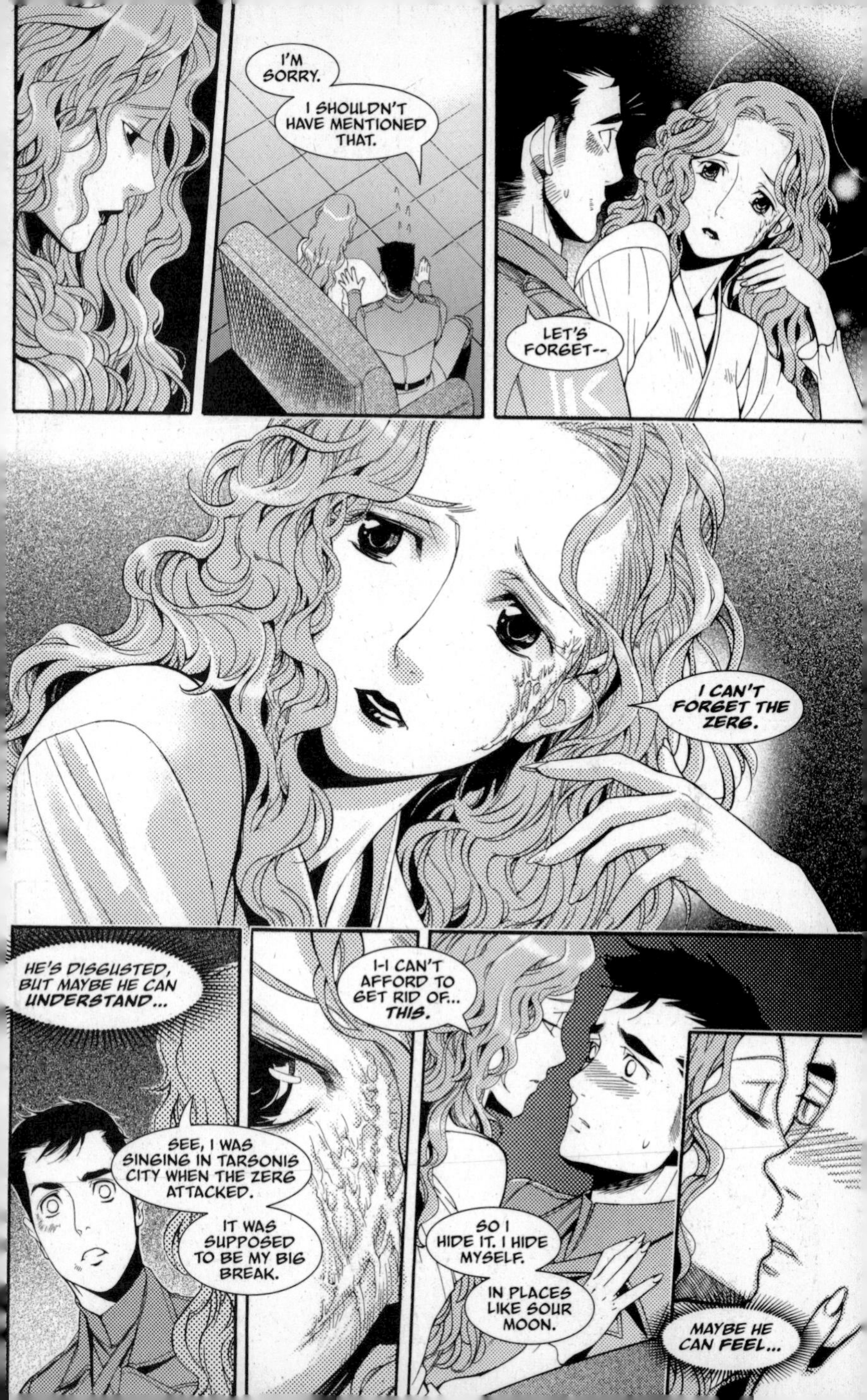
I'M SORRY.
I SHOULDN'T HAVE MENTIONED THAT.
LET'S FORGET--
I CAN'T FORGET THE ZERG.
HE'S DISGUSTED, BUT MAYBE HE CAN UNDERSTAND...
SEE, I WAS SINGING IN TARSONIS CITY WHEN THE ZERG ATTACKED.
IT WAS SUPPOSED TO BE MY BIG BREAK.
I-I CAN'T AFFORD TO GET RID OF... THIS.
SO I HIDE IT. I HIDE MYSELF.
IN PLACES LIKE SOUR MOON.
MAYBE HE CAN FEEL...

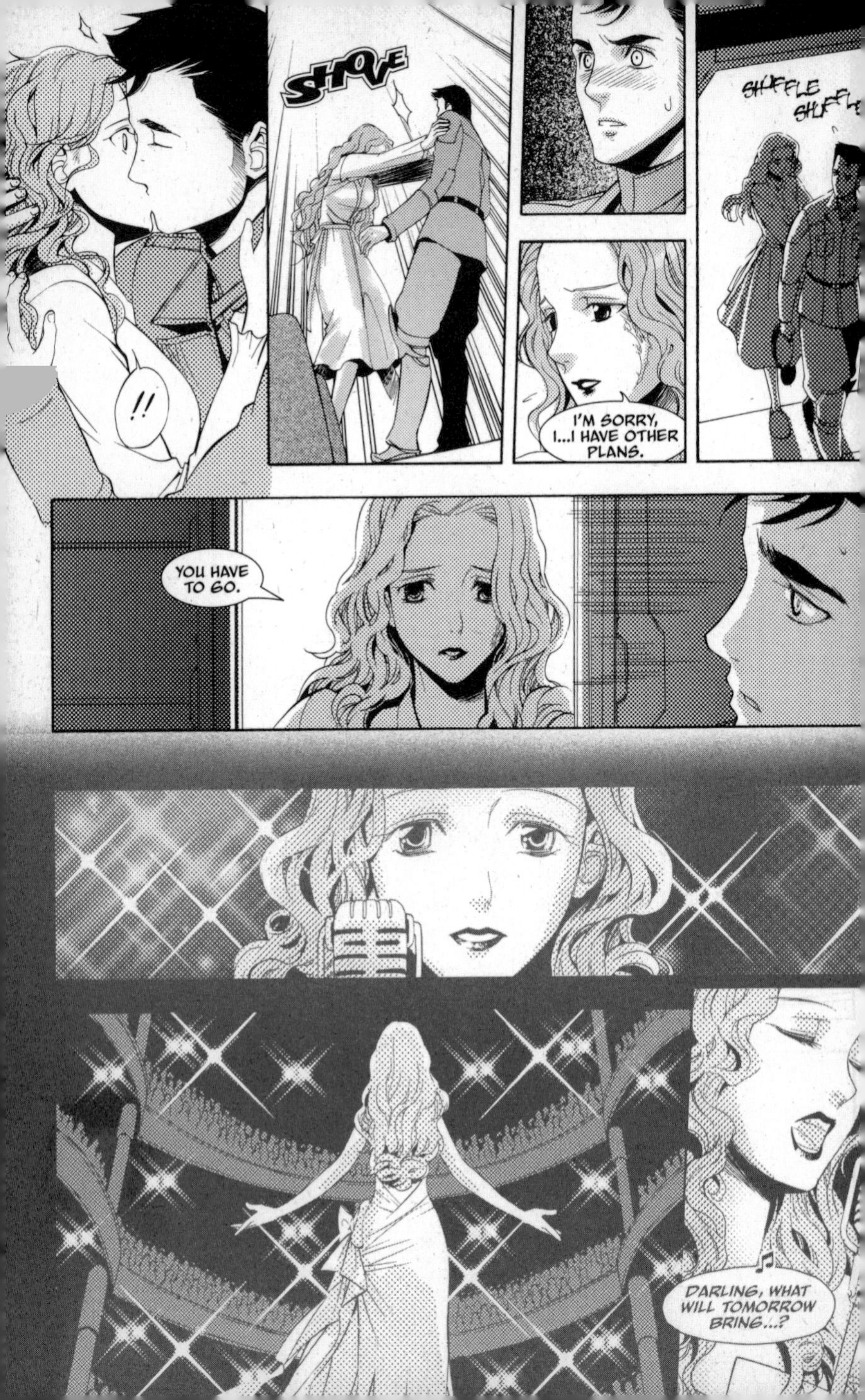
!!
SHOVE
I'M SORRY, I...I HAVE OTHER PLANS.
SHUFFLE SHUFFLE
YOU HAVE TO GO.
DARLING, WHAT WILL TOMORROW BRING...?

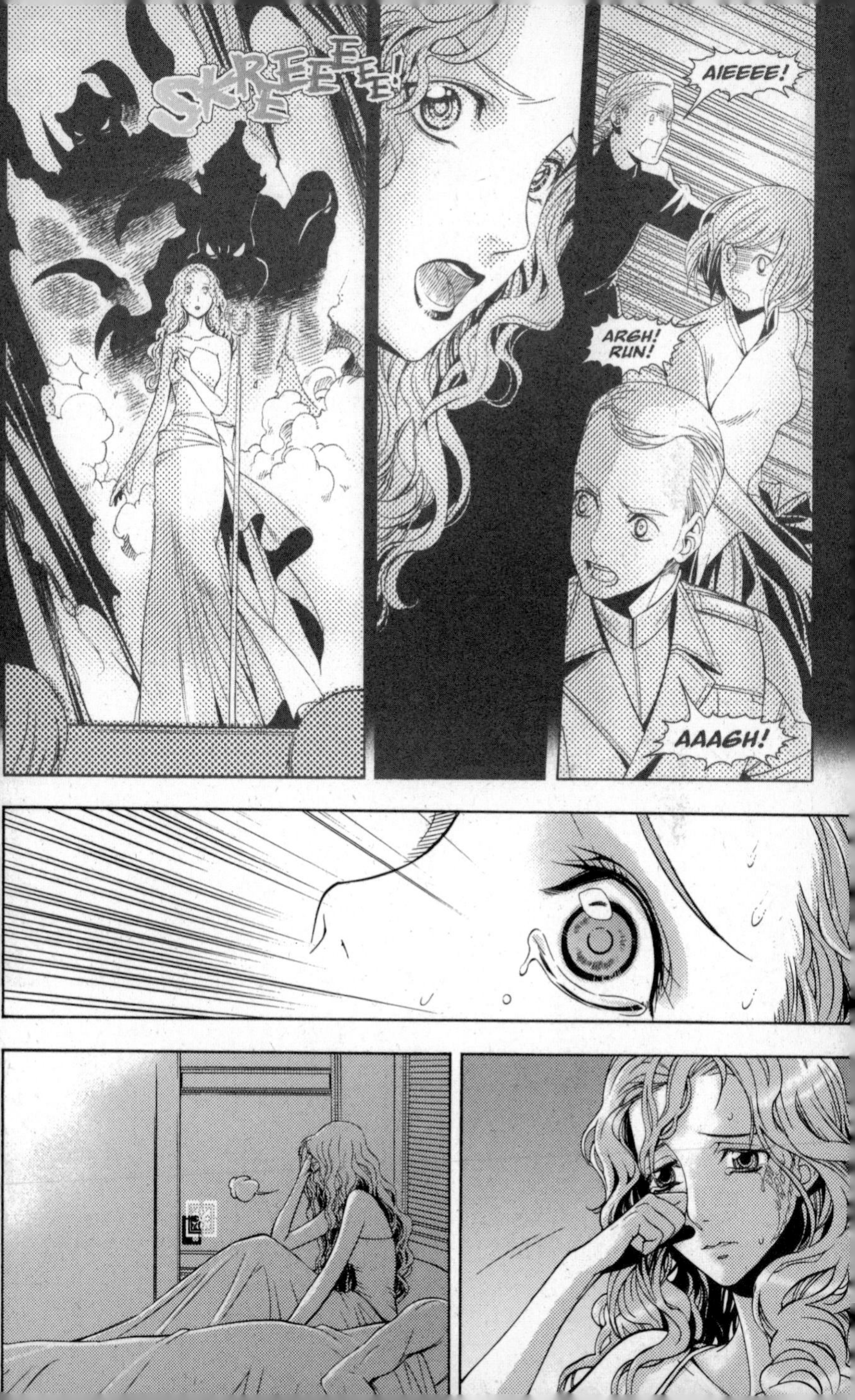

SKREEEEEEE!
AIEEEE!
ARGH! RUN!
AAAGH!

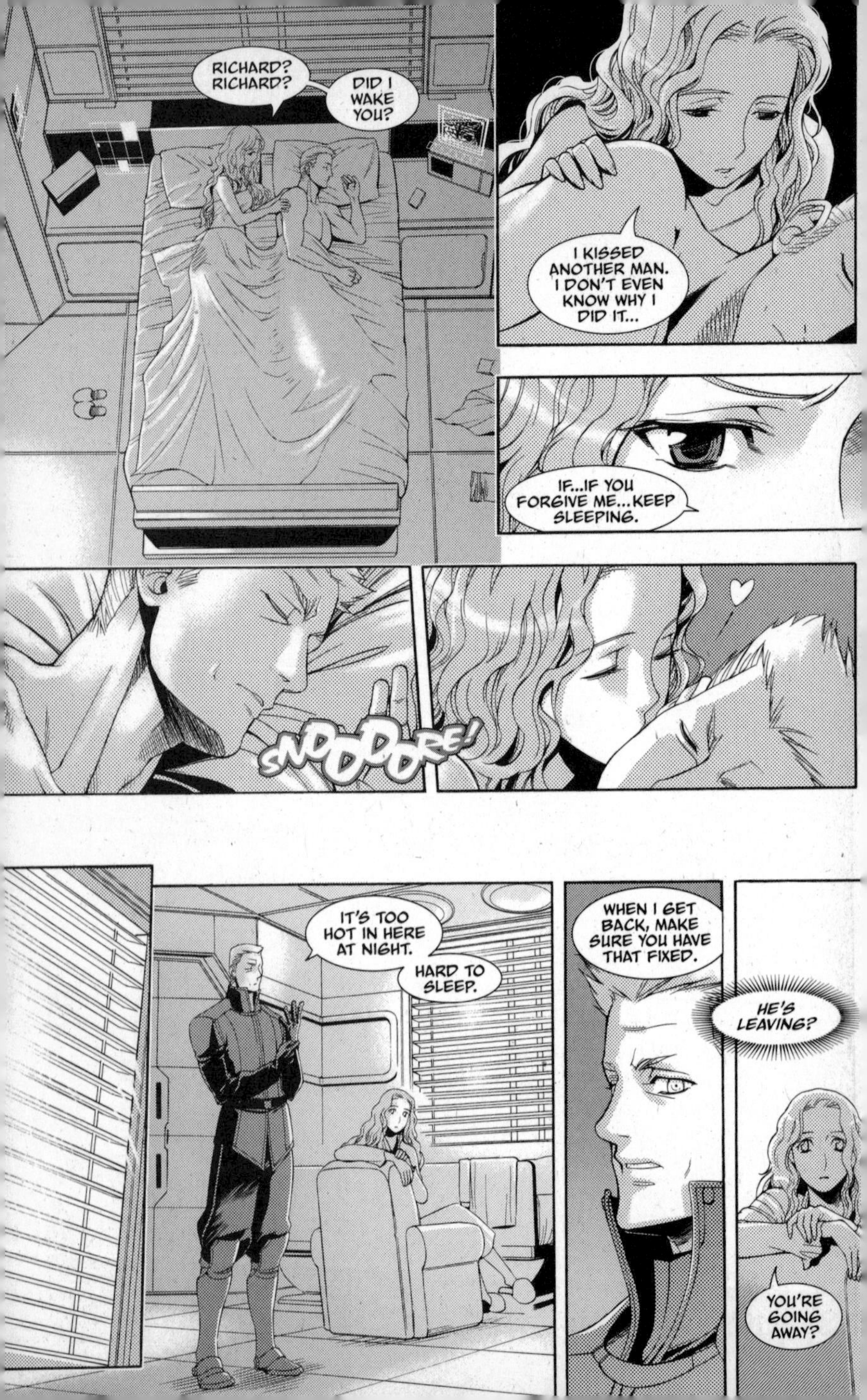
RICHARD? RICHARD?
DID I WAKE YOU?
I KISSED ANOTHER MAN. I DON'T EVEN KNOW WHY I DID IT...
IF...IF YOU FORGIVE ME...KEEP SLEEPING.
SNOOOORE!
IT'S TOO HOT IN HERE AT NIGHT.
HARD TO SLEEP.
WHEN I GET BACK, MAKE SURE YOU HAVE THAT FIXED.
HE'S LEAVING?
YOU'RE GOING AWAY?

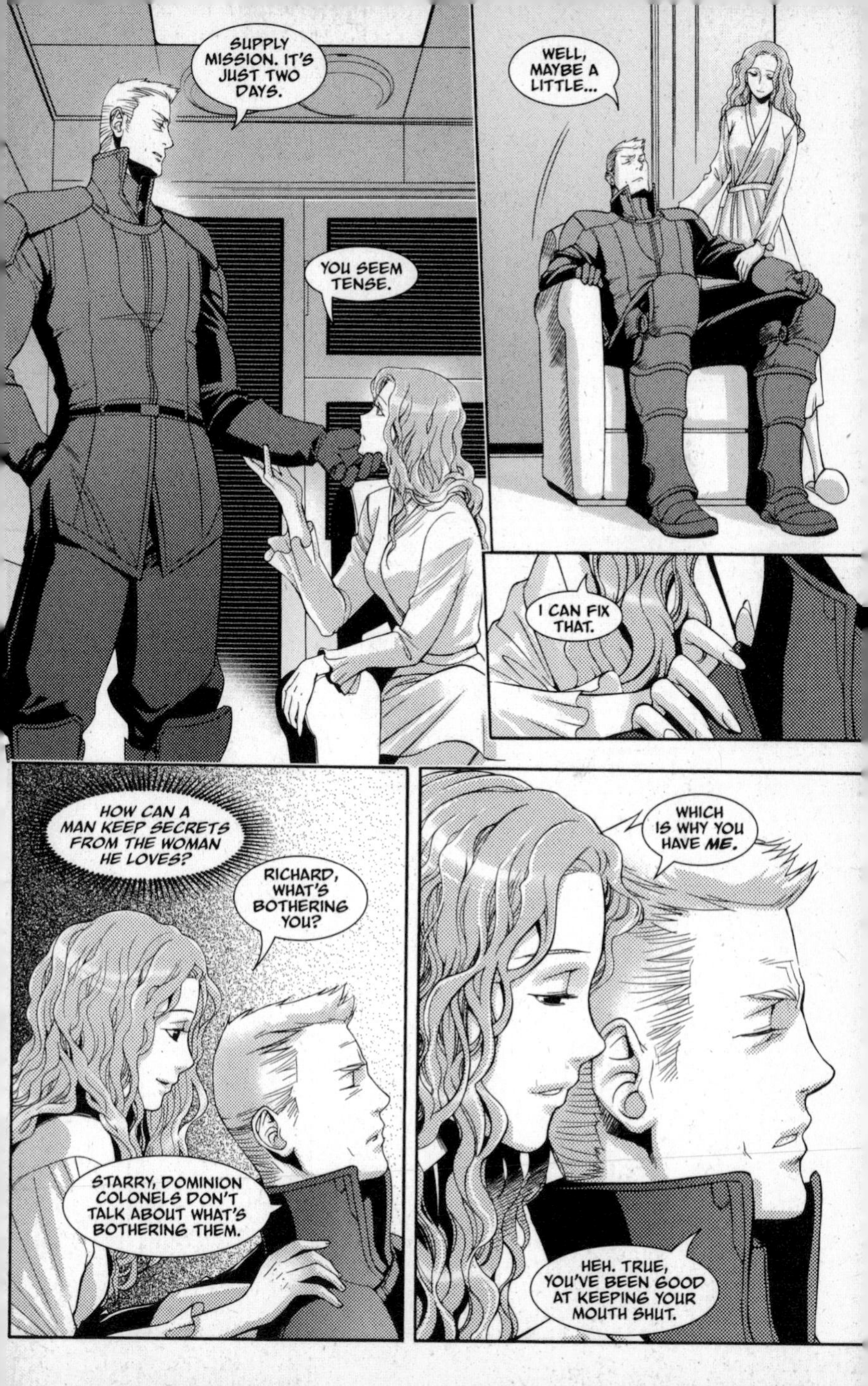
SUPPLY MISSION. IT'S JUST TWO DAYS.
YOU SEEM TENSE.
WELL, MAYBE A LITTLE...
I CAN FIX THAT.
HOW CAN A MAN KEEP SECRETS FROM THE WOMAN HE LOVES?
RICHARD, WHAT'S BOTHERING YOU?
STARRY, DOMINION COLONELS DON'T TALK ABOUT WHAT'S BOTHERING THEM.
WHICH IS WHY YOU HAVE *ME*.
HEH. TRUE, YOU'VE BEEN GOOD AT KEEPING YOUR MOUTH SHUT.

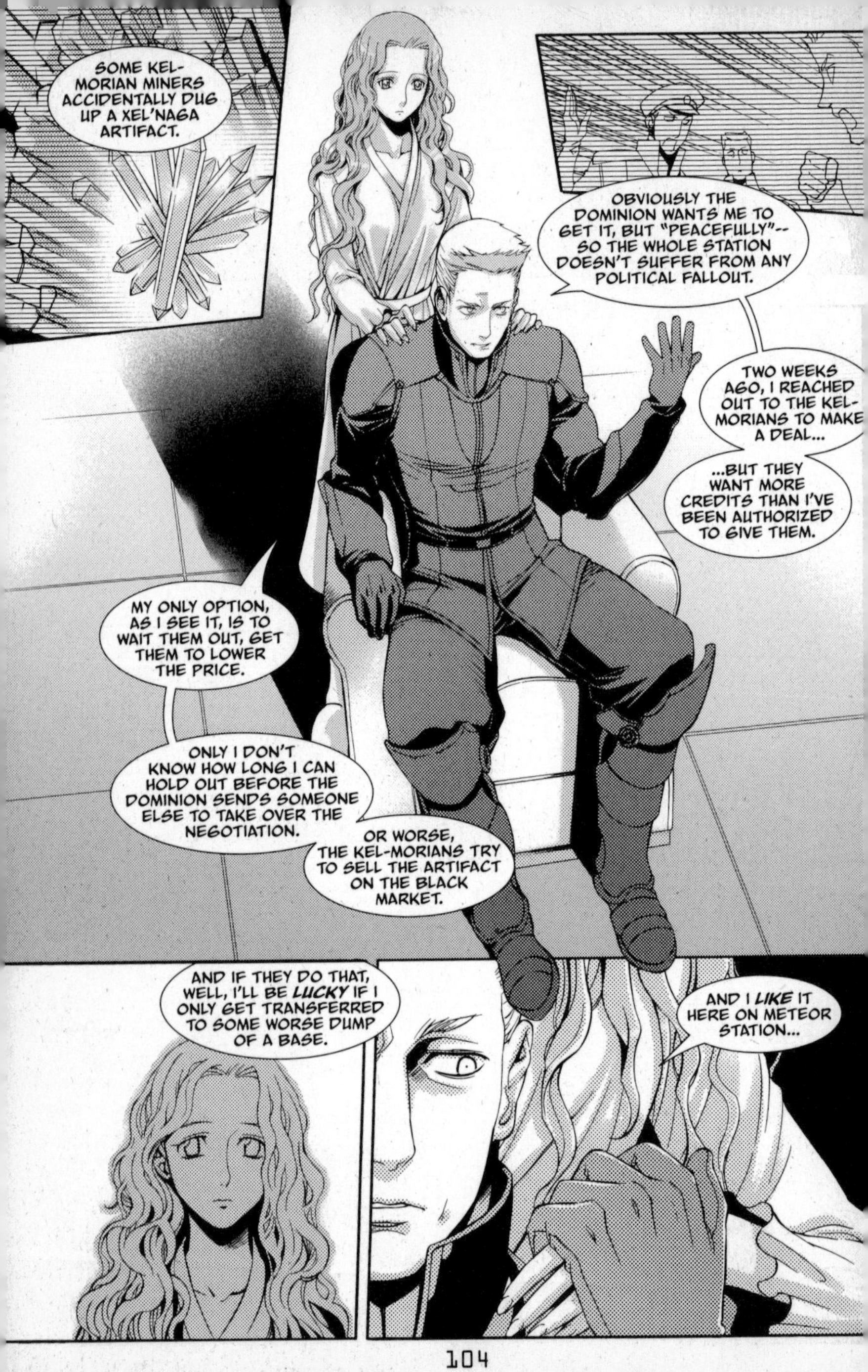
SOME KEL-MORIAN MINERS ACCIDENTALLY DUG UP A XEL'NAGA ARTIFACT.
OBVIOUSLY THE DOMINION WANTS ME TO GET IT, BUT "PEACEFULLY"-- SO THE WHOLE STATION DOESN'T SUFFER FROM ANY POLITICAL FALLOUT.
TWO WEEKS AGO, I REACHED OUT TO THE KEL-MORIANS TO MAKE A DEAL...
...BUT THEY WANT MORE CREDITS THAN I'VE BEEN AUTHORIZED TO GIVE THEM.
MY ONLY OPTION, AS I SEE IT, IS TO WAIT THEM OUT, GET THEM TO LOWER THE PRICE.
ONLY I DON'T KNOW HOW LONG I CAN HOLD OUT BEFORE THE DOMINION SENDS SOMEONE ELSE TO TAKE OVER THE NEGOTIATION.
OR WORSE, THE KEL-MORIANS TRY TO SELL THE ARTIFACT ON THE BLACK MARKET.
AND IF THEY DO THAT, WELL, I'LL BE LUCKY IF I ONLY GET TRANSFERRED TO SOME WORSE DUMP OF A BASE.
AND I LIKE IT HERE ON METEOR STATION...

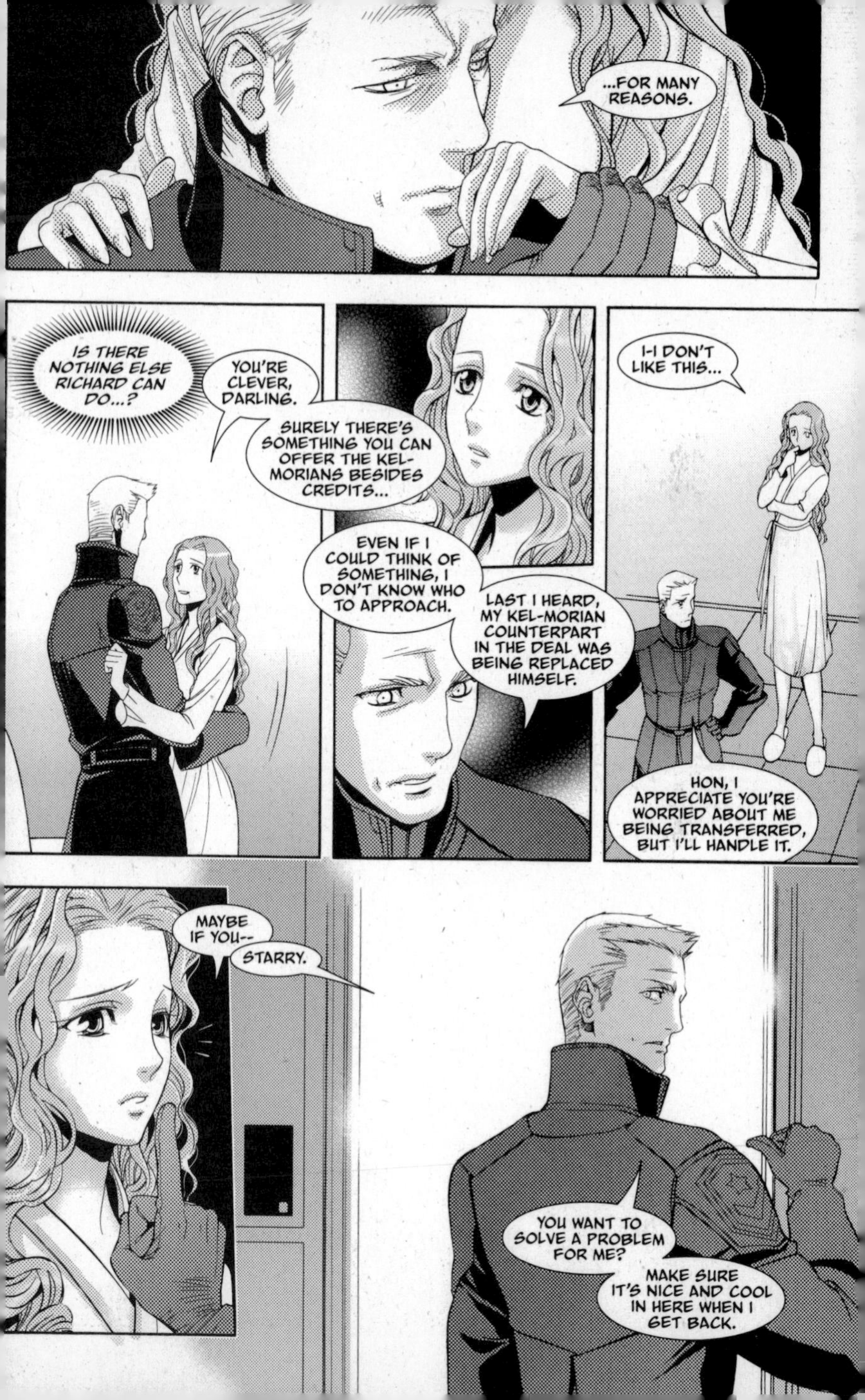
...FOR MANY REASONS.
IS THERE NOTHING ELSE RICHARD CAN DO...?
YOU'RE CLEVER, DARLING.
SURELY THERE'S SOMETHING YOU CAN OFFER THE KEL-MORIANS BESIDES CREDITS...
EVEN IF I COULD THINK OF SOMETHING, I DON'T KNOW WHO TO APPROACH.
LAST I HEARD, MY KEL-MORIAN COUNTERPART IN THE DEAL WAS BEING REPLACED HIMSELF.
I-I DON'T LIKE THIS...
HON, I APPRECIATE YOU'RE WORRIED ABOUT ME BEING TRANSFERRED, BUT I'LL HANDLE IT.
MAYBE IF YOU--
STARRY.
YOU WANT TO SOLVE A PROBLEM FOR ME?
MAKE SURE IT'S NICE AND COOL IN HERE WHEN I GET BACK.

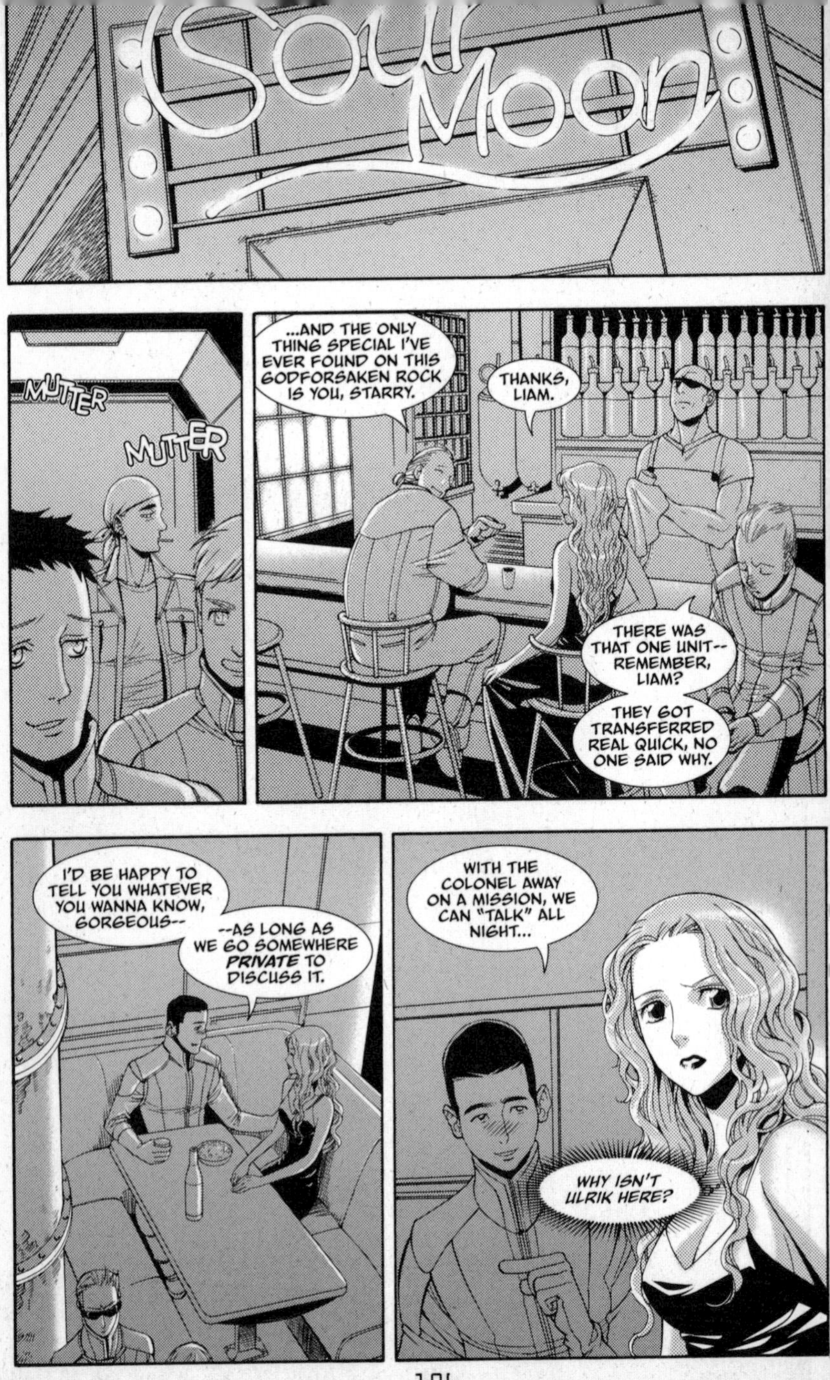
Sour Moon
MUTTER
MUTTER
...AND THE ONLY THING SPECIAL I'VE EVER FOUND ON THIS GODFORSAKEN ROCK IS YOU, STARRY.
THANKS, LIAM.
THERE WAS THAT ONE UNIT-- REMEMBER, LIAM?
THEY GOT TRANSFERRED REAL QUICK, NO ONE SAID WHY.
I'D BE HAPPY TO TELL YOU WHATEVER YOU WANNA KNOW, GORGEOUS--
--AS LONG AS WE GO SOMEWHERE *PRIVATE* TO DISCUSS IT.
WITH THE COLONEL AWAY ON A MISSION, WE CAN "TALK" ALL NIGHT...
WHY ISN'T ULRIK HERE?

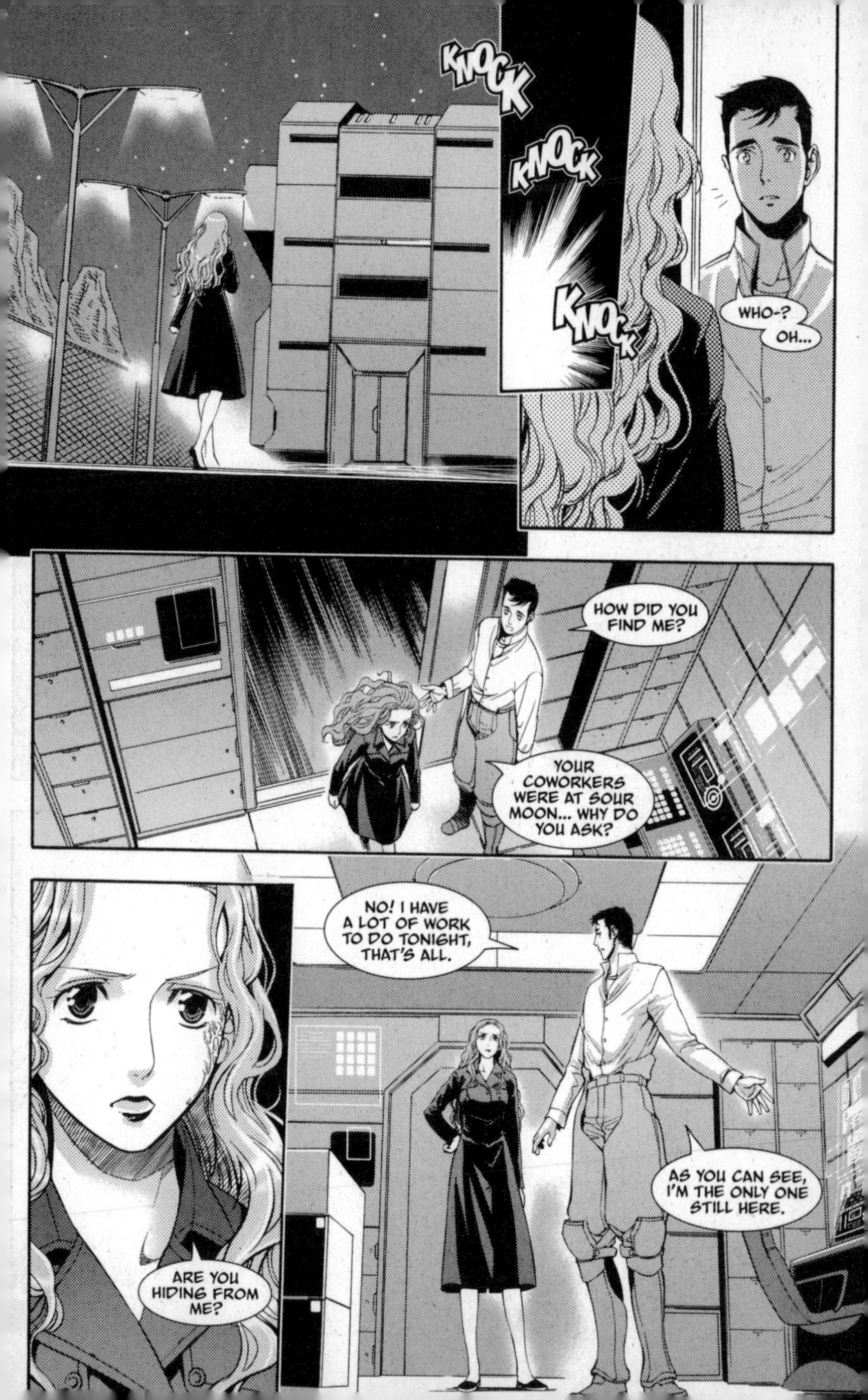
KNOCK
KNOCK
KNOCK
WHO-?
OH...
HOW DID YOU FIND ME?
YOUR COWORKERS WERE AT SOUR MOON... WHY DO YOU ASK?
ARE YOU HIDING FROM ME?
NO! I HAVE A LOT OF WORK TO DO TONIGHT, THAT'S ALL.
AS YOU CAN SEE, I'M THE ONLY ONE STILL HERE.

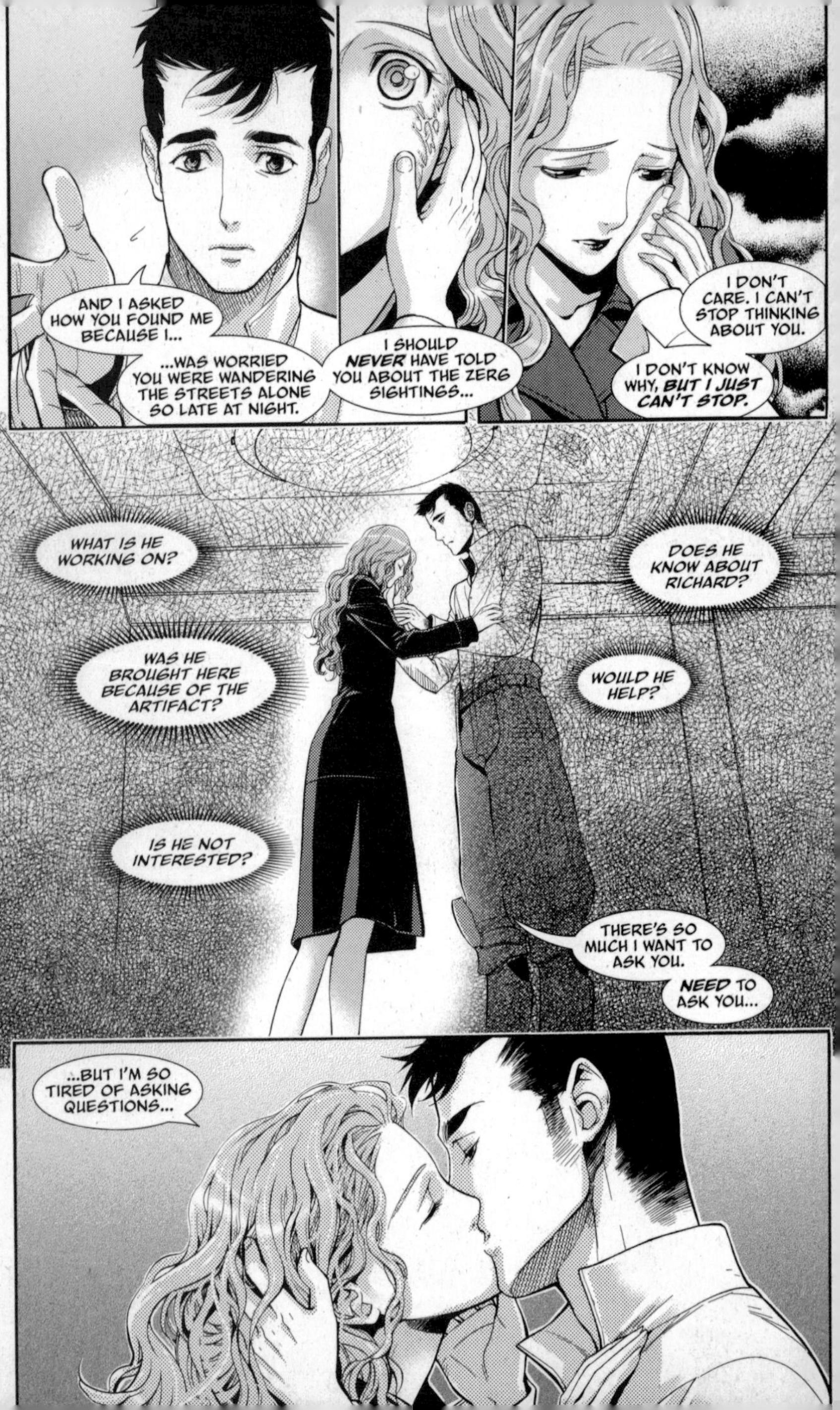
AND I ASKED HOW YOU FOUND ME BECAUSE I...
...WAS WORRIED YOU WERE WANDERING THE STREETS ALONE SO LATE AT NIGHT.
I SHOULD NEVER HAVE TOLD YOU ABOUT THE ZERG SIGHTINGS...
I DON'T CARE. I CAN'T STOP THINKING ABOUT YOU.
I DON'T KNOW WHY, BUT I JUST CAN'T STOP.
WHAT IS HE WORKING ON?
WAS HE BROUGHT HERE BECAUSE OF THE ARTIFACT?
IS HE NOT INTERESTED?
DOES HE KNOW ABOUT RICHARD?
WOULD HE HELP?
THERE'S SO MUCH I WANT TO ASK YOU.
NEED TO ASK YOU...
...BUT I'M SO TIRED OF ASKING QUESTIONS...

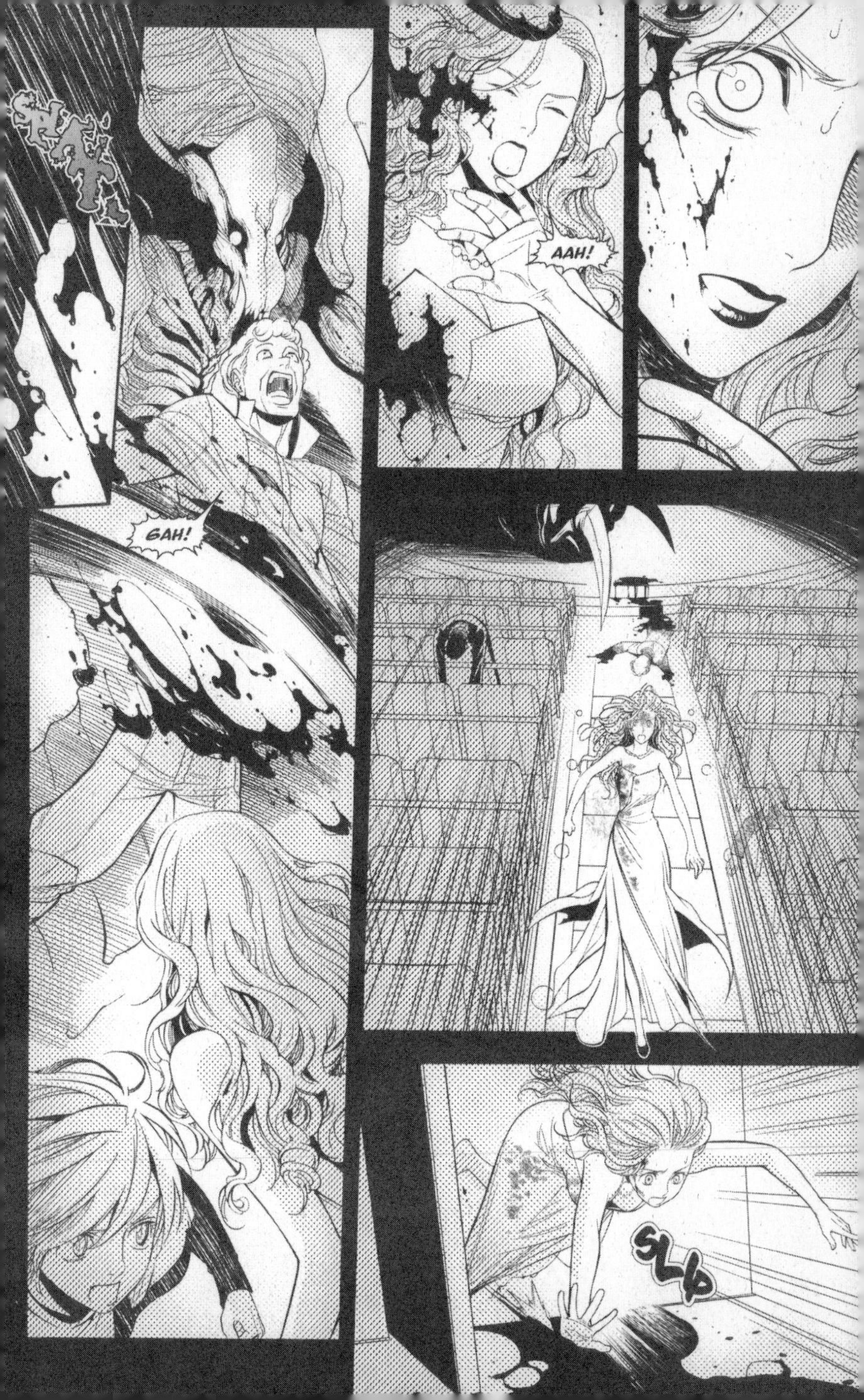

GAH!
AAH!
SLIP

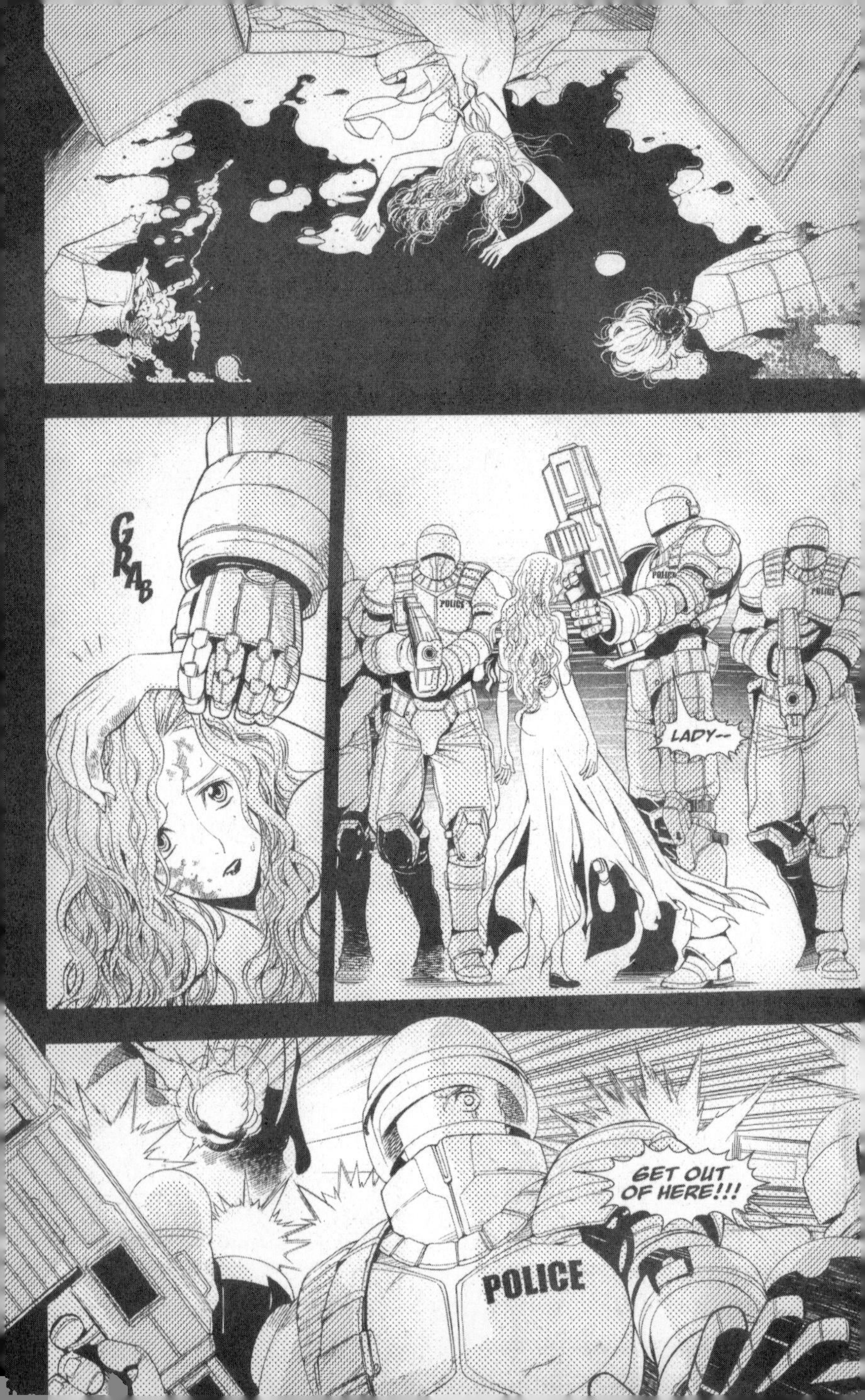
GRAB
POLICE
POLICE
POLICE
LADY--
POLICE
GET OUT OF HERE!!!

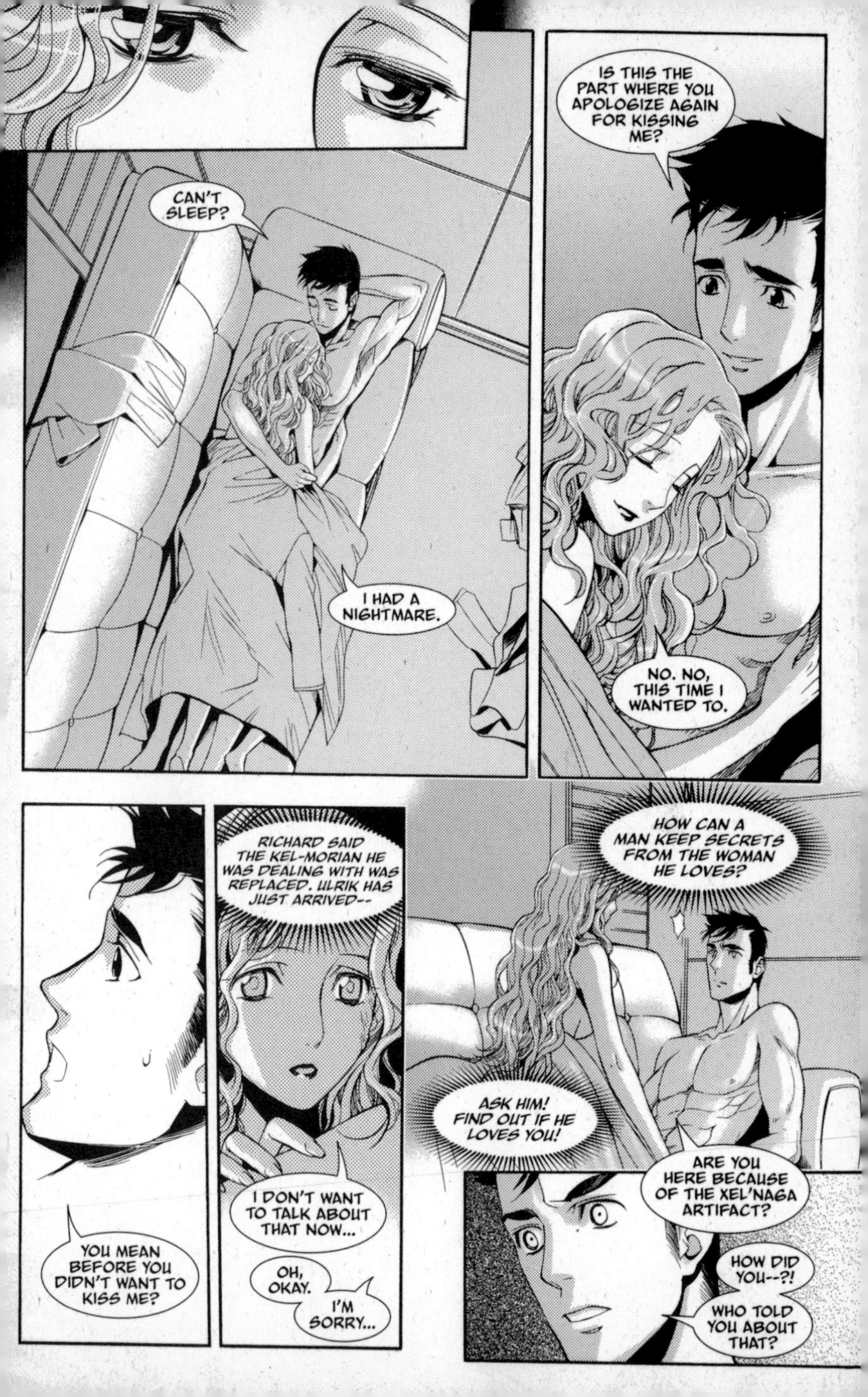
CAN'T SLEEP?
I HAD A NIGHTMARE.
IS THIS THE PART WHERE YOU APOLOGIZE AGAIN FOR KISSING ME?
NO. NO, THIS TIME I WANTED TO.
YOU MEAN BEFORE YOU DIDN'T WANT TO KISS ME?
RICHARD SAID THE KEL-MORIAN HE WAS DEALING WITH WAS REPLACED. ULRIK HAS JUST ARRIVED--
I DON'T WANT TO TALK ABOUT THAT NOW...
OH, OKAY.
I'M SORRY...
HOW CAN A MAN KEEP SECRETS FROM THE WOMAN HE LOVES?
ASK HIM! FIND OUT IF HE LOVES YOU!
ARE YOU HERE BECAUSE OF THE XEL'NAGA ARTIFACT?
HOW DID YOU--?!
WHO TOLD YOU ABOUT THAT?

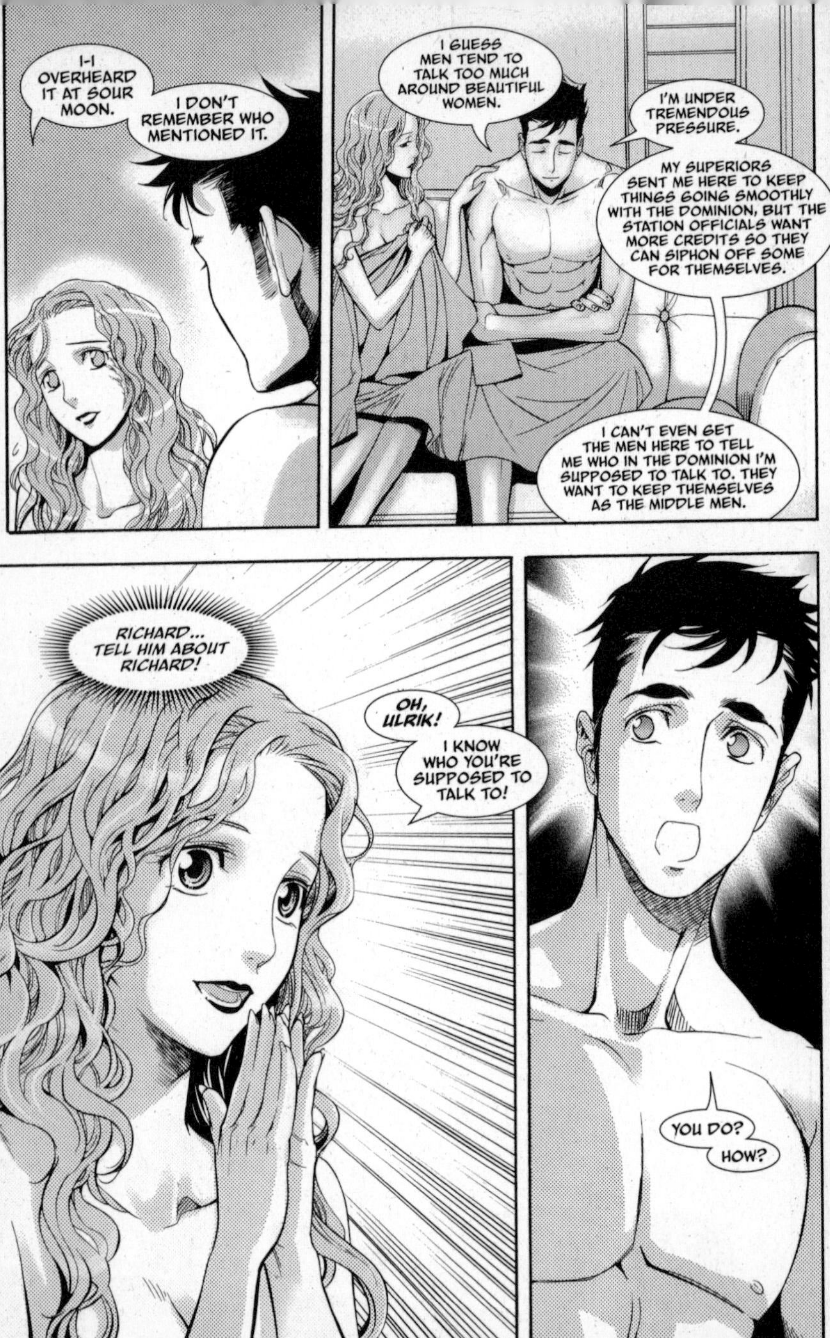
I-I OVERHEARD IT AT SOUR MOON.
I DON'T REMEMBER WHO MENTIONED IT.
I GUESS MEN TEND TO TALK TOO MUCH AROUND BEAUTIFUL WOMEN.
I'M UNDER TREMENDOUS PRESSURE.
MY SUPERIORS SENT ME HERE TO KEEP THINGS GOING SMOOTHLY WITH THE DOMINION, BUT THE STATION OFFICIALS WANT MORE CREDITS SO THEY CAN SIPHON OFF SOME FOR THEMSELVES.
I CAN'T EVEN GET THE MEN HERE TO TELL ME WHO IN THE DOMINION I'M SUPPOSED TO TALK TO. THEY WANT TO KEEP THEMSELVES AS THE MIDDLE MEN.
RICHARD... TELL HIM ABOUT RICHARD!
OH, ULRIK!
I KNOW WHO YOU'RE SUPPOSED TO TALK TO!
YOU DO?
HOW?

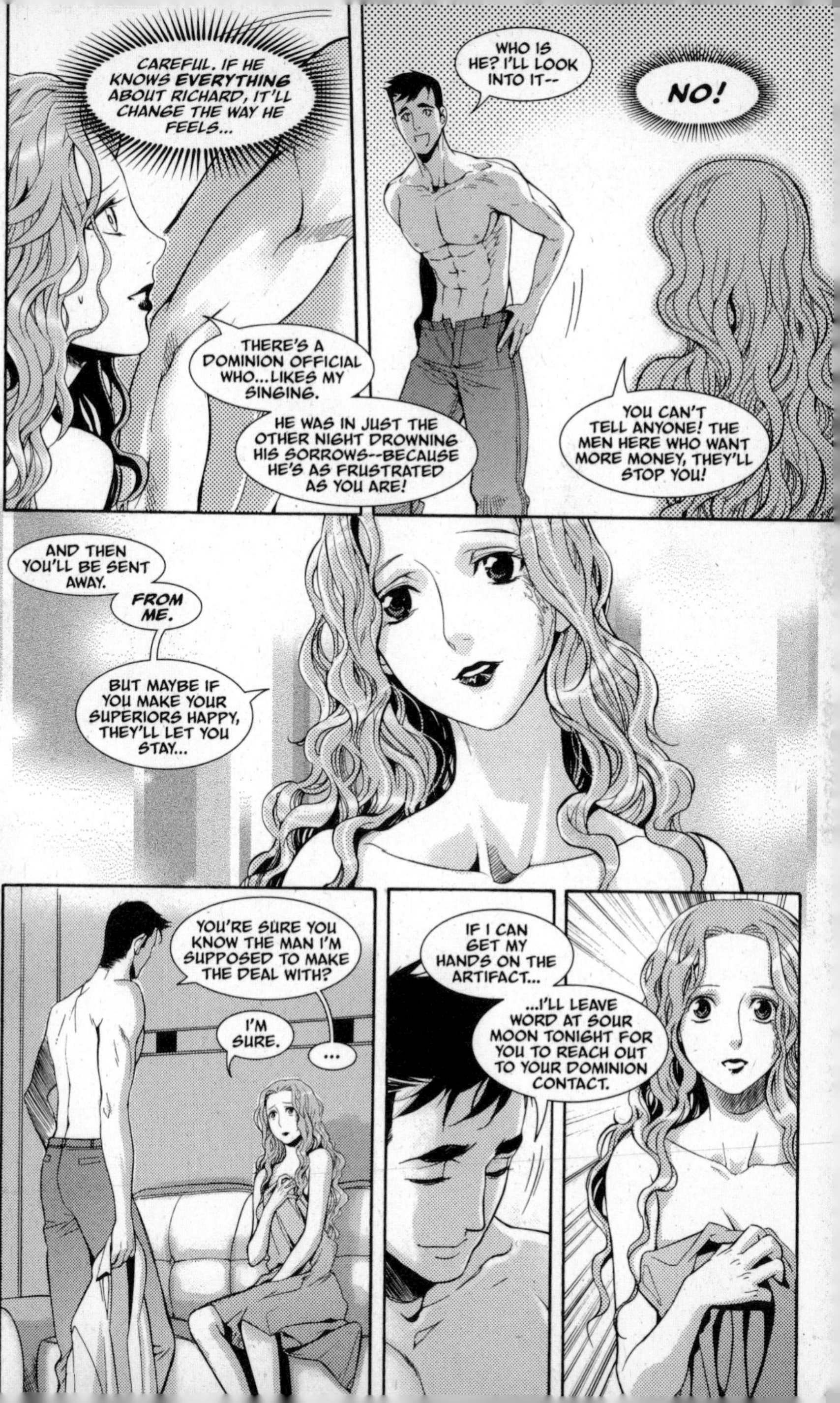
CAREFUL. IF HE KNOWS EVERYTHING ABOUT RICHARD, IT'LL CHANGE THE WAY HE FEELS...
THERE'S A DOMINION OFFICIAL WHO...LIKES MY SINGING.
HE WAS IN JUST THE OTHER NIGHT DROWNING HIS SORROWS--BECAUSE HE'S AS FRUSTRATED AS YOU ARE!
WHO IS HE? I'LL LOOK INTO IT--
NO!
YOU CAN'T TELL ANYONE! THE MEN HERE WHO WANT MORE MONEY, THEY'LL STOP YOU!
AND THEN YOU'LL BE SENT AWAY.
FROM ME.
BUT MAYBE IF YOU MAKE YOUR SUPERIORS HAPPY, THEY'LL LET YOU STAY...
YOU'RE SURE YOU KNOW THE MAN I'M SUPPOSED TO MAKE THE DEAL WITH?
I'M SURE.
...
IF I CAN GET MY HANDS ON THE ARTIFACT...
...I'LL LEAVE WORD AT SOUR MOON TONIGHT FOR YOU TO REACH OUT TO YOUR DOMINION CONTACT.

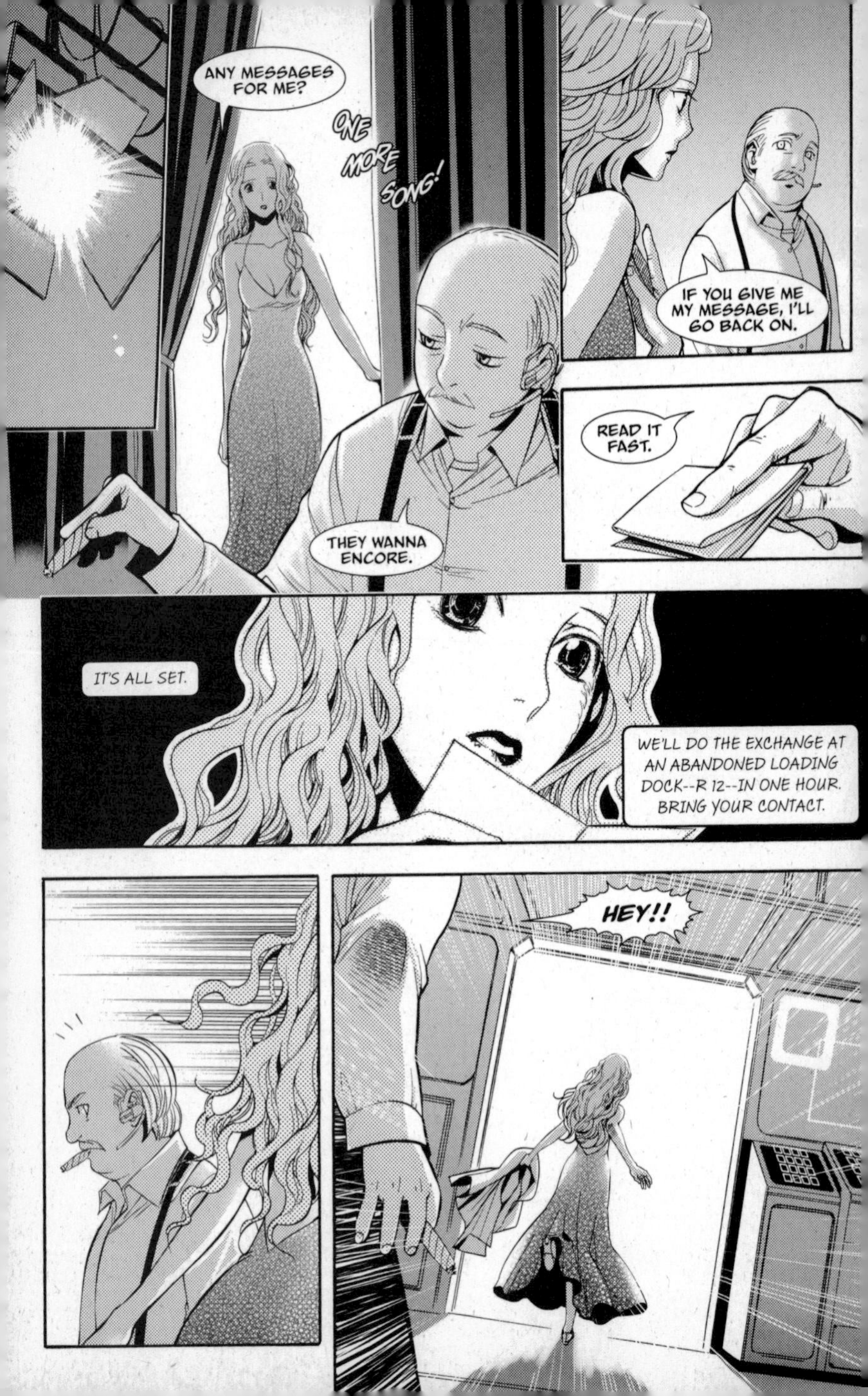
ANY MESSAGES FOR ME?
ONE MORE SONG!
THEY WANNA ENCORE.
IF YOU GIVE ME MY MESSAGE, I'LL GO BACK ON.
READ IT FAST.
IT'S ALL SET.
WE'LL DO THE EXCHANGE AT AN ABANDONED LOADING DOCK--R 12--IN ONE HOUR. BRING YOUR CONTACT.
HEY!!

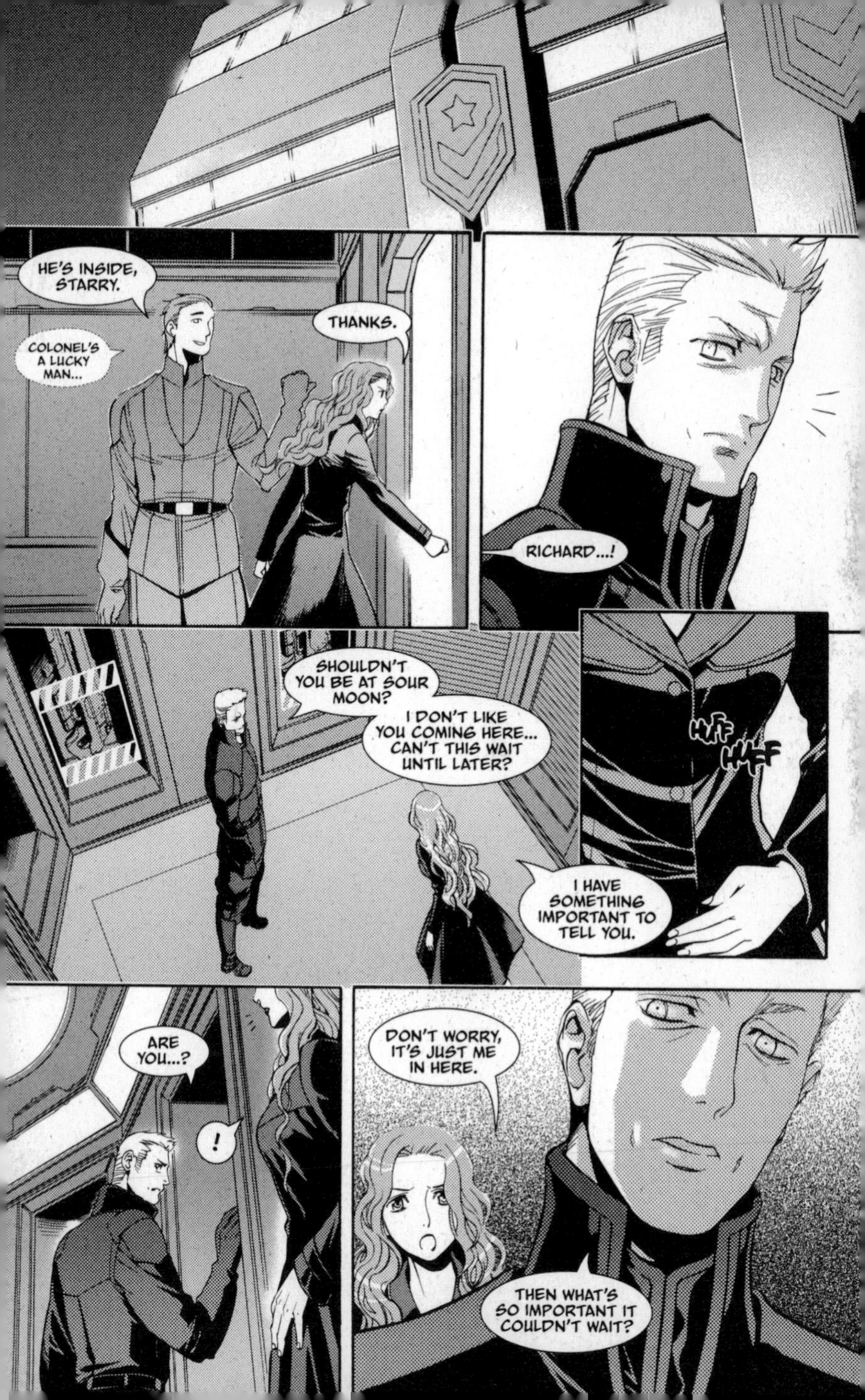
HE'S INSIDE, STARRY.
COLONEL'S A LUCKY MAN...
THANKS.
RICHARD...!
SHOULDN'T YOU BE AT SOUR MOON?
I DON'T LIKE YOU COMING HERE... CAN'T THIS WAIT UNTIL LATER?
HUFF HUFF
I HAVE SOMETHING IMPORTANT TO TELL YOU.
ARE YOU...?
!
DON'T WORRY, IT'S JUST ME IN HERE.
THEN WHAT'S SO IMPORTANT IT COULDN'T WAIT?

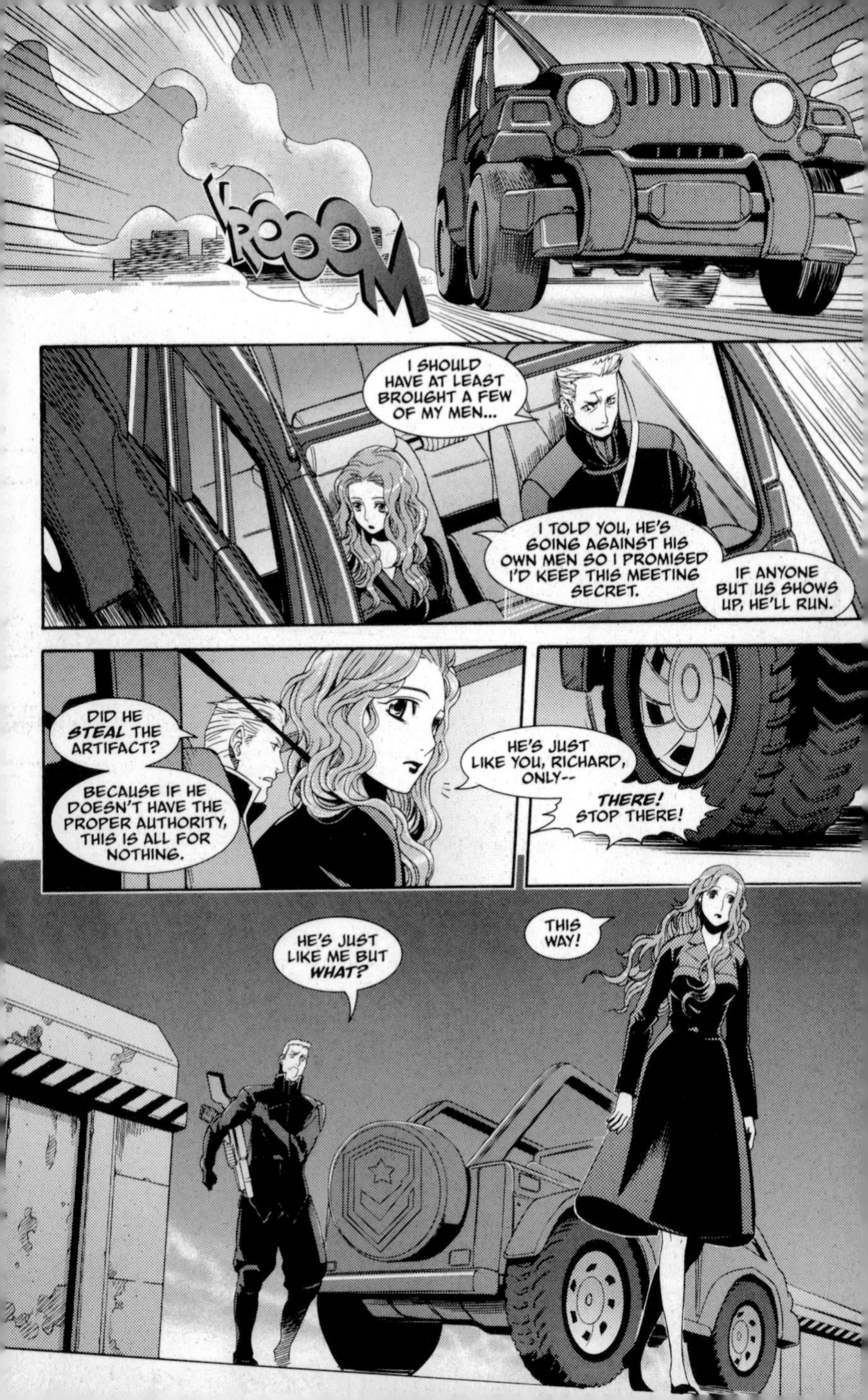
VROOOM
I SHOULD HAVE AT LEAST BROUGHT A FEW OF MY MEN...
I TOLD YOU, HE'S GOING AGAINST HIS OWN MEN SO I PROMISED I'D KEEP THIS MEETING SECRET.
IF ANYONE BUT US SHOWS UP, HE'LL RUN.
DID HE *STEAL* THE ARTIFACT?
BECAUSE IF HE DOESN'T HAVE THE PROPER AUTHORITY, THIS IS ALL FOR NOTHING.
HE'S JUST LIKE YOU, RICHARD, ONLY--
THERE! STOP THERE!
HE'S JUST LIKE ME BUT *WHAT?*
THIS WAY!

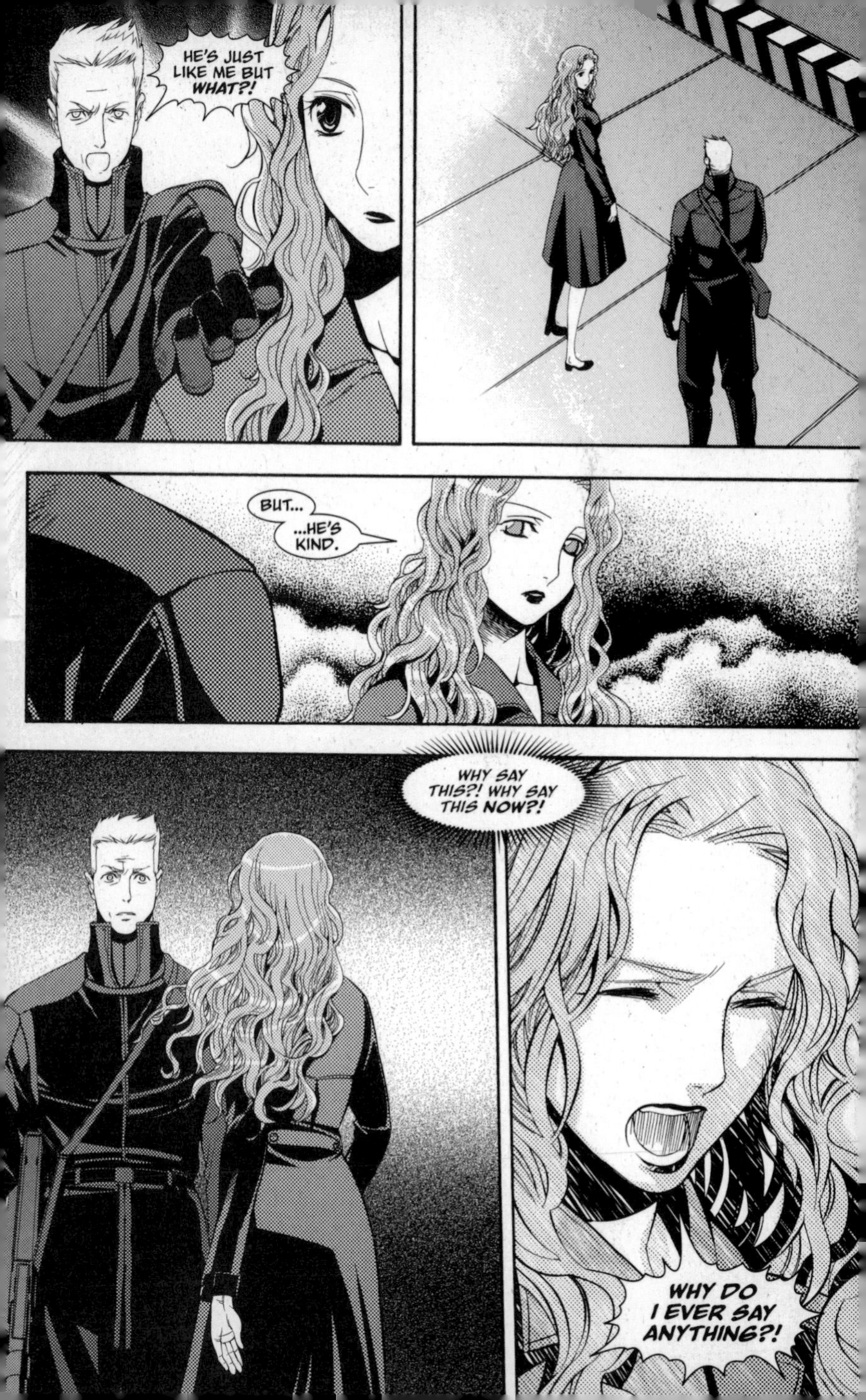
HE'S JUST LIKE ME BUT WHAT?!
BUT... ...HE'S KIND.
WHY SAY THIS?! WHY SAY THIS NOW?!
WHY DO I EVER SAY ANYTHING?!

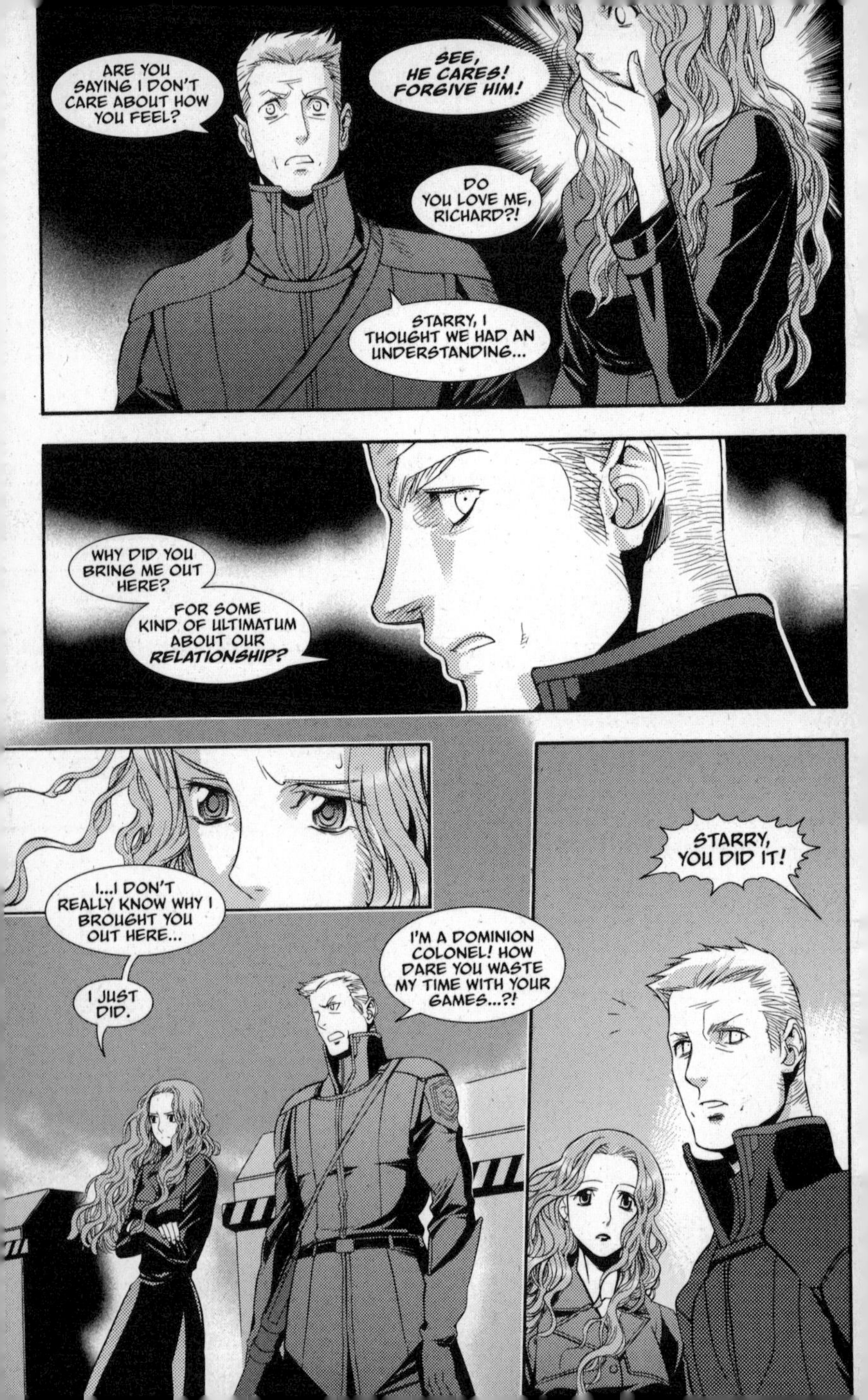
ARE YOU SAYING I DON'T CARE ABOUT HOW YOU FEEL?
SEE, HE CARES! FORGIVE HIM!
DO YOU LOVE ME, RICHARD?!
STARRY, I THOUGHT WE HAD AN UNDERSTANDING...
WHY DID YOU BRING ME OUT HERE?
FOR SOME KIND OF ULTIMATUM ABOUT OUR RELATIONSHIP?
I...I DON'T REALLY KNOW WHY I BROUGHT YOU OUT HERE...
I JUST DID.
I'M A DOMINION COLONEL! HOW DARE YOU WASTE MY TIME WITH YOUR GAMES...?!
STARRY, YOU DID IT!

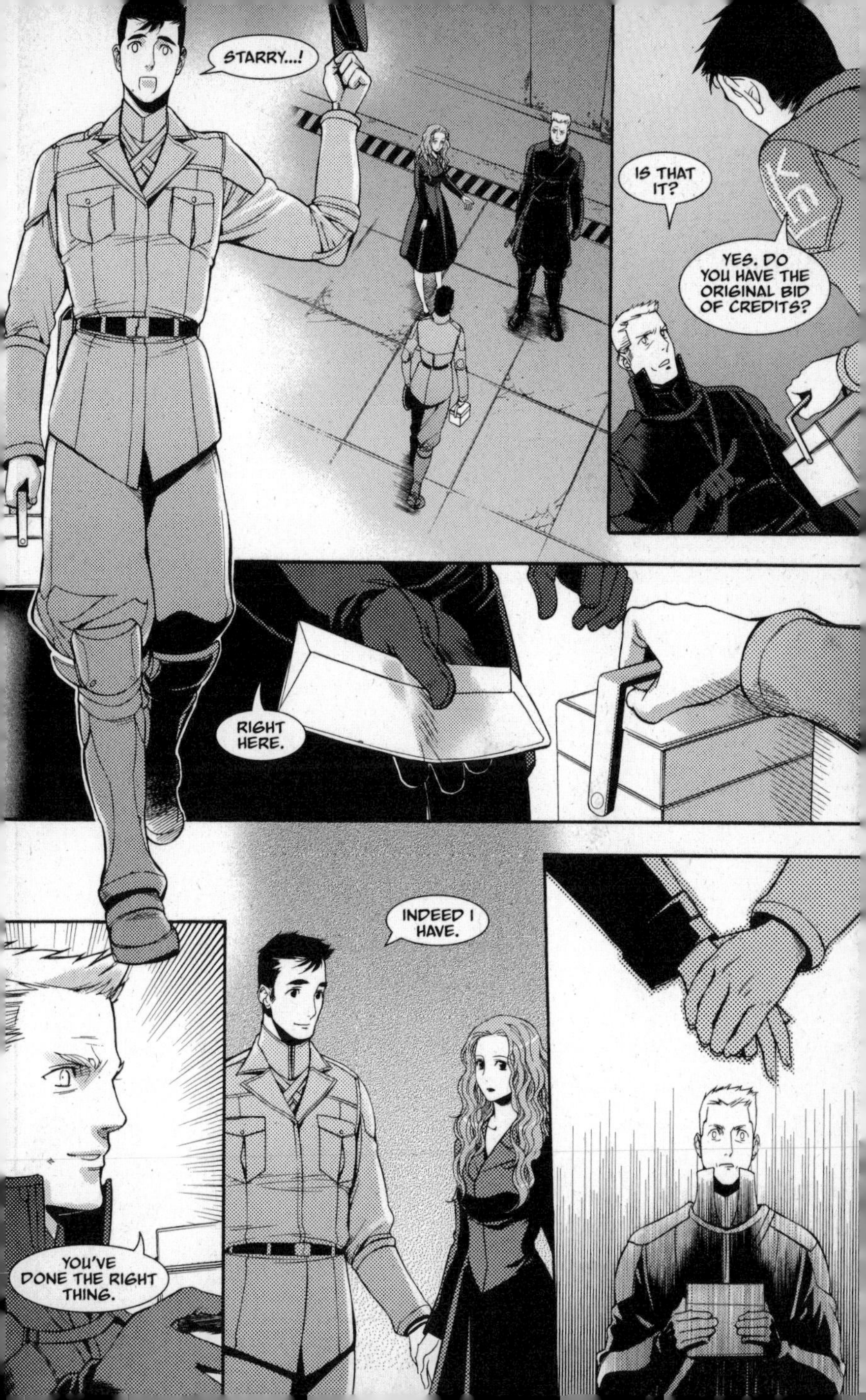
STARRY...!
IS THAT IT?
YES. DO YOU HAVE THE ORIGINAL BID OF CREDITS?
RIGHT HERE.
YOU'VE DONE THE RIGHT THING.
INDEED I HAVE.

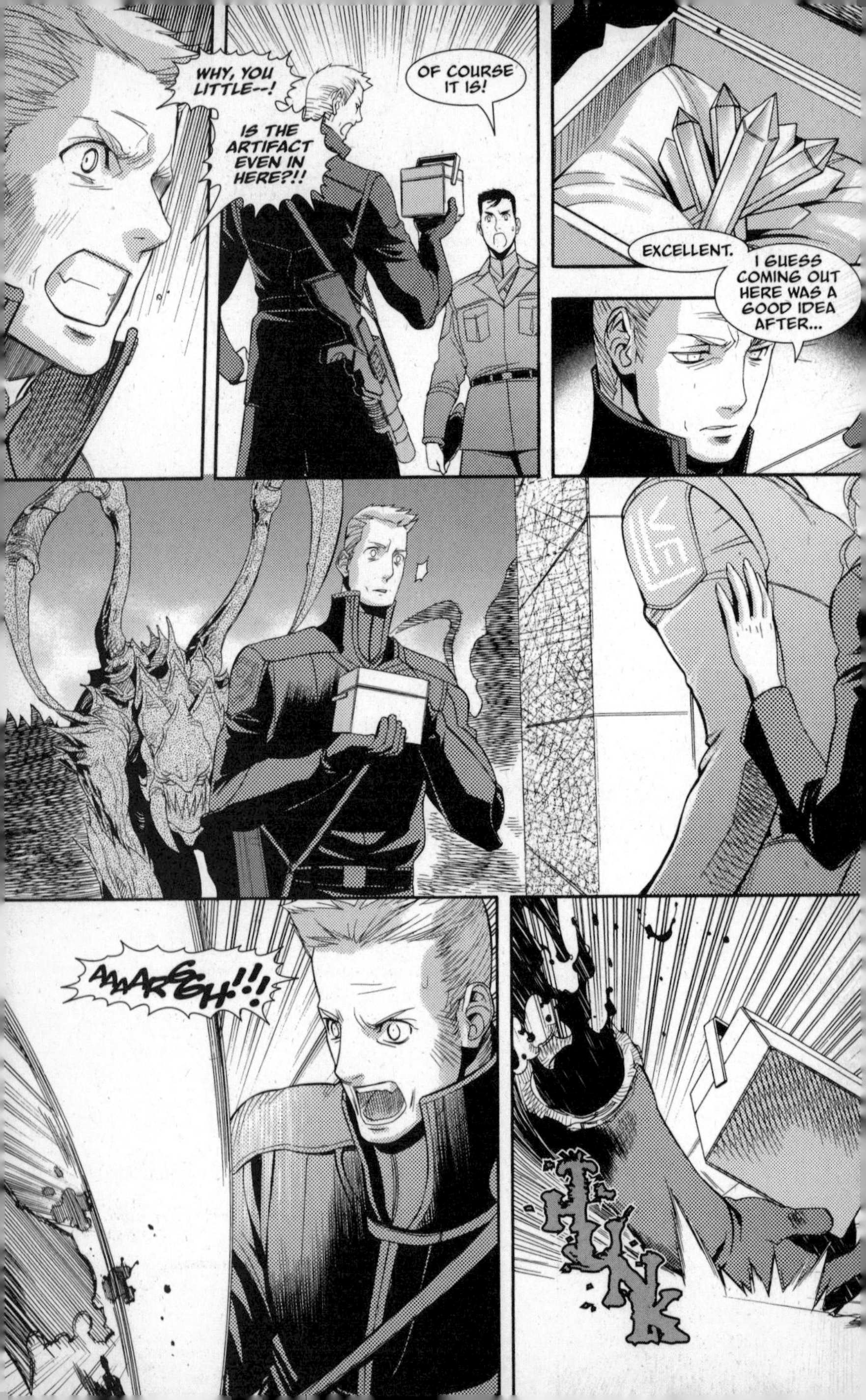

WHY, YOU LITTLE--!
IS THE ARTIFACT EVEN IN HERE?!!
OF COURSE IT IS!
EXCELLENT.
I GUESS COMING OUT HERE WAS A GOOD IDEA AFTER...
AAARGGH!!!
THUNK

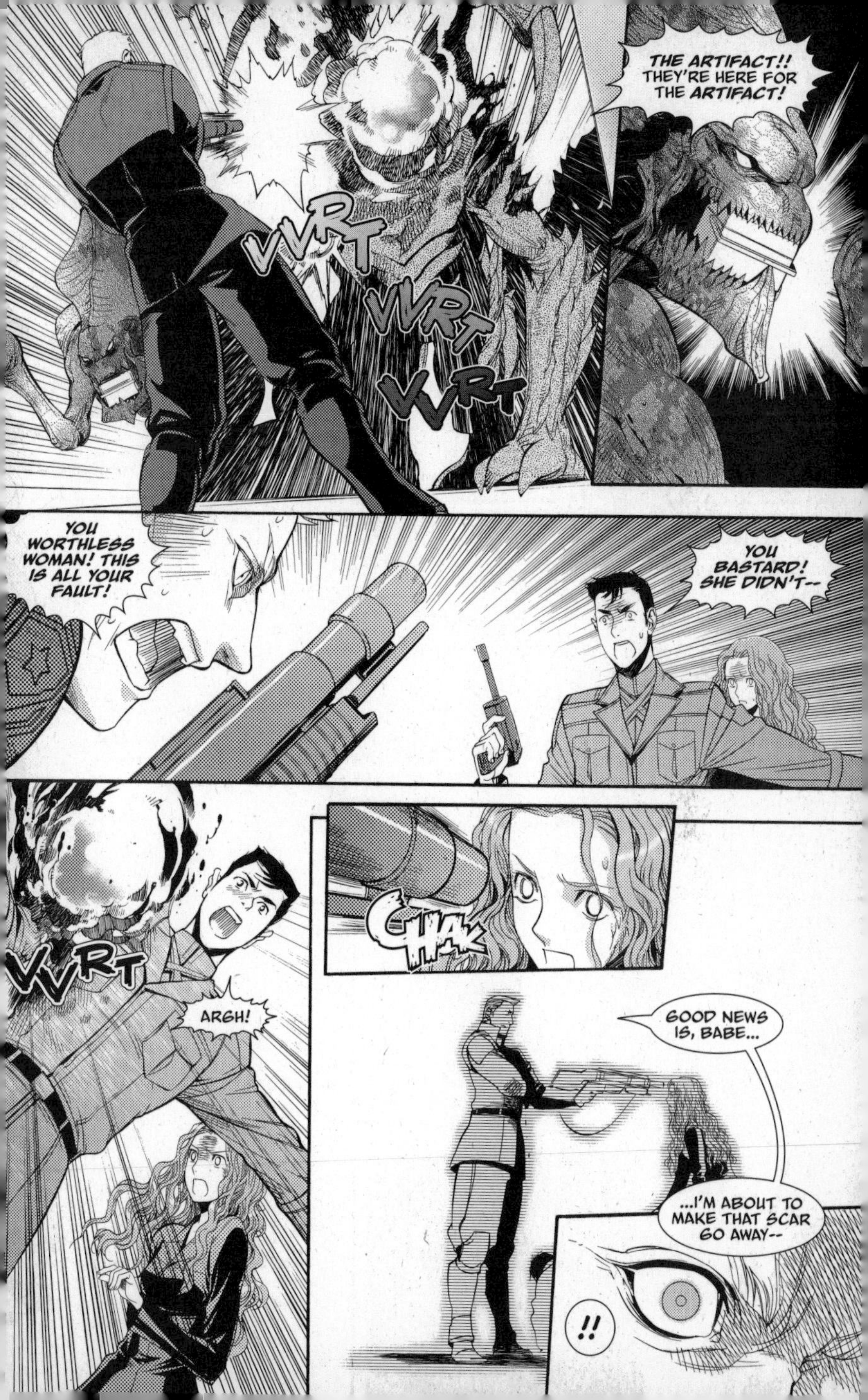
VVRT
VVRT
VVRT
THE ARTIFACT!! THEY'RE HERE FOR THE ARTIFACT!
YOU WORTHLESS WOMAN! THIS IS ALL YOUR FAULT!
YOU BASTARD! SHE DIDN'T--
VVRT
ARGH!
CHAK
GOOD NEWS IS, BABE...
...I'M ABOUT TO MAKE THAT SCAR GO AWAY--
!!

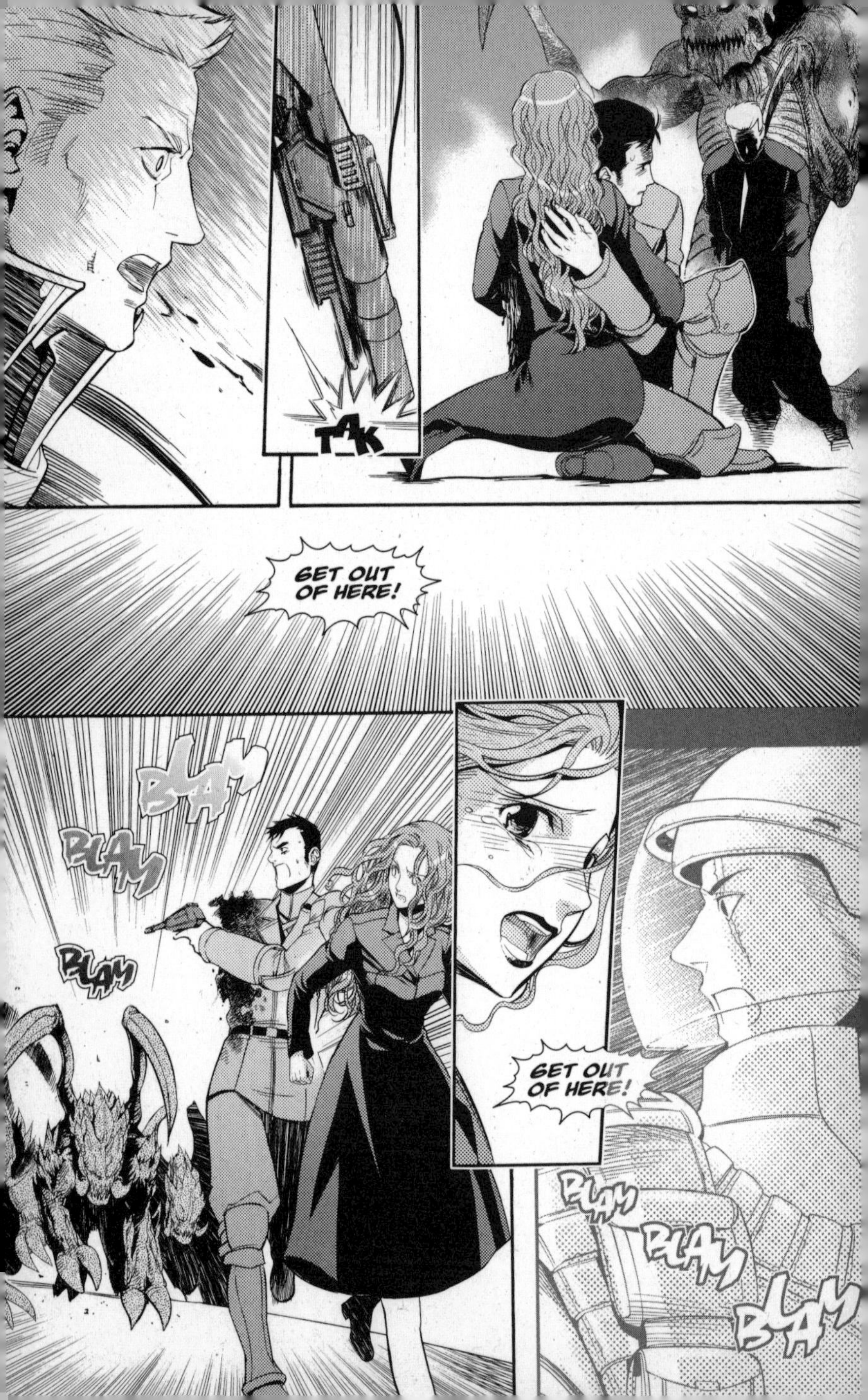
TAK
GET OUT OF HERE!
BLAM
BLAM
BLAM
GET OUT OF HERE!
BLAM
BLAM
BLAM

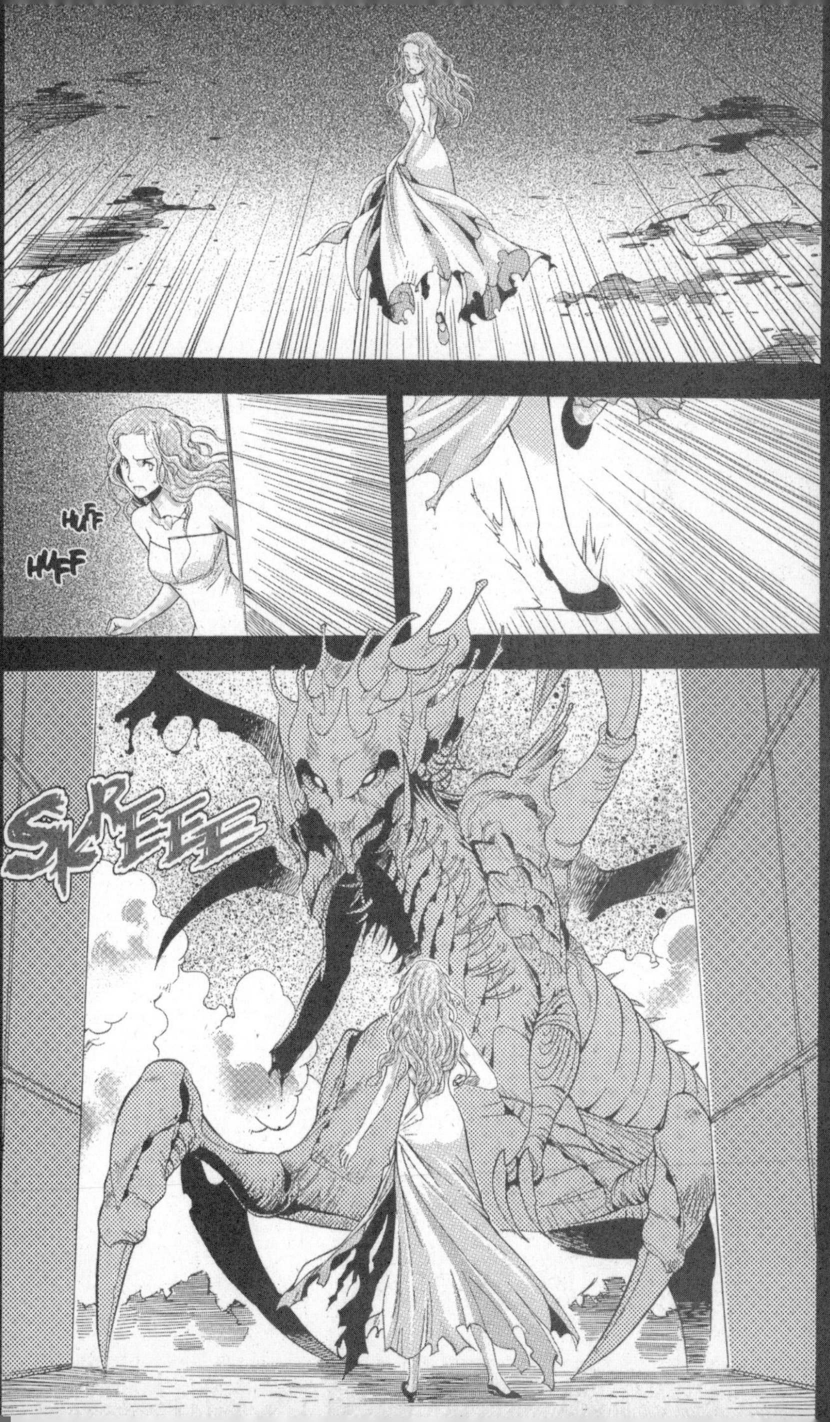
HUFF
HUFF
SKREEE

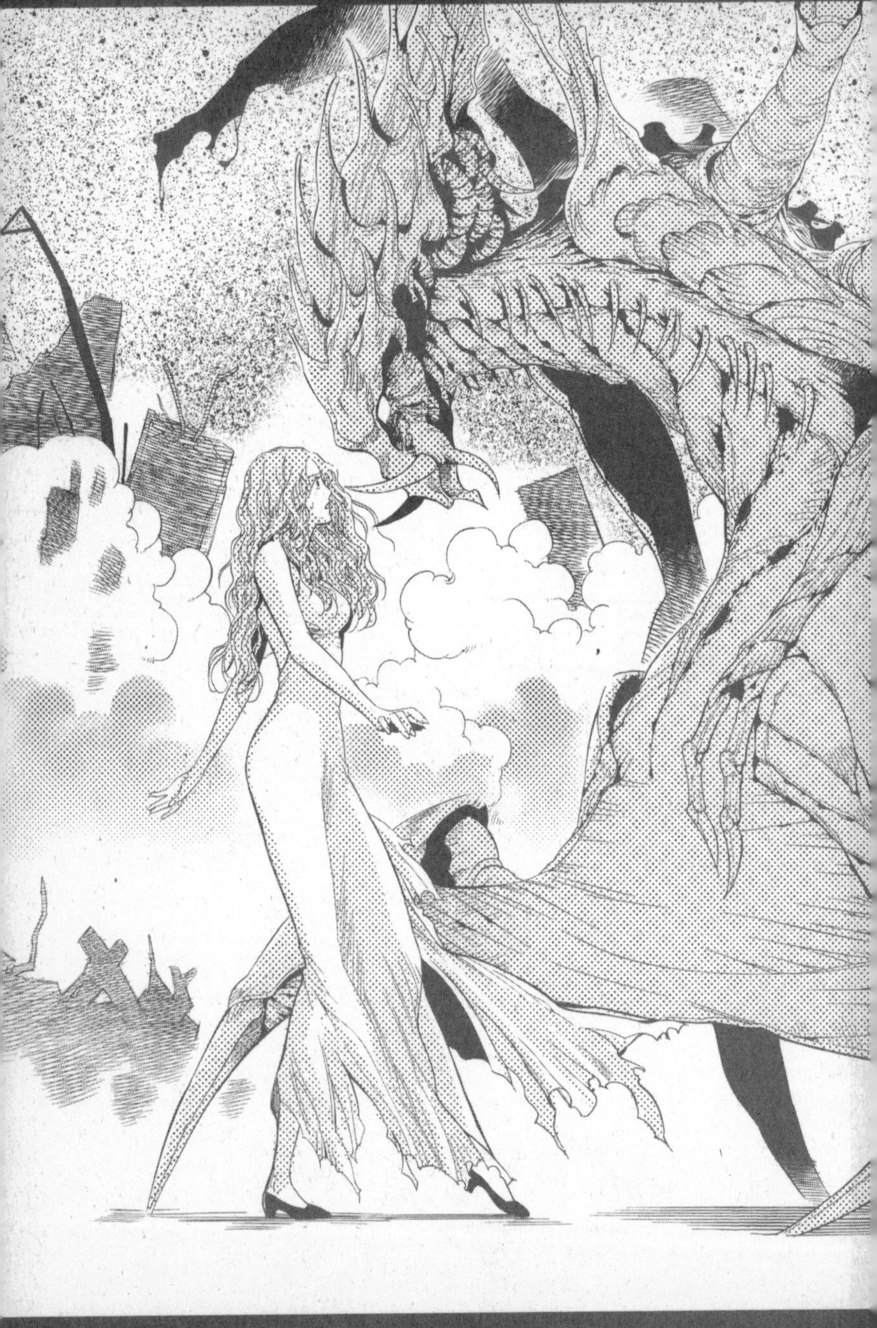

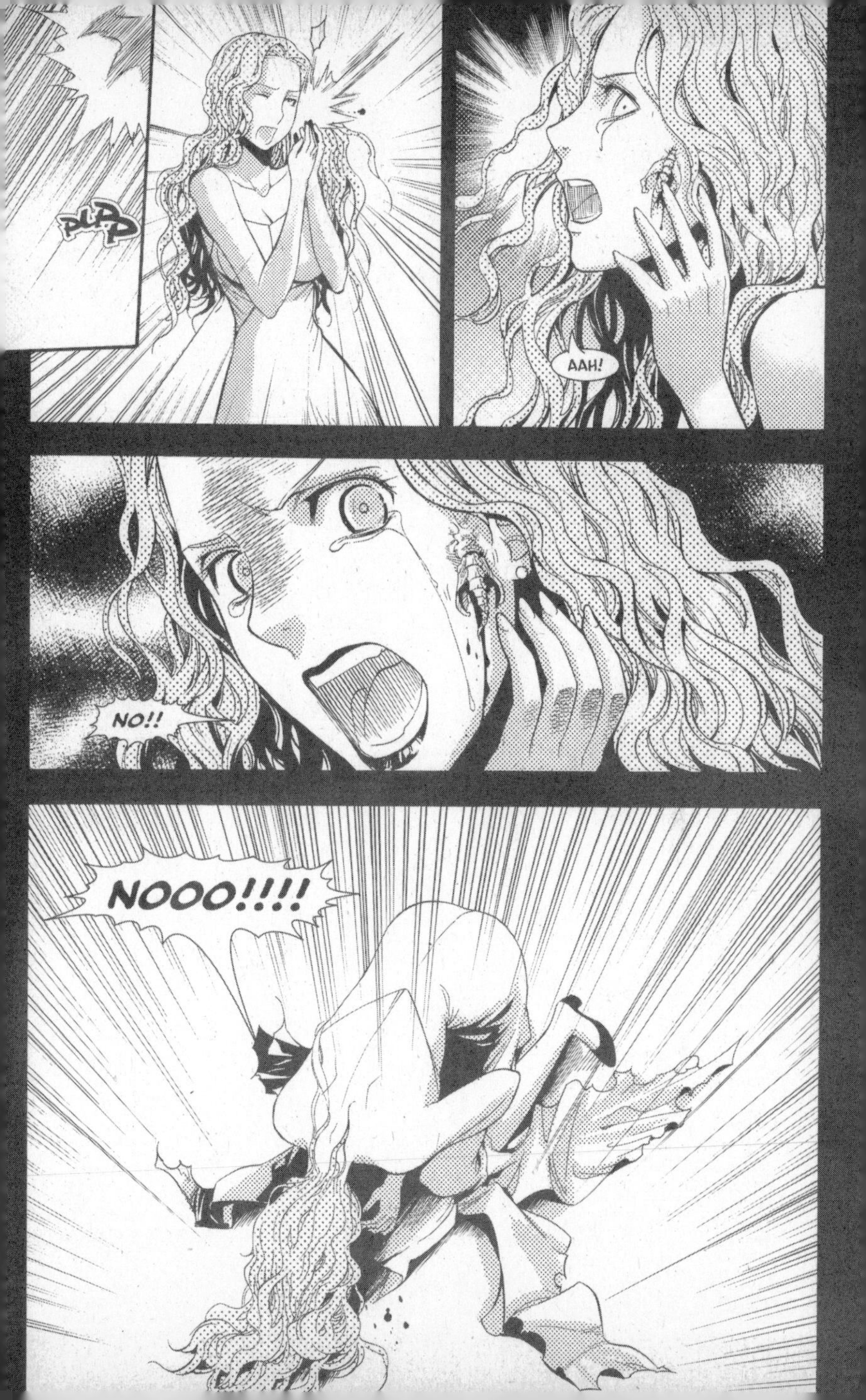
AAH!
NO!!
NOOO!!!!

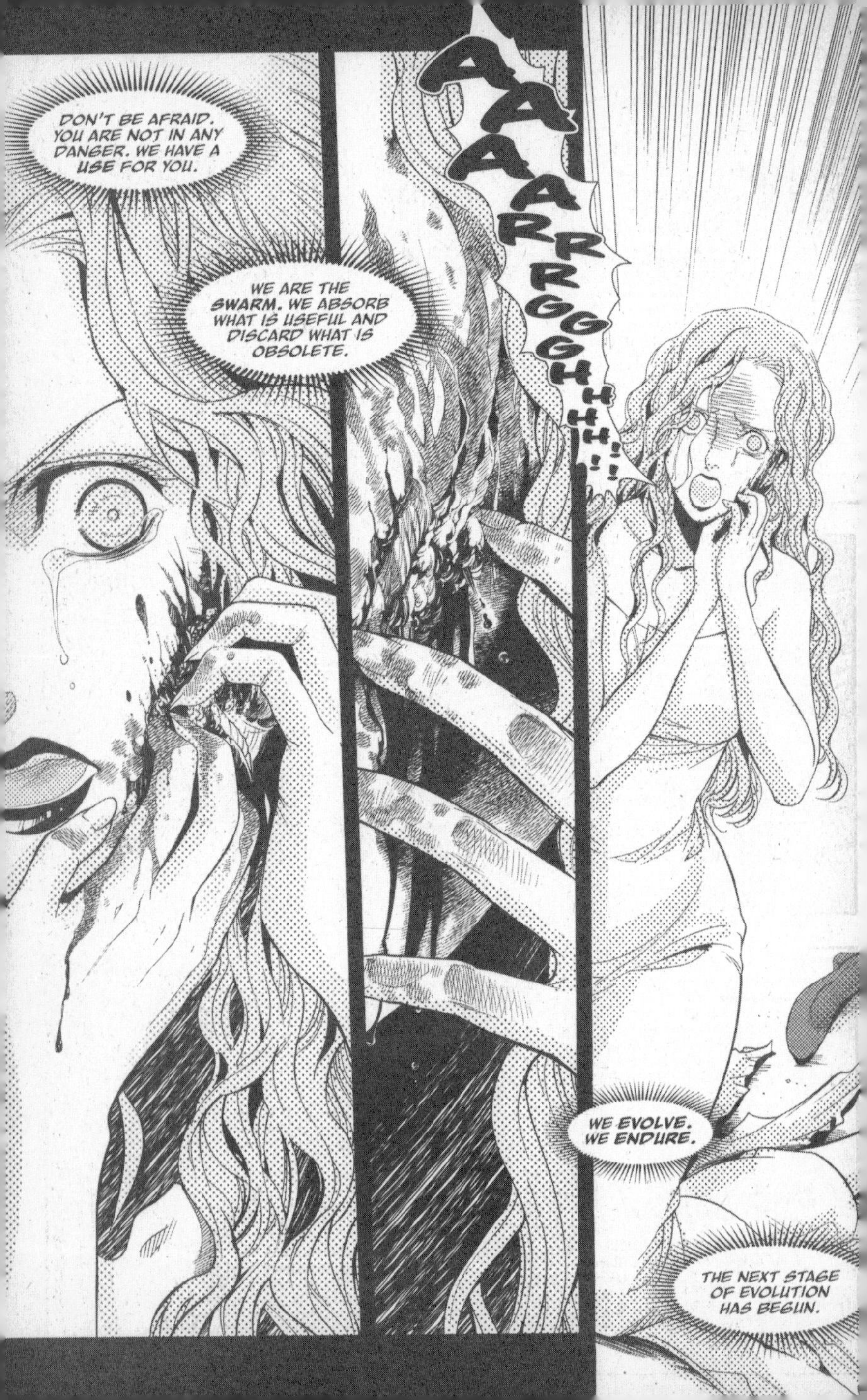
DON'T BE AFRAID. YOU ARE NOT IN ANY DANGER. WE HAVE A USE FOR YOU.
WE ARE THE SWARM. WE ABSORB WHAT IS USEFUL AND DISCARD WHAT IS OBSOLETE.
AAAARRRGGGHHHH!!
WE EVOLVE. WE ENDURE.
THE NEXT STAGE OF EVOLUTION HAS BEGUN.

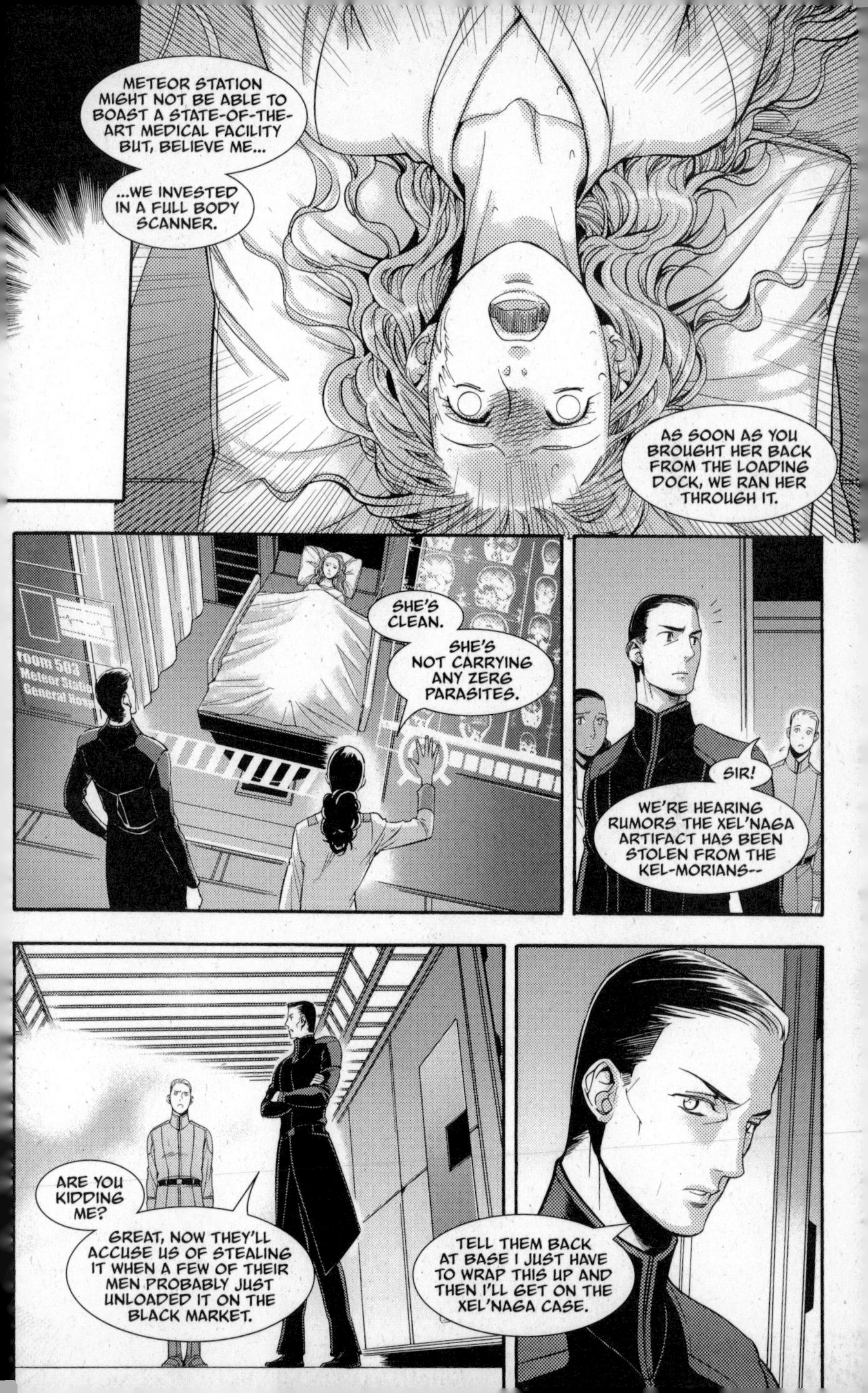
METEOR STATION MIGHT NOT BE ABLE TO BOAST A STATE-OF-THE-ART MEDICAL FACILITY BUT, BELIEVE ME...
...WE INVESTED IN A FULL BODY SCANNER.
AS SOON AS YOU BROUGHT HER BACK FROM THE LOADING DOCK, WE RAN HER THROUGH IT.
SHE'S CLEAN.
SHE'S NOT CARRYING ANY ZERG PARASITES.
SIR!
WE'RE HEARING RUMORS THE XEL'NAGA ARTIFACT HAS BEEN STOLEN FROM THE KEL-MORIANS--
ARE YOU KIDDING ME?
GREAT, NOW THEY'LL ACCUSE US OF STEALING IT WHEN A FEW OF THEIR MEN PROBABLY JUST UNLOADED IT ON THE BLACK MARKET.
TELL THEM BACK AT BASE I JUST HAVE TO WRAP THIS UP AND THEN I'LL GET ON THE XEL'NAGA CASE.

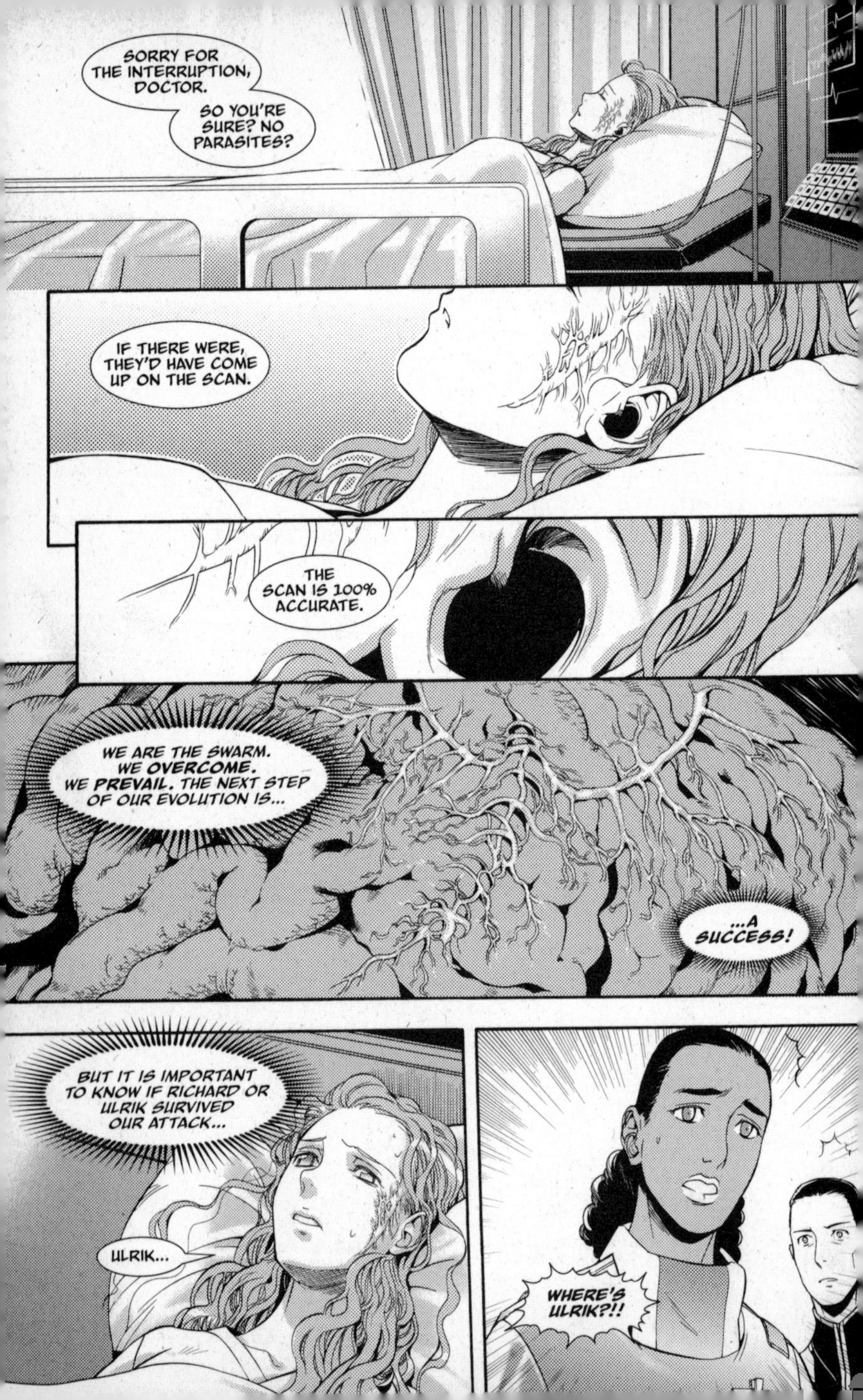

SORRY FOR THE INTERRUPTION, DOCTOR.
SO YOU'RE SURE? NO PARASITES?
IF THERE WERE, THEY'D HAVE COME UP ON THE SCAN.
THE SCAN IS 100% ACCURATE.
WE ARE THE SWARM. WE **OVERCOME**. WE **PREVAIL**. THE NEXT STEP OF OUR EVOLUTION IS...
...A SUCCESS!
BUT IT IS IMPORTANT TO KNOW IF RICHARD OR ULRIK SURVIVED OUR ATTACK...
ULRIK...
WHERE'S ULRIK?!!

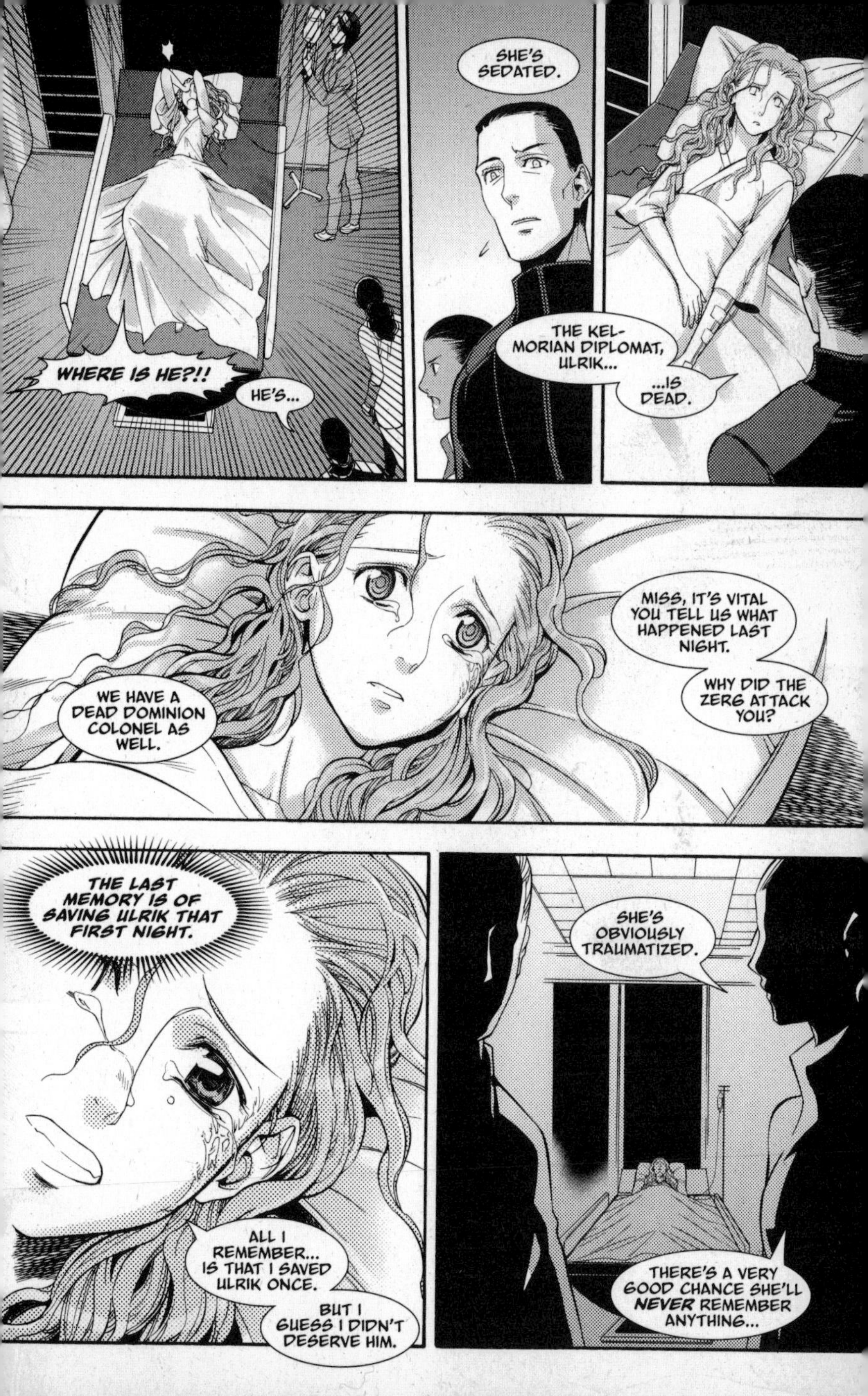
WHERE IS HE?!!
HE'S...
SHE'S SEDATED.
THE KEL-MORIAN DIPLOMAT, ULRIK...
...IS DEAD.
WE HAVE A DEAD DOMINION COLONEL AS WELL.
MISS, IT'S VITAL YOU TELL US WHAT HAPPENED LAST NIGHT.
WHY DID THE ZERG ATTACK YOU?
THE LAST MEMORY IS OF SAVING ULRIK THAT FIRST NIGHT.
ALL I REMEMBER... IS THAT I SAVED ULRIK ONCE.
BUT I GUESS I DIDN'T DESERVE HIM.
SHE'S OBVIOUSLY TRAUMATIZED.
THERE'S A VERY GOOD CHANCE SHE'LL *NEVER* REMEMBER ANYTHING...

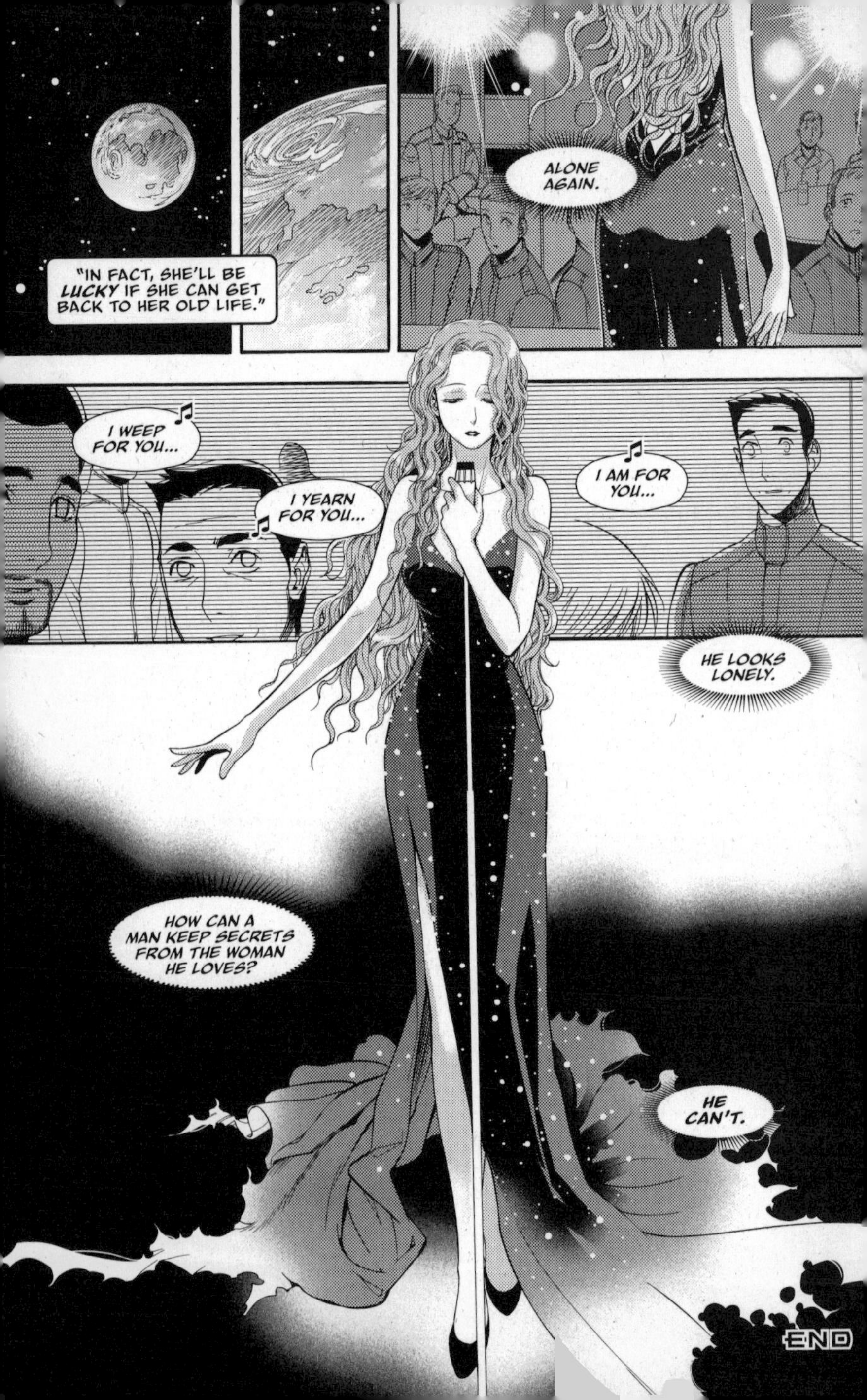
"IN FACT, SHE'LL BE LUCKY IF SHE CAN GET BACK TO HER OLD LIFE."
ALONE AGAIN.
I WEEP FOR YOU...
I YEARN FOR YOU...
I AM FOR YOU...
HE LOOKS LONELY.
HOW CAN A MAN KEEP SECRETS FROM THE WOMAN HE LOVES?
HE CAN'T.
END

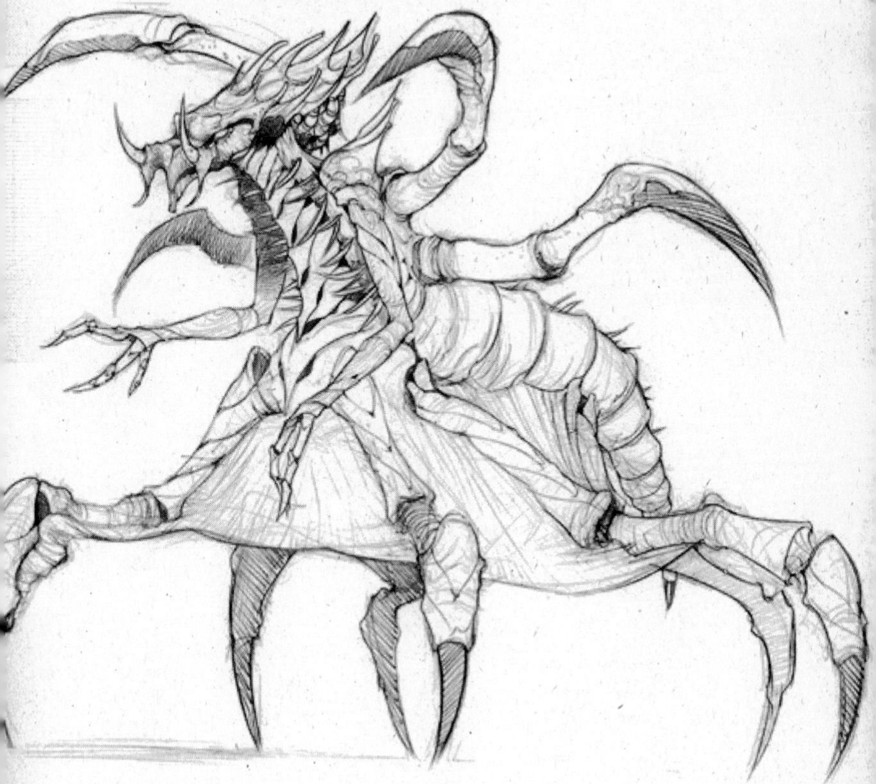

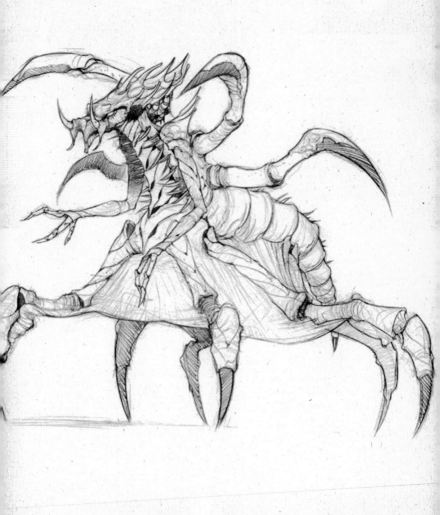

STARCRAFT

FRONTLINE
VOLUME 3

TWILIGHT ARCHON

Written by Ren Zatopek

Pencils and Inks by Noel Rodriguez
Additional Inks by Mel Joy San Juan
Tones by Mara Aum

Letterer: Michael Paolilli

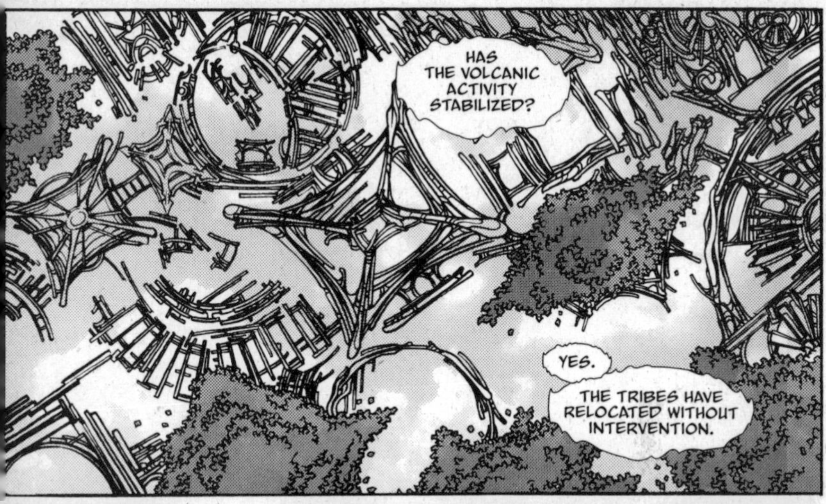
HAS THE VOLCANIC ACTIVITY STABILIZED?
YES.
THE TRIBES HAVE RELOCATED WITHOUT INTERVENTION.
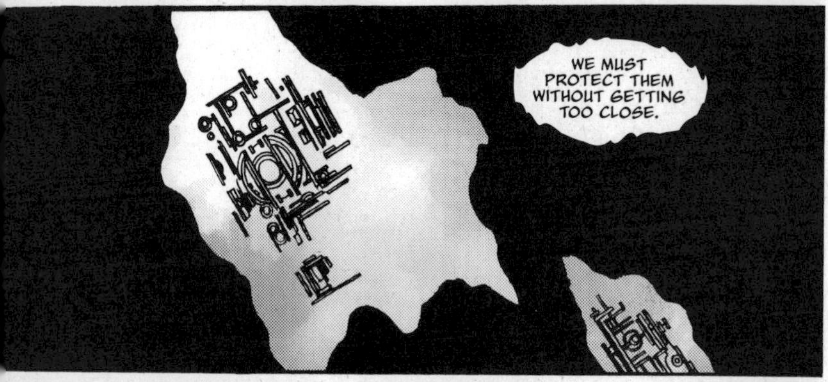
WE MUST PROTECT THEM WITHOUT GETTING TOO CLOSE.
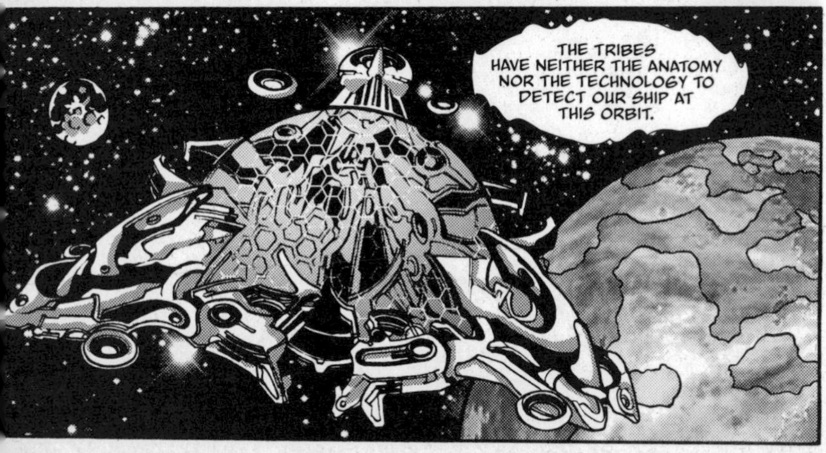
THE TRIBES HAVE NEITHER THE ANATOMY NOR THE TECHNOLOGY TO DETECT OUR SHIP AT THIS ORBIT.

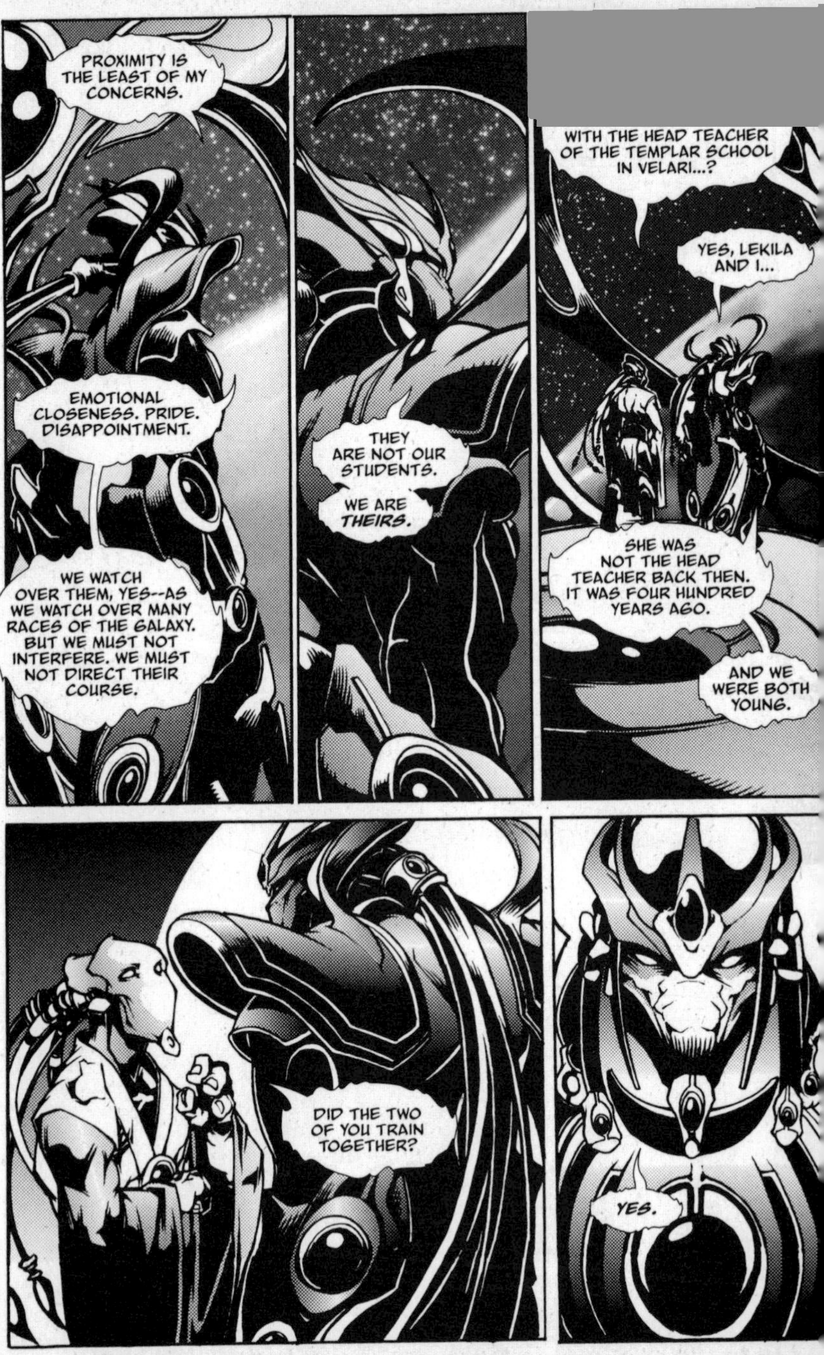
PROXIMITY IS THE LEAST OF MY CONCERNS.
EMOTIONAL CLOSENESS. PRIDE. DISAPPOINTMENT.
WE WATCH OVER THEM, YES--AS WE WATCH OVER MANY RACES OF THE GALAXY. BUT WE MUST NOT INTERFERE. WE MUST NOT DIRECT THEIR COURSE.
THEY ARE NOT OUR STUDENTS.
WE ARE *THEIRS*.
WITH THE HEAD TEACHER OF THE TEMPLAR SCHOOL IN VELARI...?
YES, LEKILA AND I...
SHE WAS NOT THE HEAD TEACHER BACK THEN. IT WAS FOUR HUNDRED YEARS AGO.
AND WE WERE BOTH YOUNG.
DID THE TWO OF YOU TRAIN TOGETHER?
YES.

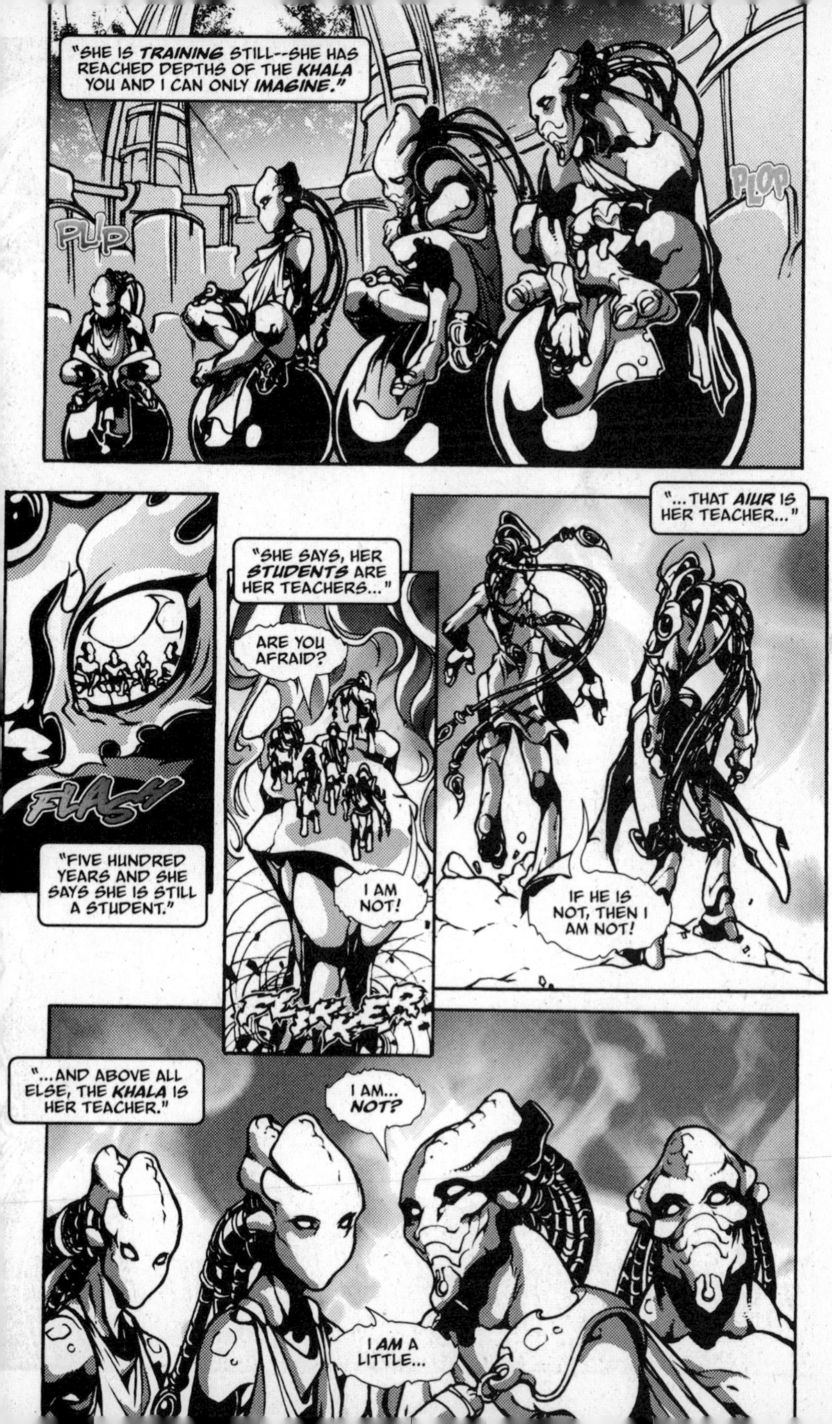
"SHE IS *TRAINING* STILL--SHE HAS REACHED DEPTHS OF THE *KHALA* YOU AND I CAN ONLY *IMAGINE*."
PLIP
PLOP
FLASH
"FIVE HUNDRED YEARS AND SHE SAYS SHE IS STILL A STUDENT."
"SHE SAYS, HER *STUDENTS* ARE HER TEACHERS..."
ARE YOU AFRAID?
I AM NOT!
"...THAT *AIUR* IS HER TEACHER..."
IF HE IS NOT, THEN I AM NOT!
"...AND ABOVE ALL ELSE, THE *KHALA* IS HER TEACHER."
I AM... *NOT?*
I *AM* A LITTLE...

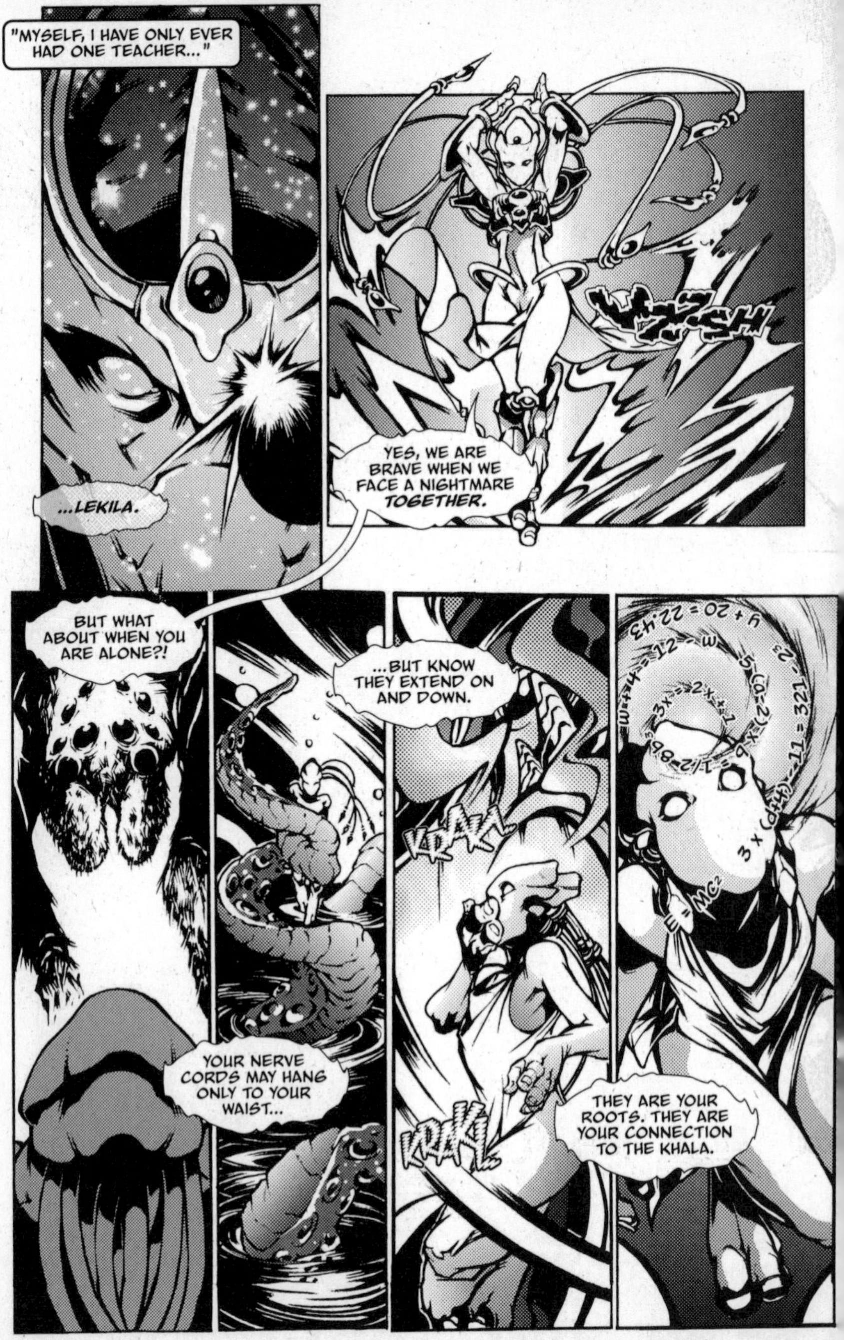
"MYSELF, I HAVE ONLY EVER HAD ONE TEACHER..."
...LEKILA.
WZZSH
YES, WE ARE BRAVE WHEN WE FACE A NIGHTMARE *TOGETHER.*
BUT WHAT ABOUT WHEN YOU ARE ALONE?!
YOUR NERVE CORDS MAY HANG ONLY TO YOUR WAIST...
...BUT KNOW THEY EXTEND ON AND DOWN.
THEY ARE YOUR ROOTS. THEY ARE YOUR CONNECTION TO THE KHALA.

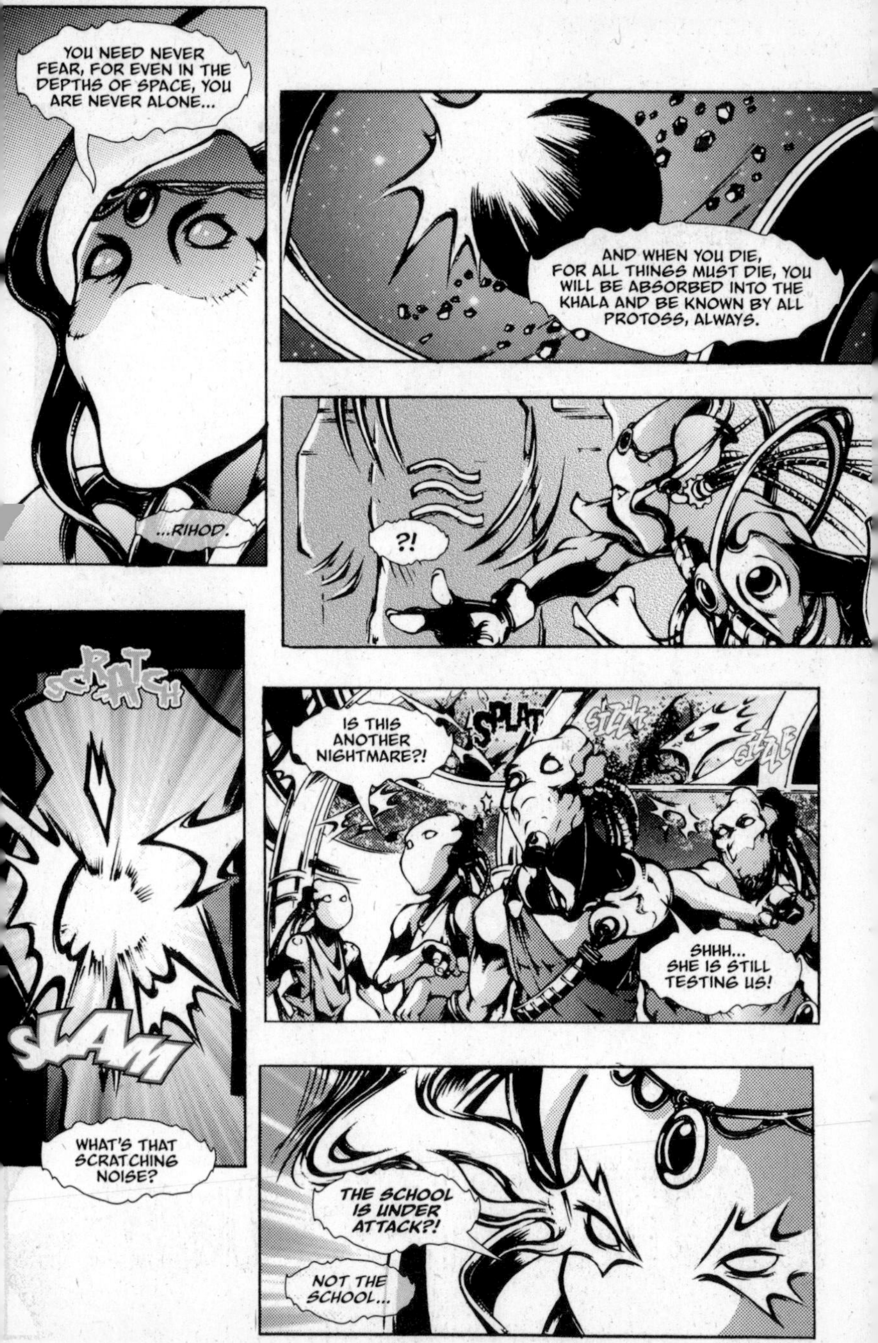
YOU NEED NEVER FEAR, FOR EVEN IN THE DEPTHS OF SPACE, YOU ARE NEVER ALONE...
...RIHOD.
AND WHEN YOU DIE, FOR ALL THINGS MUST DIE, YOU WILL BE ABSORBED INTO THE KHALA AND BE KNOWN BY ALL PROTOSS, ALWAYS.
?!
SCRATCH
SLAM
WHAT'S THAT SCRATCHING NOISE?
IS THIS ANOTHER NIGHTMARE?!
SPLAT
SHHH... SHE IS STILL TESTING US!
THE SCHOOL IS UNDER ATTACK?!
NOT THE SCHOOL...

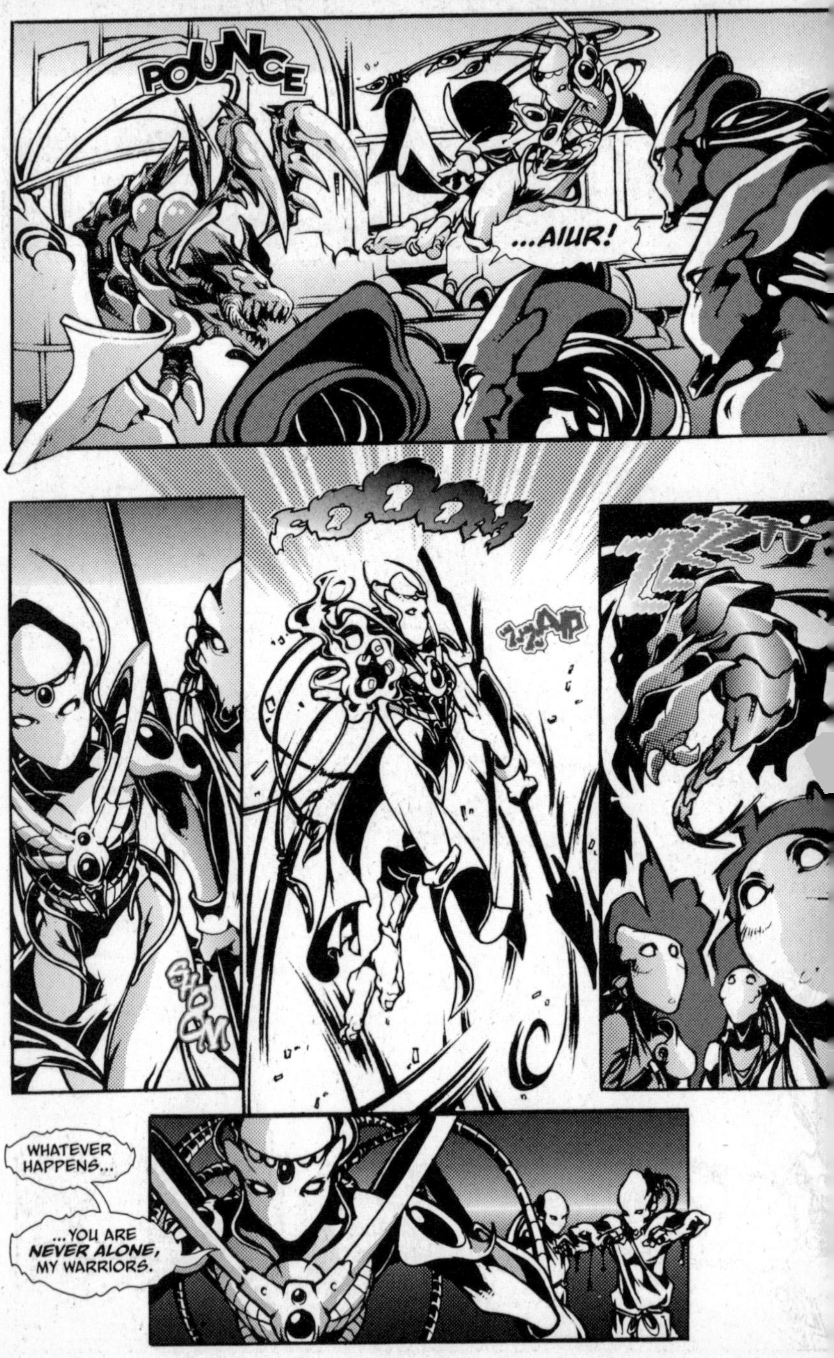
POUNCE
...AIUR!
ZAP
WHATEVER HAPPENS...
...YOU ARE NEVER ALONE, MY WARRIORS.

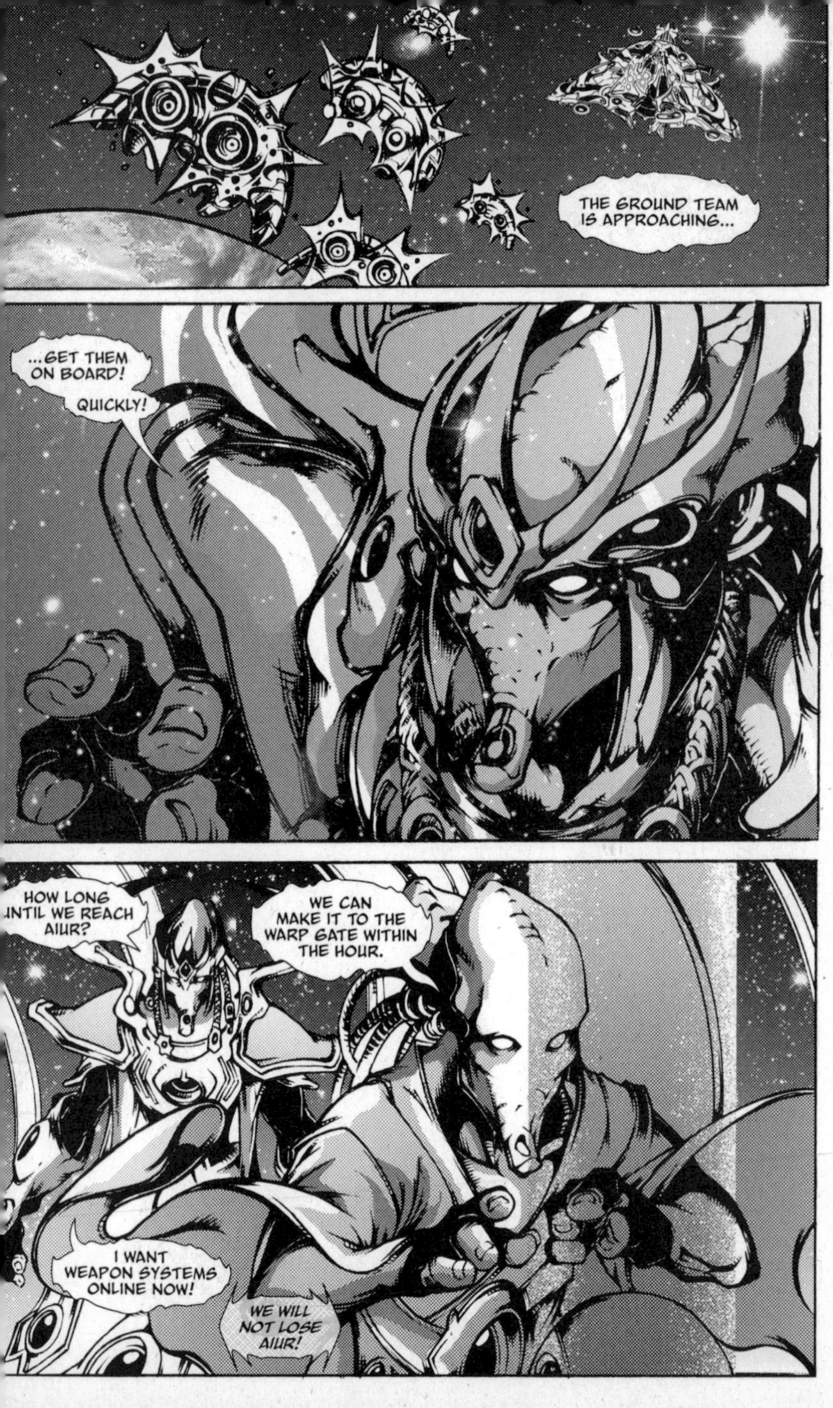
THE GROUND TEAM IS APPROACHING...
...GET THEM ON BOARD!
QUICKLY!
HOW LONG UNTIL WE REACH AIUR?
WE CAN MAKE IT TO THE WARP GATE WITHIN THE HOUR.
I WANT WEAPON SYSTEMS ONLINE NOW!
WE WILL NOT LOSE AIUR!

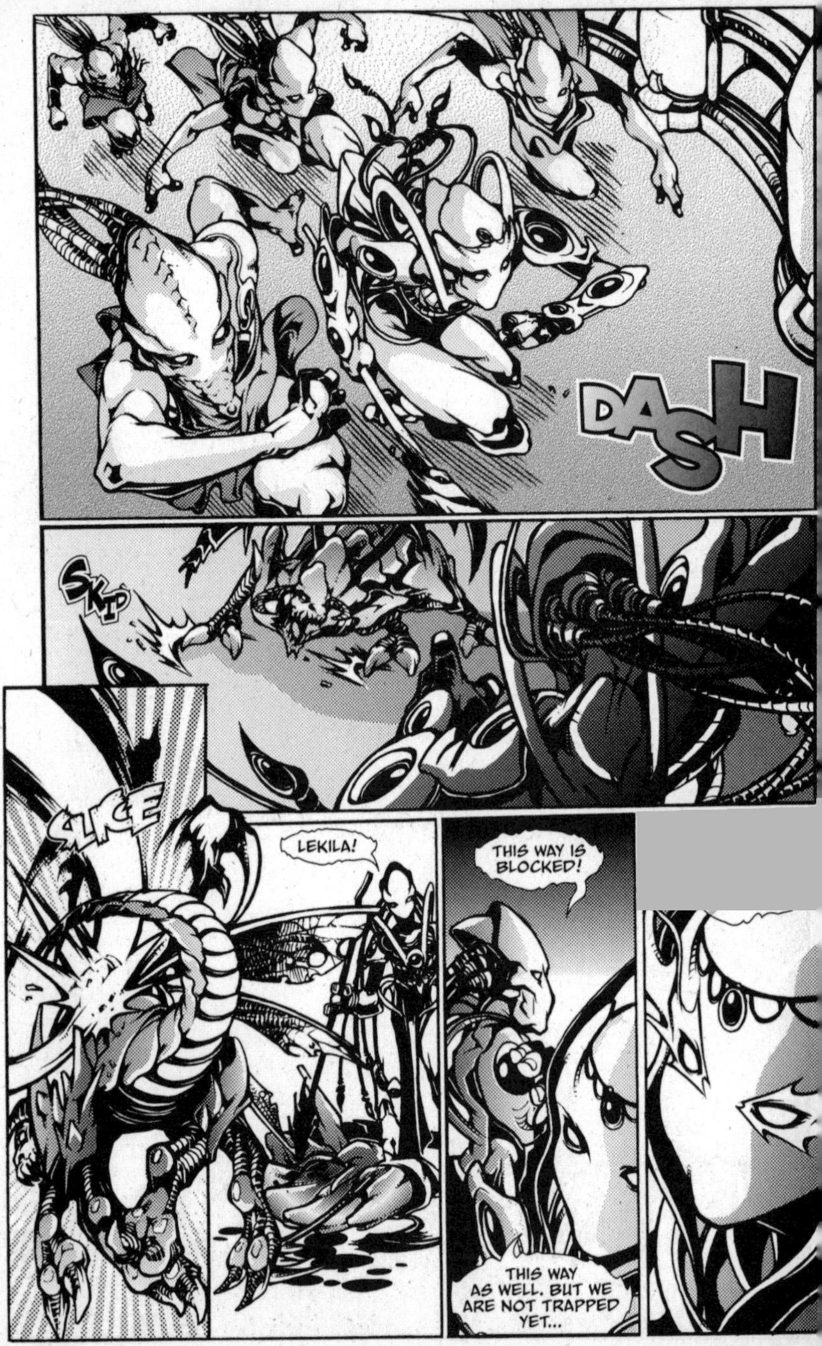
DASH
SKIP
SLICE
LEKILA!
THIS WAY IS BLOCKED!
THIS WAY AS WELL. BUT WE ARE NOT TRAPPED YET...

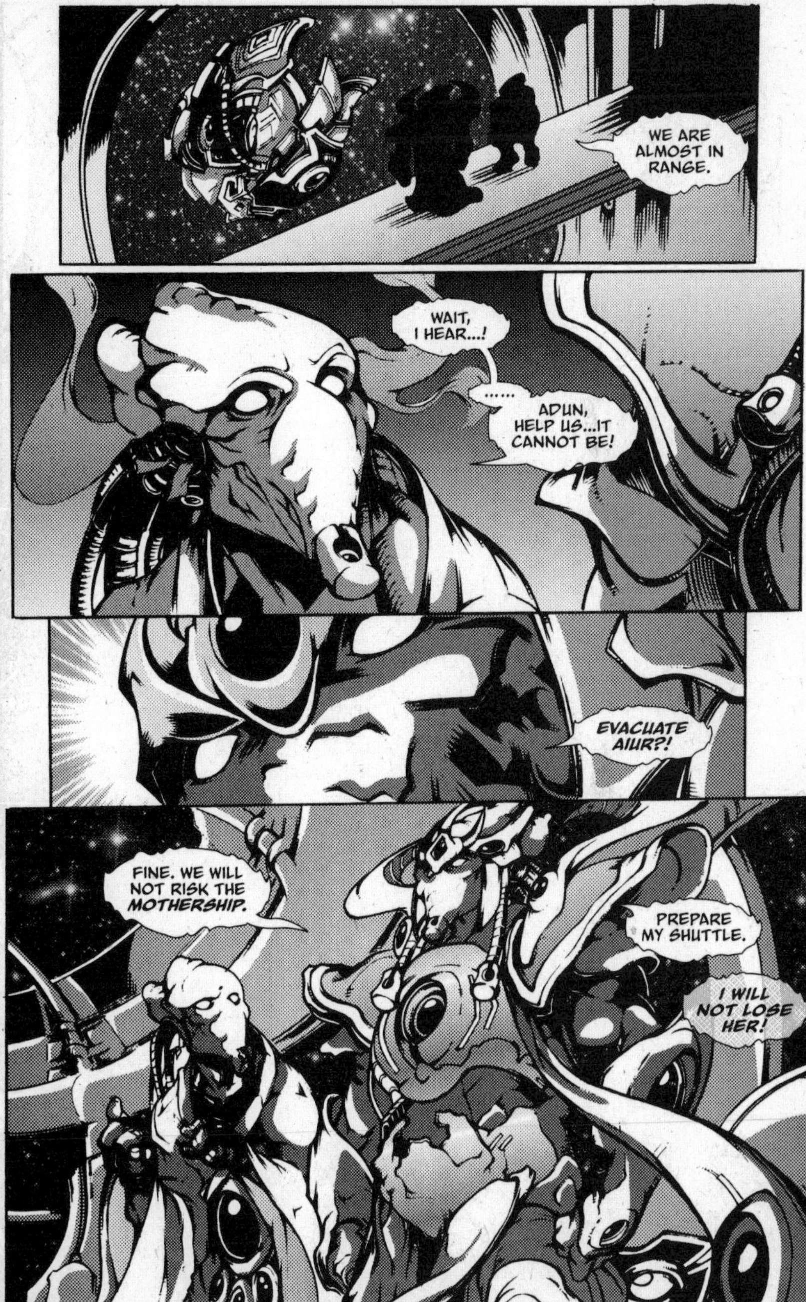
WE ARE ALMOST IN RANGE.
WAIT, I HEAR...!
......
ADUN, HELP US...IT CANNOT BE!
EVACUATE AIUR?!
FINE. WE WILL NOT RISK THE MOTHERSHIP.
PREPARE MY SHUTTLE.
I WILL NOT LOSE HER!

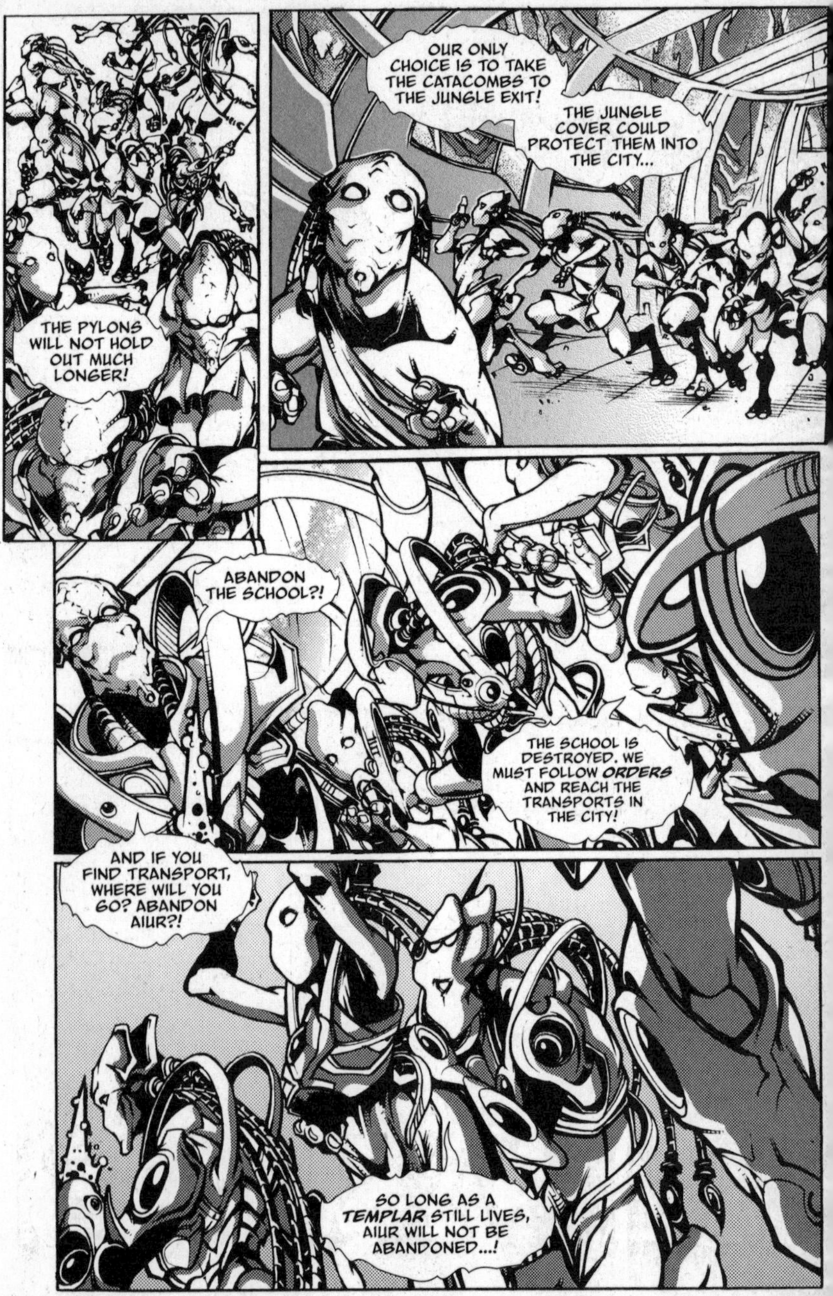
THE PYLONS WILL NOT HOLD OUT MUCH LONGER!
OUR ONLY CHOICE IS TO TAKE THE CATACOMBS TO THE JUNGLE EXIT!
THE JUNGLE COVER COULD PROTECT THEM INTO THE CITY...
ABANDON THE SCHOOL?!
THE SCHOOL IS DESTROYED. WE MUST FOLLOW ORDERS AND REACH THE TRANSPORTS IN THE CITY!
AND IF YOU FIND TRANSPORT, WHERE WILL YOU GO? ABANDON AIUR?!
SO LONG AS A TEMPLAR STILL LIVES, AIUR WILL NOT BE ABANDONED...!

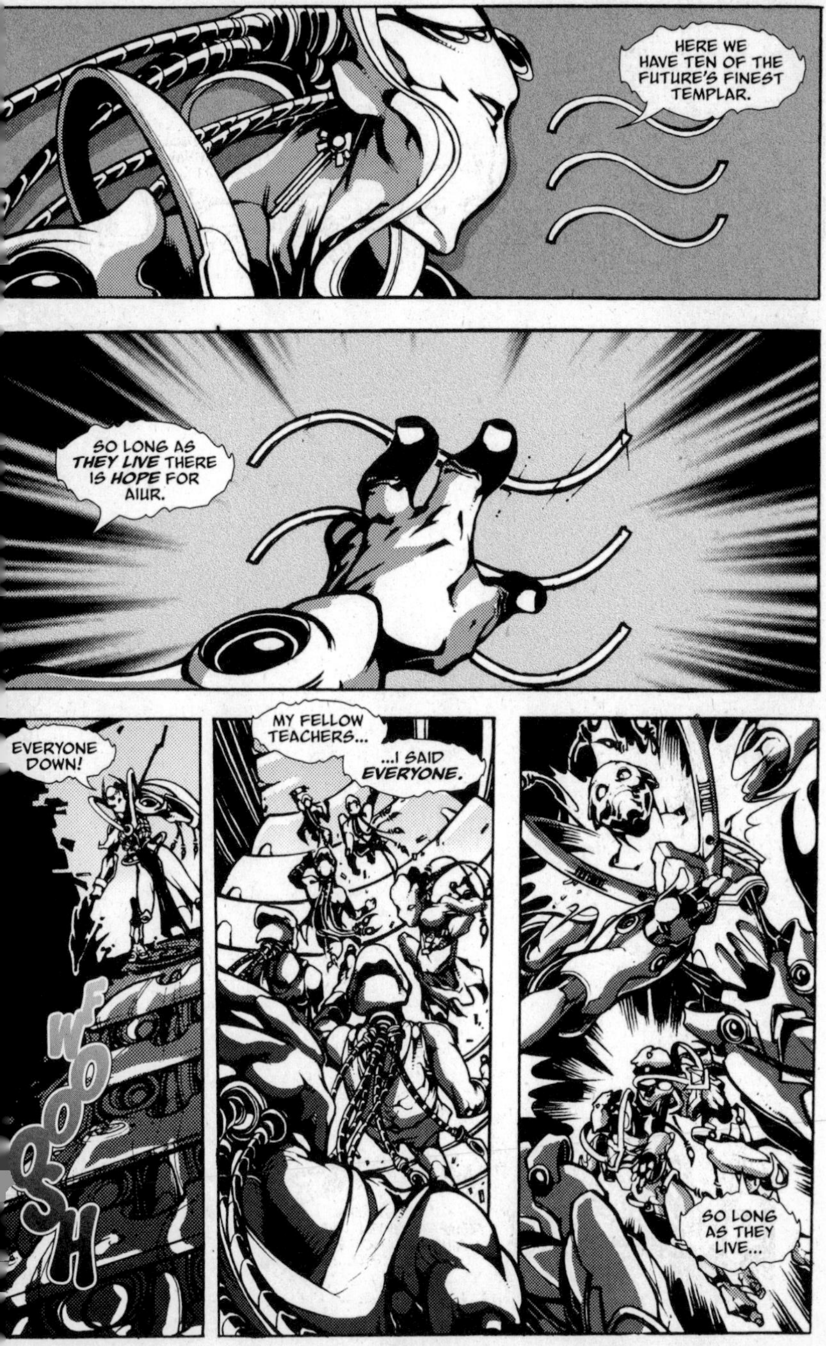
HERE WE HAVE TEN OF THE FUTURE'S FINEST TEMPLAR.
SO LONG AS *THEY LIVE* THERE IS *HOPE* FOR AIUR.
EVERYONE DOWN!
FWOOOSCH
MY FELLOW TEACHERS...
...I SAID *EVERYONE.*
SO LONG AS THEY LIVE...

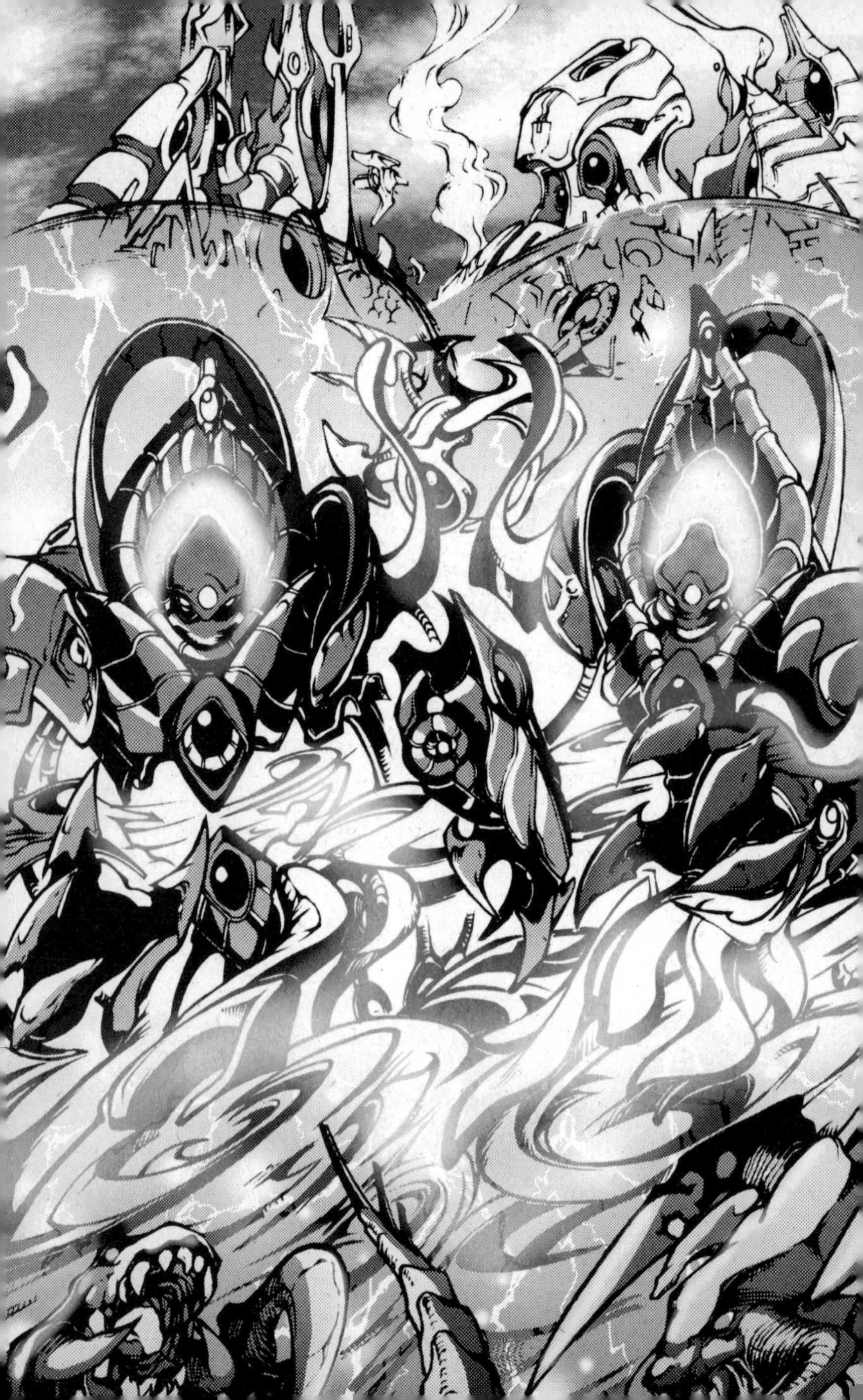

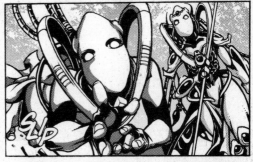

THE CREEP!

I AM NOT AFRAID!

I AM A LITTLE...

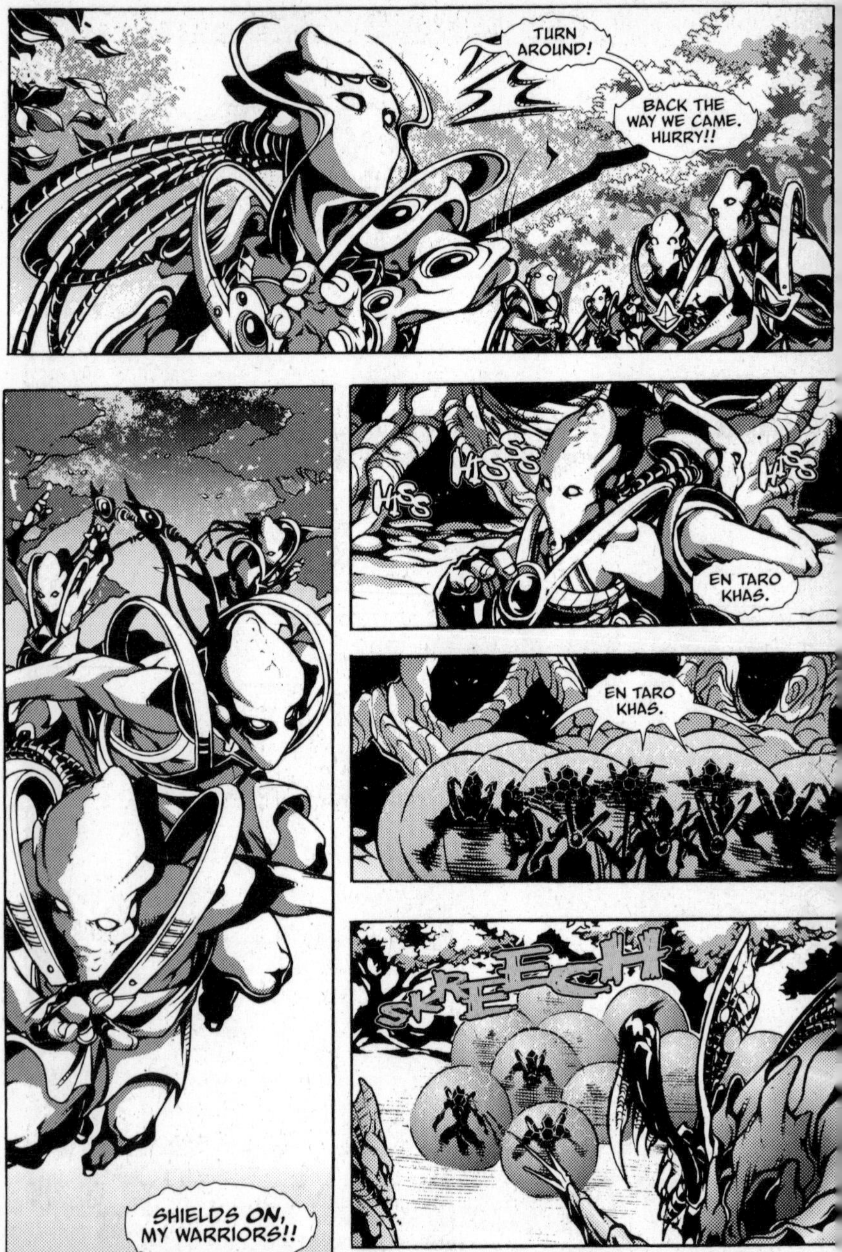
TURN AROUND!
BACK THE WAY WE CAME. HURRY!!
SHIELDS ON, MY WARRIORS!!
HISS
HISSS
HISS
EN TARO KHAS.
EN TARO KHAS.
SKREECH

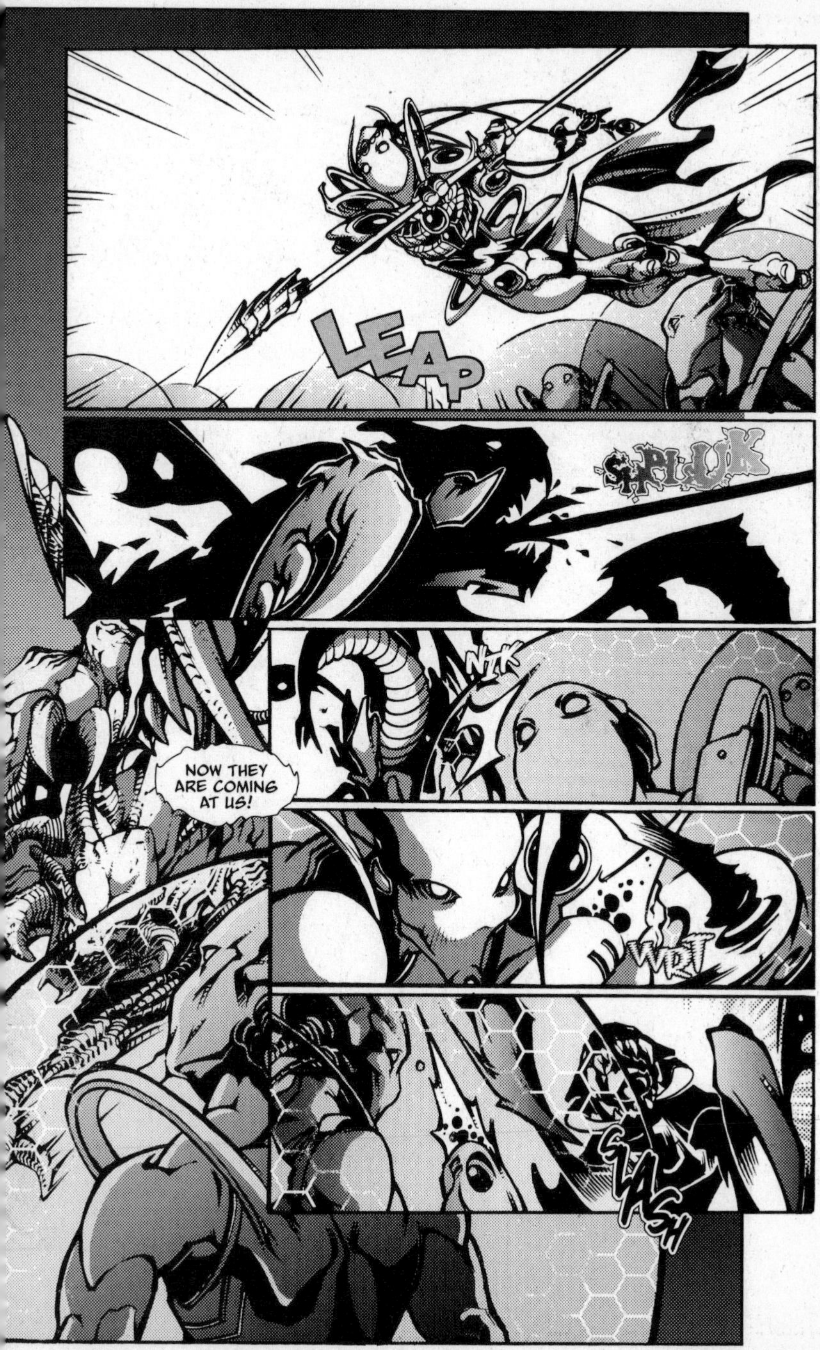
LEAP
SPLUK
NIK
NOW THEY ARE COMING AT US!
WRT
SLASH

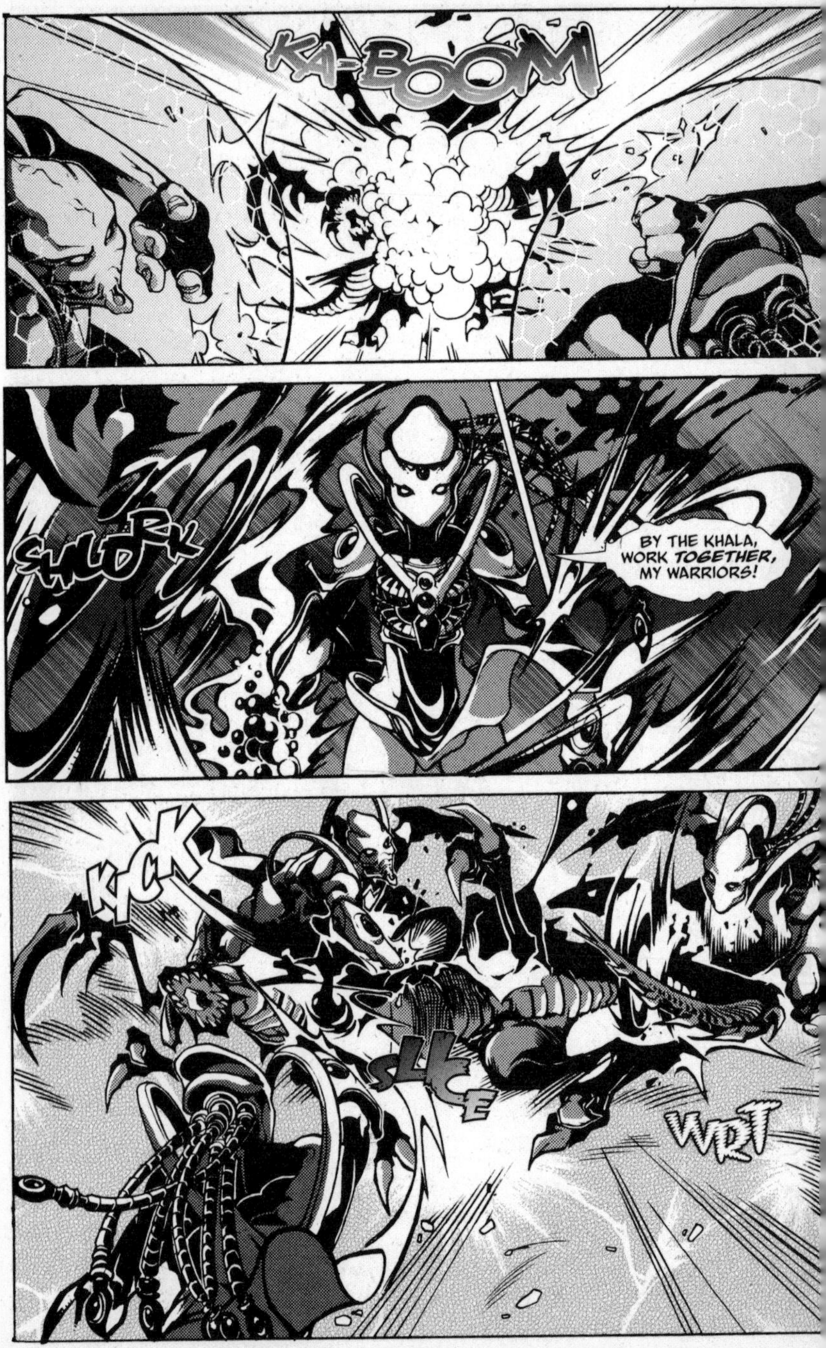
KA-BOOM
SHLORK
BY THE KHALA, WORK TOGETHER, MY WARRIORS!
KICK
SLICE
WRT

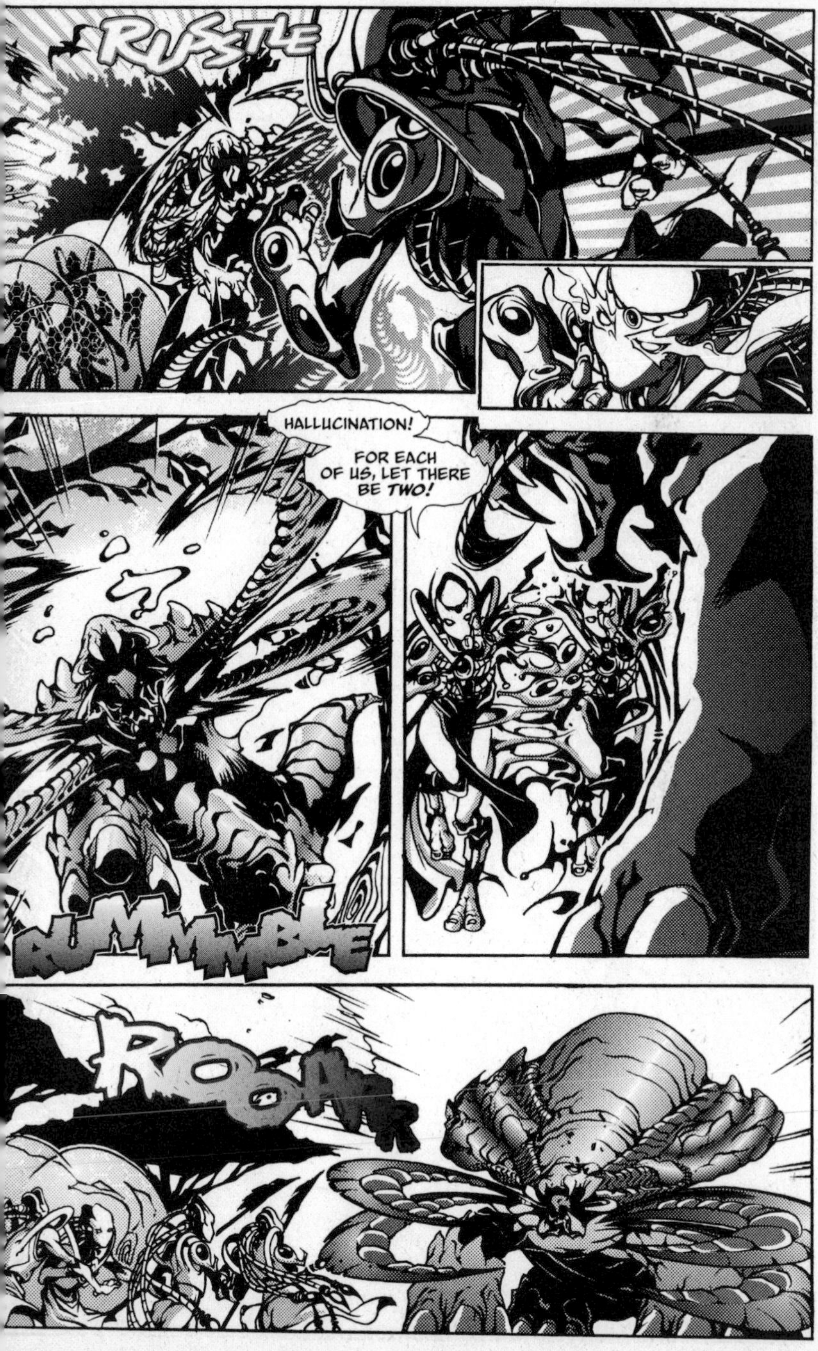
RUSSTLE
HALLUCINATION!
FOR EACH OF US, LET THERE BE *TWO!*

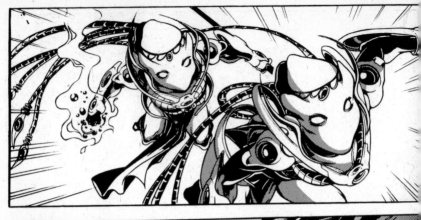

SWOOSH

POP

POP

PSIONIC STORM!

BAM

SMASH

UNH!

THE ENERGIES... HAVE FAILED.

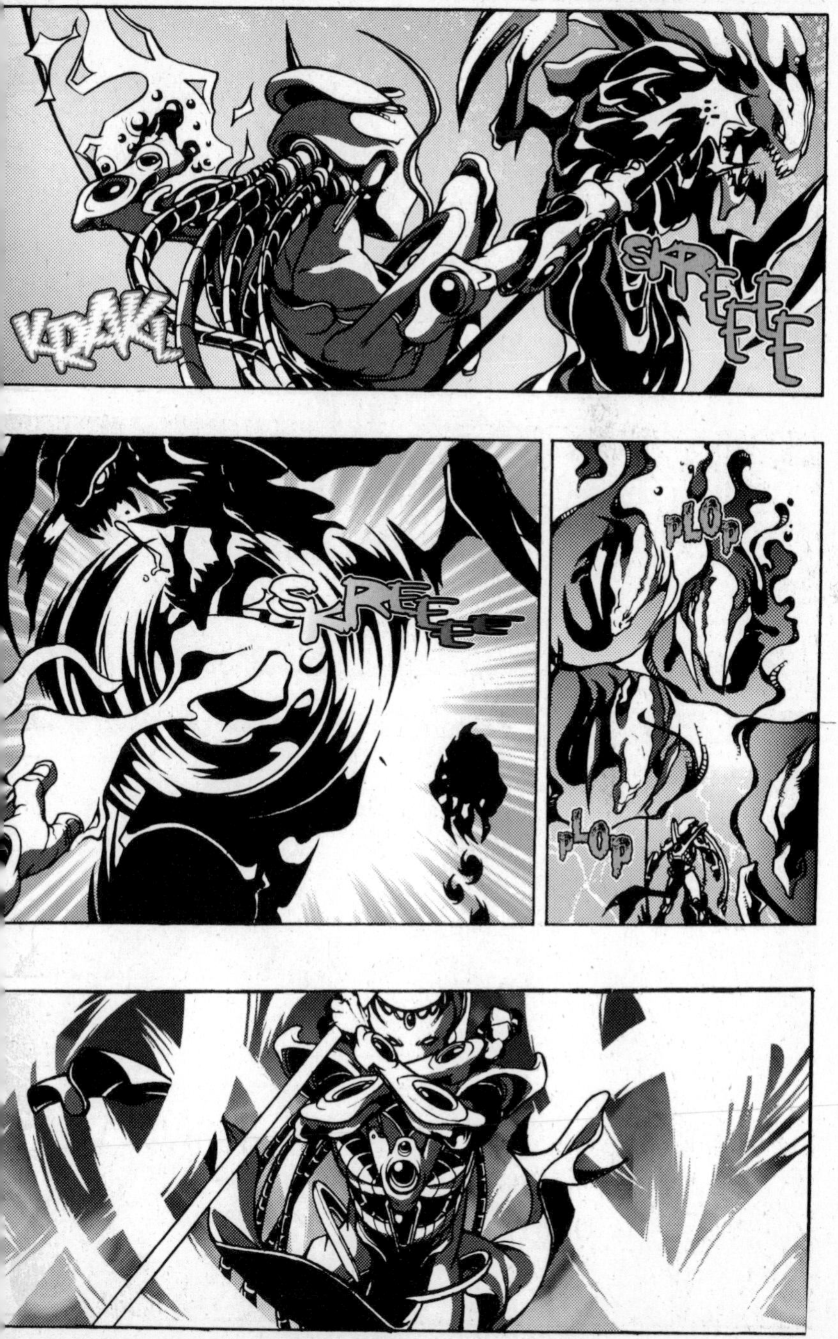
KRAKL
SKREEEEE
SKREEEE
PLOP
PLOP

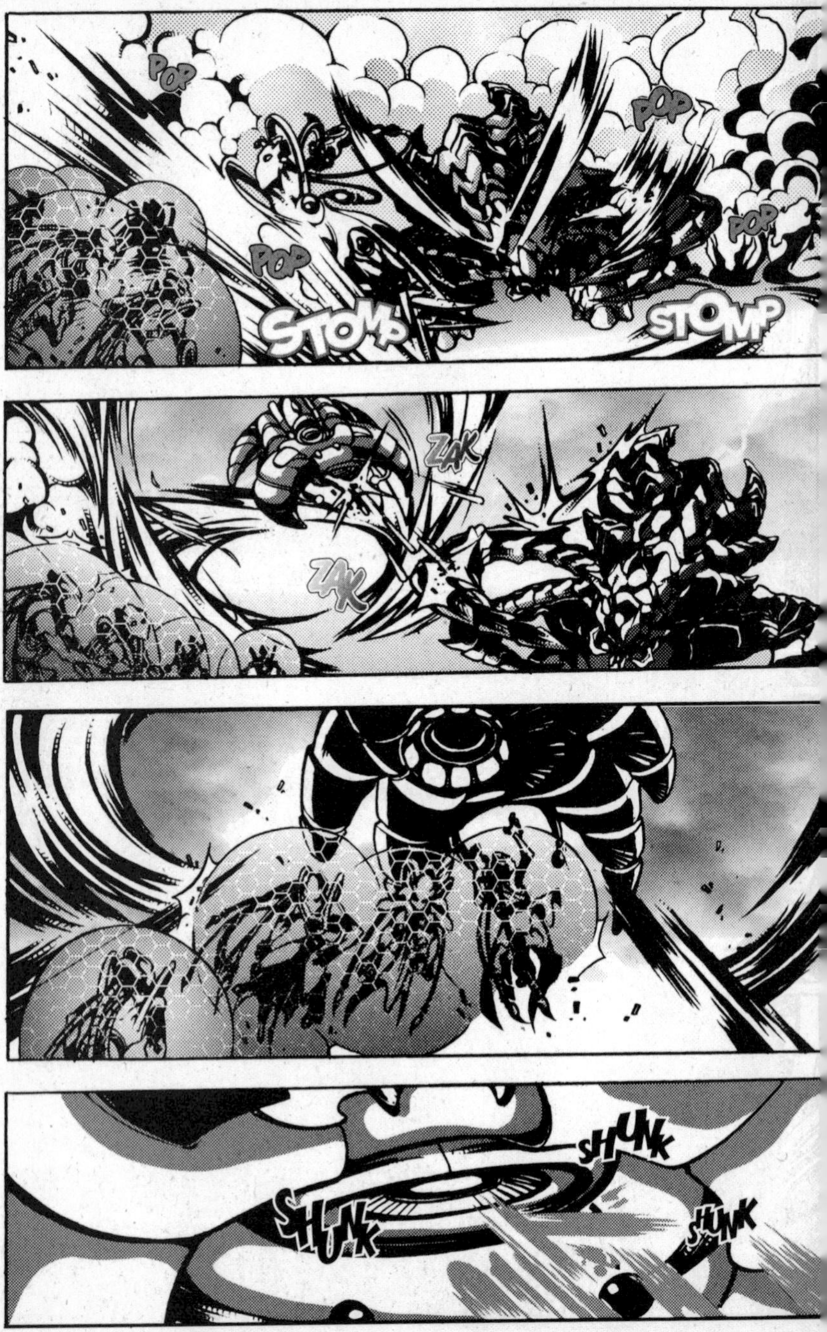
POP
POP
POP
POP
STOMP
STOMP
ZAK
ZAK
SHUNK
SHUNK
SHUNK

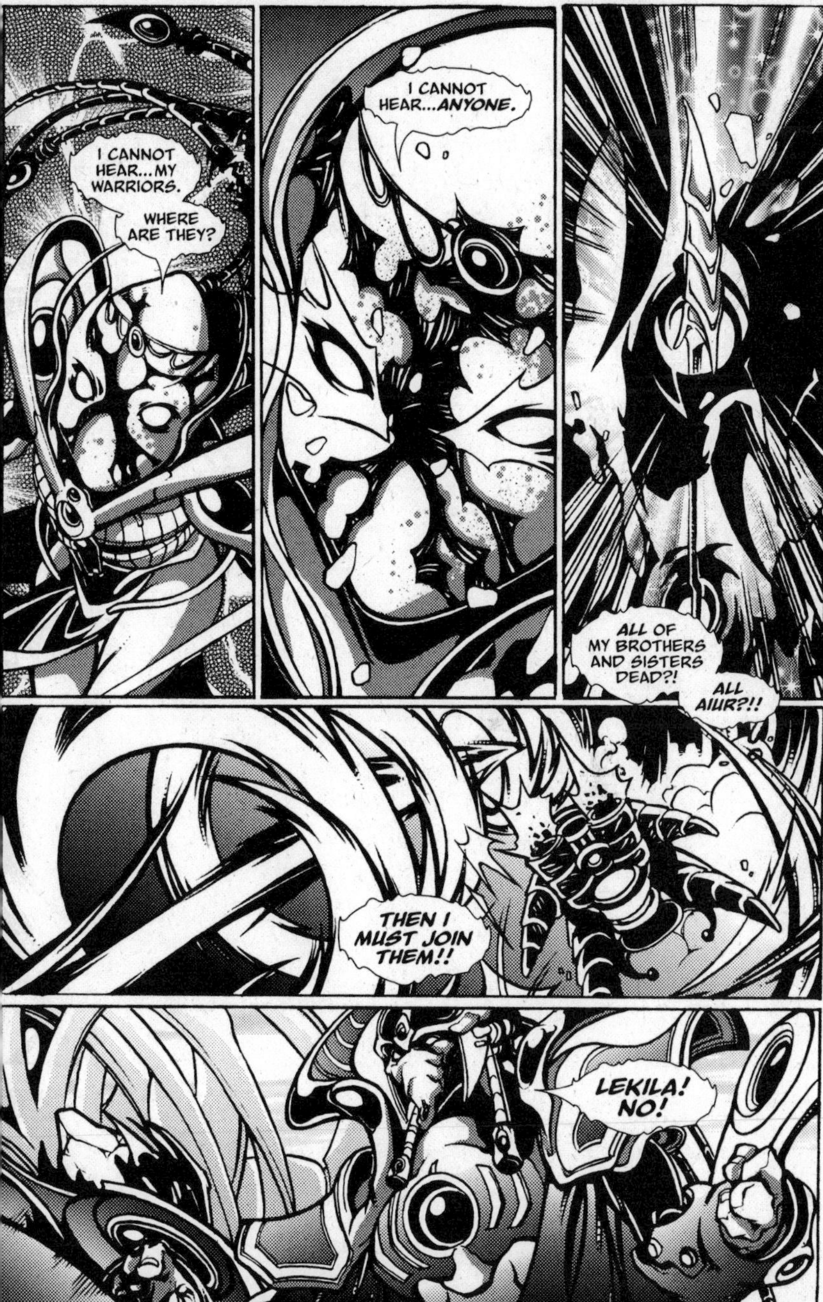
I CANNOT HEAR...MY WARRIORS.
WHERE ARE THEY?
I CANNOT HEAR...ANYONE.
ALL OF MY BROTHERS AND SISTERS DEAD?!
ALL AIUR?!!
THEN I MUST JOIN THEM!!
LEKILA! NO!

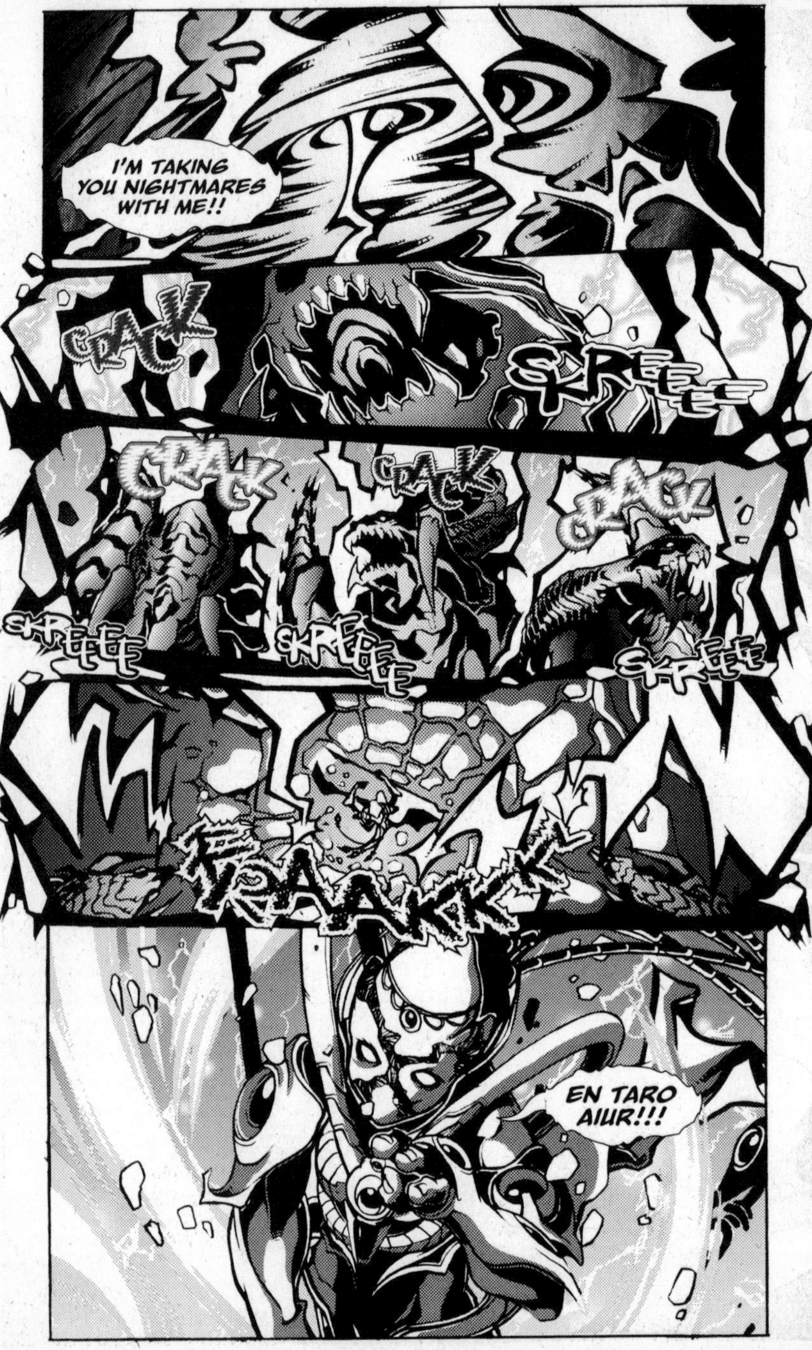
I'M TAKING YOU NIGHTMARES WITH ME!!
CRACK
SKREEEE
CRACK
CRACK
CRACK
SKREEEE
SKREEEE
SKREEEE
KRAAKKK
EN TARO AIUR!!!

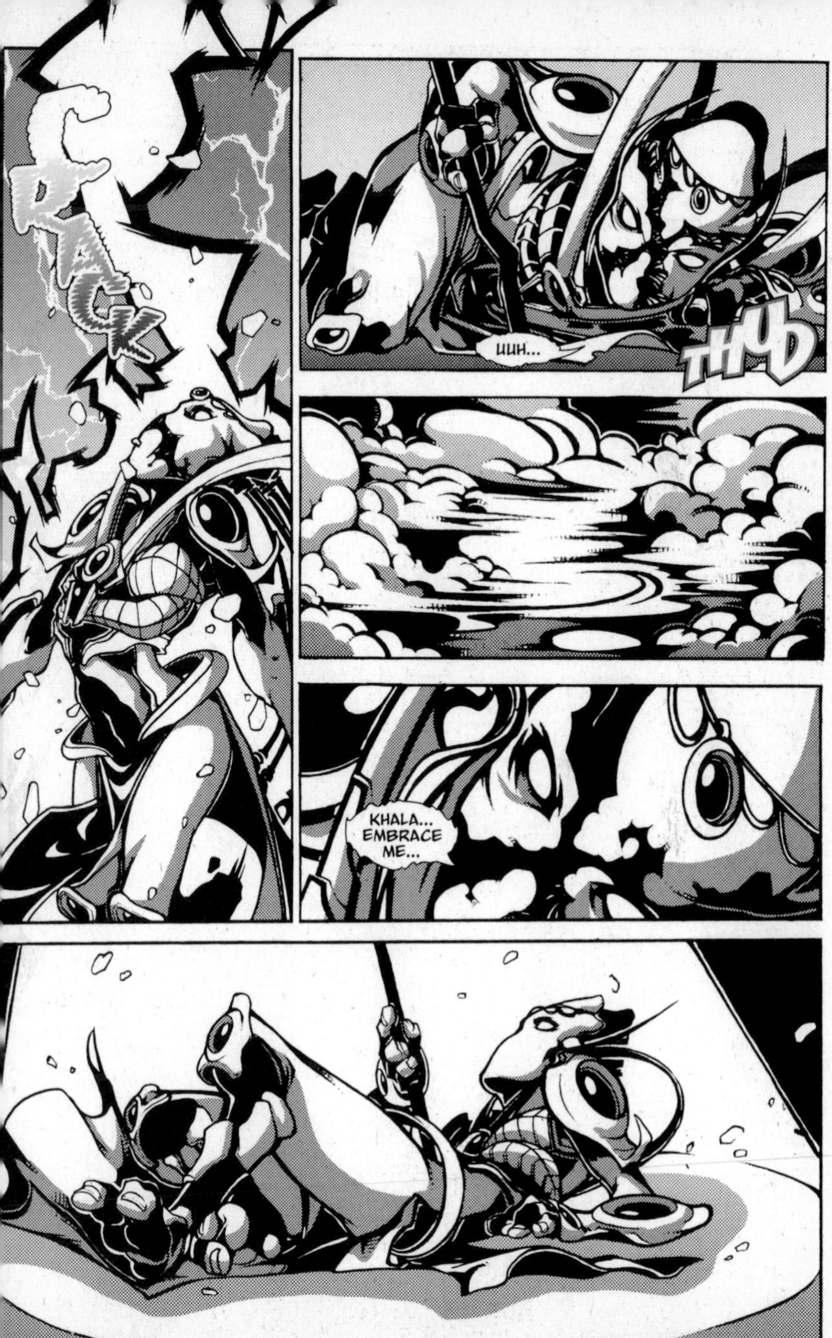
CRACK
UUH...
THUD
KHALA... EMBRACE ME...

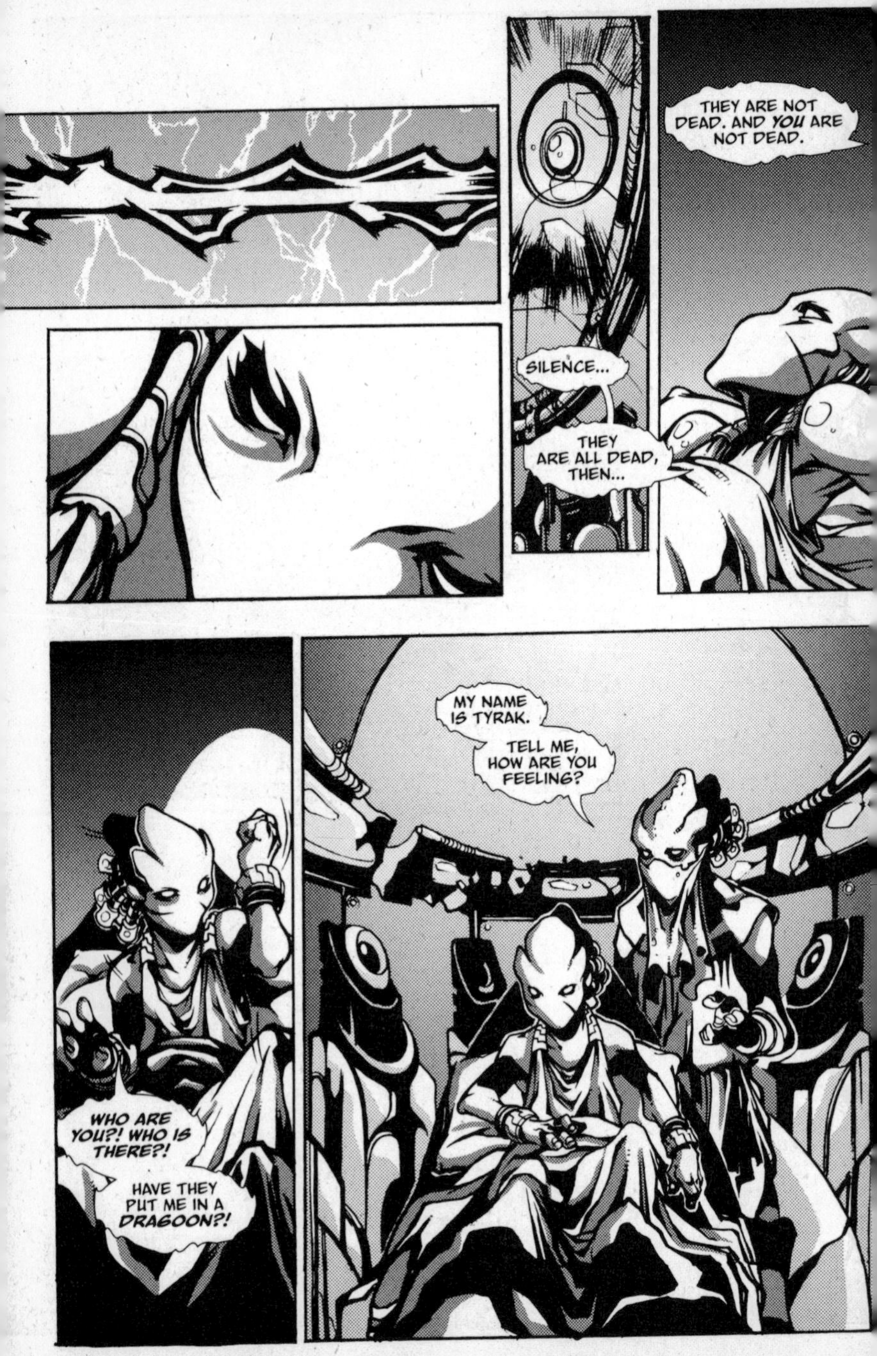
SILENCE...
THEY ARE ALL DEAD, THEN...
THEY ARE NOT DEAD. AND *YOU* ARE NOT DEAD.
WHO ARE YOU?! WHO IS THERE?!
HAVE THEY PUT ME IN A *DRAGOON*?!
MY NAME IS TYRAK.
TELL ME, HOW ARE YOU FEELING?

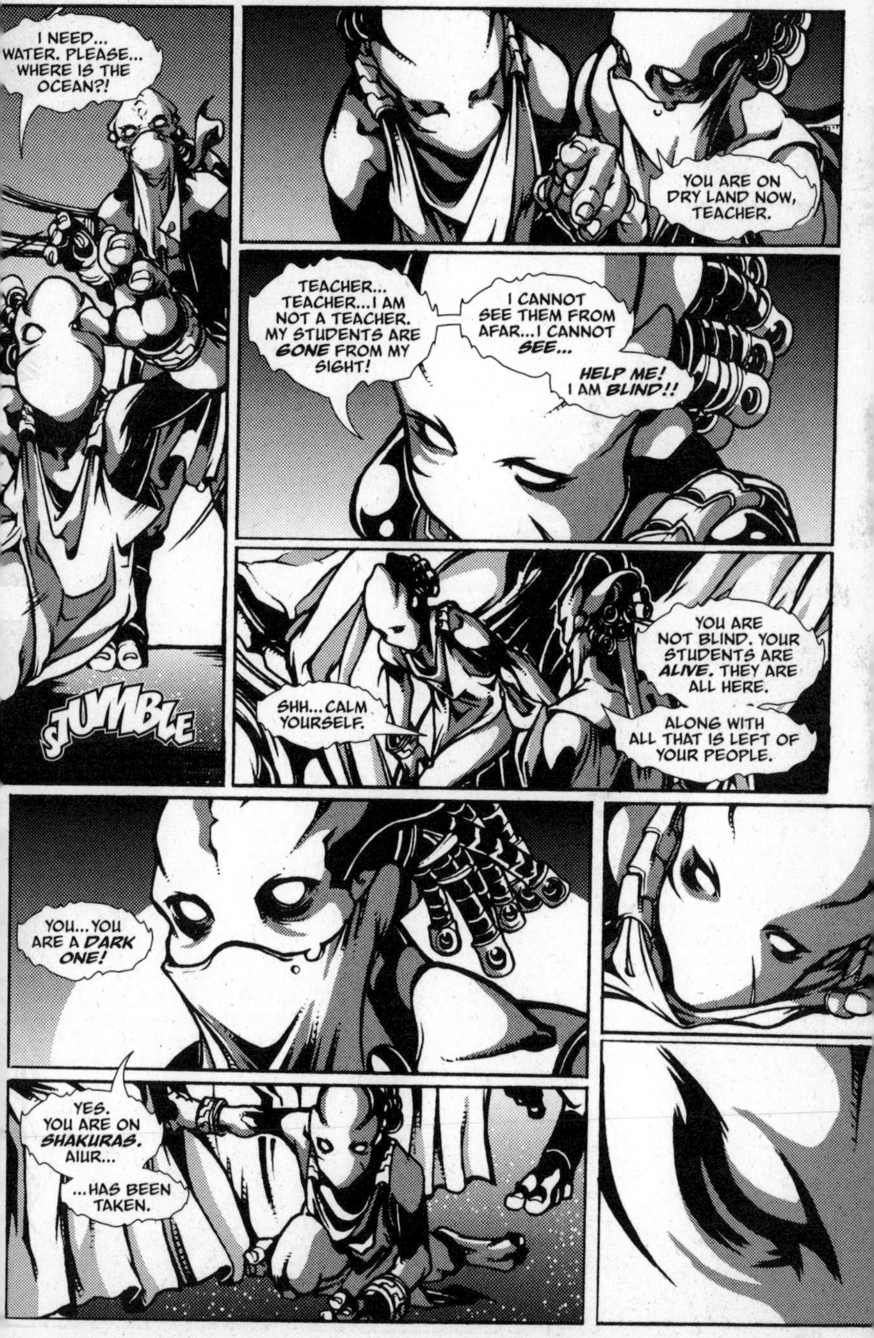
I NEED... WATER. PLEASE... WHERE IS THE OCEAN?!
STUMBLE
YOU ARE ON DRY LAND NOW, TEACHER.
TEACHER... TEACHER...I AM NOT A TEACHER. MY STUDENTS ARE *GONE* FROM MY SIGHT!
I CANNOT SEE THEM FROM AFAR...I CANNOT *SEE*...
HELP ME! I AM *BLIND!!*
SHH...CALM YOURSELF.
YOU ARE NOT BLIND. YOUR STUDENTS ARE *ALIVE.* THEY ARE ALL HERE.
ALONG WITH ALL THAT IS LEFT OF YOUR PEOPLE.
YOU...YOU ARE A *DARK ONE!*
YES. YOU ARE ON *SHAKURAS.* AIUR...
...HAS BEEN TAKEN.

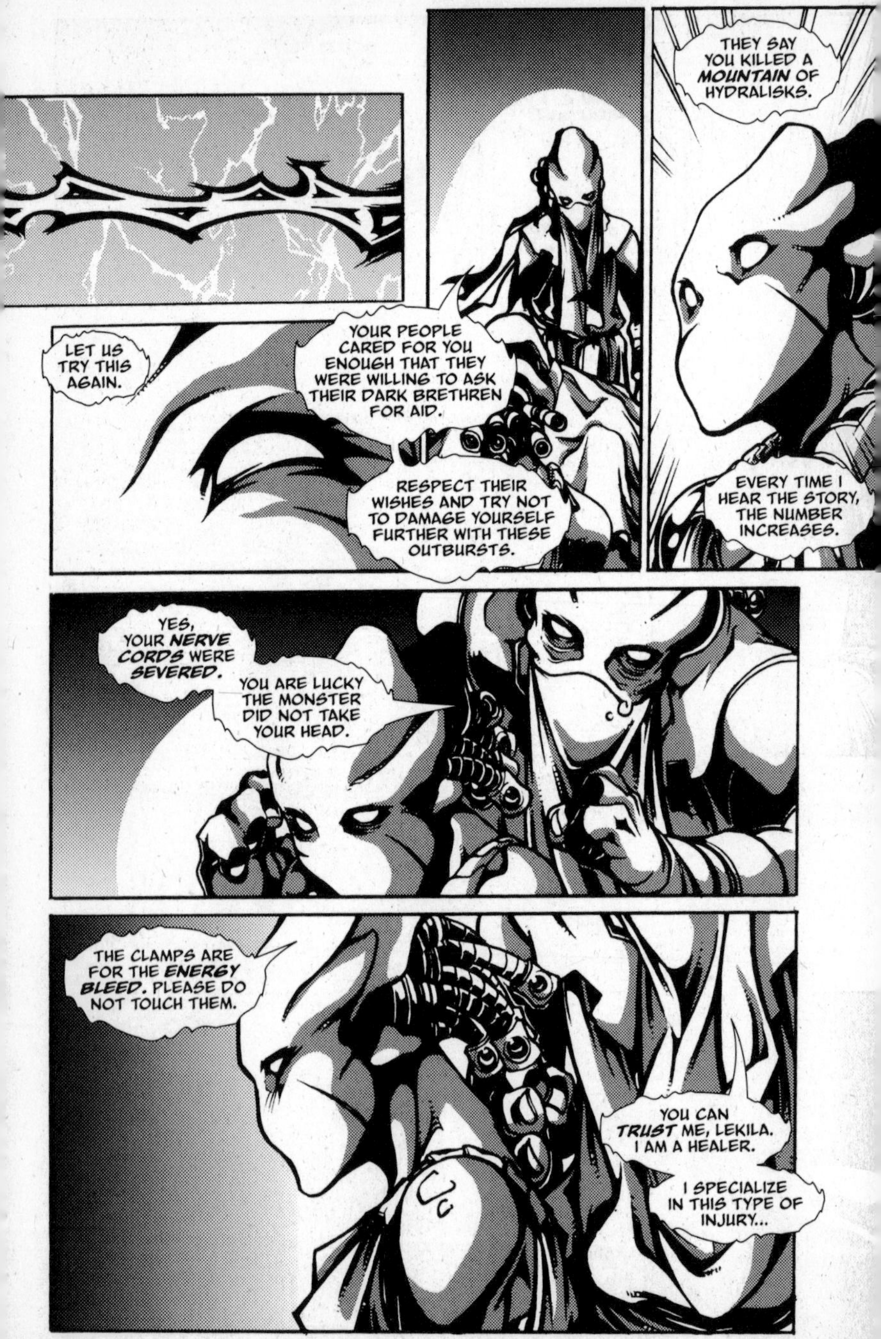
LET US TRY THIS AGAIN.
YOUR PEOPLE CARED FOR YOU ENOUGH THAT THEY WERE WILLING TO ASK THEIR DARK BRETHREN FOR AID.
RESPECT THEIR WISHES AND TRY NOT TO DAMAGE YOURSELF FURTHER WITH THESE OUTBURSTS.
THEY SAY YOU KILLED A MOUNTAIN OF HYDRALISKS.
EVERY TIME I HEAR THE STORY, THE NUMBER INCREASES.
YES, YOUR NERVE CORDS WERE SEVERED.
YOU ARE LUCKY THE MONSTER DID NOT TAKE YOUR HEAD.
THE CLAMPS ARE FOR THE ENERGY BLEED. PLEASE DO NOT TOUCH THEM.
YOU CAN TRUST ME, LEKILA. I AM A HEALER.
I SPECIALIZE IN THIS TYPE OF INJURY...

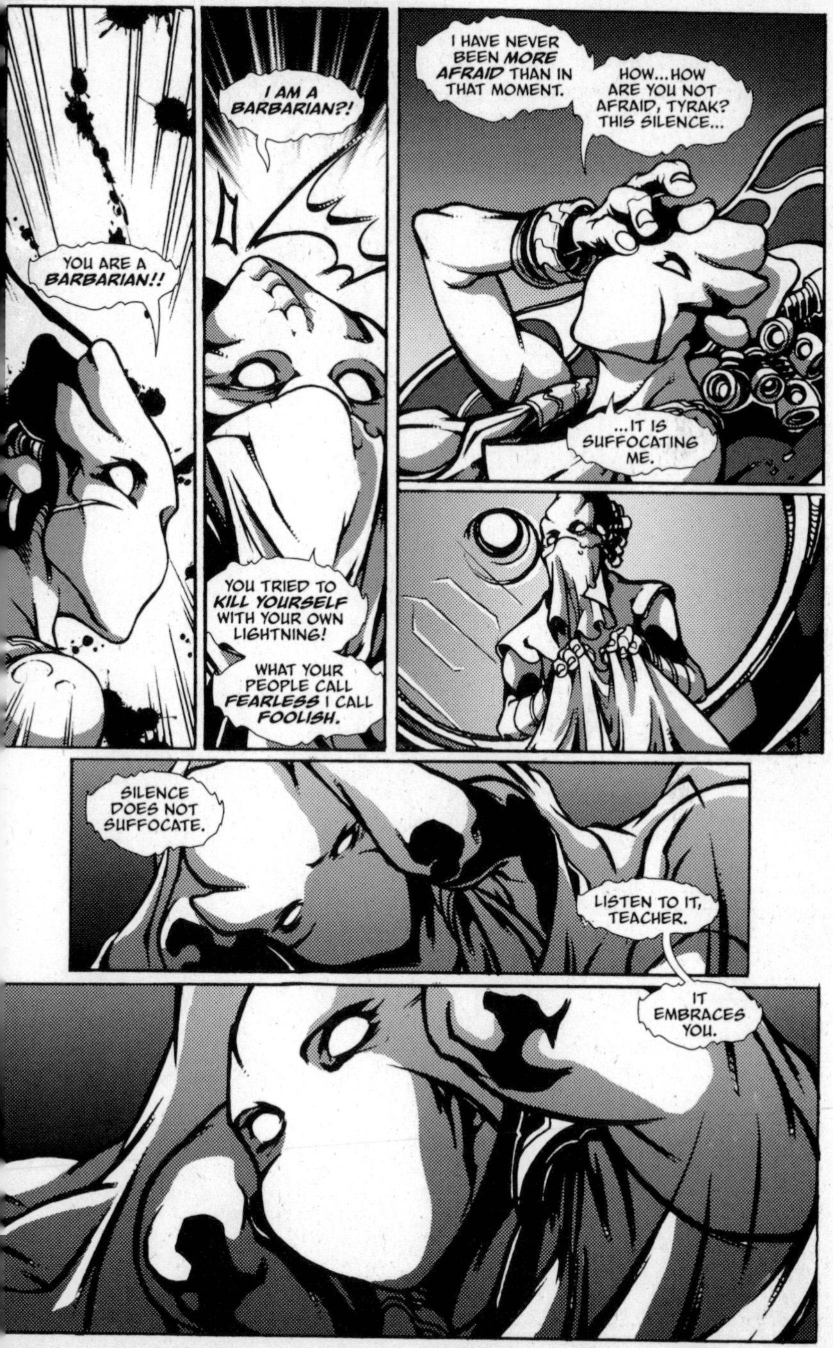
YOU ARE A BARBARIAN!!
I AM A BARBARIAN?!
YOU TRIED TO KILL YOURSELF WITH YOUR OWN LIGHTNING!
WHAT YOUR PEOPLE CALL FEARLESS I CALL FOOLISH.
I HAVE NEVER BEEN MORE AFRAID THAN IN THAT MOMENT.
HOW...HOW ARE YOU NOT AFRAID, TYRAK? THIS SILENCE...
...IT IS SUFFOCATING ME.
SILENCE DOES NOT SUFFOCATE.
LISTEN TO IT, TEACHER.
IT EMBRACES YOU.

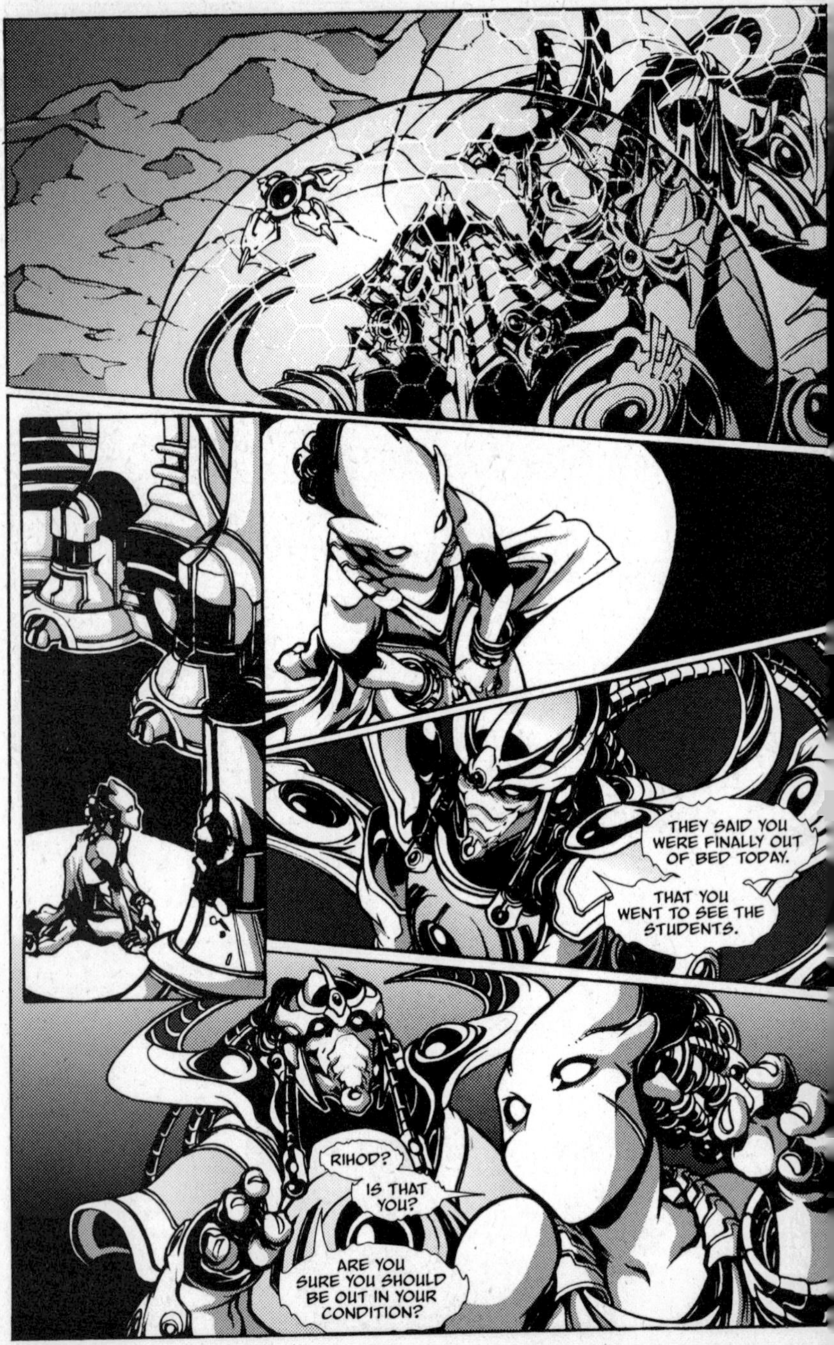
THEY SAID YOU WERE FINALLY OUT OF BED TODAY.
THAT YOU WENT TO SEE THE STUDENTS.
RIHOD?
IS THAT YOU?
ARE YOU SURE YOU SHOULD BE OUT IN YOUR CONDITION?

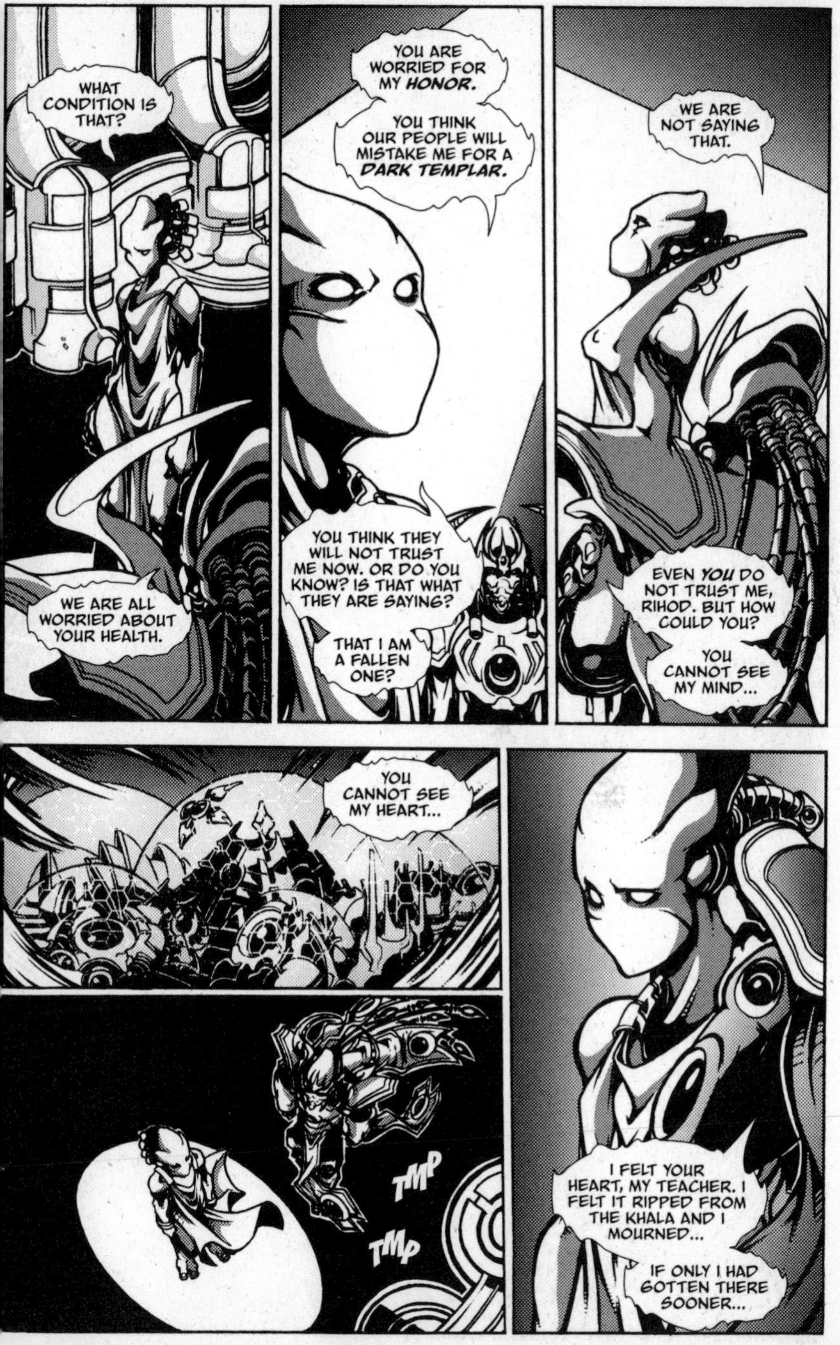
WHAT CONDITION IS THAT?
WE ARE ALL WORRIED ABOUT YOUR HEALTH.
YOU ARE WORRIED FOR MY *HONOR.*
YOU THINK OUR PEOPLE WILL MISTAKE ME FOR A *DARK TEMPLAR.*
YOU THINK THEY WILL NOT TRUST ME NOW. OR DO YOU KNOW? IS THAT WHAT THEY ARE SAYING?
THAT I AM A FALLEN ONE?
WE ARE NOT SAYING THAT.
EVEN *YOU* DO NOT TRUST ME, RIHOD. BUT HOW COULD YOU?
YOU CANNOT SEE MY MIND...
YOU CANNOT SEE MY HEART...
TMP
TMP
I FELT YOUR HEART, MY TEACHER. I FELT IT RIPPED FROM THE KHALA AND I MOURNED...
IF ONLY I HAD GOTTEN THERE SOONER...

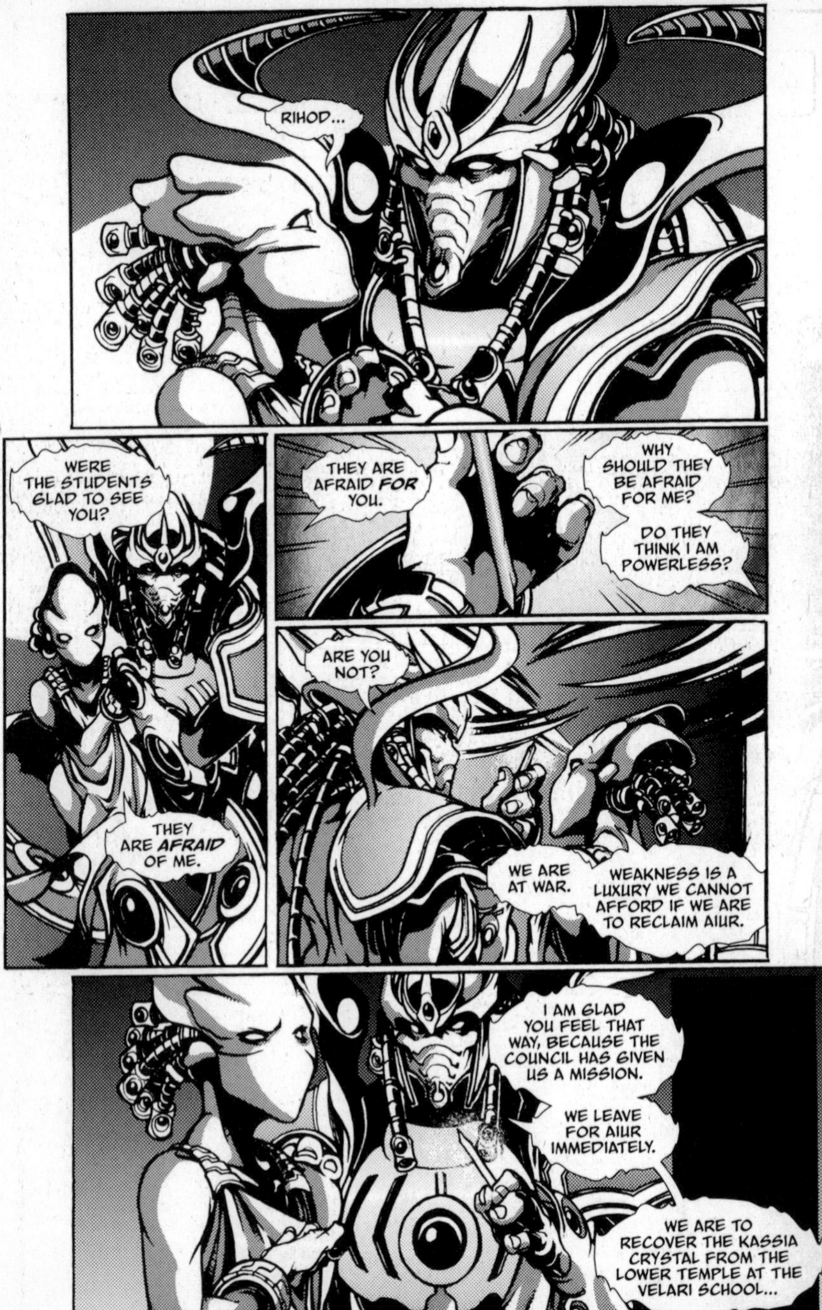
RIHOD...
WERE THE STUDENTS GLAD TO SEE YOU?
THEY ARE *AFRAID* OF ME.
THEY ARE AFRAID *FOR* YOU.
WHY SHOULD THEY BE AFRAID FOR ME?
DO THEY THINK I AM POWERLESS?
ARE YOU NOT?
WE ARE AT WAR.
WEAKNESS IS A LUXURY WE CANNOT AFFORD IF WE ARE TO RECLAIM AIUR.
I AM GLAD YOU FEEL THAT WAY, BECAUSE THE COUNCIL HAS GIVEN US A MISSION.
WE LEAVE FOR AIUR IMMEDIATELY.
WE ARE TO RECOVER THE KASSIA CRYSTAL FROM THE LOWER TEMPLE AT THE VELARI SCHOOL...

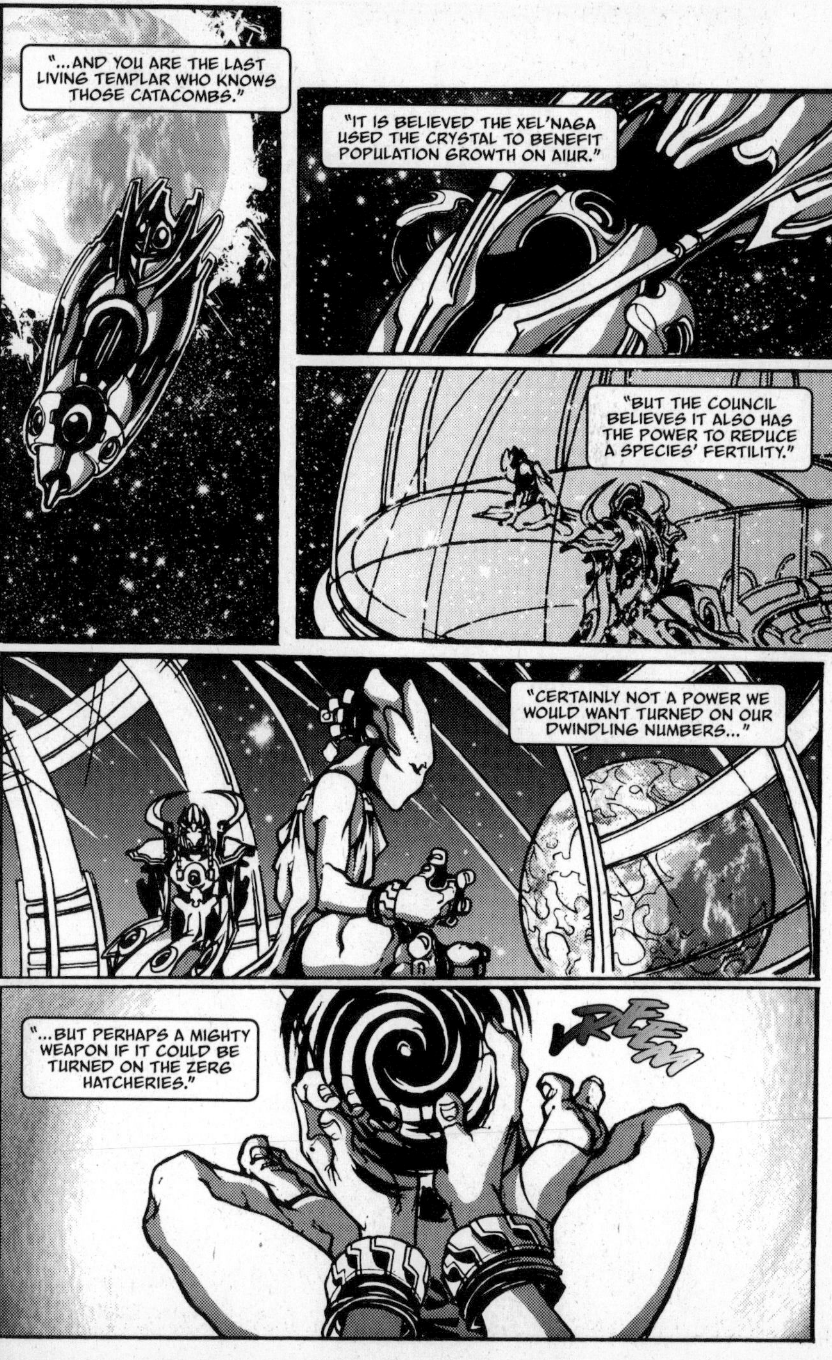
"...AND YOU ARE THE LAST LIVING TEMPLAR WHO KNOWS THOSE CATACOMBS."
"IT IS BELIEVED THE XEL'NAGA USED THE CRYSTAL TO BENEFIT POPULATION GROWTH ON AIUR."
"BUT THE COUNCIL BELIEVES IT ALSO HAS THE POWER TO REDUCE A SPECIES' FERTILITY."
"CERTAINLY NOT A POWER WE WOULD WANT TURNED ON OUR DWINDLING NUMBERS..."
"...BUT PERHAPS A MIGHTY WEAPON IF IT COULD BE TURNED ON THE ZERG HATCHERIES."
VREEM

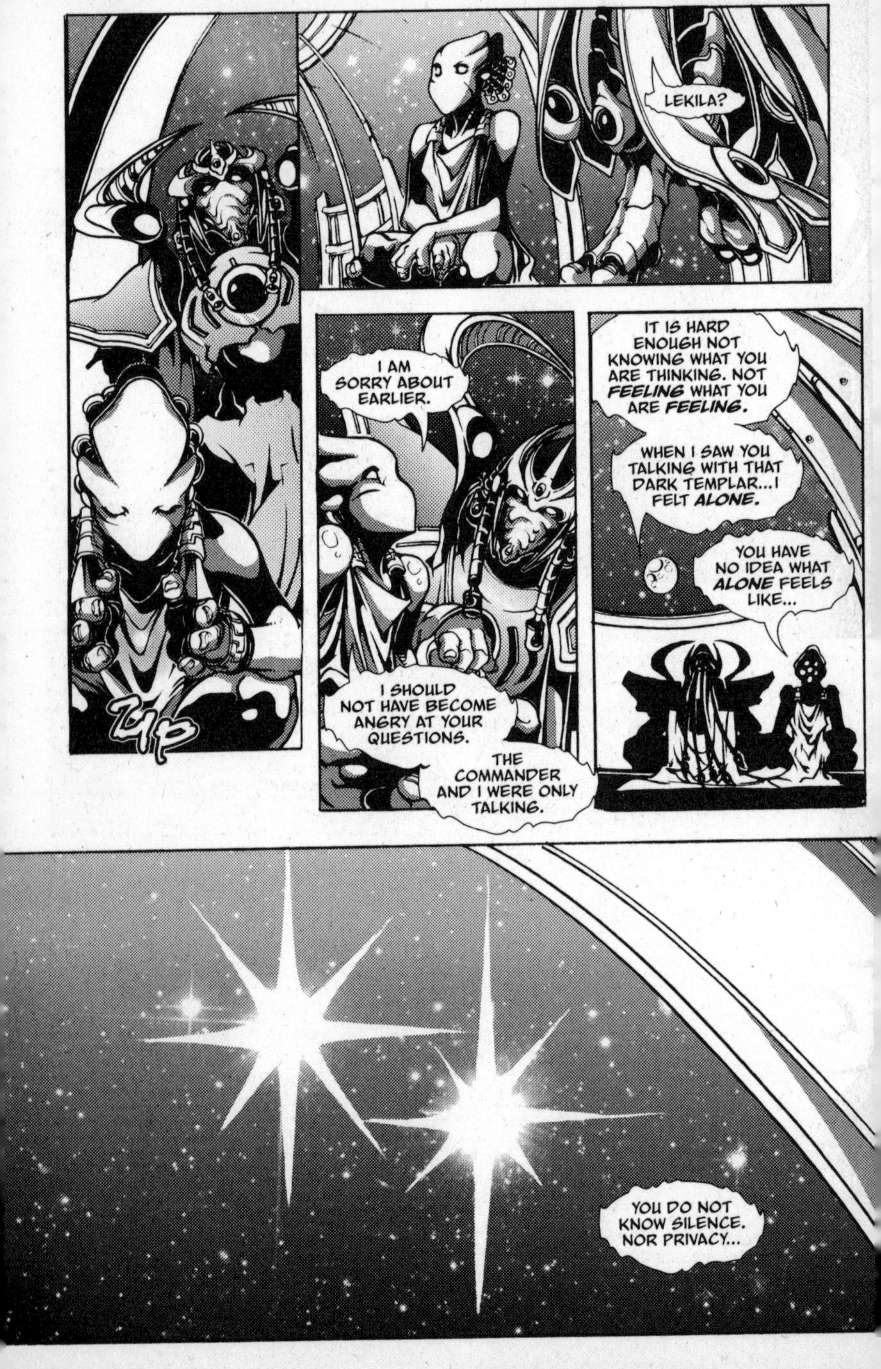

ZIP
LEKILA?
I AM SORRY ABOUT EARLIER.
I SHOULD NOT HAVE BECOME ANGRY AT YOUR QUESTIONS.
THE COMMANDER AND I WERE ONLY TALKING.
IT IS HARD ENOUGH NOT KNOWING WHAT YOU ARE THINKING. NOT FEELING WHAT YOU ARE FEELING.
WHEN I SAW YOU TALKING WITH THAT DARK TEMPLAR...I FELT ALONE.
YOU HAVE NO IDEA WHAT ALONE FEELS LIKE...
YOU DO NOT KNOW SILENCE. NOR PRIVACY...

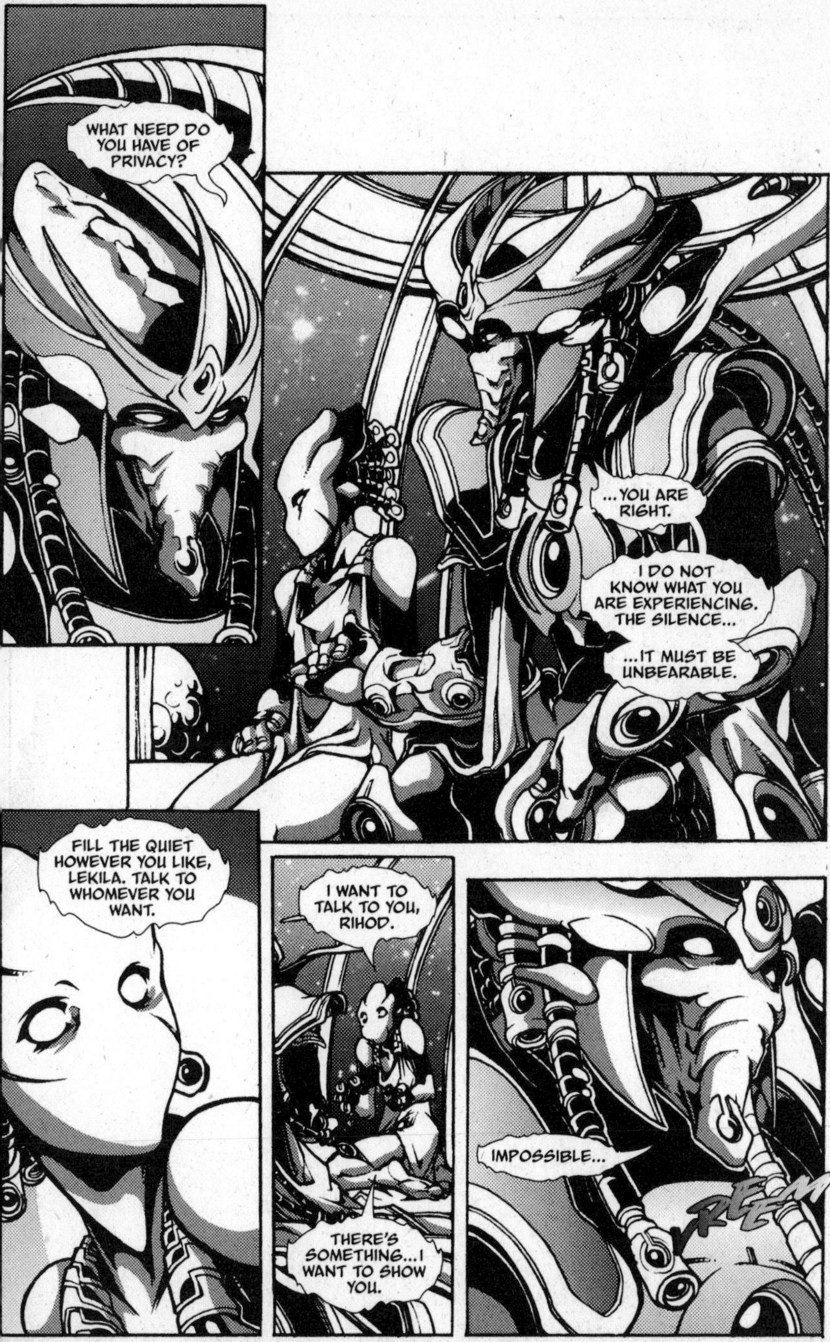
WHAT NEED DO YOU HAVE OF PRIVACY?
...YOU ARE RIGHT.
I DO NOT KNOW WHAT YOU ARE EXPERIENCING. THE SILENCE...
...IT MUST BE UNBEARABLE.
FILL THE QUIET HOWEVER YOU LIKE, LEKILA. TALK TO WHOMEVER YOU WANT.
I WANT TO TALK TO YOU, RIHOD.
THERE'S SOMETHING...I WANT TO SHOW YOU.
IMPOSSIBLE...

Velari School
Catacombs

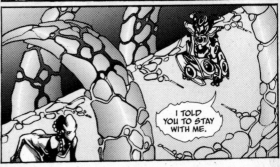

I TOLD YOU TO STAY WITH ME.

AND I TOLD *YOU* TO KEEP UP!

THIS WAY.

FOLLOW HER.

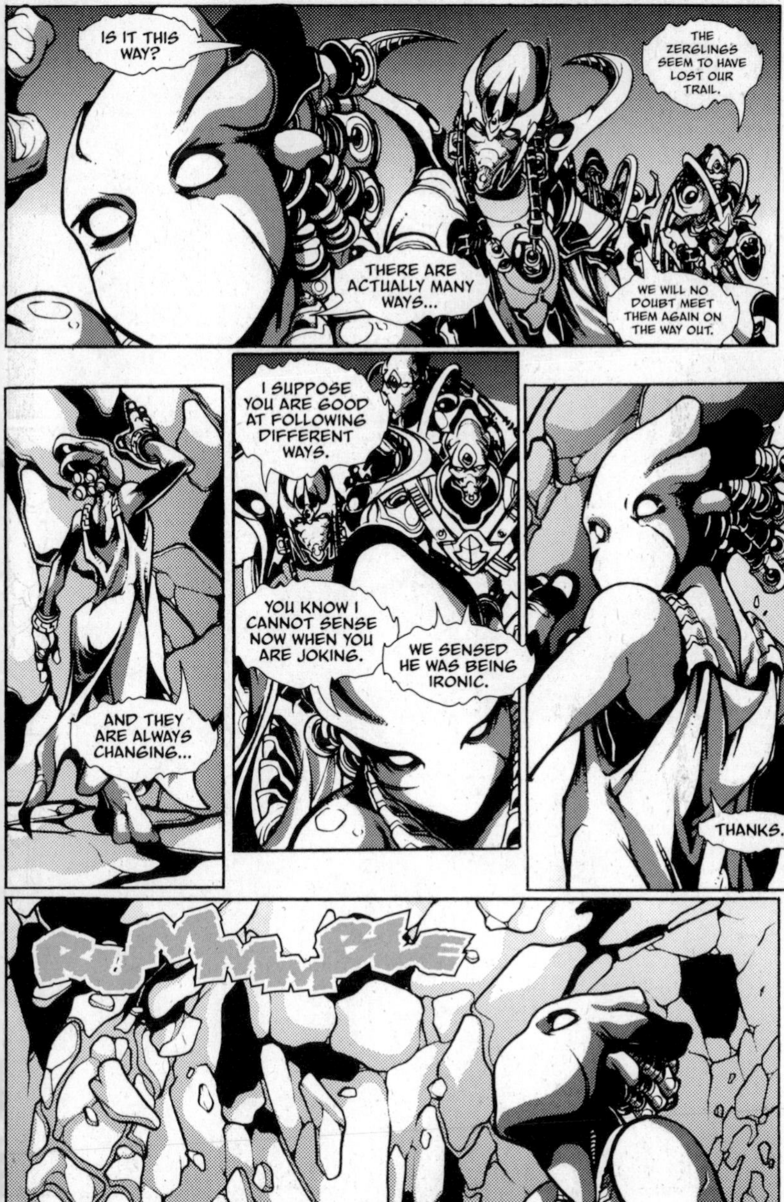
IS IT THIS WAY?
THE ZERGLINGS SEEM TO HAVE LOST OUR TRAIL.
THERE ARE ACTUALLY MANY WAYS...
WE WILL NO DOUBT MEET THEM AGAIN ON THE WAY OUT.
AND THEY ARE ALWAYS CHANGING...
I SUPPOSE YOU ARE GOOD AT FOLLOWING DIFFERENT WAYS.
YOU KNOW I CANNOT SENSE NOW WHEN YOU ARE JOKING.
WE SENSED HE WAS BEING IRONIC.
THANKS...
RUMMMBLE

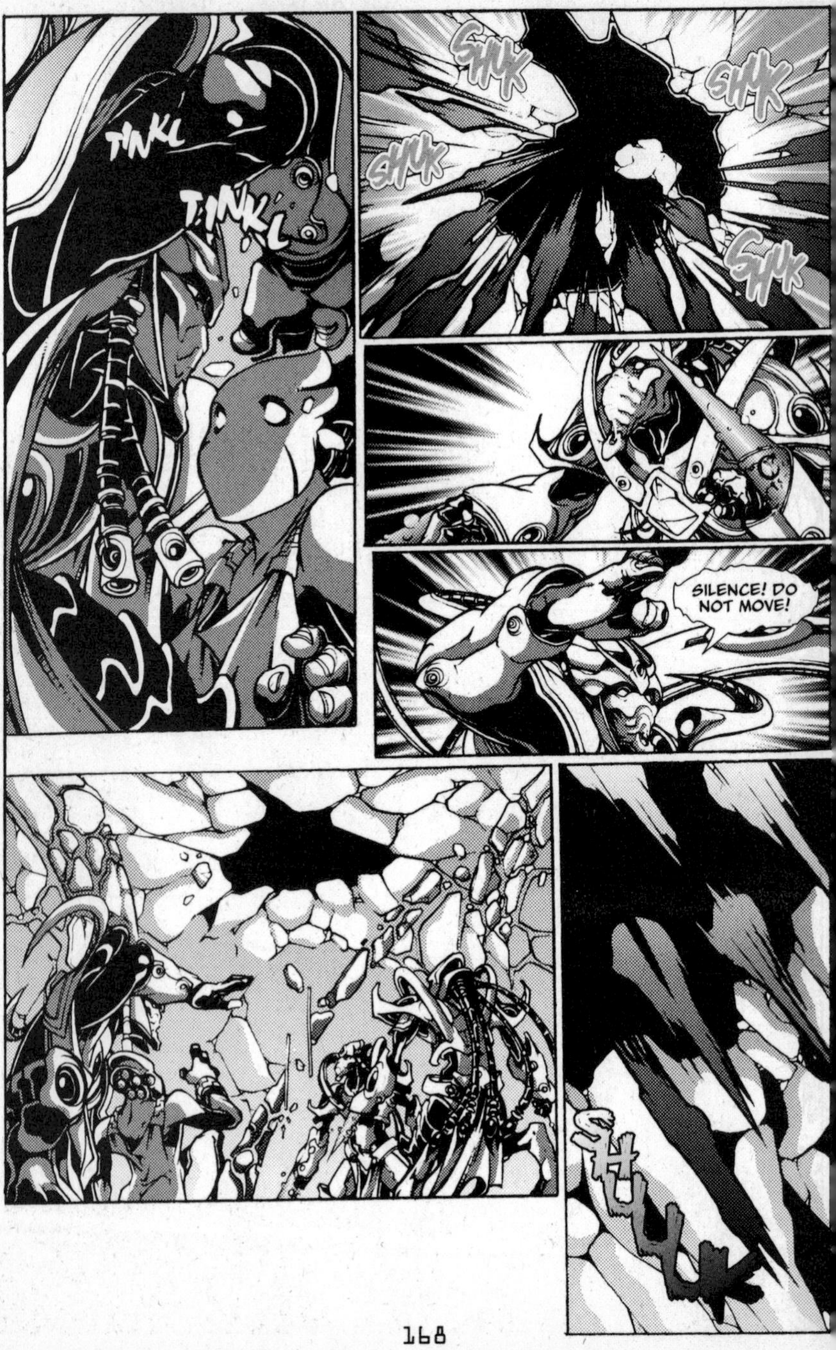
TINKL
TINKL
SHUK
SHUK
SHUK
SHUK
SILENCE! DO NOT MOVE!
SHUUK

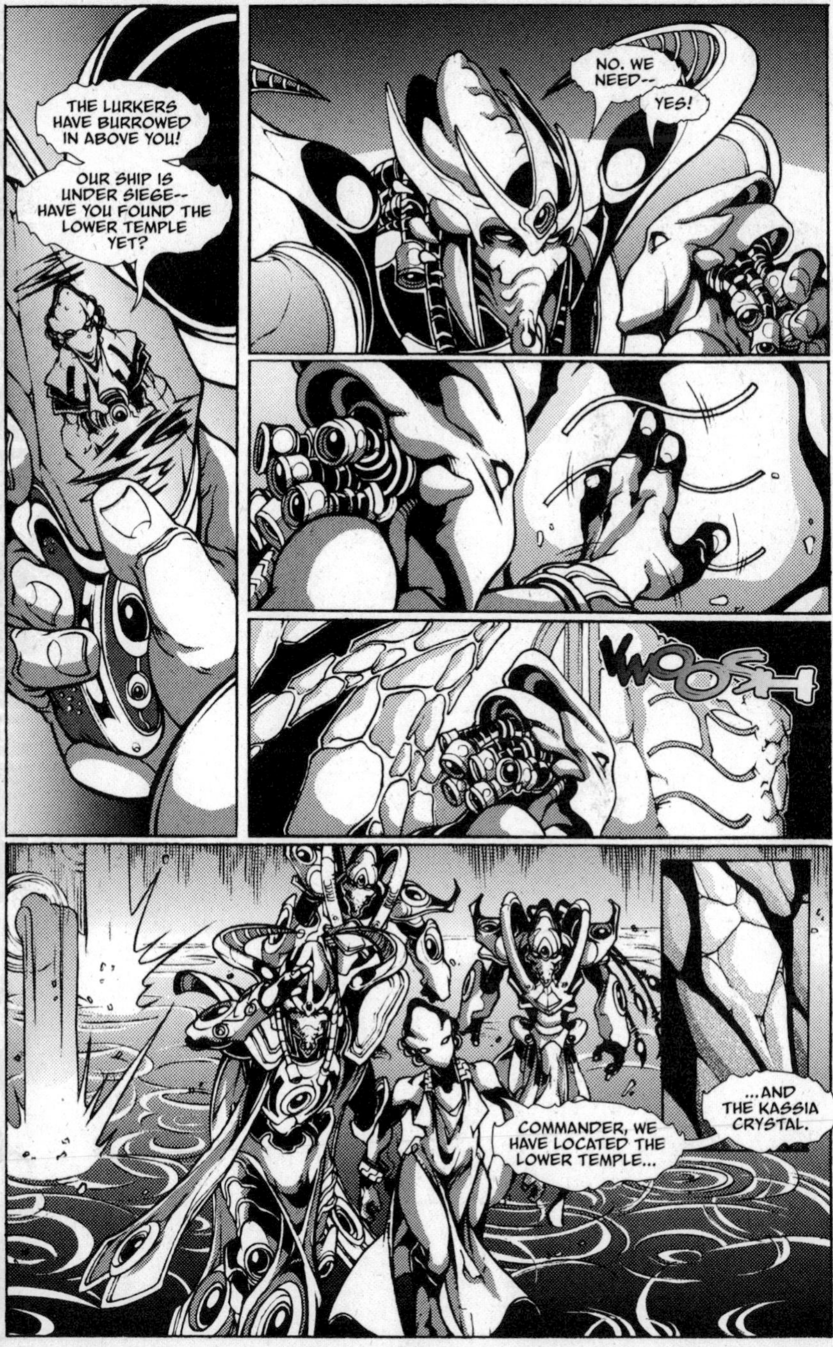
THE LURKERS HAVE BURROWED IN ABOVE YOU!
OUR SHIP IS UNDER SIEGE-- HAVE YOU FOUND THE LOWER TEMPLE YET?
NO. WE NEED--
YES!
VWOOSH
COMMANDER, WE HAVE LOCATED THE LOWER TEMPLE...
...AND THE KASSIA CRYSTAL.

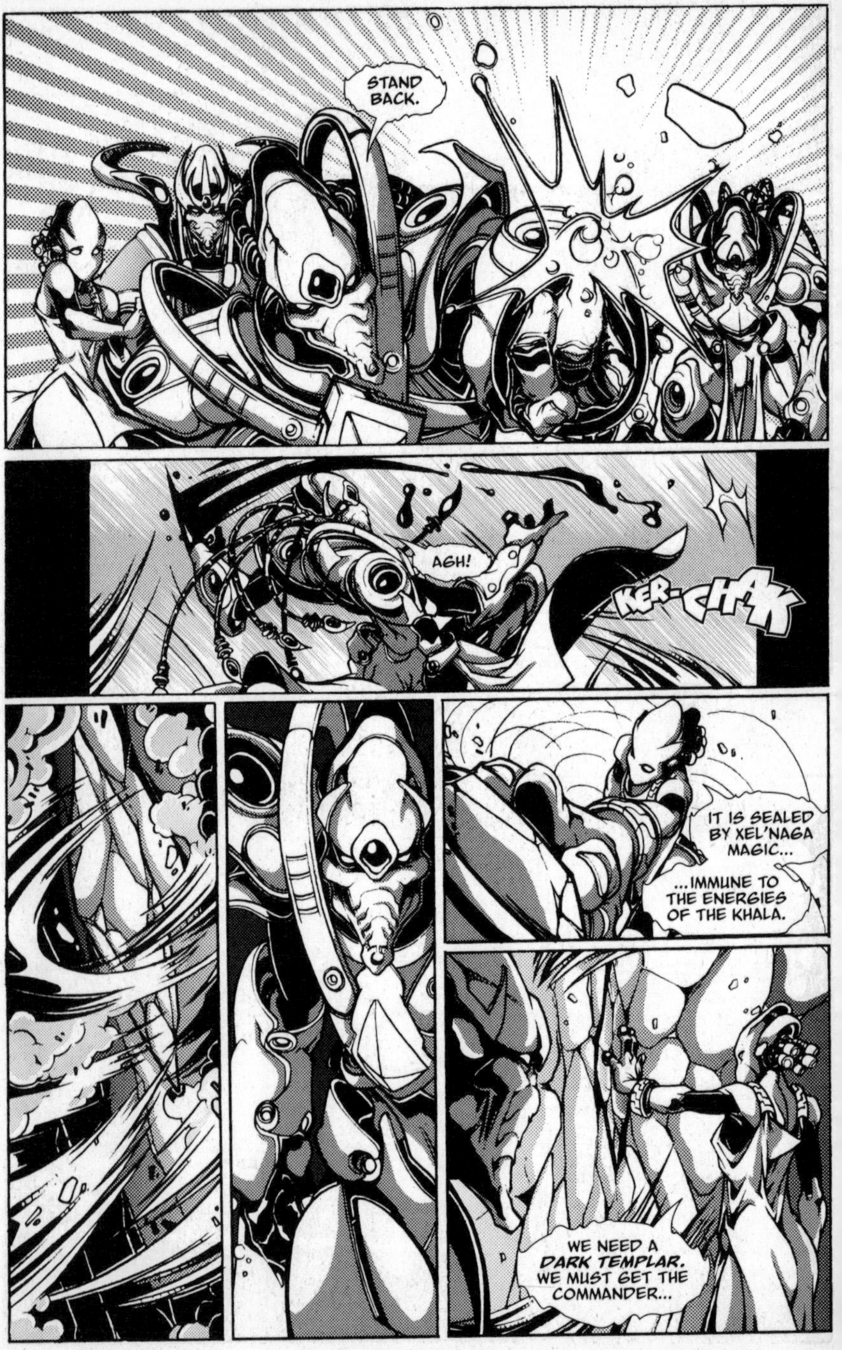
STAND BACK.
AGH!
KER-CHAK
IT IS SEALED BY XEL'NAGA MAGIC...
...IMMUNE TO THE ENERGIES OF THE KHALA.
WE NEED A *DARK TEMPLAR.* WE MUST GET THE COMMANDER...

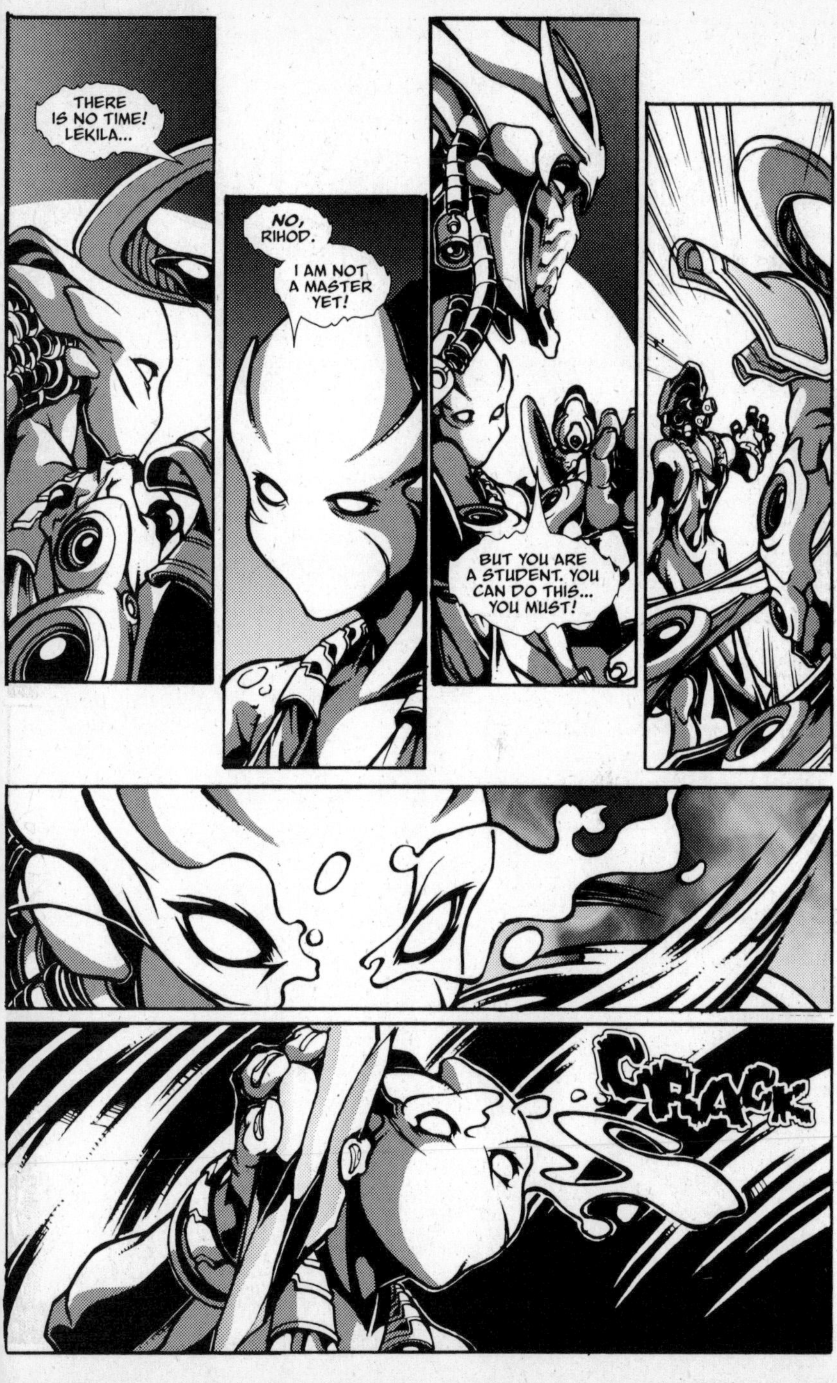
THERE IS NO TIME! LEKILA...
NO, RIHOD.
I AM NOT A MASTER YET!
BUT YOU ARE A STUDENT. YOU CAN DO THIS... YOU MUST!
CRACK

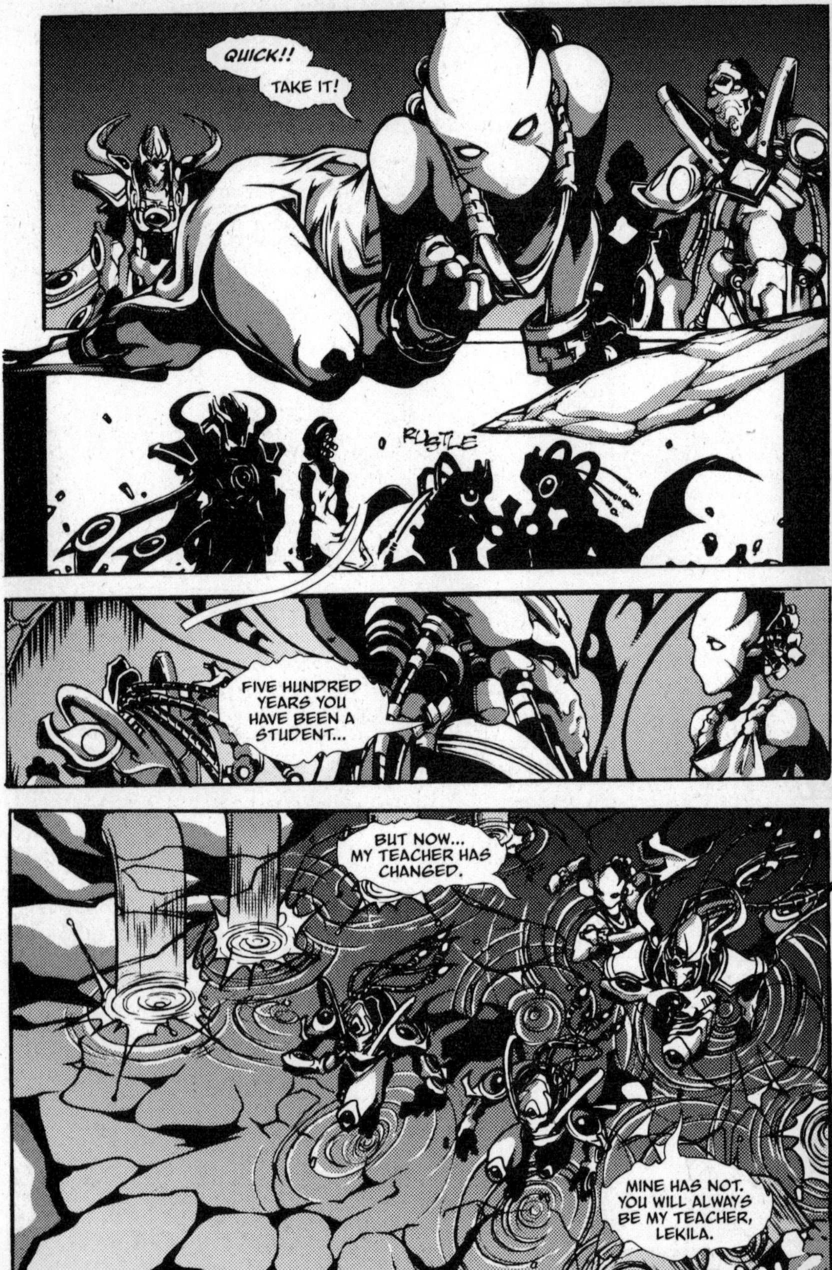
QUICK!!
TAKE IT!
RUSTLE
FIVE HUNDRED YEARS YOU HAVE BEEN A STUDENT...
BUT NOW... MY TEACHER HAS CHANGED.
MINE HAS NOT. YOU WILL ALWAYS BE MY TEACHER, LEKILA.

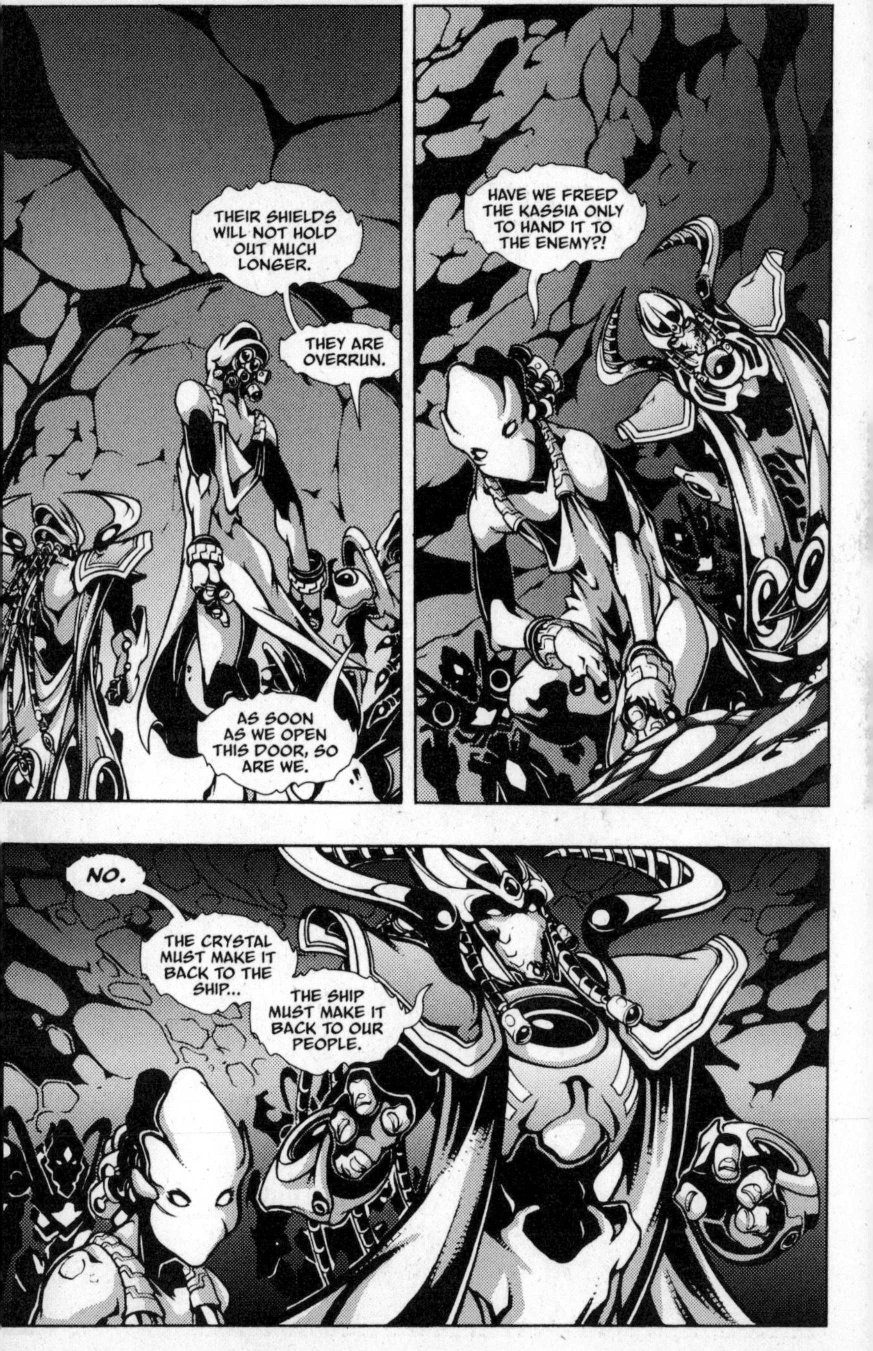
THEIR SHIELDS WILL NOT HOLD OUT MUCH LONGER.
THEY ARE OVERRUN.
AS SOON AS WE OPEN THIS DOOR, SO ARE WE.
HAVE WE FREED THE KASSIA ONLY TO HAND IT TO THE ENEMY?!
NO.
THE CRYSTAL MUST MAKE IT BACK TO THE SHIP...
THE SHIP MUST MAKE IT BACK TO OUR PEOPLE.

RIHOD...

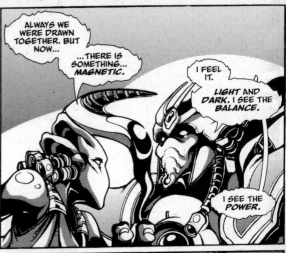

ALWAYS WE WERE DRAWN TOGETHER. BUT NOW...

...THERE IS SOMETHING... MAGNETIC.

I FEEL IT.

LIGHT AND DARK. I SEE THE BALANCE.

I SEE THE POWER.

DO YOU SEE THAT ONE CANNOT BE WITHOUT THE OTHER?

I SEE THAT I CANNOT BE WITHOUT YOU.

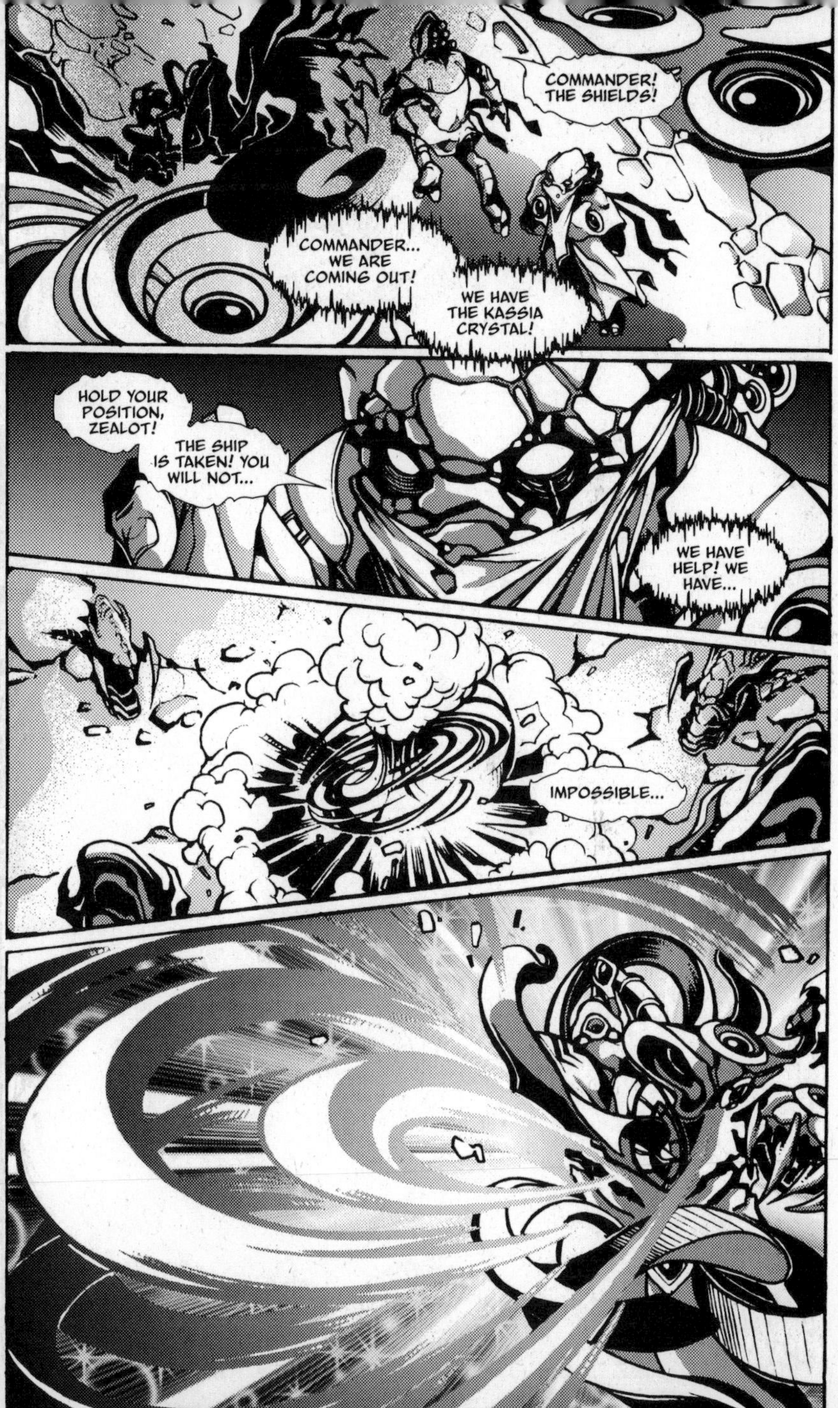
COMMANDER! THE SHIELDS!
COMMANDER... WE ARE COMING OUT!
WE HAVE THE KASSIA CRYSTAL!
HOLD YOUR POSITION, ZEALOT!
THE SHIP IS TAKEN! YOU WILL NOT...
WE HAVE HELP! WE HAVE...
IMPOSSIBLE...

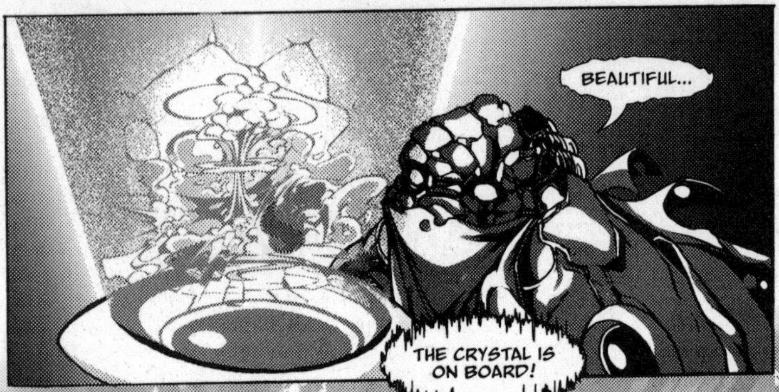
BEAUTIFUL...
THE CRYSTAL IS ON BOARD!
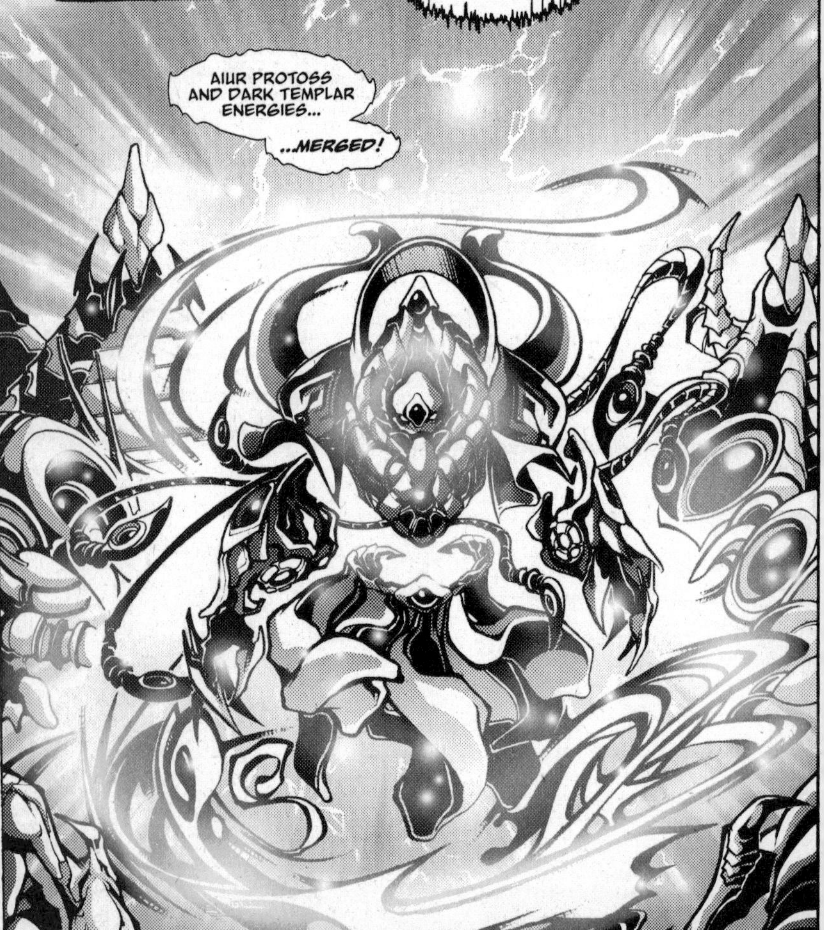
AIUR PROTOSS AND DARK TEMPLAR ENERGIES...
...MERGED!

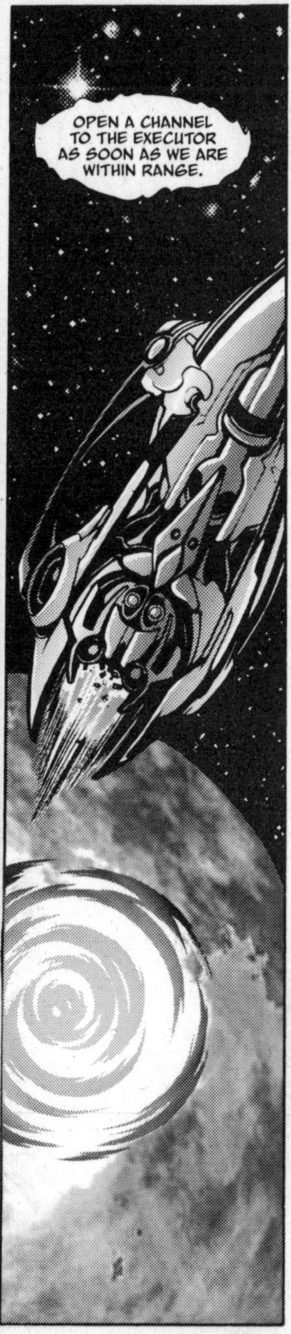
OPEN A CHANNEL TO THE EXECUTOR AS SOON AS WE ARE WITHIN RANGE.

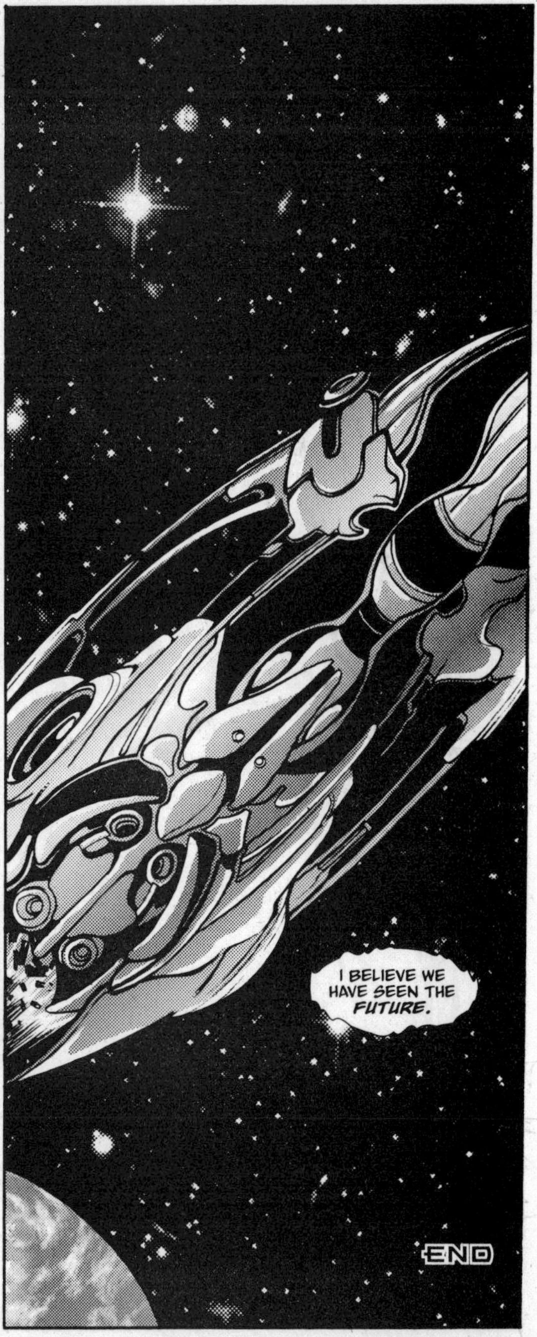
I BELIEVE WE HAVE SEEN THE *FUTURE.*
END

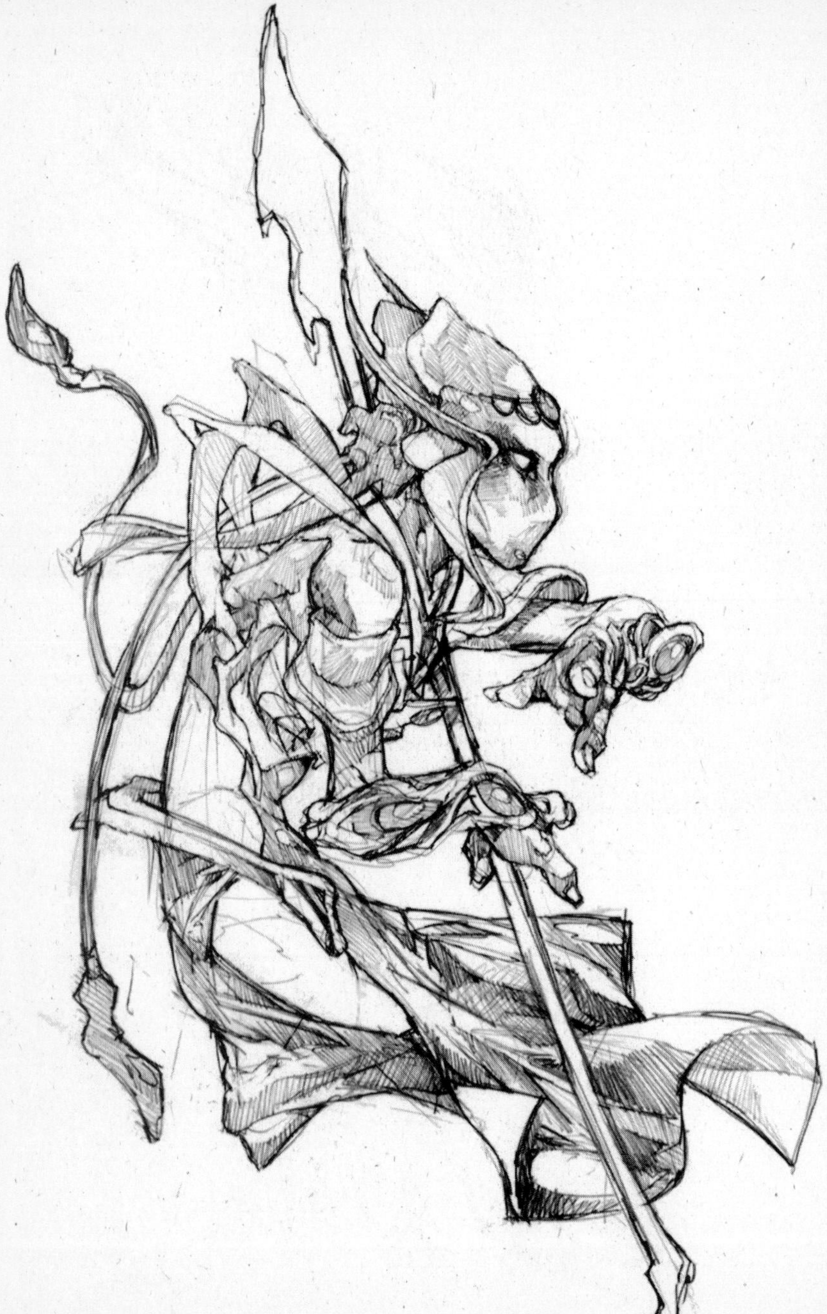

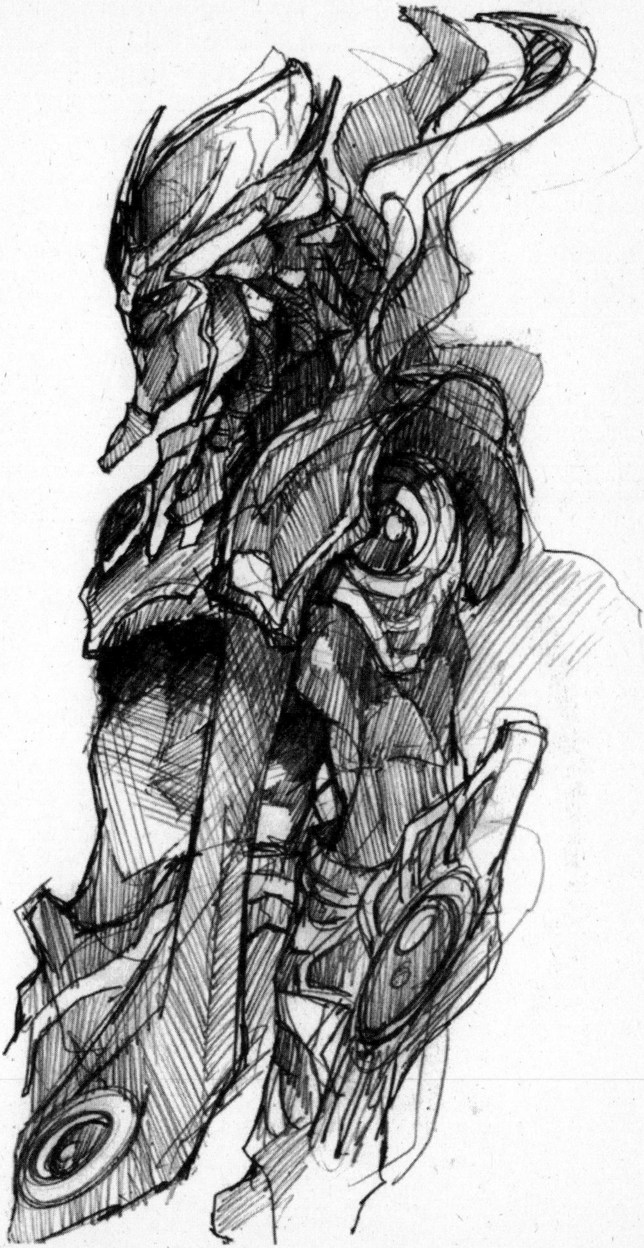

PAUL BENJAMIN

Paul Benjamin is a writer, editor, supermodel and video game writer/producer based in Austin, Texas. His comic book and graphic novel work ranges from his original manga series *Pantheon High* to *Marvel Adventures Hulk* and *Marvel Adventures Spider-Man*. His stories have appeared in numerous other Marvel titles as well as TOKYOPOP's *Star Trek: the manga* and *StarCraft: Frontline* series. Paul's video game writing and producing credits include Sega's *The Incredible Hulk* and Activision's *Spider-Man: Web of Shadows* for the Nintendo DS as well as the upcoming *X-Men Origins: Wolverine* for Wii and PlayStation 2 and Electronic Arts' *G.I. JOE: The Rise of COBRA* for many platforms. And, of course, everyone is familiar with Paul's long list of credits as a supermodel. For more info, go to http://www.thepaulbenjamin.com.

DAVE SHRAMEK

Dave Shramek is a game designer and writer in Austin, Texas. As is so often the case, he settled there after graduating from the University of Texas with a degree in Radio, Television and Film. Much to the delight of his parents, he was able to turn this normally unemployable degree into an actual profession with regular employment opportunities in the game development rich environment of Austin. He currently resides there with his ambitions of global dominance and an unhealthy addiction to Tex-Mex.

JOSH ELDER

Josh Elder is the handsome and brilliant writer of *Mail Order Ninja*, which he's pretty sure has been acclaimed by some critic, somewhere. A graduate of Northwestern University with a degree in Film, Joshua currently resides in the quaint, little Midwestern town of Chicago, Illinois. A longtime *StarCraft* fanboy, Josh is still geekgasming over the fact that he gets to write for *Frontline*. But Josh also played football, so he isn't a total dork. But he also played Dungeons & Dragons. So yeah, he kind of is a total dork.

GRACE RANDOLPH

Grace Randolph is a comedic actor and writer born and raised in New York City. Previously she's written *Justice League Unlimited #41* for DC Comics plus "Newsworthy" for *StarCraft: Frontline* and "Warrior: Divided" for *Warcraft: Legends,* both for TOKYOPOP. Her upcoming work is an adaptation of Meg Cabot's *Jinx* for manga, the sequel to "Warrior: Divided," and *Muppets: Peter Pan* for Boom! Studios. Outside of comics, Grace is the host/writer/producer of the webshow *Beyond the Trailer,* which is distributed by Next New Networks. Grace also studies at the Upright Citizens Brigade Theatre (UCB) where she has written, performed and produced the shows "Situation: Awkward" and "Igor On Strike." Visit her informative--and awesome!--website at www.gracerandolph.com.

REN ZATOPEK

Ren Zatopek is a medicine woman by day and a screenwriter and story analyst by night. She first worked with TOKYOPOP writing the English adaptation of Youn In-Wan's *Deja Vu*. She was asked to create a story for the *StarCraft* anthology because of her physical similarities to the protoss: long hair, psionic powers and knees that bend backwards. Ren knows there is no cow level.

ARTISTS:

HECTOR SEVILLA

Hector Sevilla hails from Chihuahua, Mexico. He is a huge fan of *StarCraft*, and never imagined he would ever help create a part of the *StarCraft* universe. He thanks Kathy Schilling, Paul Morrissey and Blizzard for the wonderful opportunity--and Hope Donovan for her great patience. In addition, Hector has created *Lullaby,* and is working on *Leviticus Cross* and Konami's *Lunar Knights.* He dedicates this manga to his parents for all the love and support they show each day to him. You can see more of his art at http://elsevilla.deviantart.com

RAMANDA KAMARGA

Like a superhero, **Ramanda Kamarga** holds a regular job during the day and draws comics at night. An avid gamer, he shares his free time with his wife and his PSP. Ramanda's previous works include *G.I. JOE: Sigma Six*, *Bristol Board Jungle*, TOKYOPOP's *Psy*Comm* volumes 2 & 3, and of course *StarCraft: Frontline*. To see more of his stuff, just visit his website at www.ramandakamarga.com.

SEUNG-HUI KYE

After publishing thirteen manwha and illustrating two light novels in South Korea, **Seung-hui Kye** decided to move on. In 2008, she made her Japanese manga debut with the oneshot story "Kuroi Ude" in *MiChao!* magazine, published through Kodansha. And now she is excited to make her English-language debut in such a superb manga as *StarCraft: Frontline.*

NOEL RODRIGUEZ

Noel Rodriguez began drawing, inking and coloring manga at age seventeen in his native Philippines for the local market. Before long, he was discovered by Glass House Graphics. Noel began working out of their Manila offices on such Western manga projects as *Dream Knight* and his own co-creation, *Warlords of Oz.* He is happiest drawing *StarCraft* and only recently discovered food.

Deception, betrayal, hubris, cruelty...and that was just getting the creative teams for this anthology signed up! I kid. The **StarCraft** world may be brutal, but you couldn't ask for a crackier team of minutemen...er, I mean, a finer crack team of manga creators!

First, a big congratulations to those on their second **Frontline** tour of duty: writers Paul Benjamin, Dave Shramek, Grace Randolph, Josh Elder and artist Ramanda Kamarga. And also thanks to our most decorated veteran, Hector Sevilla, on his third story in as many volumes—you rock, Hector! Last but not least, a little fresh blood never hurt a campaign, and commendable rookies Ren Zatopek, Noel Rodriguez and Seung-hui Kye shocked our system into high gear with the rocket-like force of their incredible craft.

As always, our deepest thanks goes to the guiding forces at Blizzard. I'd like to thank our immediate contacts at Blizzard—Jason Bischoff, Micky Neilson, Rob Tokar and Evelyn Fredericksen—for their ongoing support of our soldiers on the **Frontline**. You keep us reaching for the stars—and upon missing, we still end up on motherships.

And speaking of stars, fast-approaching thunders the star-studded fourth installment of **StarCraft: Frontline**. Featuring **Wings of Liberty** main character Jim Raynor in a story written by Chris Metzen himself, you faithful readers will also be treated to David Gerrold's (the writer of **Star Trek's** "Trouble with Tribbles") first foray into the **StarCraft** universe—as well as a sneak peak into TOKYOPOP's upcoming **Ghost Academy** trilogy!

And very lastly, thanks to my fellow squad members at TOKYOPOP, editor Troy "Short Bus Off a Short Cliff" Lewter and layout artist/**StarCraft** expert Michael "I Can Do It" Paolilli. Rock and roll!

Hope Donovan
Editor

STARCRAFT

FRONTLINE

IN THE NEXT VOLUME...

You've just read four stories of isolation, courage, despair and redemption...but still you look toward the future, fixing your eyes upon further *StarCraft* adventures that await you on the near horizon...

Chris Metzen, Blizzard Entertainment's Senior Vice President, Creative Development, brings you a never-before-seen story of Jim Raynor's past that leads directly into the highly anticipated videogame **StarCraft II: Wings of Liberty**...

Colin Phash is inducted into the Ghost Academy while his father Corbin runs for his life from that which Colin is to become...

A sneak peak at **StarCraft II**'s *reaper unit in a tale of revenge that explodes across the* **StarCraft** *universe and invites the wrath of a protoss dark templar...*

A brave team of protoss dark templar face down an ancient evil threatening to envelop the Koprulu sector in madness...

So suit up in your marine armor, get on the FRONTLINE, and prepare yourself for another intense barrage of *StarCraft* stories!

STARCRAFT!
FRONTLINE VOLUME 4

COMING
OCTOBER 2009

WARCRAFT®

LEGENDS
VOLUME FOUR

SNEAK PEEK

The smell of engine exhaust saturates your flight
suit, the ringing of a long since detonated mortar
still echoes in your ears, the vibrations of the ship's
engine pulses in your very core like a second heartbeat...though your exciting ride through the thrilling
universe of *StarCraft* may have ended for today--your
adventure has just begun! For now it's time to head
for the untamed lands of Azeroth and experience the
thrilling fantasy-adventure that is *Warcraft: Legends*.
TOKYOPOP is proud to present this series of anthologies
set in the World of Warcraft, Blizzard's global MMORPG
phenomenon. On the next page you'll find a sneak peak of
"Bloodsail Buccaneer," one of the four stories featured in
Warcraft: Legends Volume 4.

A thrilling high-seas tale written by Dan Jolley and drawn by Fernando
Heinz Furukawa, "Bloodsail Buccaneer" is the story of a slacker teenager
named Jimmy Blackridge and his two partners in mischief, Liam and Bram.
The three boys venture to the coast of Westfall, seeking the perfect fishing
spot...but instead find themselves kidnapped and forced to join the crew of
the most cutthroat pirates to ever sail the South Seas. They will quickly have
to learn what it means to be men if they are to survive the deadliest voyage
they will ever take...

Warcraft: Legends Volume 4 is available now!

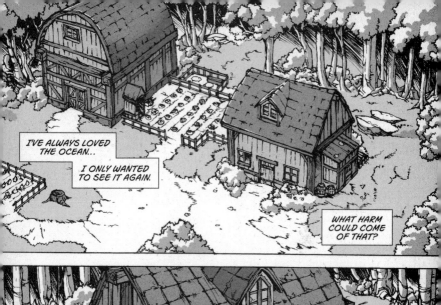

I'VE ALWAYS LOVED THE OCEAN...

I ONLY WANTED TO SEE IT AGAIN.

WHAT HARM COULD COME OF THAT?

JIMMY...!

JIMMY!

JIMMY BLACKRIDGE!!

GET YOUR NARROW BACKSIDE OUT OF BED RIGHT NOW!!

AAAH!!

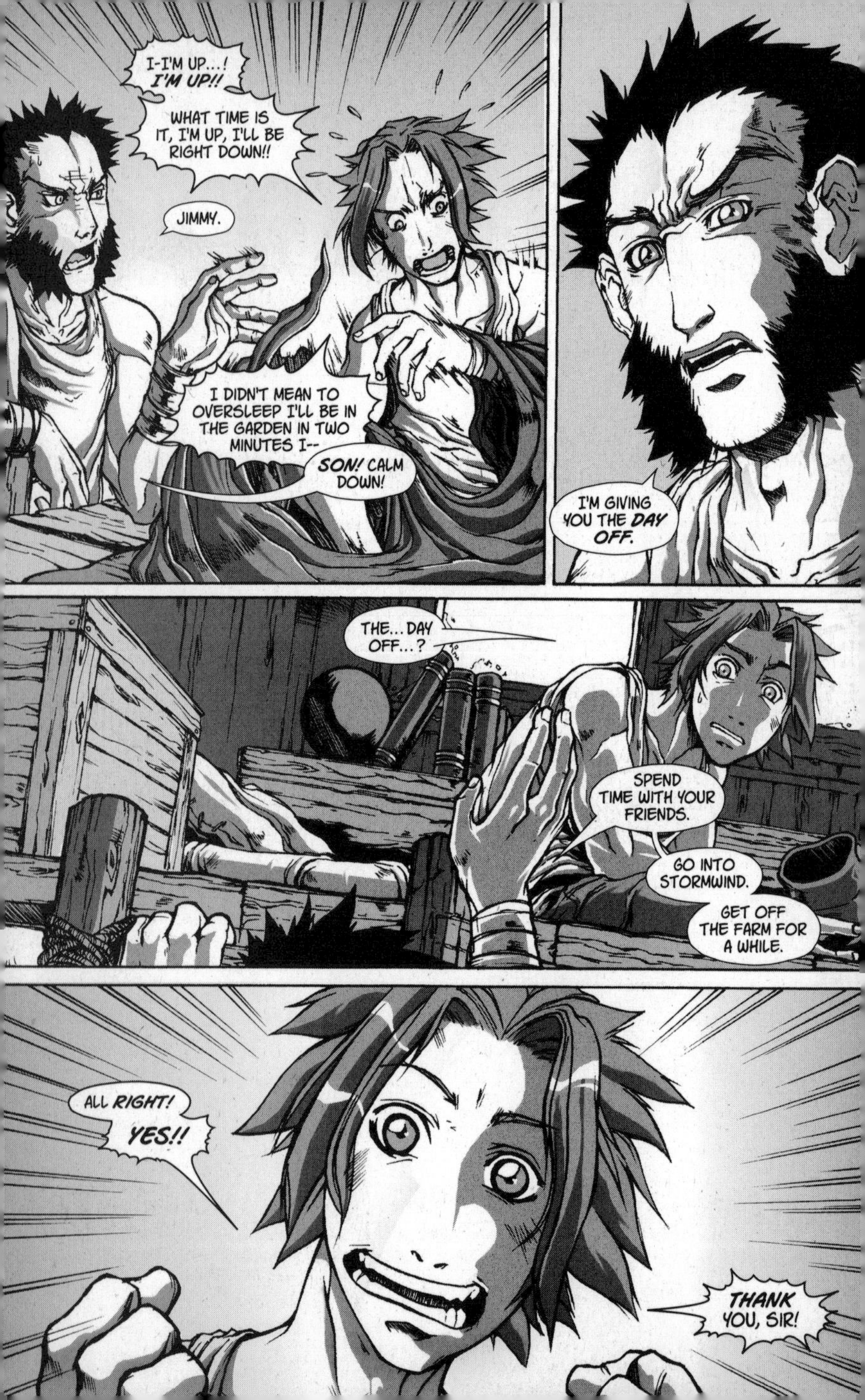
I-I'M UP...! I'M UP!!
WHAT TIME IS IT, I'M UP, I'LL BE RIGHT DOWN!!
JIMMY.
I DIDN'T MEAN TO OVERSLEEP I'LL BE IN THE GARDEN IN TWO MINUTES I--
SON! CALM DOWN!
I'M GIVING YOU THE DAY OFF.
THE... DAY OFF...?
SPEND TIME WITH YOUR FRIENDS.
GO INTO STORMWIND.
GET OFF THE FARM FOR A WHILE.
ALL RIGHT!
YES!!
THANK YOU, SIR!

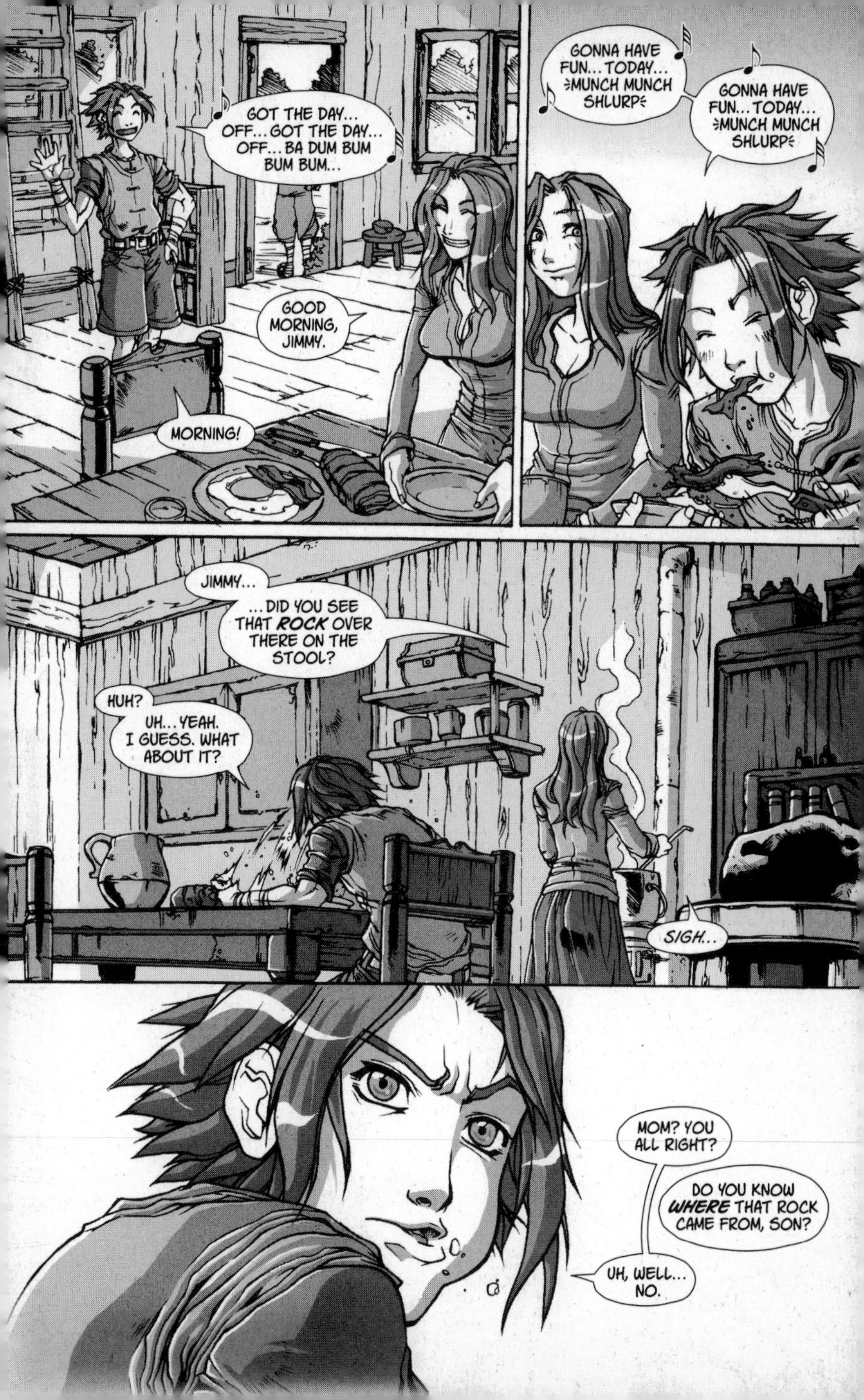
GOT THE DAY... OFF... GOT THE DAY... OFF... BA DUM BUM BUM BUM...
GOOD MORNING, JIMMY.
MORNING!
GONNA HAVE FUN... TODAY... MUNCH MUNCH SHLURP
GONNA HAVE FUN... TODAY... MUNCH MUNCH SHLURP
JIMMY...
...DID YOU SEE THAT ROCK OVER THERE ON THE STOOL?
HUH?
UH... YEAH. I GUESS. WHAT ABOUT IT?
SIGH...
MOM? YOU ALL RIGHT?
DO YOU KNOW WHERE THAT ROCK CAME FROM, SON?
UH, WELL... NO.

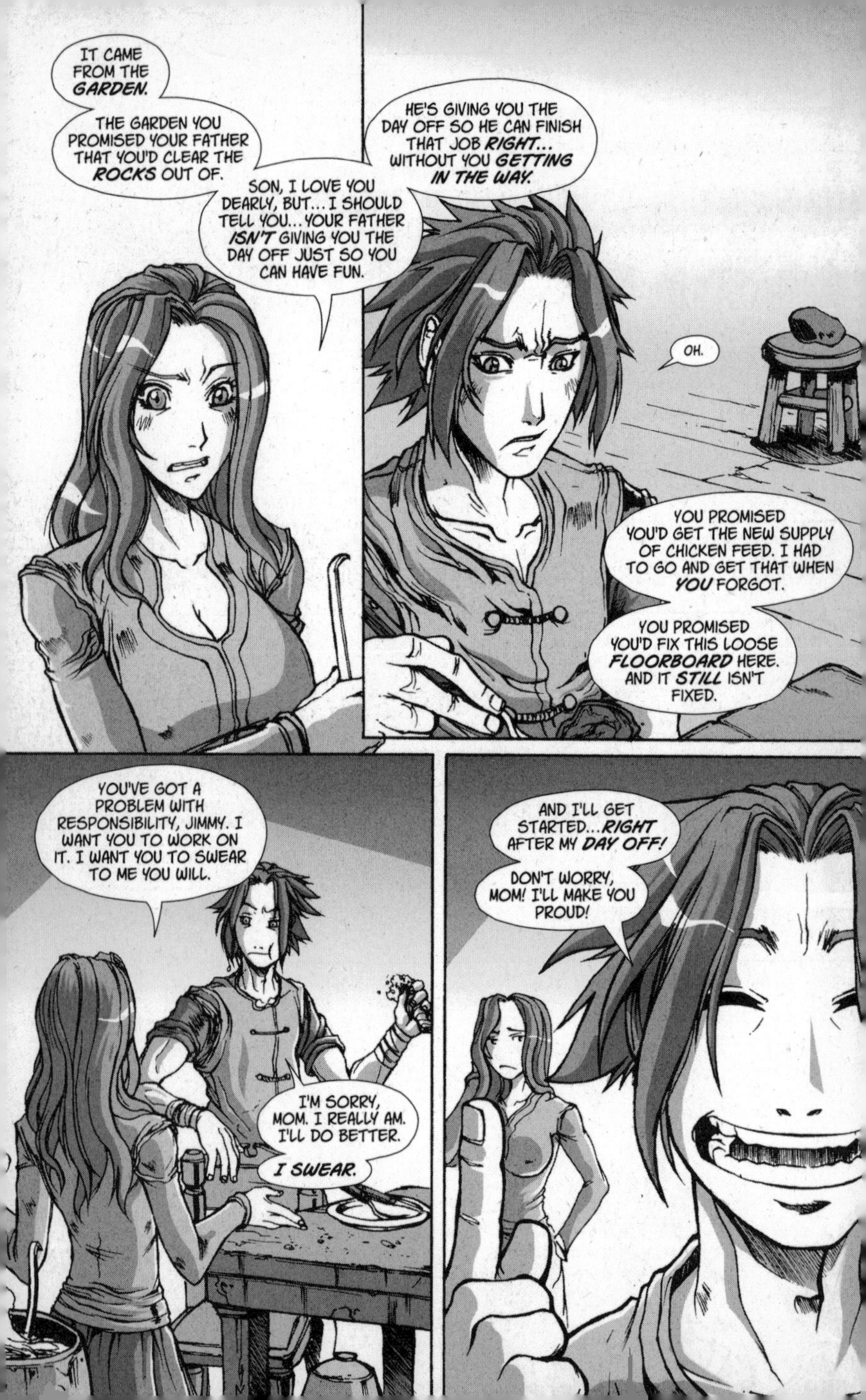

IT CAME FROM THE **GARDEN.**
THE GARDEN YOU PROMISED YOUR FATHER THAT YOU'D CLEAR THE **ROCKS** OUT OF.
SON, I LOVE YOU DEARLY, BUT... I SHOULD TELL YOU... YOUR FATHER ***ISN'T*** GIVING YOU THE DAY OFF JUST SO YOU CAN HAVE FUN.
HE'S GIVING YOU THE DAY OFF SO HE CAN FINISH THAT JOB ***RIGHT...*** WITHOUT YOU ***GETTING IN THE WAY.***
OH.
YOU PROMISED YOU'D GET THE NEW SUPPLY OF CHICKEN FEED. I HAD TO GO AND GET THAT WHEN ***YOU*** FORGOT.
YOU PROMISED YOU'D FIX THIS LOOSE ***FLOORBOARD*** HERE. AND IT ***STILL*** ISN'T FIXED.
YOU'VE GOT A PROBLEM WITH RESPONSIBILITY, JIMMY. I WANT YOU TO WORK ON IT. I WANT YOU TO SWEAR TO ME YOU WILL.
I'M SORRY, MOM. I REALLY AM. I'LL DO BETTER.
I SWEAR.
AND I'LL GET STARTED... ***RIGHT*** AFTER MY ***DAY OFF!***
DON'T WORRY, MOM! I'LL MAKE YOU PROUD!

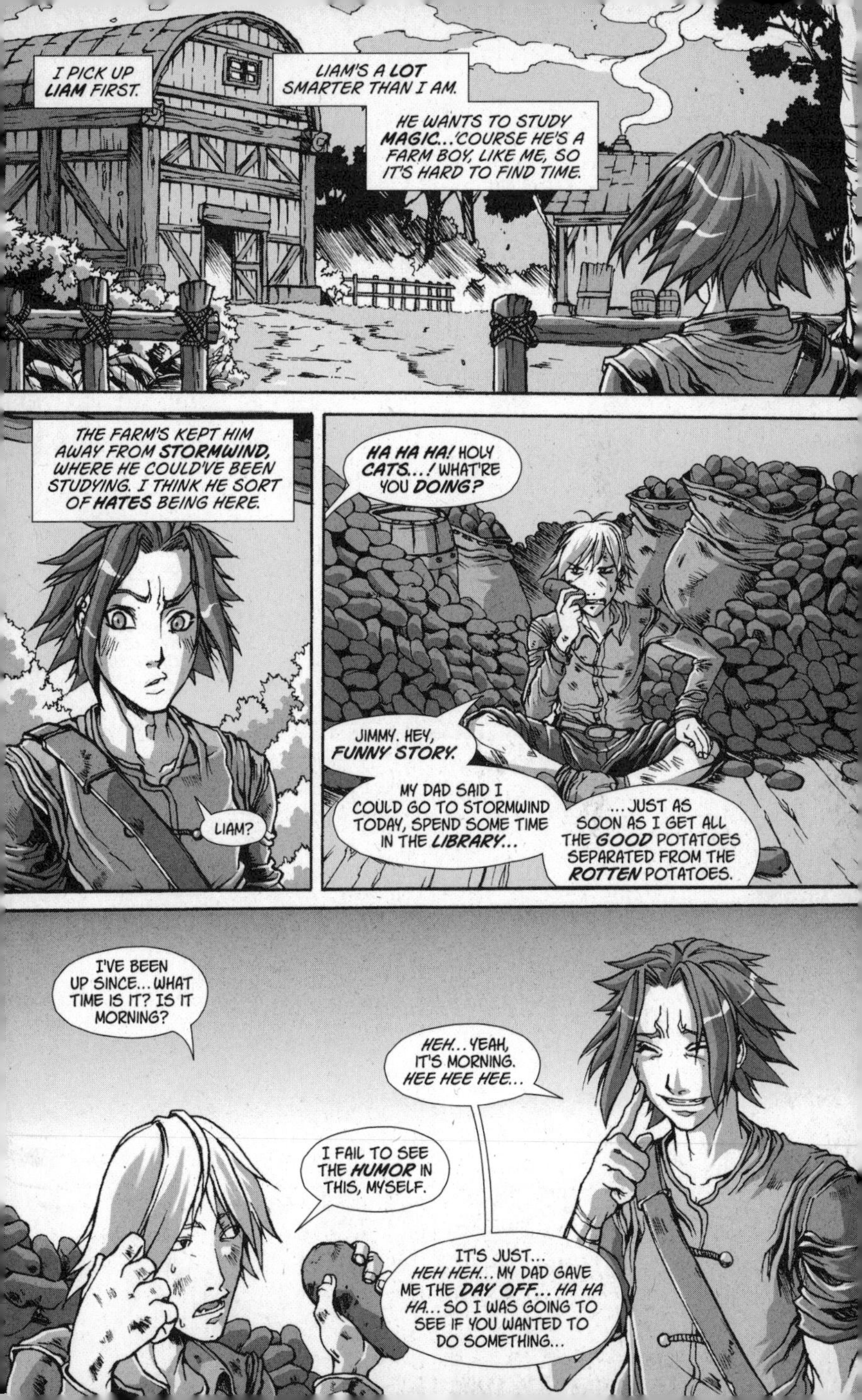
I PICK UP LIAM FIRST.
LIAM'S A LOT SMARTER THAN I AM.
HE WANTS TO STUDY MAGIC...'COURSE HE'S A FARM BOY, LIKE ME, SO IT'S HARD TO FIND TIME.
THE FARM'S KEPT HIM AWAY FROM STORMWIND, WHERE HE COULD'VE BEEN STUDYING. I THINK HE SORT OF HATES BEING HERE.
LIAM?
HA HA HA! HOLY CATS...! WHAT'RE YOU DOING?
JIMMY. HEY, FUNNY STORY.
MY DAD SAID I COULD GO TO STORMWIND TODAY, SPEND SOME TIME IN THE LIBRARY...
...JUST AS SOON AS I GET ALL THE GOOD POTATOES SEPARATED FROM THE ROTTEN POTATOES.
I'VE BEEN UP SINCE... WHAT TIME IS IT? IS IT MORNING?
HEH... YEAH, IT'S MORNING. HEE HEE HEE...
I FAIL TO SEE THE HUMOR IN THIS, MYSELF.
IT'S JUST... HEH HEH... MY DAD GAVE ME THE DAY OFF... HA HA HA... SO I WAS GOING TO SEE IF YOU WANTED TO DO SOMETHING...

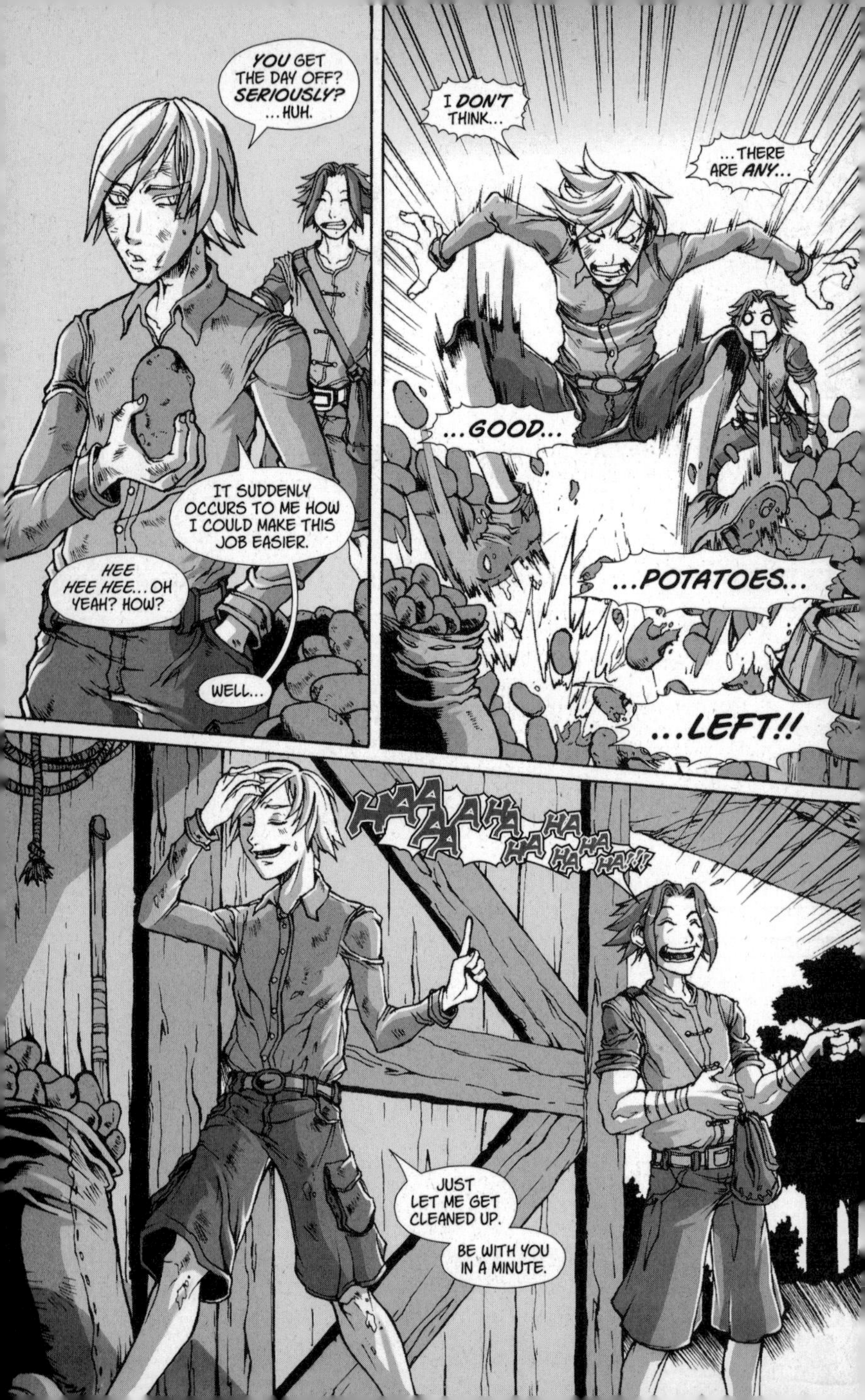
YOU GET THE DAY OFF? SERIOUSLY? ...HUH.
IT SUDDENLY OCCURS TO ME HOW I COULD MAKE THIS JOB EASIER.
HEE HEE HEE... OH YEAH? HOW?
WELL...
I DON'T THINK...
...THERE ARE ANY...
...GOOD...
...POTATOES...
...LEFT!!
HAAAAAHA HA HA HA HA HA!!!
JUST LET ME GET CLEANED UP.
BE WITH YOU IN A MINUTE.

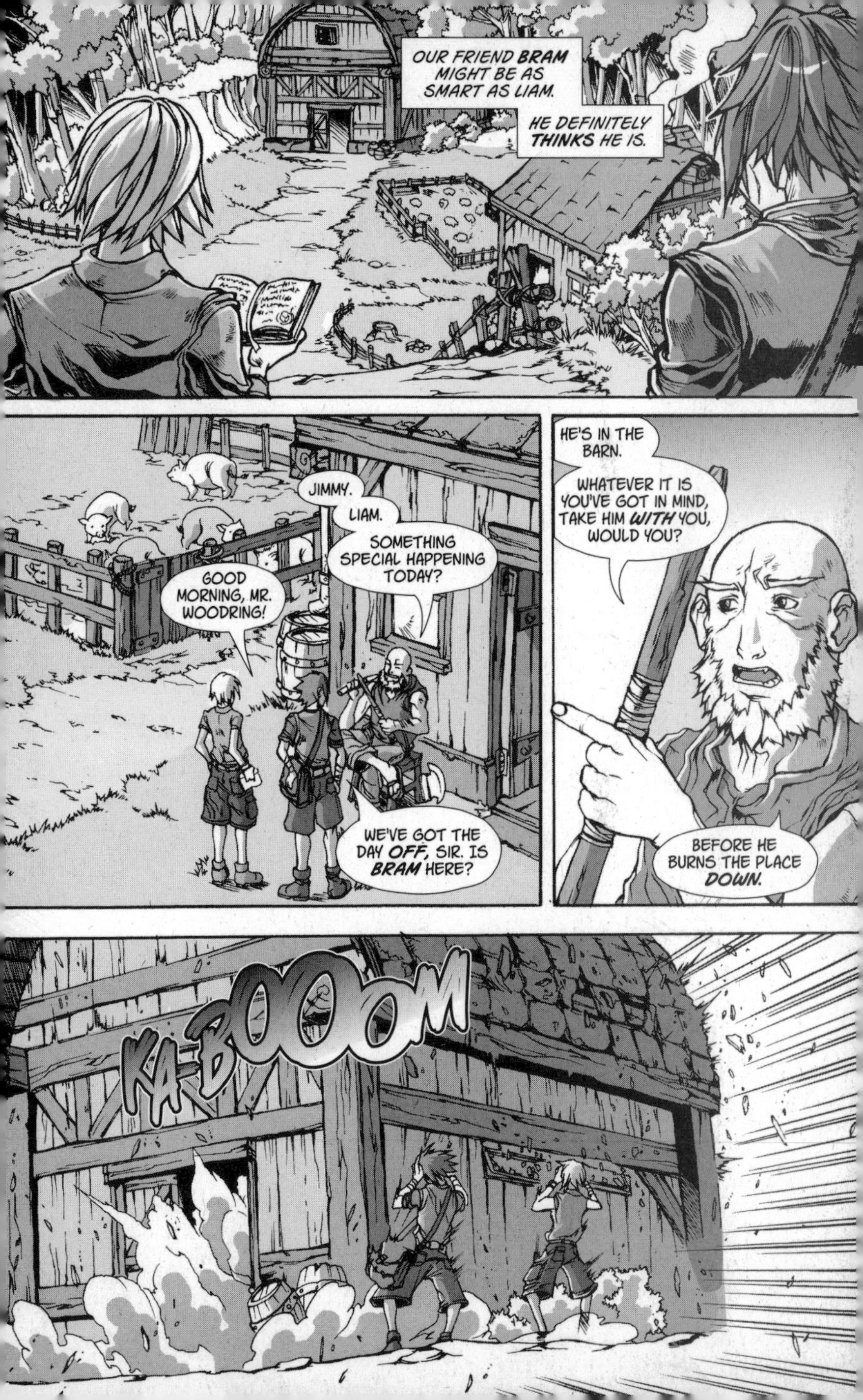
OUR FRIEND BRAM MIGHT BE AS SMART AS LIAM.
HE DEFINITELY THINKS HE IS.
JIMMY.
LIAM.
SOMETHING SPECIAL HAPPENING TODAY?
GOOD MORNING, MR. WOODRING!
WE'VE GOT THE DAY OFF, SIR. IS BRAM HERE?
HE'S IN THE BARN.
WHATEVER IT IS YOU'VE GOT IN MIND, TAKE HIM WITH YOU, WOULD YOU?
BEFORE HE BURNS THE PLACE DOWN.
KA-BOOOM

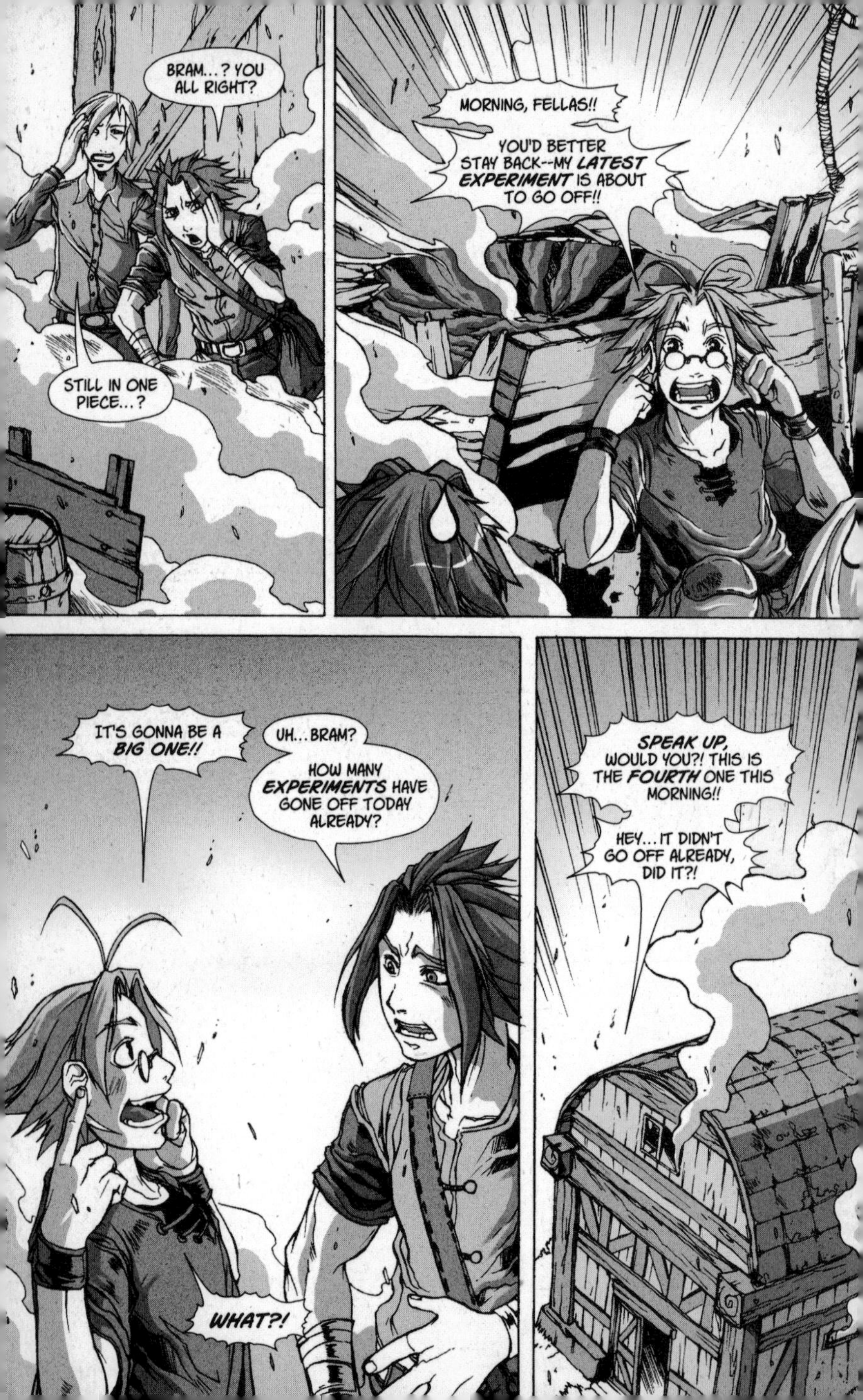
BRAM...? YOU ALL RIGHT?
STILL IN ONE PIECE...?
MORNING, FELLAS!!
YOU'D BETTER STAY BACK--MY *LATEST EXPERIMENT* IS ABOUT TO GO OFF!!
IT'S GONNA BE A *BIG ONE!!*
UH...BRAM?
HOW MANY *EXPERIMENTS* HAVE GONE OFF TODAY ALREADY?
WHAT?!
SPEAK UP, WOULD YOU?! THIS IS THE *FOURTH* ONE THIS MORNING!!
HEY...IT DIDN'T GO OFF ALREADY, DID IT?!

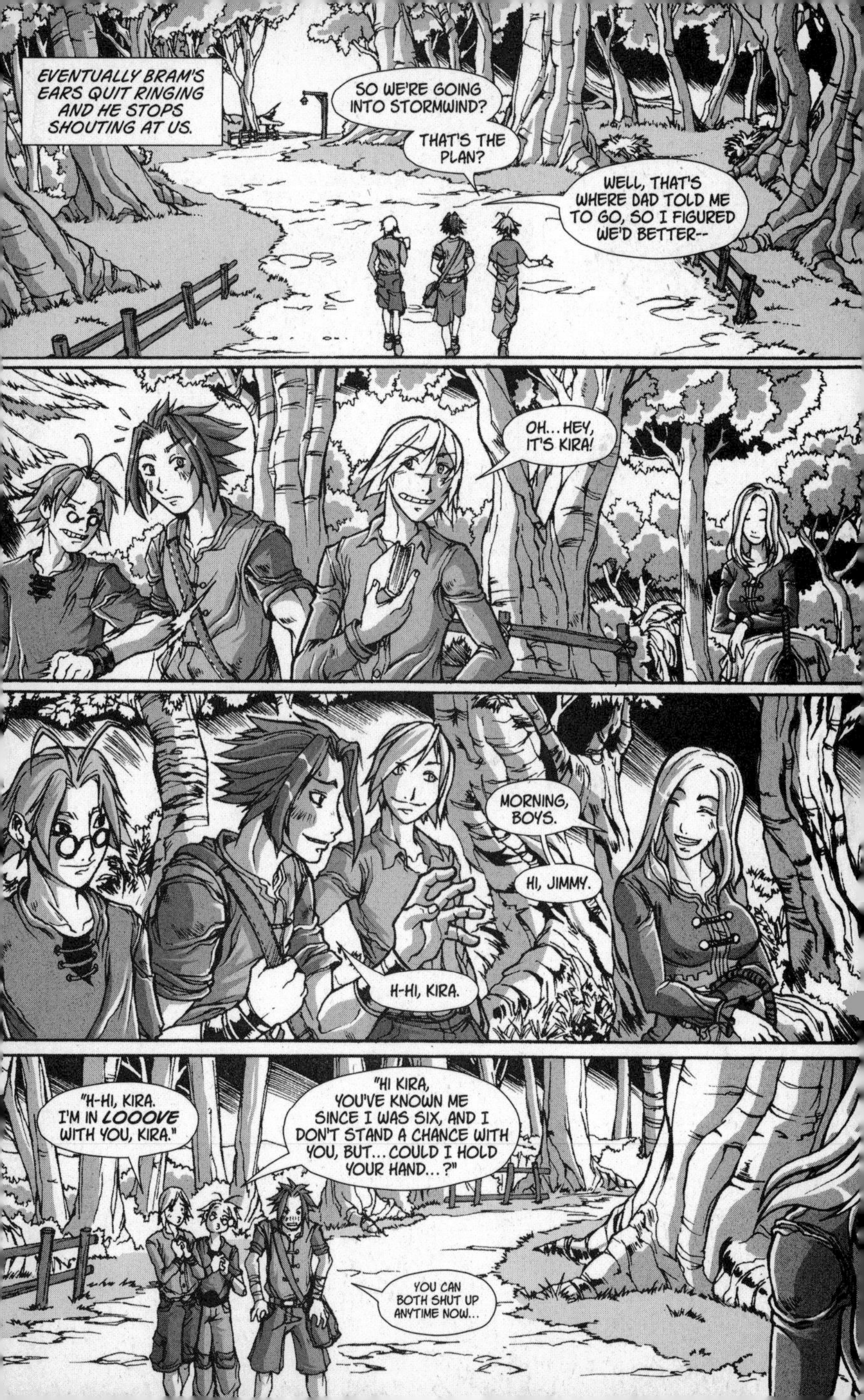
EVENTUALLY BRAM'S EARS QUIT RINGING AND HE STOPS SHOUTING AT US.
SO WE'RE GOING INTO STORMWIND?
THAT'S THE PLAN?
WELL, THAT'S WHERE DAD TOLD ME TO GO, SO I FIGURED WE'D BETTER--
OH... HEY, IT'S KIRA!
MORNING, BOYS.
HI, JIMMY.
H-HI, KIRA.
"H-HI, KIRA. I'M IN LOOOVE WITH YOU, KIRA."
"HI KIRA, YOU'VE KNOWN ME SINCE I WAS SIX, AND I DON'T STAND A CHANCE WITH YOU, BUT... COULD I HOLD YOUR HAND...?"
YOU CAN BOTH SHUT UP ANYTIME NOW...

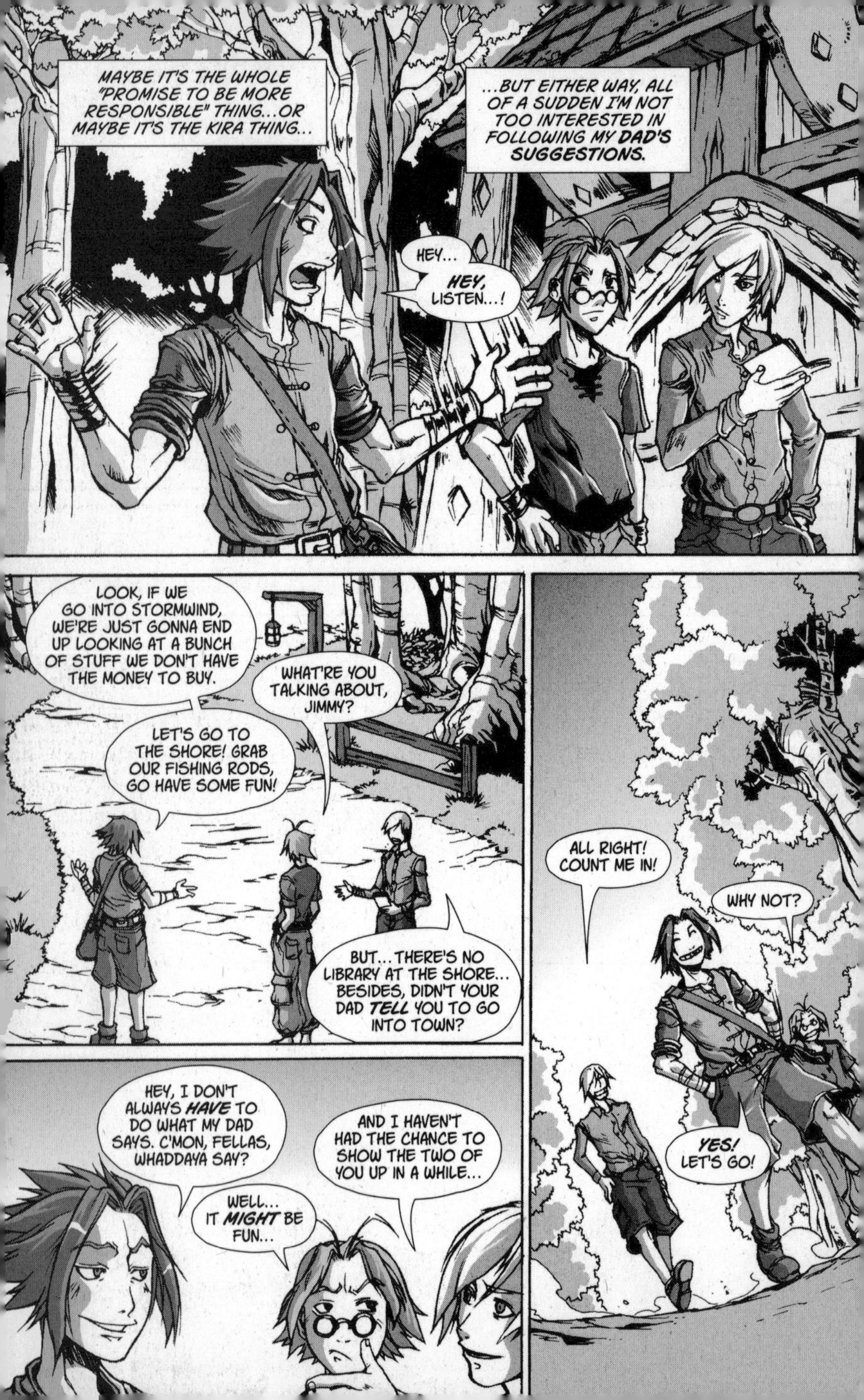
MAYBE IT'S THE WHOLE "PROMISE TO BE MORE RESPONSIBLE" THING...OR MAYBE IT'S THE KIRA THING...
...BUT EITHER WAY, ALL OF A SUDDEN I'M NOT TOO INTERESTED IN FOLLOWING MY **DAD'S** SUGGESTIONS.
HEY...
HEY, LISTEN...!
LOOK, IF WE GO INTO STORMWIND, WE'RE JUST GONNA END UP LOOKING AT A BUNCH OF STUFF WE DON'T HAVE THE MONEY TO BUY.
WHAT'RE YOU TALKING ABOUT, JIMMY?
LET'S GO TO THE SHORE! GRAB OUR FISHING RODS, GO HAVE SOME FUN!
BUT... THERE'S NO LIBRARY AT THE SHORE... BESIDES, DIDN'T YOUR DAD ***TELL*** YOU TO GO INTO TOWN?
HEY, I DON'T ALWAYS ***HAVE*** TO DO WHAT MY DAD SAYS. C'MON, FELLAS, WHADDAYA SAY?
AND I HAVEN'T HAD THE CHANCE TO SHOW THE TWO OF YOU UP IN A WHILE...
WELL... IT ***MIGHT*** BE FUN...
ALL RIGHT! COUNT ME IN!
WHY NOT?
YES! LET'S GO!

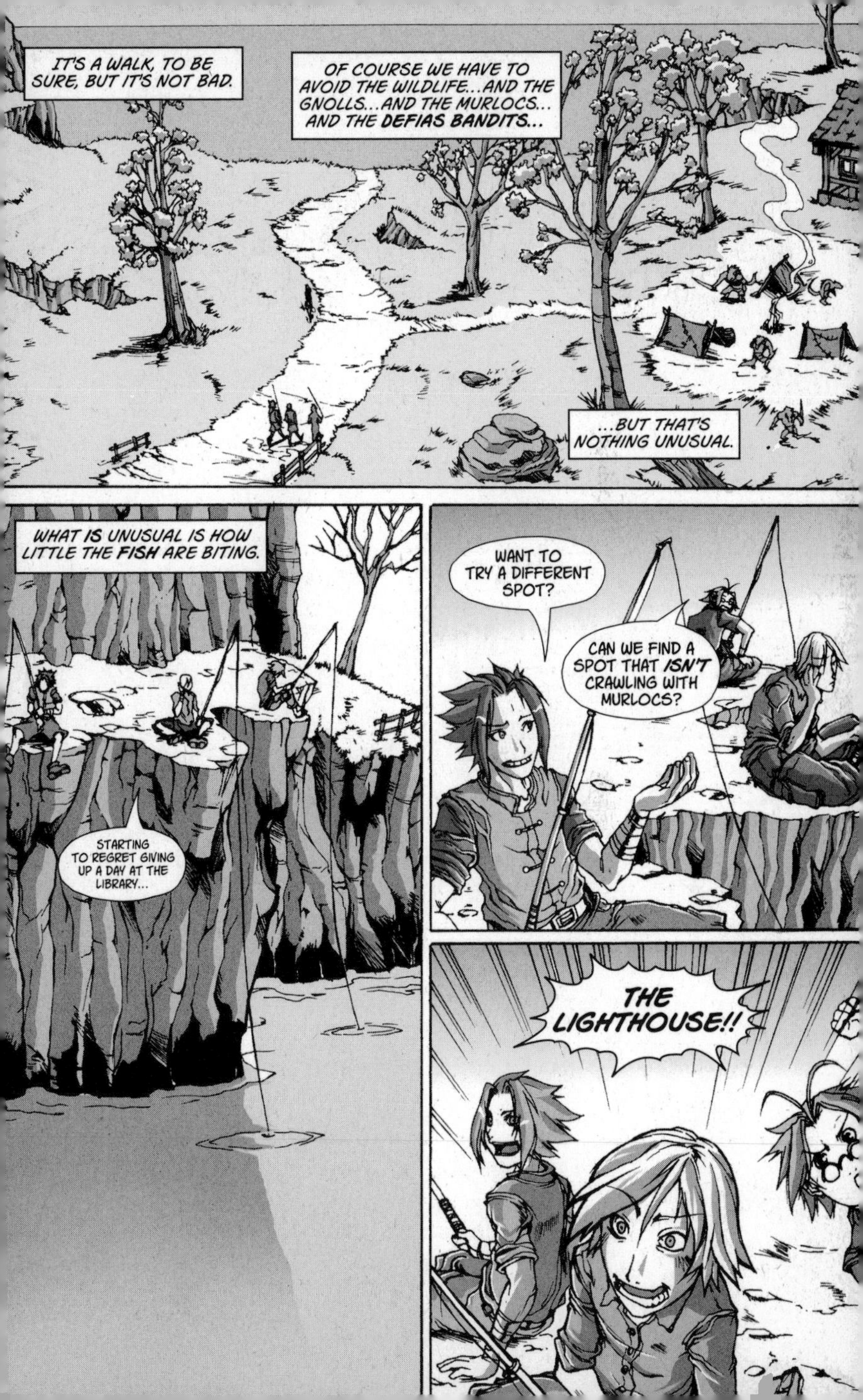
IT'S A WALK, TO BE SURE, BUT IT'S NOT BAD.
OF COURSE WE HAVE TO AVOID THE WILDLIFE...AND THE GNOLLS...AND THE MURLOCS... AND THE DEFIAS BANDITS...
...BUT THAT'S NOTHING UNUSUAL.
WHAT IS UNUSUAL IS HOW LITTLE THE FISH ARE BITING.
STARTING TO REGRET GIVING UP A DAY AT THE LIBRARY...
WANT TO TRY A DIFFERENT SPOT?
CAN WE FIND A SPOT THAT ISN'T CRAWLING WITH MURLOCS?
THE LIGHTHOUSE!!

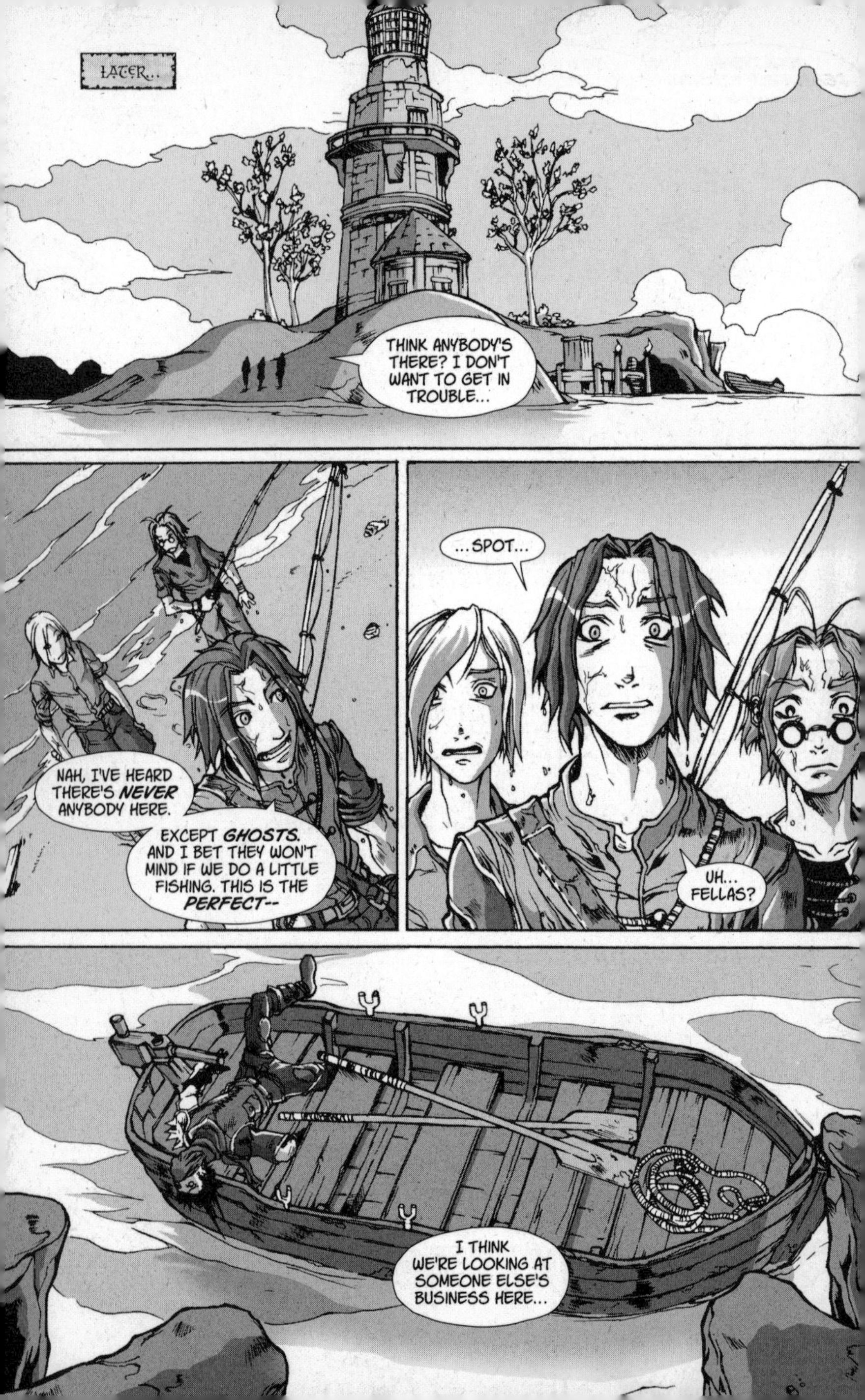
LATER...
THINK ANYBODY'S THERE? I DON'T WANT TO GET IN TROUBLE...
NAH, I'VE HEARD THERE'S *NEVER* ANYBODY HERE.
EXCEPT *GHOSTS*. AND I BET THEY WON'T MIND IF WE DO A LITTLE FISHING. THIS IS THE *PERFECT*--
...SPOT...
UH... FELLAS?
I THINK WE'RE LOOKING AT SOMEONE ELSE'S BUSINESS HERE...

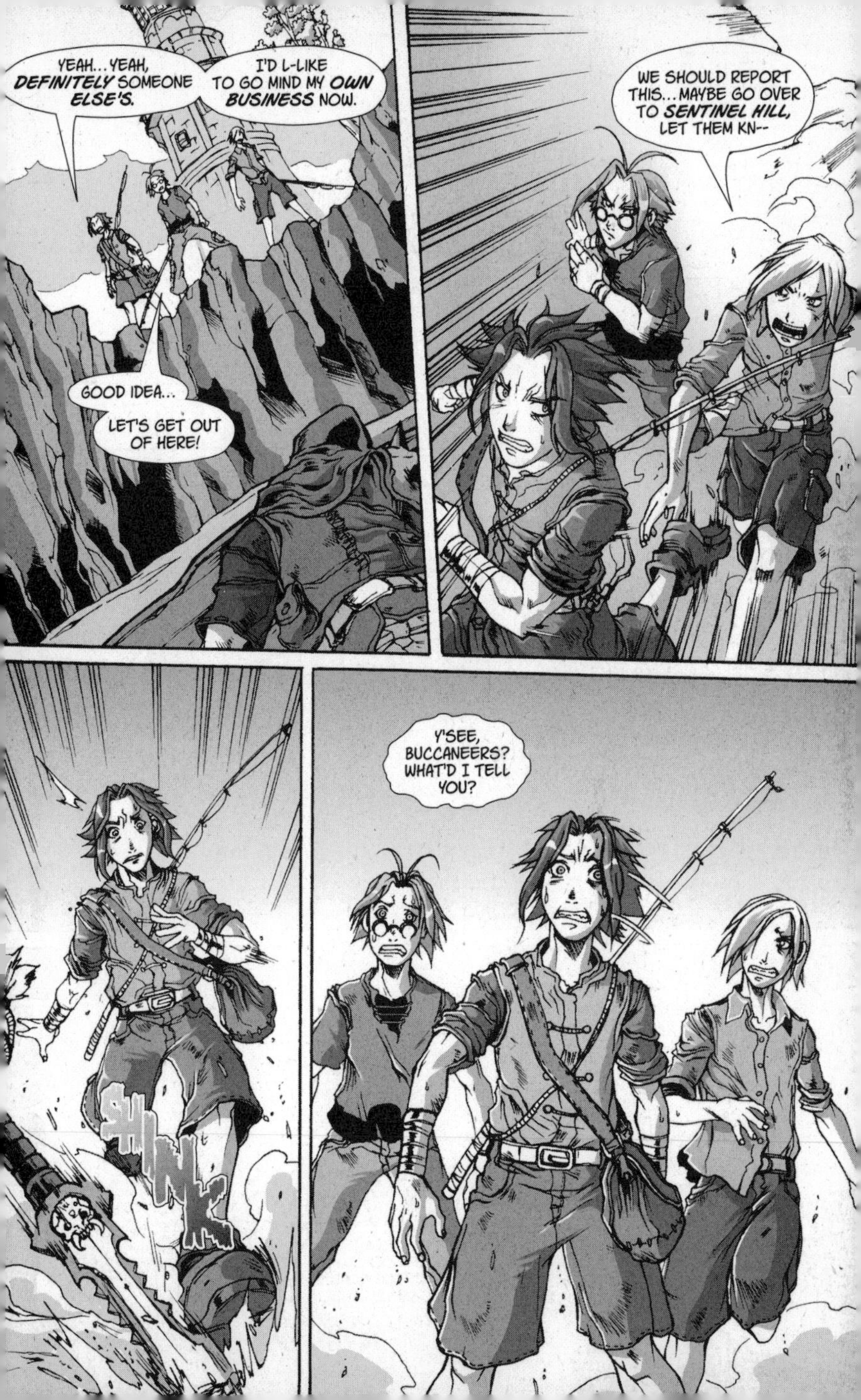
YEAH... YEAH, DEFINITELY SOMEONE ELSE'S.
I'D L-LIKE TO GO MIND MY OWN BUSINESS NOW.
GOOD IDEA...
LET'S GET OUT OF HERE!
WE SHOULD REPORT THIS... MAYBE GO OVER TO SENTINEL HILL, LET THEM KN--
SHINK
Y'SEE, BUCCANEERS? WHAT'D I TELL YOU?

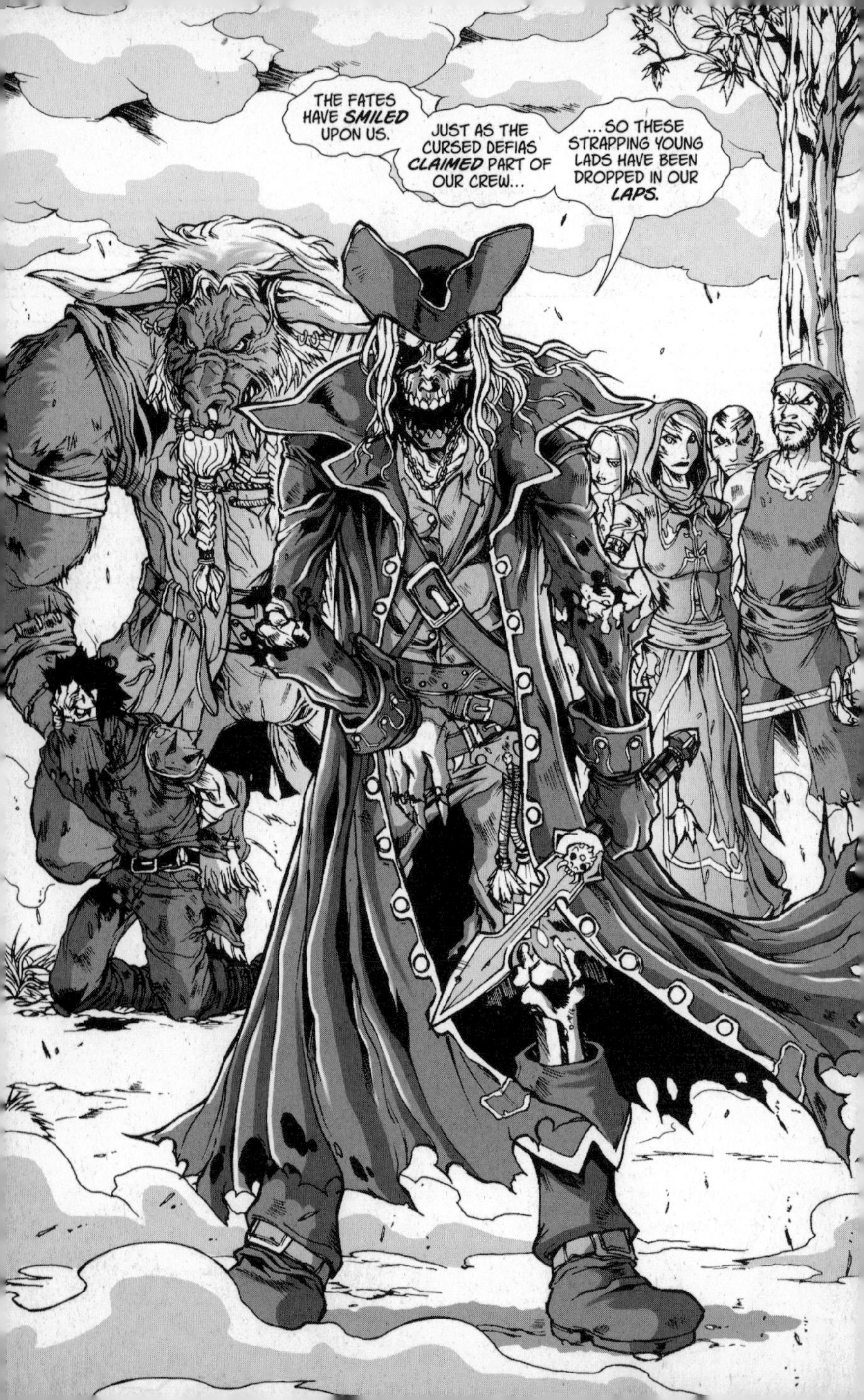
THE FATES HAVE SMILED UPON US.
JUST AS THE CURSED DEFIAS CLAIMED PART OF OUR CREW...
...SO THESE STRAPPING YOUNG LADS HAVE BEEN DROPPED IN OUR LAPS.

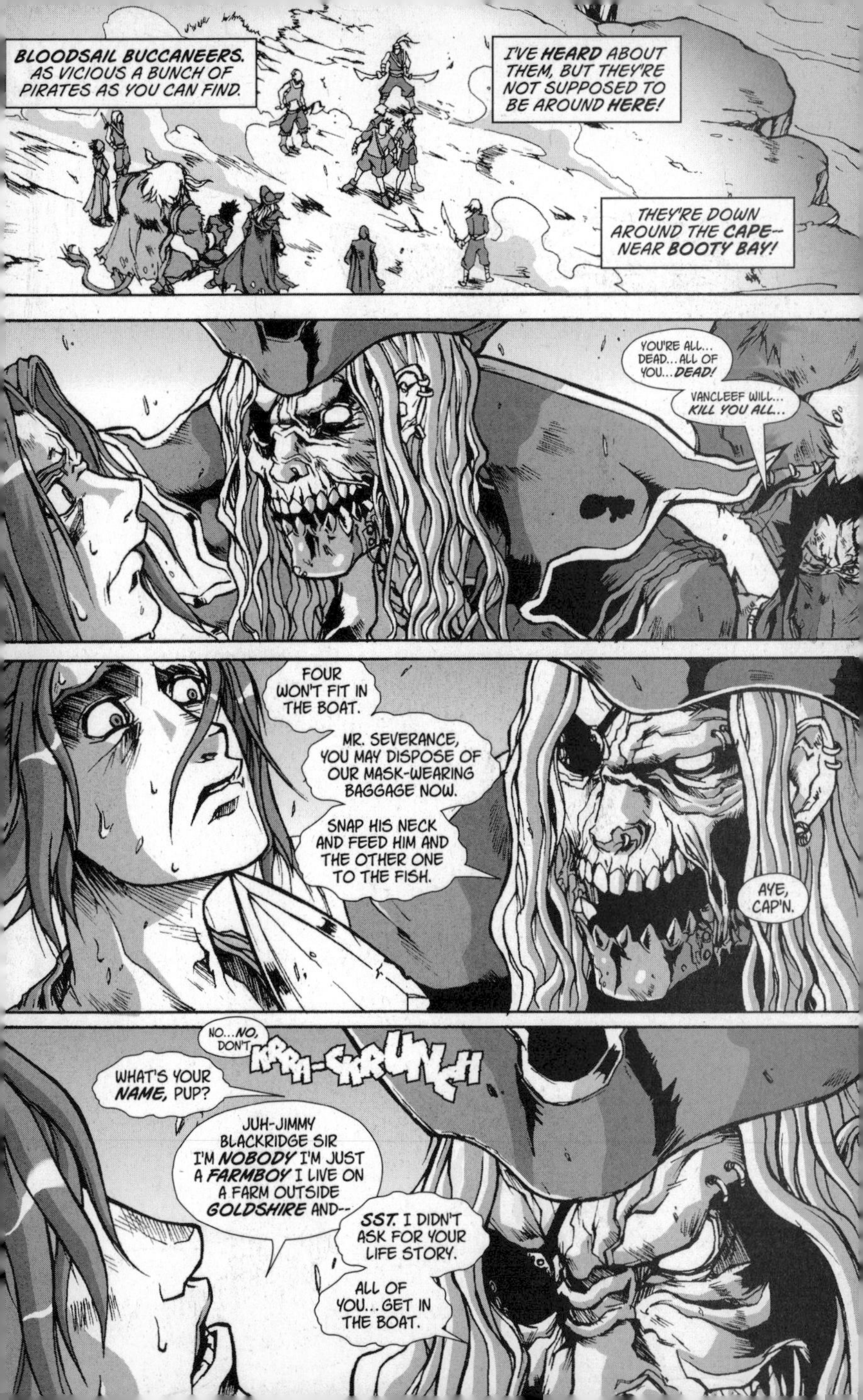
BLOODSAIL BUCCANEERS. AS VICIOUS A BUNCH OF PIRATES AS YOU CAN FIND.
I'VE HEARD ABOUT THEM, BUT THEY'RE NOT SUPPOSED TO BE AROUND HERE!
THEY'RE DOWN AROUND THE CAPE-- NEAR BOOTY BAY!
YOU'RE ALL... DEAD... ALL OF YOU... DEAD!
VANCLEEF WILL... KILL YOU ALL...
FOUR WON'T FIT IN THE BOAT.
MR. SEVERANCE, YOU MAY DISPOSE OF OUR MASK-WEARING BAGGAGE NOW.
SNAP HIS NECK AND FEED HIM AND THE OTHER ONE TO THE FISH.
AYE, CAP'N.
WHAT'S YOUR NAME, PUP?
NO... NO, DON'T
KRRA-SKRUNCH
JUH-JIMMY BLACKRIDGE SIR I'M NOBODY I'M JUST A FARMBOY I LIVE ON A FARM OUTSIDE GOLDSHIRE AND--
SST. I DIDN'T ASK FOR YOUR LIFE STORY.
ALL OF YOU... GET IN THE BOAT.

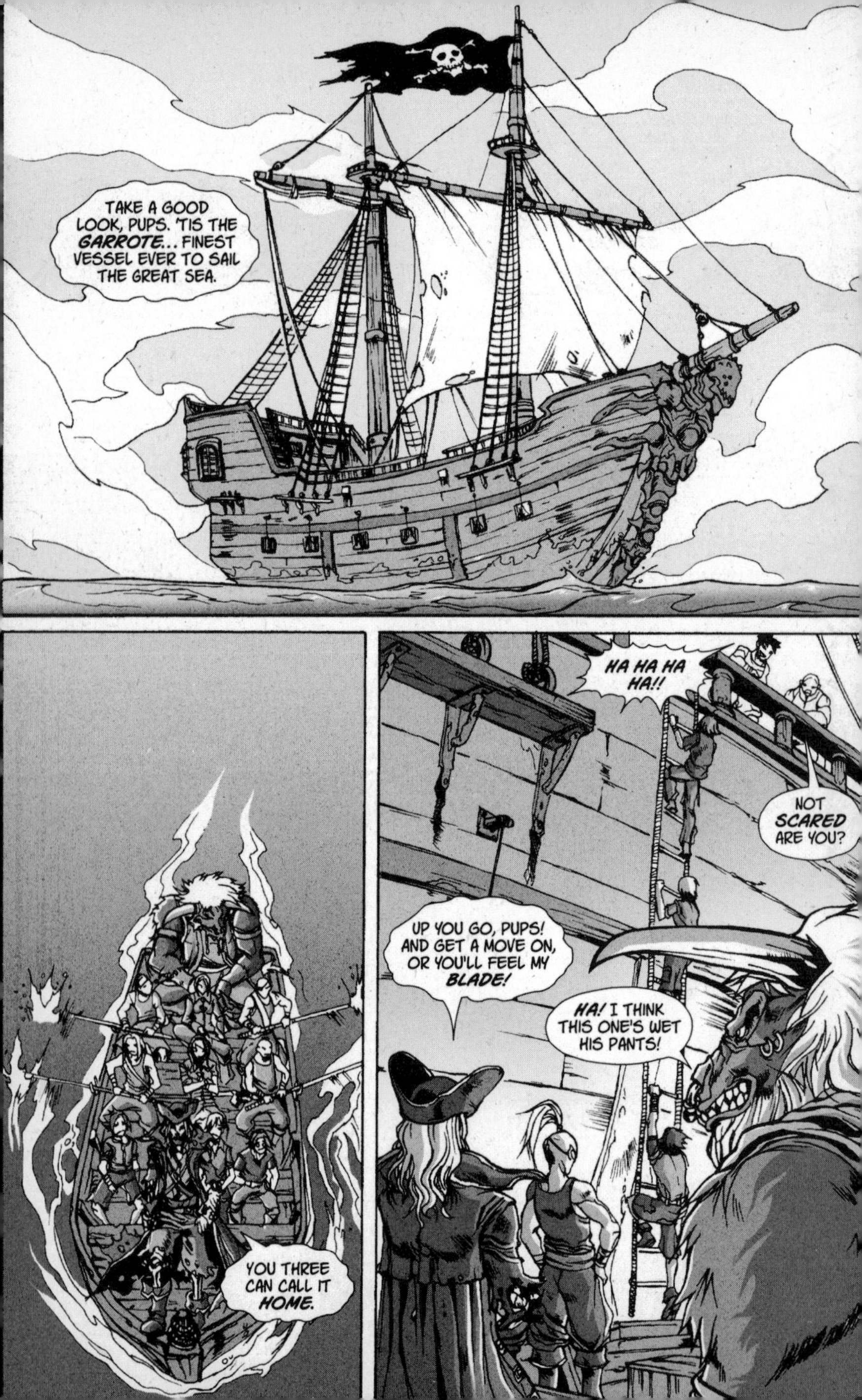
TAKE A GOOD LOOK, PUPS. 'TIS THE GARROTE... FINEST VESSEL EVER TO SAIL THE GREAT SEA.
YOU THREE CAN CALL IT HOME.
HA HA HA HA!!
NOT SCARED ARE YOU?
UP YOU GO, PUPS! AND GET A MOVE ON, OR YOU'LL FEEL MY BLADE!
HA! I THINK THIS ONE'S WET HIS PANTS!

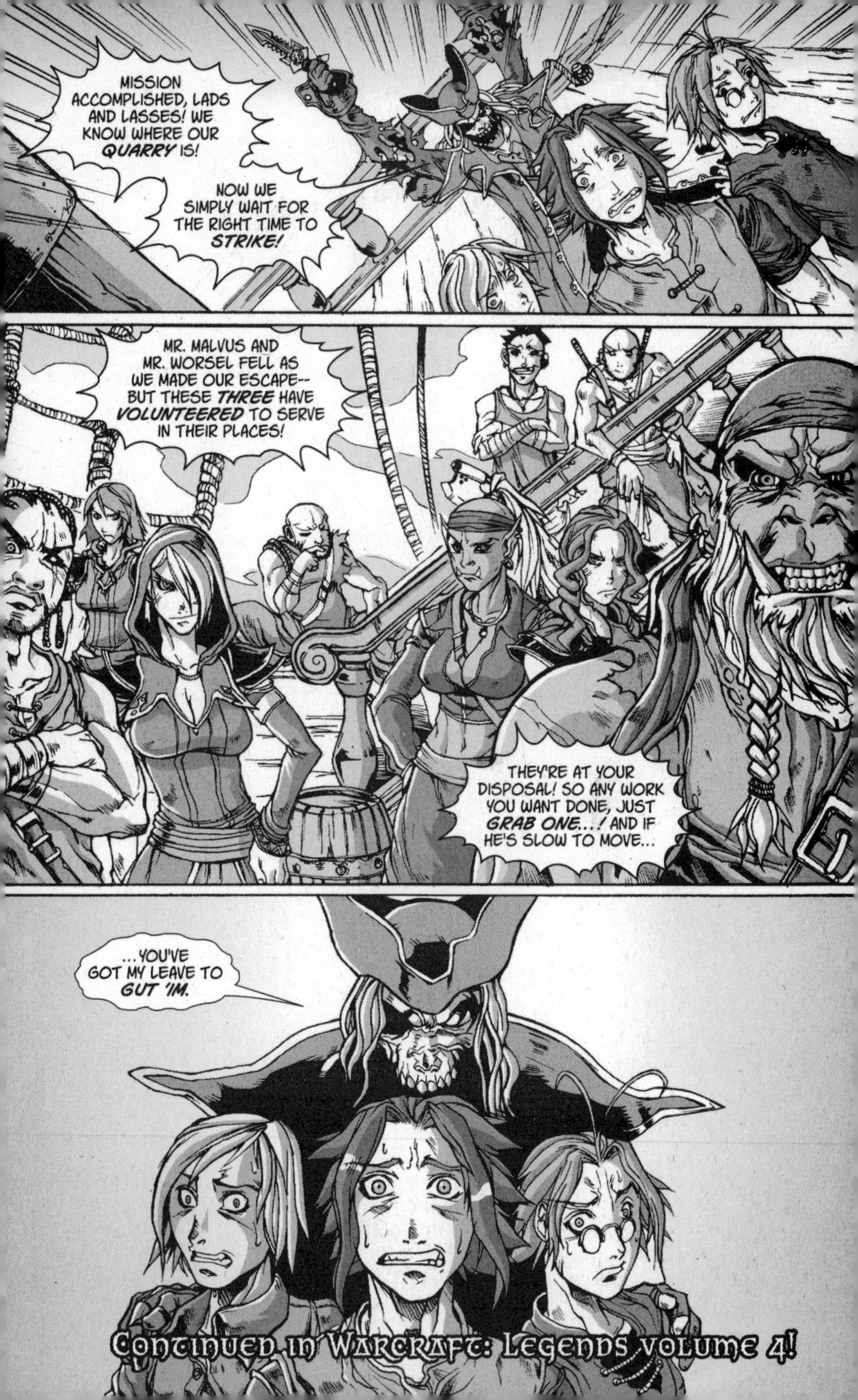
MISSION ACCOMPLISHED, LADS AND LASSES! WE KNOW WHERE OUR QUARRY IS!
NOW WE SIMPLY WAIT FOR THE RIGHT TIME TO STRIKE!
MR. MALVUS AND MR. WORSEL FELL AS WE MADE OUR ESCAPE-- BUT THESE THREE HAVE VOLUNTEERED TO SERVE IN THEIR PLACES!
THEY'RE AT YOUR DISPOSAL! SO ANY WORK YOU WANT DONE, JUST GRAB ONE...! AND IF HE'S SLOW TO MOVE...
...YOU'VE GOT MY LEAVE TO GUT 'IM.
Continued in Warcraft: Legends volume 4!

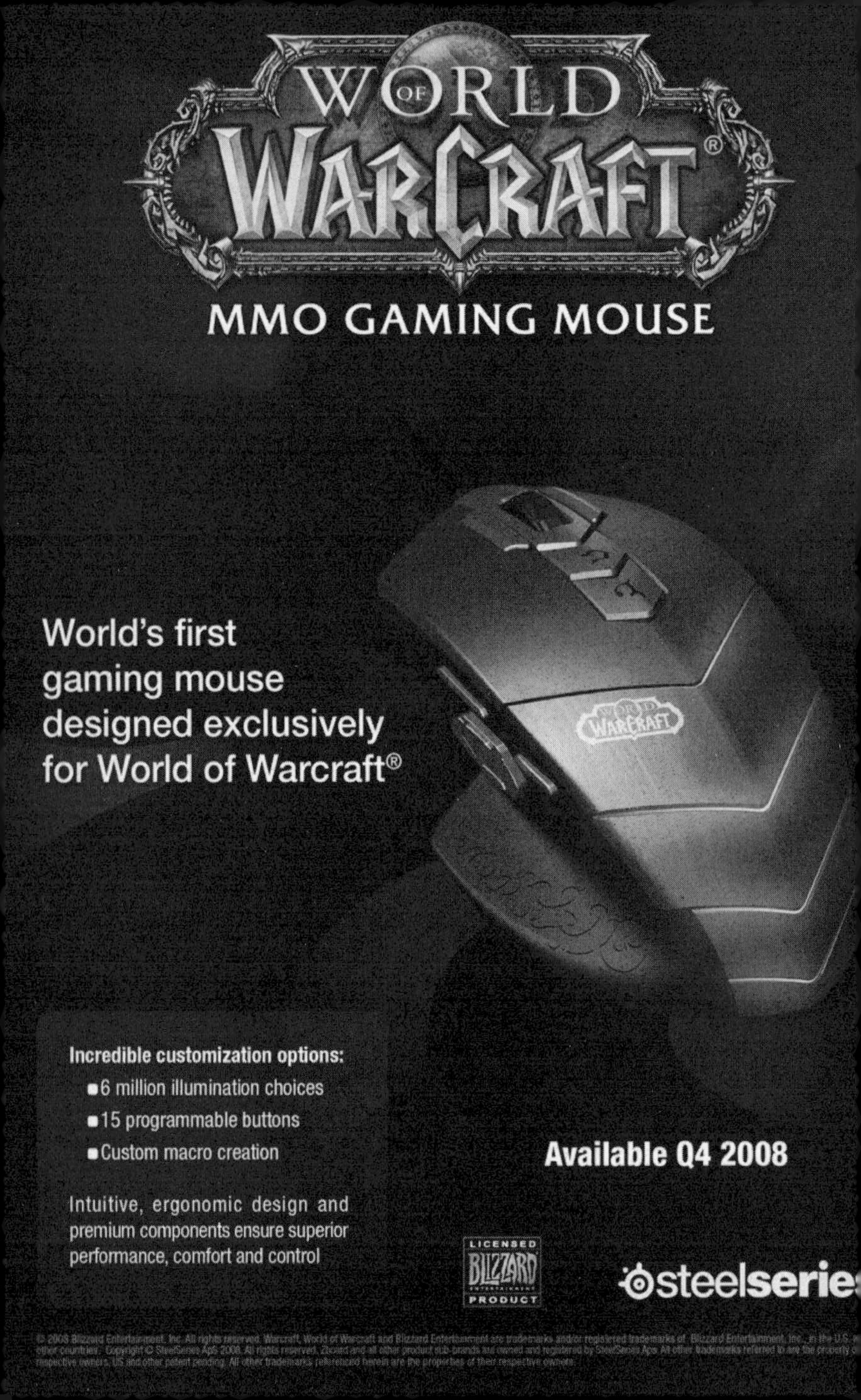
WORLD OF WARCRAFT®
MMO GAMING MOUSE
World's first gaming mouse designed exclusively for World of Warcraft®
Incredible customization options:
6 million illumination choices
15 programmable buttons
Custom macro creation
Intuitive, ergonomic design and premium components ensure superior performance, comfort and control
Available Q4 2008
LICENSED BLIZZARD ENTERTAINMENT PRODUCT
steelseries

EPIC BATTLES
IN THE PALM OF YOUR HAND

World of Warcraft® Collectible Miniatures Game
- Premium miniatures with detailed paints designed by Studio McVey
- Standard and deluxe starter sets plus three-figure boosters
- Innovative game play utilizing the unique detachable UBase

Coming Fall 2008!

For more information, visit

WOWMINIS.COM

Actual Gameplay.

TEEN
T™
Blood
Suggestive Themes
Use of Alcohol
Violence
ESRB CONTENT RATING www.esrb.org
Game Experience May Change
During Online Play

NO. I'D RATHER KILL RATS.

With millions of players online, World of Warcraft has made gaming
history — and now it's never been easier to join the adventure.
Simply visit **www.warcraft.com**, download the FREE TRIAL and join
thousands of mighty heroes for ten days of bold online adventure.
A World Awaits...

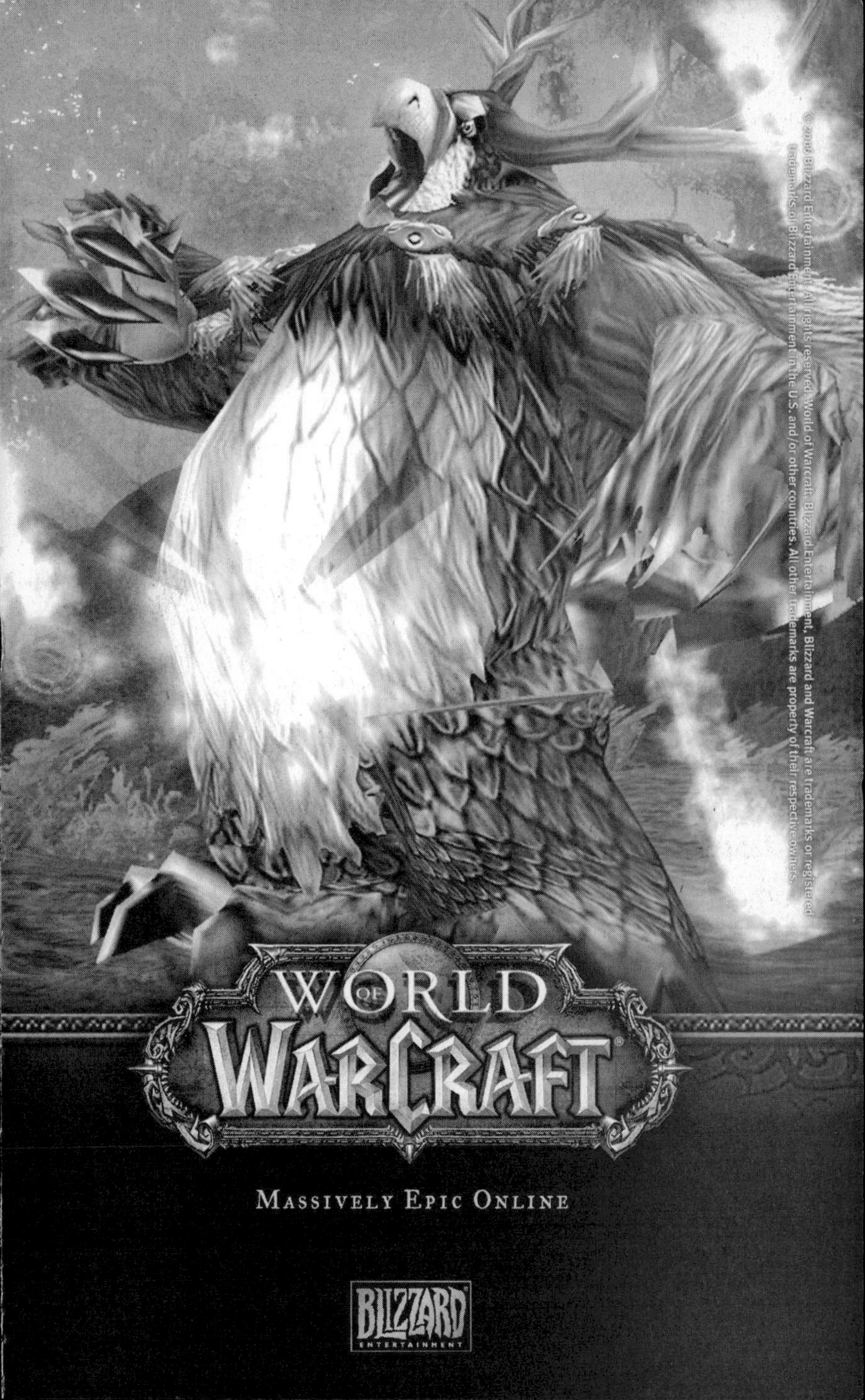

WORLD OF WARCRAFT®

MASSIVELY EPIC ONLINE

BLIZZARD® ENTERTAINMENT

Legends Forged Daily
WORLD OF WARCRAFT
The ADVENTURE GAME
Explosive Trap
Rotten Ghoul
Grab your sword, ready your spells, and set off for adventure in the World of Warcraft! Vanquish diabolical monsters (as well as your fellow heroes) through intrigue and in open battle!
Play one of four unique characters, each with their own abilities and style of play. Ultimately, only one hero can be the best – will it be you?
FANTASY FLIGHT GAMES
LICENSED BLIZZARD PRODUCT
WWW.FANTASYFLIGHTGAMES.COM
© 2008 Blizzard Entertainment, Inc. All rights reserved. Warcraft, World of Warcraft and Blizzard Entertainment are trademarks and/or registered trademarks of Blizzard Entertainment, Inc., in the U.S. and/or other countries.